YANKEES

YANKEES:
AN ILLUSTRATED HISTORY

GEORGE SULLIVAN
AND JOHN POWERS

PRENTICE-HALL, INC., ENGLEWOOD CLIFFS, NEW JERSEY 07632

Other books by the authors:

George Sullivan

The Picture History of the Boston Celtics

The Picture History of the Boston Red Sox

The Flying Fisherman (*with R.V. "Gadabout" Gaddis*)

John Powers

The Short Season: A Boston Celtics Diary, 1977–1978

Library of Congress Cataloging in Publication Data

Sullivan, George
  Yankees.

  Bibliography: p.
  1. New York Yankees (Baseball team)—History.
I. Powers, John
GV875.N4S84 1982   796.357′64′097471   82–10187
ISBN 0-13-971820-6
ISBN 0-13-971812-5 (pbk.)

Book Designer: Joan Ann Jacobus
Art Director: Hal Siegel
Editorial/production supervision by Inkwell
Manufacturing buyer: Ed Leone

This book is available to businesses and organizations at a
special discount when ordered in large quantities. For information, contact General Publishing Division, Special Sales,
Prentice-Hall, Inc., Englewood Cliffs, N.J. 07632

Prentice-Hall International, Inc., London
Prentice-Hall of Australia Pty. Limited, Sydney
Prentice-Hall of Canada Inc., Toronto
Prentice-Hall of India Private Limited, New Delhi
Prentice-Hall of Japan, Inc., Tokyo
Prentice-Hall of Southeast Asia Pte., Ltd., Singapore
Whitehall Books Limited, Wellington, New Zealand

For three All-Stars: Sean, George and Lisa.

G.S.

And for Evan, who was Rookie of the Year on at least one ballot.

J.P.

Acknowledgments

Our boxscore has a long assist column.

Particular thanks go to the Yankees organization, which could not have been more cooperative—from principal owner George Steinbrenner, president Lou Saban and vice president/general counsel Ed Broderick through the entire Yankee lineup, on and off the field.

Special recognition goes to David Szen, the Yankees' zealous director of publications. No request stumped him—no clipping or statistic too elusive, no photo too remote.

The Yankees' help in locating and providing a wealth of photographs was extraordinary. So was that of the National Baseball Hall of Fame and Museum at Cooperstown, New York. Librarian Jack Redding was always accommodating as he probed his files tirelessly day after day for notable Yankee photos in the archives of that baseball mecca on the shores of Lake Otsego.

Other important help was supplied in a variety of ways by Alan Aronson, Frank O'Brien, John Frederickson and Betsy Leesman.

The advice and patience of Prentice-Hall senior editor Saul Cohen also is appreciated, along with that of Fred Dahl of Inkwell. So was the help of literary agent Bill Berger.

Finally, we are grateful to our partners behind this Sullivan/Powers double-play combination—Betty Sullivan and Elaine Powers—for their support throughout all these extra innings. Like the Yankees, they are champions.

George Sullivan and John Powers
Boston, Massachusetts

CONTENTS

Opening Day at Yankee Stadium, April 18, 1923.

Bobby Murcer, the League's top power pinch hitter, 1981.

The newly renovated Yankee Stadium, 1976.

THE YANKEE WAY

They were America's best road show when a certain Ohio schoolboy was growing up in the thirties, a collection of summer heroes who appeared just long enough in your town to reaffirm their invulnerability.

Gehrig, DiMaggio, and the rest of them would check into the Hotel Cleveland, perform flawlessly for three days at Municipal Stadium, then move on to Detroit, Chicago, and the world championship.

"When the Yankees came to town it was like Barnum and Bailey coming to town," George Steinbrenner would reminisce after he'd bought the club decades later. "The excitement."

The New York Yankees have been larger than life ever since a wealthy brewery owner named Ruppert imported a boisterous manchild named Ruth and built a stadium in the Bronx to accommodate him.

Joe McCarthy, who managed the club during Steinbrenner's childhood, deliberately had the uniforms cut half a size large and the caps squared off. The Yankees, he reasoned, would thus appear more intimidating to rivals.

The amateur psychology was unnecessary. Any baseball team that won seven pennants in eight years was likely to be imposing enough in street clothes.

When manager Miller Huggins realized that the Pirates were watching his Yankees take batting practice before the 1927 World Series, he had Babe Ruth, Lou Gehrig, and Bob Meusel casually stage a home run derby for their benefit.

"Do they do this all the time?" Pittsburgh

shortstop Glenn Wright gulped, as ball after ball plopped into Forbes Field's upper deck.

Most of the time. For six decades the Yankees have been a most enduring anachronism—a baseball team that performs, more often than not, with the instincts, continuity, and success of a blue-chip corporation.

Rooting for New York, as the cliché had it, was like rooting for U.S. Steel—the players even wore pinstripes. The Yankees were crisp, dignified, and dispassionate.

And their employers, from Jacob Ruppert to Steinbrenner, believed that those qualities were part of a club tradition, a certain way of conducting business.

The Yankee Way was a 10-game lead by Independence Day, a clinched pennant by Labor Day, and champagne in October.

The Yankee Way was generations of players—from Gehrig to DiMaggio, from Mickey Mantle to Thurman Munson—who never wore another uniform and who either retired with a handful of championship rings or wept when traded away.

The Yankee Way was also a front office that took those championships as its due. "Fine, fine, McCardy," Ruppert would tell McCarthy after each Series triumph in the thirties. "Do it again next year."

By the fifties, championship money was routinely figured into a player's salary. "Don't forget you get a World Series share," a club executive assured pitcher Jim Bouton in 1963 while offering him a $9000 contract. "You can always count on that."

For decades, until Steinbrenner spent handsome sums to rebuild the franchise in the late Seventies, the New York front office was corporate America in microcosm.

It coolly looted the Red Sox roster in the early twenties once it realized that Boston owner Harry Frazee was desperate for ready cash. It used the downtrodden Kansas City Athletics as a separate farm system in the fifties, exchanging used-up veterans for promising young talent. And it paid salaries that were no higher than they had to be.

"What do you fellows think I am, a millionaire?" Ruppert, a millionaire, told his players in the twenties, thus setting the negotiating stance for decades to come.

Gehrig, a walking embodiment of Yankee virtues, never earned more than $37,000. Other employees were frequently treated as replacement parts, their service records given cursory consideration. After winning ten pennants in a dozen years, manager Casey Stengel was shunted aside at age 70.

To baseball fans and rivals who resented their monopoly, the Yankees appeared smug, insensitive and tightfisted. But what Yankee-haters resented most was their monotonous consistency, one Chinese-style dynasty rising from the ashes of its predecessor, producing nearly 7000 victories in all, 33 American League pennants, and 22 world championships.

By 1954, after New York had dominated baseball for six of the previous seven years, Douglass Wallop would write an enormously popular, if wistful tale—"The Year the Yankees Lost the Pennant" (later to be a Broadway and film hit, "Damn Yankees"). Even the devil, Wallop mused, was a Yankee fan.

From 1921 until 1929, New York lost only two pennant races. From 1936 until 1944, they lost one. From 1947 until 1965, only three. "Every year is next year," New York sportswriter Roger Kahn typed moments after the final game of the 1952 World Series, "for the New York Yankees."

It was the farm system, carefully stocked and replenished since the days of general manager Ed Barrow, that produced New York's autumn monopolies.

"It's good to see some good young players coming into the league," well-traveled American League manager Jimmy Dykes would say in 1963. "But why do they always have to be wearing the Yankee uniform?"

There was always another .350 hitter ripening in Newark, a 20-game winner waiting in Kansas City. The year Ruth left, creaky with age and dissipation, a Yankee scout was scribbling notes on a San Francisco minor-leaguer named DiMaggio. When DiMaggio retired, Stengel merely beckoned to the "the kid," Mantle.

Thus the Yankees linked generation to generation and championship to championship. Whatever the year, there was always a Hall of Famer three cubicles away to point to as an example.

Gehrig played 2130 straight games, shrugging off split fingers, beanings, and lumbago until his body literally gave out on him. DiMaggio performed flawlessly, spoke softly, and picked up all dinner checks. "When you eat with the dago," he informed the greenest rookie, "the dago pays."

Mantle stuffed bleeding abscesses with gauze and went out to play on rickety knees in August heat.

A team code evolved, unspoken unless it was violated. "You're with the Yankees now," McCarthy admonished newcomer Jake Powell, who'd just administered a hotfoot to a teammate in a Boston train station. "We don't do those things."

It might be a road show, but Barnum and Bailey it wasn't. The club furnished three sets of pinstripes, so the players would always be immaculately turned out. Off the field, coats and ties were the rule. From the day McCarthy had the card table broken apart with an axe in 1931, the

Yankee clubhouse was considered a place of business. When former player Billy Martin arrived in August of 1975 to take over a club that had fallen 10 games behind Boston, he quickly pinpointed the clubhouse atmosphere as one reason.

"It wasn't the Yankee clubhouse the way I remembered it," he remarked. "Anyone who wanted to was running around."

When seasons went sour, as they did from time to time (and from 1965 through 1969, when the talent simply ran out), divergence from the Yankee Way was invariably listed as a reason.

"The trouble with this club," growled one veteran, as the 1930 club slipped to third, "is that there are too many fellows on it who aren't Yankees."

When a franchise that had had only three managers in 28 years went through three in 1946, a New York sportswriter named Will Wedge summed up thusly: "It grows more and more un-Yankeelike."

It meant something to play for New York. DiMaggio's own story, published in 1946, was entitled *Lucky to be a Yankee.* After he retired, Mantle had nightmares about hearing the Stadium loudspeaker announcing his name and not being able to get there.

Rollie Sheldon wept when the front office traded him. John Blanchard, who said he'd rather sit on the bench as a third-string Yankee catcher than start anywhere else, was crestfallen when he was dealt to Kansas City. "I don't want to play every day," he said. "I want to stay here."

That was the Yankee Way.

Manager Ralph Houk (l) and coach Jim Turner.

Mickey Mantle at bat despite his most physically painful season, 1959.

ALL THE SEASONS

1903–1914

They began as one of Byron Bancroft Johnson's daydreams and grew out of his hatred for the National League and his bitterness toward New York Giants manager John McGraw.

The New York Highlanders played in a wooden ballpark on a rocky hilltop in uptown Manhattan, their record fluctuating wildly from year to year. They were known by any number of last names—the Hill Dwellers, Cliffmen, Gordon Highlanders, Porch Climbers or Burglars—but their first name would remain New York.

To Ban Johnson, whose embryonic American League was embroiled in a fierce struggle for primacy with its established National League cousins, that was the important thing. You could not be taken seriously without a New York franchise.

How Johnson finally got one there in 1903 was the product of a chain reaction that began in the previous season, after he'd indefinitely suspended McGraw, then the Baltimore Orioles' manager, for abusing umpires.

So McGraw had gotten Giant owner John T. Brush to buy the team and free half a dozen players to sign with National League clubs. And when the Orioles were unable to field a team against St. Louis one afternoon, Johnson revoked the Baltimore franchise, stretched the roster with temporary filler from other league clubs and appointed Wilbert Robinson as manager.

Then he moved the club to New York that fall and raided National League rosters—most notably Pittsburgh's—to build a contender. The only thing Johnson lacked was land for a ball park, and Brush and partner Andrew Freedman had vowed to make that impossible.

They had friends in Tammany Hall, the corrupt but powerful political organization that had run New York for decades. Any likely parcel of land, Johnson was told, would either be unavailable to him or would soon have streets cut through it.

But during the winter a derbied gambler named Frank Farrell turned up at Johnson's office with a certified check for $25,000 and a plot of ground in mind. He and his sidekick William Devery, an unusually wealthy retired police chief with an ample belly, would buy the Orioles for $18,000, Farrell said, and build a stadium along Broadway on Washington Heights between 165th and 168th Streets.

The $25,000 check was a token of good faith. "That's a pretty big forfeit, Mr. Farrell," Johnson reminded him. New York *Sun* sports editor Joe Vila, who'd accompanied Farrell, snickered. "He bets that much," he assured Johnson, "on a horse race."

Besides the cash, Farrell and Devery had political friends of their own. Within three months they'd bought the land (a former Revolutionary War battlefield; workers unearthed bullets, gunstocks, grapeshot and bayonets), surrounded it with a wooden fence, leveled the hummocky ground and erected a grandstand and bleachers that would accommodate 15,000 spectators.

"You could look from the stands," said infielder Jimmy Austin, "and see all the way down the Hudson River." Hilltop Park was neither as large nor dignified as the Polo Grounds, where the Giants gamboled, and it was barely ready for opening day—right fielder Willie Keeler nearly fell into an unfilled ditch chasing a fly.

But it was a stadium in New York, and the club that played inside quickly became a pennant challenger under new manager Clark Griffith, a seven-time 20-game winner who doubled as a starting pitcher that year—at age thirty-three—and won fourteen games.

They were christened the Highlanders, a name recognizing both the elevation of their workplace and figurehead President Joseph W. Gordon (the Gordon Highlanders were—and are—a legendary Scottish regiment). But newspapers called them anything that fit conveniently into a headline.

Their first-year roster was a pastiche of seven rookies and refugees from eleven clubs, and injuries and poor hitting consigned them to fourth place, 17 games behind Boston. But relying on a sturdy righthanded spitballer named Happy Jack Chesbro to pitch every third day, the Highlanders fought Boston down to the season's final game in 1904.

As Keeler, whose secret was to "hit 'em where they ain't," built a .343 average out of 162 singles, Chesbro started 51 games, completed 48 and won 41—a league record that still stands. Yet he blew the pennant with a single spitter that got away in the season's final inning as he pitched his third game in four days.

Defending champion Boston (then called the Pilgrims) had come to New York for the concluding doubleheader leading by a game and a half, and were greeted by a crowd of 28,540 that clustered fifteen deep around the Hilltop outfield. With the score 2–2 in the ninth inning of the opener Boston's Lou Criger beat out an infield hit, went to third on a bunt and a grounder, and lumbered home when Chesbro's 2–2 pitch to Fred Parent sailed over catcher Red Kleinow's head to the chicken-wire backstop.

Criger, hardly the fastest man in the game, scored without sliding. The Highlanders, who'd won 92 games, would never again come so close to a pennant.

The 1905 season proved grim. At one point every regular was on the disabled list; the Highlanders had to borrow catcher Mike Powers from the Athletics to fill in for eleven games. Chesbro, who'd been 41–13, slumped to 19–13; his teammates followed, dropping to 71–78 and sixth place, 21½ games behind Philadelphia.

But along the way they'd found a nimble first baseman named Hal Chase (dubbed Prince Hal), who was probably the best fielder ever to play the position, a rollicking free spirit who lured crowds to Hilltop Park that otherwise had no reason to come.

Chase would hit .323 and steal 28 bases in 1906 and New York would contend throughout the season, winning five consecutive doubleheaders and holding first place several times. But erratic pitching—the fewest complete games (99) and fourth-highest ERA (2.78) in the league—undid them and the Highlanders finished second, three games behind Chicago.

Thus began a period of ineptitude and confusion that would continue—except for the 1910 season—until Farrell and Devery sold the club in 1915.

The 1907 Highlanders were a second-division club almost from the start and finished fifth, eight games below .500. Farrell had taken over as club president; now he and Devery would shout from behind the dugout and proffer unwanted advice to Griffith on lineups and strategy.

By the middle of 1908, with attendance off (it had dipped from 434,700 to 305,500 in two years), his club destined for the cellar, and the interference from Farrell and Devery unabated, Griffith quit in June, thus beginning a procession of five managers in the next six years.

The first was shortstop Norman Elberfeld,

Wee Willie Keeler bunting.

Outside Hilltop Park.

Maisel making a force play at third base.

Big Bill Devery, co-owner.

Frank Farrell, co-owner.

Clarke Griffith, first manager.

Hal Chase.

Jack Chesbro, first pitching ace.

nicknamed The Tabasco Kid for his spicy tongue. He and Chase grated against each other from the start and, as dissension mounted, Chase jumped the club and pitched for a renegade league in California, waiting for the crash he guessed lay ahead.

The Highlanders quickly fell to last place and ended up with what would be the worst record in franchise history, 51–103. Along the way Washington's Walter Johnson shut them out three times in four days and Boston's forty-one-year-old Cy Young threw a 27-batter no-hitter at them.

So Elberfeld gave way to George Stallings, a Southern miracle worker who would later bring the 1914 Braves from the basement to the National League pennant in less than three months. With Chase back in the lineup, and an infusion of young talent around him, the Highlanders climbed back into the first division for most of the 1909 season, finished fifth as attendance set a franchise record (501,000) and carried their momentum forth into 1910.

With Stallings alternating patience and harsh words New York challenged throughout the season. "He was a fine manager," Austin would insist. "One of the best. We finished in second place and he deserved a lot of the credit for that."

But before the season ended Stallings was gone, too. He had also had his difficulties with Chase, who had complained to the owners about him. When Farrell and Devery backed Chase, Stallings resigned, eleven games from the end of the season. So Chase, who'd never particularly cared for any kind of authority, was made manager.

"God, what a way to run a ball club," Austin groaned. "Well, you know how good a manager Hal Chase was." A sixth-place manager, as it turned out, sitting uneasily astride a .500 club full of former teammates who wouldn't respond to him. It was the second of six unsuccessful player-to-manager experiments that New York would try over the years (Elberfeld, Roger Peckinpaugh in 1914, Bob Shawkey in 1930, Bill Dickey in 1946, Yogi Berra in 1964); by the fall of 1911 Chase was back at first base and a minor-league manager named Harry Wolverton, who was fond of sombreros and sleek cigars, was in charge.

Wolverton was given a ceremonial wreath on opening day of the 1912 season, which some wags later joked should have been saved for his professional funeral that autumn. The Highlanders came entirely undone under his direction, losing 102 games and reverting to eighth.

The only constant was a pack of unruly fans who stood a dozen deep along the baselines and behind the plate and hooted at visitors. One of them had singled out Detroit's Ty Cobb on May 16. "There's going to be trouble if that fellow isn't stopped," Cobb warned Wolverton. When he

Ty Cobb sliding into New York's Jimmy Austin.

Ban Johnson, League founder.

Kid Elberfeld.

Branch Rickey.

John Anderson, who stole second with the bases loaded.

Roy Hartzell.

Hilltop Park by the Boston bench on the final day of the 1904 season.

*Al Orth, a good early-day
New York pitcher.*

*Wid Conroy, the Yankees'
original third baseman.*

wasn't, Cobb went into the stands and beat the man bloody. Johnson immediately suspended Cobb, and when the Tigers threatened to go on strike to support him, Johnson vowed to suspend the entire team.

When the Tigers carried out their threat, manager Hugh Jennings rounded up a bunch of Philadelphia sandlotters to play the next game against the Athletics, which Detroit promptly lost, 24–2. A theology student named Allan Travers, who would become a Catholic priest, made major league history by allowing all 24 runs and promptly retired with a lifetime 15.75 earned-run average as his teammates made nine errors behind him). Finally, after Cobb's penalty was reduced to a ten-day suspension and a fifty dollar fine, the Tigers returned.

The Highlanders, meanwhile, sank to their natural level and Farrell and Devery shucked Wolverton at the end of the season. In his place they hired Cubs first baseman-manager Frank Chance (of Tinker-to-Evers-to-Chance fame) who'd managed Chicago to four pennants and two world championships in five years and had been labeled the "Peerless Leader."

If the club remained hapless, at least the field manager's name and address could be changed. In the spring of 1913 New York *Press* sports editor Jim Price, tired of trying to cram the word "Highlanders" into his headlines, began using "Yankees" instead. So the team, which figured it might smell sweeter by any other name, adopted it.

They also decided to abandon the rickety instability of Hilltop Park and share the Polo Grounds with their National League neighbors, the Giants.

In 1910, when fire had raced through the Polo Grounds and left the Giants homeless, the Highlanders had offered them squatting privileges atop Washington Heights. Now the Giants were reciprocating with roomier quarters in a tonier neighborhood—Eighth Avenue between 155th and 157th streets.

Yet the Yankees proved no more adept or successful than the Highlanders had been. "The season of 1913 opened with nothing to speak of," George Moreland wrote in *Balldom,* his "Britannica of Baseball," "except that Chance was handed about as poor a lot of ball players as any man ever undertook to mold into a ball club."

Only four men—catcher Ed Sweeney, outfielders Birdie Cree and Harry Wolter, and utility man Roy Hartzell—were left from the awful 1912 club, but even that proved to be no benefit. Forty-five men would wear the Yankee uniform before the summer was done, including seven catchers.

The record was better, if 57–94 and seventh place can be considered an improvement. At-tendance jumped from 242,194 to 357,551, but that was mostly due to the change in address. The Yankees were less promising and more anonymous than the club Griffith had left in exasperation six years earlier.

When 1914 began Chance was still in the manager's chair—but Chase was gone. Chase, who knew that Chance had gone deaf in one ear from one beaning too many, had delighted in sitting to his deaf side and mimicking Chance's orders. Finally Sweeney, who liked Chance, exploded.

"I'm no stool pigeon," he told Chase. "But you're not going to make fun of the big guy in front of me any more." Thus made aware, Chance took away the first-base job that Chase had held since 1905, ordered him into street clothes and traded him to the White Sox early in the 1913 season for sore-footed third baseman Rollie Zeider and incompetent first baseman Babe Borton.

"Chance traded Chase," Mark Roth wrote in the New York *Globe,* "for a bunion and an onion." Neither pleased the owners, who eventually fired Chance two weeks before the end of the 1914 season.

And once again, as they'd done when they replaced Griffith with Elberfeld and Stallings with Chase, Farrell and Devery elevated a player, this time shortstop Roger Peckinpaugh.

The season would turn out with a slightly nicer odor—70–84 and sixth place—but little else changed. The club was still a laughingstock, followed by rowdies and peopled with journeymen who rarely looked at or cared about the standings.

"The Yankees at that time were what we used to call a 'joy club,'" Peckinpaugh admitted. "Lots of joy and lots of losing. Nobody thought we could win and most of the time we didn't. But it didn't seem to bother the boys too much. They would start singing songs in the infield right in the middle of a game."

But Farrell, whose luck at the racetrack had fled, was singing the blues. His club hadn't had a winning season or finished better than sixth since 1910. The move to the Polo Grounds, where the Giants had won three straight National League pennants, had only served to display the Yankees as stylistic hoboes by comparison.

Worst of all, the club had been a bust at the gate. Only once since the franchise had been moved from Baltimore in 1903 had attendance surpassed 500,000 for a season; usually it was less than 350,000.

Farrell was quarrelling with Devery, and Johnson, as league president, was sorely disappointed in what he had hoped would become the cornerstone of the American League.

Meanwhile, two millionaire sportsmen had been sitting in companion boxes at the Polo

Grounds with some regularity. They were watching the Giants, of course, who were the city's fashionable club. Their names were Jacob Ruppert and Tillinghast L'Hommedieu Huston and they were looking for a plaything.

1915

All Ruppert and Huston had in common was a rooting interest in the Giants, a season's box at the Polo Grounds and enough ready cash to indulge their caprices.

Colonel Jacob Ruppert had inherited millions and added to them by shrewd management of his father's uptown brewery; Captain Tillinghast L'Hommedieu Huston had made his fortune as a civil engineer in Cuba after the Spanish-American War. Giants manager John McGraw had introduced them as mutually affluent sportsmen and they began passing summer afternoons together behind the team dugout.

Neither was a stranger to professional baseball. Huston loved ball parks and the men that haunted them. Ruppert had passed up earlier chances to buy the Giants and the Chicago Cubs. After owner John T. Brush died in 1912, both men approached McGraw about buying the club.

"No," McGraw replied. "No chance." Brush's widow and daughters wanted to retain ownership. "But if you really want to buy a ball club," McGraw continued, "I think I can get one for you. How about the Yankees? I hear Farrell and Devery are fed up and want out."

That was hardly what Ruppert and Huston had in mind. The Yankees were haphazard and mediocre, playing before sections of empty seats at the Polo Grounds. The Giants were the city's fashionable team and Ruppert and Huston were fashionably rich enough to fancy them as a diversion.

Ruppert was a forty-seven-year-old bachelor clubman who owned a Fifth Avenue town house and a Rhenish castle on the Hudson across from West Point, and lived meticulously well, changing clothes several times daily—assisted by a valet—from a vast wardrobe. He raced horses, raised Saint Bernards for show, maintained a yacht and called everybody by his last name.

His colonelcy was honorary, given him at age twenty-two by Governor David B. Hill. The extent of Ruppert's military service was member-

ship in the socially correct Company B of the New York National Guard's 7th Regiment.

Huston's captaincy, though, had been earned—with an engineering unit in Cuba, where he lived for a decade after the Spanish–American war, modernizing harbors and planning Havana's sewerage system. When he returned to New York he was a man of considerable means, wealthy enough to maintain a 30,000-acre hunting preserve in Georgia with a lodge where cronies sipped aged corn whiskey by the fire and swapped stories. First names were good enough for Cap Huston, who lived from day to day with the rumpled informality of an unmade four-poster bed.

Where Ruppert was immaculately barbered and crisply turned out, Huston wore the same wrinkled suit for days and jammed a derby over his ears. A New York newspaperman dubbed him "The Man in the Iron Hat." Yet when he decided to build an estate on Butler Island in the middle of Georgia's Altamaha River, Huston used the Petit Trianon at Versailles as a model. "Marie Antoinette could sure pick houses," he mused, "even if she didn't have much luck with her boyfriends."

For all his earthiness there was a touch of the dilettante to Huston, and the Yankees hardly seemed a suitable plaything. But they were available and, after two years of friendly persuasion by McGraw and American League President Ban Johnson, Huston and Ruppert decided to gamble. "See Farrell," they told McGraw. "Ask him if they want to sell."

A deal was quickly struck. Farrell's passion for the racetrack had left him desperately short of cash and he and Devery were quarrelling frequently. The prospect of splitting $460,000 and parting company was irresistible. Once they sold the club on January 11, 1915, Farrell and Devery never spoke again and pursued their separate paths to poverty. Devery, his real estate holdings gone sour, was dead within four years, leaving debts of $1,023; Farrell died in 1926 with assets of $1,072.

Meanwhile, Ruppert and Huston had inherited something of an urban renewal project at the foot of Coogan's Bluff. The Yankees had finished in the American League's second division for the four previous seasons and were drawing fewer than 360,000 spectators a year.

So Ruppert installed himself as president and set about reorganizing the club. He knew little about baseball; as a child he'd captained his neighborhood nine only because he'd bought them equipment and uniforms. But Jake Ruppert could run a company.

He signed on Harry Sparrow—who'd put together the White Sox–Giants world tour the winter before—as business manager and hired two road secretaries to help him. Wild Bill Dono-

Ruppert.

Ray Fisher, 18–11 record and Yankees' top ERA: 2.11

Ray Caldwell, Yankee ace with 19–16 record.

van, a former Detroit pitcher who'd just managed Providence (and a young left-hander named George Ruth) to the International League pennant, was brought in as field manager. Players were more difficult to come by.

"I want to win," Ruppert had insisted. "Every day I want to win ten-nothing. Close games make me nervous."

Yet except for first baseman Wally Pipp, who was acquired from the Tigers for the $7,500 waiver price, and pitcher Bob Shawkey, for whom Ruppert paid the Athletics a steep $85,000, the Yankees were forced to field virtually the same lineup for the 1915 season.

And while they began the year in dignified new pinstriped uniforms they ended it with virtually the same record, 69–83, in fifth place. Neither Ruppert nor Huston had ever finished fifth in anything.

1916

Seven years filled with endless railroad tracks, hotel rooms and travel bags had driven him back to the farm, and nothing manager Connie Mack could say had changed his mind. J. Franklin Baker, the best third baseman in the game, had retired at age twenty-eight from the Philadelphia Athletics after the 1914 season and gone back to Trappe, Maryland, and the pastoral life.

A fifty-game lark with the town team in nearby Upland had satisfied his competitive urges during the summer of 1915—or had it? Yankee manager Bill Donovan guessed that a spark still burned in Baker that might be fanned by the prospect of playing in New York. So during the next winter he approached Philadelphia, which still owned Baker's rights, for permission to talk to him.

Mack, convinced that Baker would still prefer Philadelphia if he ever changed his mind, agreed. And so, surprisingly enough, did Baker, provided Mack would sell his rights. The price was $35,000—and Home Run Baker was wearing pinstripes. He'd earned the nickname five years earlier by crashing two home runs off Giant aces Christy Mathewson and Rube Marquard in successive games to propel the A's to the world championship, and had become the cornerstone of Mack's "Hundred-Thousand-Dollar Infield," playing alongside Jack Barry, Stuffy McInnis and Eddie Collins.

"Home Run" Baker.

New York manager Wild Bill Donovan.

Baker was everything the Yankees wanted—a durable, aggressive fielder who once had knocked down Ty Cobb after being spiked, a superior base-stealer, and a power hitter in a dead-ball era. More important, he was a proven draw at the gate which the Yankees, having attracted only 256,000 customers in 1915, needed desperately.

Once Donovan installed him at third and shifted Fritz Maisel to the outfield, Baker's impact was immediate. No Yankee since Hal Chase had lured quite as many spectators to the Polo Grounds (attendance doubled overnight) and the club reponded with a hustling style that quickly involved them in the pennant race for the first time in six years.

The euphoria was short-lived. In midseason Baker crashed into the grandstand chasing a pop foul and missed fifty games with broken ribs; it was one in a series of injuries that soon made hash of the starting lineup. Donovan was forced to use seven outfielders and only center fielder. Lee Magee started more than 110 games. Except for Bob Shawkey (23–14) and Nick Cullop (12–6), the pitching grew uninspired. By season's end the club had fallen to fourth, 11 games behind the Red Sox. Still, it was a landmark season. Not since 1910 had the Yankees finished in the first division and only once, in 1909, had more paying customers filed through the turnstiles.

Yankees drilling in training camp.

1917

Captain Tillinghast L'Hommedieu Huston, a war veteran who could foresee disjointed times as well as any man, had decided that spring training and baseball bats should have a dual purpose. So while America prepared for battle and the American League for the 1917 season, the Yankees did both.

Huston brought Army drill sergeants to Macon, Georgia, to teach his people how to present arms with a Louisville Slugger, then went overseas himself as an officer with the 18th Engineers. France was in turmoil, and before long the Yankees were, too.

Once again the club started aggressively—George Mogridge's no-hitter at Fenway Park on April 24 is still the only one by a Yankee left-hander. Yet by July their best hope was another first-division finish; by August even that seemed a fantasy.

Wally Pipp was the League home run champ for the second year in a row.

Ray Caldwell pitched 9⅔ hitless innings of relief.

New York's team batting average—.239—was the worst in the league and the pitching dismal across the board. Only Urban Shocker (8–5) and Slim Love (6–5) posted winning seasons. Mogridge, the April hero, finished at 9–11.

And worst of all to owner Jacob Ruppert's corporate mind, attendance had fallen off dramatically, from 469,000 to 330,000. The colonel rarely attended games now or consulted with Bill Donovan, his beleaguered manager, brooding instead at his brewery at the corner of Third Avenue and 90th Street.

Finally, after the club had finished sixth, 28½ games behind Chicago, the manager was summoned downtown. "I like you, Donovan," Ruppert admitted. "But we have to make some changes around here."

"I know it, colonel," Donovan conceded. So after three years, 239 losses and two second-division efforts the Wild Bill era ended (he would die six years later, at forty-seven, in a freakish train wreck). And Ruppert called American League President Ban Johnson, who'd urged him into this quagmire several years before, for advice.

"Get Miller Huggins," he was told.

1918

He was born in Cincinnati to English parents who preferred cricket and wanted him to be a lawyer. Instead, Miller Huggins had turned second baseman and player-manager and applied his intensity, intelligence and quick wit to the dugout. Huggins had actually earned a law degree from the University of Cincinnati, passed the bar and established a practice before turning to baseball. While laconic among strangers he was humorous and digressive with intimates, read widely, favored pipe tobacco over cut plug and followed the stock market. And he knew baseball intimately and had played it well.

His only failing, thought American League President Ban Johnson, was that Huggins was working in the wrong league. Johnson despised the National League, and when Yankee President Jacob Ruppert asked him to suggest a replacement for Wild Bill Donovan for the 1918 season Johnson immediately recommended Huggins.

Only two roadblocks loomed. Huggins, who'd just brought the St. Louis Cardinals from the cellar to third place and owned stock in the franchise, didn't want the job. And Ruppert's partner, Cap Huston, didn't want Huggins, preferring Brooklyn manager "Uncle" Wilbert Robinson.

It proved easier to change Huggins' mind, and *The Sporting News* publisher J. G. Taylor Spink began trying as soon as Huggins arrived in New York for the National League meetings in December. Why didn't Huggins go up to the brewery for a chat with the colonel, he urged. No, Huggins told Spink, I'm happy where I am.

"If you won't go willingly," Spink replied, "I'll hit you on the head and drag you there."

"All right," Huggins conceded. "To please you, I'll go."

Ruppert quickly offered Huggins the job—and the reverberations from France, where Huston was serving with the 18th Engineers, was immediate. A stream of telegrams, invective and letters to Huston's cronies in the New York press followed, causing a split between the partners that was never repaired.

Ruppert's real offense had been the brusque treatment accorded Robinson, whom Huston hunted and drank with at his Dover Hall lodge in Georgia during the off-season. "I don't think [Ruppert] cared for me," Robinson would tell friends afterward. "And personally, I didn't care a lot for him."

Robinson, at fifty-four, was still hearty and

Ruppert and new manager Miller Huggins.

Cap Huston (right) with Dodger pilot Wilbert Robinson.

vigorous. He'd led the Dodgers to the pennant a year earlier, would win another in 1920 and would manage for fourteen more years. Yet his interview with Ruppert was brief.

"No," the colonel had decided. "You will not do. For one thing, you are too old." Robinson had stalked out of the office and cabled Huston, who'd called Ruppert, who'd shrugged and gone off to pursue a man sixteen years younger and more tautly wound.

Though Huggins stood only five foot six and weighed 140 pounds, he had played thirteen seasons for Cincinnati and St. Louis as a nimble fielder (which brought the nickname "Little Everywhere") and a leadoff man with a knack for reaching base. As a manager he was inventive yet driven, pacing the foul line from his third-base coaching box with shoulders hunched. He stressed fundamentals and discipline and the Yankees quickly bore his mark.

In a span of less than a month the club executed a league-record eight sacrifices (six of them bunts) to beat star southpaw Babe Ruth in Boston, turned a game-ending triple play to snuff out Detroit, and hung in with Cleveland for nineteen innings (with Indian pitcher Stan Coveleski going the distance) before losing.

Such proficiency and spirit was a welcome novelty, and in a normal year might have produced a contender, but 1918 was anything but normal. War shortened the season by twenty-six games, ending it on Labor Day, and played havoc with rosters. The Yankees lost eleven men to the armed forces (Huston's training-camp drill sergeants had been worthwhile after all), including first baseman Wally Pipp and pitcher Bob Shawkey, and finished fourth, three games below .500.

Still, the season marked a return to the first division and promised future stability—so long as Huston, now a colonel himself, was laying railroad track in France.

1919

For three months, while his record sank to 5–10, he had suspected his Boston teammates were deliberately playing carelessly behind him. Now, on a July evening at Comiskey Park, Carl Mays was convinced of it.

Several Chicago batters had reached base on errors, and a throw from catcher Wally Schang

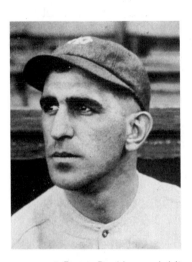

Roger Peckinpaugh hit safely in 29 straight games—the most until DiMaggio's 56 in 1941.

Del Pratt, second baseman, combined with Peckinpaugh as the Yankees' double-play combination.

Bob Shawkey returned from the war and posted his second 20-victory season.

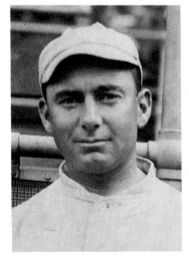

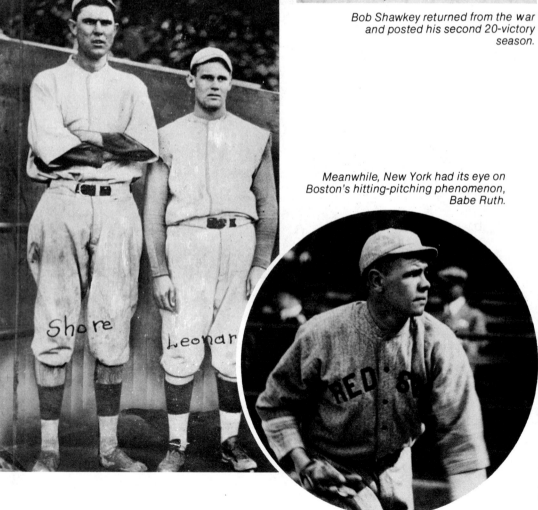

Duffy Lewis, Ernie Shore, and Dutch Leonard (pictured in Boston uniforms) were obtained from the Red Sox at the start of the talent flow from Boston to New York.

Meanwhile, New York had its eye on Boston's hitting-pitching phenomenon, Babe Ruth.

that was supposed to nail a runner at second base had somehow bounced off Mays's head. When the inning was done he stormed off the mound and into the clubhouse.

"I'll never pitch for this club again," he growled at manager Ed Barrow, who had learned to take such outbursts philosophically. Mays was a peevish loner whose temper frayed easily.

"Tell Carl to forget about it and get back in the game," Barrow told pitcher Sam Jones, but Mays had already dressed and packed his gear. "Tell Barrow I've gone fishing," he told Jones—and disappeared.

Thus began an unprecedented dispute that ended up in New York State Supreme Court, plunged the American League (not to mention its standings) into chaos, and precipitated the demise of the league's founder and president, Ban Johnson. It also gave the Yankees a 20-game winner.

Mays did go fishing, and returned to Boston to find that Johnson had not only ordered him suspended but forbidden the club from trading him. But Boston owner Harry Frazee soon shipped him to New York anyway, for $40,000 and two mediocre pitchers named Allan Russell and Bob McGraw. And the Yankees, who badly needed a stopper to supplement Bob Shawkey, immediately put Mays into uniform and on the mound.

So the battle lines were drawn, with Johnson instructing his umpires to keep Mays from playing and the league owners split into factions.

New York President Jacob Ruppert had a natural ally in Frazee, and found another in Chicago's Charles Comiskey, who'd been eager to curb Johnson's virtually unlimited powers. They ultimately slapped Johnson and the five loyalist owners with a $500,000 lawsuit and obtained an injunction that allowed Mays to pitch for the Yankees, who were battling Chicago and Cleveland for the pennant.

To nobody's surprise, Mays's impact on the club was immediate. At twenty-seven he'd been a superior pitcher for Boston, teaming with Babe Ruth to win two pennants in three years. His specialty was a fastball thrown submarine-style that would literally kill—and would a year later when Cleveland shortstop Ray Chapman died hours after being beaned.

Mays was both durable and prolific; in the first days of the 1918 pennant race he'd won both ends of a doubleheader and taken it as a matter of course.

Mays won his first game in pinstripes, only hours after Yankee management had served the umpiring staff with an injunction before a doubleheader at St. Louis on August 7, and went on to win nine of twelve games for the club—depending upon whose records you wanted to believe. John-son had ruled that Mays's victories would not count in the standings; consequently newspapers kept two sets, with Mays and without.

So when the season ended New York had finished either third or fourth, according to which version you preferred. Johnson preferred fourth and refused to award the third-place money the club thought it had earned, so Ruppert and partner Cap Huston paid the difference out of their own coffers. And at the winter meetings the colonels, Frazee, and Comiskey made their move against Johnson.

They forced Cincinnati owner August Herrmann, who chaired the three-man National Commission that Johnson dominated, to resign. Finally, the commission, which served as the sport's ruling body in those days, conceded New York both its third place and the cash that came with it.

A year later, in the wake of the Black Sox scandal, the commission was shelved and replaced by baseball Commissioner Kenesaw Mountain Landis—the game's first czar—as Johnson's influence dwindled. With one stroke Ruppert and Huston had improved their pitching staff decisively, quashed Johnson and continued an exodus of players from Boston to New York that would change both franchises permanently.

1920

He was born of uncertain parentage above a waterfront saloon in Baltimore, grew up speaking German and spent his youth in a Catholic school for orphans and incorrigibles.

He had an enormous appetite for food, drink and women, a casual disdain for training rules and a complete inability to remember names. A Washington pitcher named Joe Engel noticed him at a schoolboy baseball game in Maryland and mentioned him to Baltimore President Jack Dunn. "I think his name," Engel said, "is Ruth."

George Herman Ruth: and by 1919, at age twenty-four, he was the cornerstone of the Red Sox franchise, a superb lefthanded pitcher who'd been shifted to the outfield because Boston needed his bat—and his drawing power—in the lineup every day.

Nobody, not even the entire pennant-winning White Sox, hit as many home runs as Ruth did (29) that year, or did it with as much flair.

He was broad-shouldered and profane, carrying a blacksmith's torso atop spindly legs, which caused him to round the bases with a pigeon-toed gait. There was nobody remotely like him in a New York uniform, yet he might never have worn one had Boston owner Harry Frazee not been on the verge of bankruptcy.

He was a Broadway producer who'd bought the franchise on credit from Joseph Lannin and John I. Taylor three years earlier. When several of his shows flopped and Lannin and Taylor were pressing him for payment, Frazee walked several doors down 42nd Street to the Yankee front office and asked President Jacob Ruppert for a $500,000 loan. Ruppert asked for Ruth and a mortgage on Fenway Park.

So Frazee called his manager, Ed Barrow, on a Sunday in January 1920, and told him to drop by the bar at the fashionable Hotel Knickerbocker that evening.

"You're going to be sore as hell at me for what I'm going to tell you," Frazee began.

"You're going to sell the Big Fellow," Barrow guessed. "I expected it, Harry. But let me tell you this—you're going to ruin yourself and the Red Sox in Boston for a long time to come."

"I can't help it," Frazee shrugged. "I'm up against the wall. I need money desperately."

Ruppert would pay him about $100,000 (reports vary from $100,000 to $139,000) outright and loan him $350,000 with the ball park as security. "Gentlemen," the colonel would inform a group of New York newspapermen. "We have just bought Babe Root."

The reaction was immediate—outrage in Boston, where Ruth had helped produce three pennants, delight in New York, and concern among the Yankees' landlords, the Giants, who'd monopolized both the hearts and pocketbooks of Manhattan fans for more than four decades.

The Giants felt the impact in spring training. Before the trade they'd arranged a barnstorming tour with the Red Sox, hoping to capitalize on their own natural lure and Ruth's big bat. Instead, the Yankees, preceding the Giants on the tour, were cleaning up at the gate. And so was Ruth, his salary now doubled to $20,000.

It was an omen of what was to come at the Polo Grounds during the regular season; with Ruth attracting spectators who couldn't tell a fastball from a slider, the Yankees shattered the Giants' major-league attendance record, drawing 1,289,422 (double their 1919 figure), which still stands as a mark for daytime play.

Not that it was any surprise. Ruth was already established as the league's most popular player. By age twenty-three he'd had a five-cent cigar named after him. He'd arrived in the majors at age nineteen, and the next season won 18 games for Boston's world champions. "He would

have been the greatest left-handed pitcher of his generation," guessed Detroit's Ty Cobb.

From the moment a Catholic clergyman discovered him catching in an intramural league at St. Mary's Industrial School, an overgrown nineteen-year-old in blue overalls, Ruth had seemed larger than life.

"The ball was three feet off the ground going through the box," Brother Gilbert noticed, "and three feet off the ground when it got to second base. I knew that with an arm like that he could be made into a pitcher."

Engel watched Ruth strike out eighteen college freshmen one afternoon and informed Dunn, who signed Ruth to a $600 contract sight unseen and brought him to the Orioles' 1914 training camp at Fayetteville, North Carolina. Until then Ruth had never been on a train, had more than five dollars in his pocket or been given unlimited breakfast privileges.

"You mean I can eat anything I want and it won't cost me anything?" Ruth asked Dunn.

"Sure. Anything."

After Ruth had eaten three stacks of wheatcakes and ham, his new teammates stood aghast. "I wouldn't have believed it," said sportswriter Roger Pippen, "if I hadn't seen it."

Presently Dunn led Ruth, a six-foot-two, 220-pound manchild, out to the diamond, "Here comes Dunnie," crowed one Oriole, "with his latest babe."

After Ruth beat both of the previous year's pennant winners, the Athletics and the Giants, in exhibition games, his future seemed assured. By the end of the International League season his salary had been tripled and Dunn had sold him to Boston in a package deal with Ernie Shore and Ben Egan for what amounted to $2,900.

By the end of 1919 Ruth had won 89 games plus all three of his World Series starts and had been shifted to the outfield where he led the American League in home runs (29), runs (103), runs batted in (114), slugging average (.657) and total bases (284)—all for a sixth-place club.

With Ruth's passage from one franchise to the other the Red Sox sank gradually into the cellar, where they finished during nine of the next twelve years. The Yankees grew into the sport's most enduring dynasty.

The 1920 season produced their first stirrings, a 95–59 record (their best ever) in a pennant race that went down to the final week. The club's success was tied directly to Ruth's, and his was prodigious that year—a .376 batting average, 137 runs batted in and an incredible 54 home runs, more than every team in either league save the Phillies.

But their pennant duel with Cleveland was marred by the death of Indian shortstop Ray Chapman in mid-August, beaned by a submarine

Ruth at practice, surrounded by writers and photographers.

Ruth at bat for the Yankees.

Ruppert and Huggins watch Ruth's blasts.

Carl Mays, the Yankee pitcher who threw a ball that killed Cleveland batter Ray Chapman.

ball from New York pitcher Carl Mays. Possibly it was a brush-back pitch; Chapman did like to crowd the plate.

"I've always had a horror of hitting a player," Mays said. "Poor Chapman was one of the hardest to pitch to. The ball I pitched was a straight one on the inside. I expected Chapman to be able to gauge it."

In any case Chapman never moved. The ball fractured his skull and he died at five o'clock the next morning. His teammates dedicated the remainder of the season to Chapman and went on to win the pennant by two games over Chicago. The Yankees would finish third, as they had the year before, but this was hardly the same team. The Big Fellow and Harry Frazee's theatrical woes had changed that for all time.

1921

The ball had skimmed viciously along the grass toward right field and Aaron Ward, a second baseman himself, simply assumed it had gone through. He'd been leading off first, had seen Home Run Baker rip Art Nehf's pitch, sensed Giant second baseman Johnny Rawlings lunging for it and thought instinctively of third base.

This was the bottom half of the ninth inning of the eighth game of the Yankees' first World Series appearance, and Ward represented the tying run that would keep them alive. Instead, he became the final out of the Giants' first world championship in sixteen years as Rawlings, George Kelly and Frankie Frisch combined for a 4–3–5 double play that stands as one of the most bizarre and dramatic of all Series finishes. "You won't see one play like that in ten years," moaned Babe Ruth.

It left the Yankees—who'd won the first two games and held a 4–0 lead in the third—stunned and their partisans frozen in their seats for minutes afterwards, while Giant fans exulted around them.

Thus ended their most successful season to that point, a season in which the Yankees won their first American League pennant, drew 1.2 million paying customers to the Polo Grounds and created a roistering image for themselves both on and off the diamond.

Their symbol was Ruth, whose daytime feats in the batter's box were merely a prelude to excessive nights at the dining table and behind the wheel.

Since the front office (with manager Miller Huggins's misgivings) allowed the players to drive their own cars from city to city during Eastern road trips, Ruth organized a merry crew of highwaymen to share his twelve-cylinder, fire-engine-red Packard roadster at 110 miles an hour.

One night after a game at Washington Ruth tipped the car over on a curve thirty miles from Philadelphia while singing "The Trail of the Lonesome Pine." Then he shrugged and called a cab, arriving in the city to find headlines claiming "BABE RUTH KILLED IN AUTO ACCIDENT."

An exaggeration, as Mark Twain would say. Ruth hit a home run against the Athletics the next day and went on to enjoy his best season, smashing a record 59 home runs, knocking in a league-leading 170 runs and batting .378. "Nobody gave me a good ball to hit," he mused. "But if they were anywhere near the plate I took a cut at them."

So did his teammates, who accounted for 134 of the American League's 477 homers that year. With Carl Mays (27–9), Waite Hoyt (19–13) and Bob Shawkey (18–12) anchoring a pitching staff that led the league in complete games, strikeouts and earned-run averages, the Yankees quickly took control of the pennant race, aided by a new policy of noninterference from the front office.

Three years of fussing from Jacob Ruppert and meddling by Cap Huston had driven Huggins to distraction. But when business manager Harry Sparrow had died late in 1920 the colonels hired Boston manager Ed Barrow as general manager, and gave him authority over day-to-day operations.

Barrow, who'd dealt with Ruth, Mays and Ernie Shore of the Yankees during their days as Red Sox, quickly moved to reassure Huggins.

Waite Hoyt, 19–13 record.

Wally Schang, the new catcher.

Ed Barrow, general manager.

Ruth displays his controversial elbow infection.

Huggins (left) and Tris Speaker, manager of the Indians.

Aaron Ward.

"I know what you've been up against," Barrow told him. "You're the manager and you'll not be second-guessed by me. Your job is to win, mine is to see that you get the players you need to win. I'll take responsibility for every deal I make. What do you want right now?"

"Well, I could use about eight players," Huggins replied. "But I'll take what I can get."

Before the season Barrow had put together a deal with Boston—who else?—exchanging Muddy Ruel, Herb Thormahlen, Sam Vick and Del Pratt for Hoyt, Wally Schang, Harry Harper and Mike McNally. And Huggins molded his nine for the New Era.

The pennant race came down to a weekend series at the Polo Grounds against the world champion Indians in late September, with the Yankees leading by two percentage points. Hoyt won the opener, 4–2. Then New York battered half a dozen Cleveland pitchers, 21–7, and went two games up. But Cleveland's George Uhle dazzled the Yankees, 9–0, and presented Huggins with a knotty pitching problem to think through.

He had used most of what was in his bullpen in game three. Did he go back to Hoyt? Or gamble with Jack Quinn, who'd beaten the Indians at League Park earlier in the month but hadn't worked since?

"Fellows, I'm up against it," Huggins told his staff shortly before game time. "I don't know who to pitch."

The players opted for Quinn, but Cleveland riddled him for three runs before he could retire a man. The Yankees answered with four in the bottom of the inning and, with Hoyt relieving, managed to nurse the lead into the ninth while dusk was falling rapidly.

With two out and Mays now pitching, the Indians loaded the bases and sent catcher Steve O'Neill to the plate and a nervous Ruppert from his box seat to the New York bullpen where he joined his players—and fidgeted.

"Hofmann, you think we'll win?" he asked a reserve catcher. "Say yes, Hofmann, don't tell me no. You think Mays can get this man O'Neill, Hofmann? Is O'Neill good?"

Mays blew his first pitch past O'Neill.

"What is it, is it a strike, Hofmann?"

"Yes, one strike," Hofmann replied. "Two to go."

"Two more. Oh fellows, win this game for me. Please win this game for me. If you win it I'll give you anything. I'll give you the brewery."

Ruppert fretted all the way to a full count whereupon Mays, helped by the dying light, got O'Neill to swing at a pitch in the dirt. The Yankees went on to win the pennant by 4½ games, but Ruppert kept the brewery.

More elusive game remained in the form of Ruppert's uptown landlords, the Giants, who'd erased a 7½-game Pittsburgh lead in the final six weeks to win the National League pennant.

It was the first World Series played entirely in the same park and the last of the revived best-of-nine format. With Mays and Hoyt each hurling 3–0 shutouts the Yankees quickly swept the first two games. No club had ever done that and still lost the Series, and when they grabbed a 4–0 lead in the third inning of game three a sweep seemed conceivable.

But the Giants chased Shawkey with four runs in the bottom half of the inning, racked relievers Quinn and Rip Collins for eight more in the seventh, won 13–5 and tied the Series two days later.

Meanwhile, Ruth, who'd developed an elbow abscess, could barely swing a bat. He struck out three times as the Yankees won game five and repaired to the bench for the final three games, while New York *Sun* sports editor Joe Vila questioned his resilience in print.

That produced an angry outburst from Ruth prior to game six. "You're accusing me of not having any guts," Ruth shouted at Vila. "Now if you have any, print a picture of my arm with this hole in it and let your readers see my side of it."

The Yankees never won another game. Trailing 1–0 in the bottom of the ninth in game eight Huggins had Ruth bat for Wally Pipp, but he managed only a grounder to first. Then Ward walked, bringing Baker to the plate.

"He was a tough lefthanded pull hitter," said Rawlings, "and I would have been playing him over toward first base anyway. But with a man on first I figured Baker would be trying to hit behind him and edged over even more."

Ward never saw Rawlings knock down Baker's grounder and make the play at first from the seat of his pants. So Kelly, whose arm was not to be trifled with, fired across the diamond to Frisch, who tagged Ward sliding.

"He jumped into me," Frisch said. "He tumbled me over pretty good, trying to knock the ball out of my hands. They all did in those days."

Particularly when a world championship and Manhattan bragging rights were involved.

1922

The turbulence had begun during the previous autumn, only hours after the Yankees had lost the World Series to the Giants. Commissioner Kene-

The site of Yankee Stadium.

saw Mountain Landis had received word that Babe Ruth and several of his teammates, most notably outfielder Bob Meusel, catcher Wally Schang and pitcher Carl Mays, were taking the midnight train to Buffalo for a barnstorming tour, in defiance of Landis's edict against them.

Distressed, Landis ordered Ruth to telephone him. "Babe, you'd better not make that trip," warned Landis, who felt such tours diminished the World Series. "If you do there will be a lot of consequences."

Sorry, Ruth told him, I'm already committed. Schang and Mays backed out, but Ruth, Meusel and two reserve pitchers went anyway. After three games Yankee co-owner Cap Huston paid off the promoters to abort the tour and Landis set down the punishment—Ruth and Meusel's World Series shares would be withheld and they would be suspended for the first thirty-nine games of the 1922 season.

Thus began a year during which the Yankees squabbled with their manager and fought among themselves, the Giants evicted them from the Polo Grounds, Huston split with partner Jacob Ruppert, and the club was swept in a World Series for the last time until 1963.

Though Ruth was banned until mid-May he was allowed to work with the club at its new spring training headquarters in New Orleans, which meant sumptuous meals at Antoine's, evenings awash in cocktails at the Little Club across from the hotel, and a generally undisciplined atmosphere.

"YANKEES TRAINING ON SCOTCH" read one New York headline, which so alarmed the front office that they hired a private detective to trail the team on its first western swing and report to both the club and a perturbed Landis.

Yet roistering seemed to agree with the Yankees. When Ruth and Meusel returned to a

Huggins (right) greets Everett Scott, who was acquired from the Red Sox.

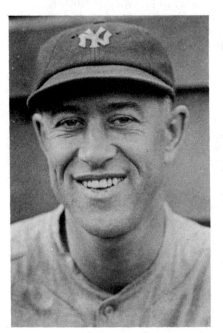

"Bullet Joe" Bush and . . .
Joe Dugan, also acquired from
the Red Sox.

Whitey Witt, who was hit on the head with a
pop bottle during a crucial series in St. Louis.

sold-out Polo Grounds on May 20 the club was in first place. The only rival that threatened was St. Louis—unless the Yankees self-destructed, which actually seemed conceivable.

As the season headed into August with the Browns still chasing them, Yankee composure unraveled on a western trip. Wally Pipp and Ruth exchanged punches in St. Louis after Ruth had criticized Pipp's fielding. In Detroit reserve catcher Al DeVormer fought with Mays one day, Fred Hofmann the next.

Finally, manager Miller Huggins threatened to fine and suspend any brawlers and the club turned its attention to a pivotal September series in St. Louis, where brown beer barrels had been set on street corners for contributions for gifts for the Browns once they clinched the pennant.

Instead, New York took two of three in a riotous series during which center fielder Whitey Witt was beaned and gashed by a bottle. The barrels were dumped into the gutter and the money given to charity. Three weeks later the Yankees won the pennant by a single game and prepared for another, more bitter Series duel with their landlords, this time with a stronger lineup.

During another pre-season raiding party on Boston's roster, general manager Ed Barrow had acquired shortstop Everett Scott, the league's best fielder, plus right-handers Joe Bush (26–7) and Sam Jones (13–13) for shortstop Roger Peckinpaugh and pitchers Harry Collins and Jack Collins. Witt had been bought from the Athletics in April and Joe Dugan, the league's best third baseman, was acquired from the Red Sox in July—which outraged St. Louis fans and American League President Ban Johnson and ultimately produced a June 1 trading deadline.

Yet the Series was a disaster. The Giants wiped out a 2-0 Yankee lead in the eighth with four consecutive singles before Bush retired a man and grabbed the opener. And after the Yankees had climbed out of a three-run deficit to tie game two umpire George Hildebrand, anticipating darkness, called the game after ten innings, with forty-five minutes of daylight remaining.

"It was crazy," Dugan would say. "The people were milling around yelling. They were mad at everybody. They could have played another inning or two anyway. It was broad daylight. Everyone was laughing. It was a joke among the players."

Not so with Landis, who was hounded across Eighth Avenue by angry spectators demanding refunds, and who decided to turn over the profits to charity.

All of which merely prolonged the inevitable. Ruth, who batted .118 for the Series without a home run, was concluding a miserable season during which he was suspended several times, chased hecklers and wrangled frequently with Huggins.

"If you don't want to play ball, why don't you go home?" the manager would shout. "You go home!" Ruth would retort. "If you don't like the way I play ball, why don't you fire me?"

As Ruth slumped in the Series, so did the Yankees. The Giants blanked them in game three, held Ruth hitless, heckled him and finally hooted him out of their clubhouse when he turned up to warn them about the "personal stuff" they'd been shouting.

After erasing a 2–0 deficit to take game four, the Giants closed it out the following afternoon after Huggins, with the Yankees leading 3–2 in the eighth, ordered a reluctant Bush to walk Pep Youngs, thus loading the bases with two out.

George Kelly, who'd thrown out Aaron Ward to kill off the Yankees in the 1921 Series, hit Bush's next pitch into left-center field, scoring two runs and ending it.

Huston, who'd disliked Huggins ever since he'd been hired instead of Brooklyn manager Wilbert Robinson in 1918, brooded all the way to the press headquarters downtown where he smashed a row of cocktail glasses. "Miller Huggins," he vowed, "has managed his last game for the Yankees."

Instead, Huston had watched his last game as co-owner. Barrow, fed up with the colonels' bickering, threatened to quit unless the lines of authority were more clearly drawn. On May 1 Ruppert bought out Huston for $1.5 million and continued work on his own stadium on a 240,000-square-foot plot of land at 161st Street and River Avenue in the Bronx. It would be The House that Ruth Built—and Ruppert paid for.

1923

For a decade they had been fellow residents and business rivals, competing for the same spectator dollar. But the Giants were the landlords at the Polo Grounds, the Yankees their tenants, as Giant owner Charles Stoneham was quick to remind them.

As long as the tenants were no financial or artistic threat to the landlords, they'd been tolerated. But the arrival of Babe Ruth in 1920 had changed that relationship permanently. Where the Yankees had drawn 619,000 customers the previous year that number soared to 1,290,000, which was 100,000 more than the Giants at-

THE NEW HOME OF THE AMERICAN LEAGUE BASEBALL CLUB OF NEW YORK
· THE · OSBORN · ENGINEERING · CO · · CLEVELAND ·

Rendering of Yankee Stadium that would never be fully encircled as planned

Opening day at Yankee Stadium, April 18, 1923.

tracted while finishing second in the National League.

When that trend continued in 1921 Giant manager John McGraw, who'd urged Jacob Ruppert and Cap Huston to buy the Yankees a decade earlier, approached Stoneham about an eviction notice.

"The Yankees will have to build a park in Queens or some other out-of-the-way place," McGraw told him. "Let them go away and wither on the vine."

Stoneham had served notice on Ruppert during the middle of the 1922 season—and found that the Colonel had anticipated him. During the winter of 1921 Ruppert had bought for $600,000 from the estate of William Ward Astor a ten-acre parcel across the Harlem River between 157th and 161st streets.

Now he called a Cleveland engineering company and ordered plans and specifications drawn and told White Construction Company that it had one year and $1.9 million to build him a house for Babe Ruth.

The stadium would be in the Bronx, yet it could be reached in sixteen minutes by subway from the club offices downtown. The result was well worth the trip—a massive triple-tiered piece of cement-and-steel wedding cake that *The New York Times* labeled "a skyscraper among ballparks."

The contractors had needed 13,000 cubic yards of topsoil, 116,000 square feet of sod, 20,000 cubic yards of concrete, 2,200 tons of structural steel and 950,000 board feet of Pacific Coast fir for the bleachers, which stretched from foul line to foul line. As a hallmark, Ruppert added a copper frieze sixteen feet deep atop the stadium. There was no other structure like it anywhere.

Yankee Stadium would be the last privately financed ballpark in the land and Ruppert, with his systematic raiding of the Red Sox roster, had put together a ball club worthy of it.

And it was his club, finally. After he'd bought out Huston's share for $1.5 million, Ruppert had dashed off a telegram to the team in Chicago. "I now am the sole owner of the Yankees," it read. "Miller Huggins is my manager."

The roster was a manager's dream. The pitching staff—with Herb Pennock, Joe Bush, Sam Jones, Waite Hoyt, Bob Shawkey and Carl Mays—was so reliable that New York writers dubbed it the "Six-Star Final." Joe Dugan, at third base, was the game's best. Shortstop Everett Scott was the league's iron man. And a repentant and recharged Ruth was back in the outfield.

His worst year, ruined by bickering with his teammates and Huggins, a .315 average and a .118 World Series, was behind him. Now there

Lord and Lady Mountbatten attend the World Series with Ruppert.

was a new stadium to fill, a $1,000-a-week contract to live up to and a pennant to defend.

So Ruth reported to spring training at 200 pounds, his lowest weight as a Yankee, and on April 18 turned up at the Stadium for opening day eager for work.

So did a record major league crowd of nearly 65,000 New Yorkers (the announced figure of 74,200 was exaggerated) who nearly crushed Commissioner Kenesaw Mountain Landis in their eagerness to reach the turnstiles. As it was, the gates had to be closed half an hour early and 25,000 were turned away.

Inside John Philip Sousa and his 7th Regiment Band led a procession to centerfield that included Landis, Stoneham and Red Sox owner Harry Frazee, who'd sold the Yankees eleven members of their roster.

The 1922 pennant was raised to an ovation *The New York Times* said "floated across the Harlem and far beyond." Governor Al Smith threw out the first ball. And by the third inning Ruth had hit the first home run in his house, a three-run shot into the right field bleachers that sent the Yankees on to a 4–1 victory over Boston.

It was the first of 41 home runs that summer, as Ruth enjoyed his best year for average (.393), hits (205) and doubles (45), won the American League's MVP Award unanimously and helped the club draw a million spectators, thus burying McGraw's prophecy that "the fans will soon forget about them over there."

The Yankees, hardly coincidentally, won the pennant by sixteen games over Detroit and met the Giants for their third straight subway Series. This time it was no longer landlord versus tenant but neighbor against neighbor and McGraw was

Sad Sam Jones was the Yankees' top pitcher at 21–8 with a no-hitter.

Lou Gehrig made his Yankee debut at the age of 20, hitting .423 in 13 games, including the first of his 493 career home runs.

Casey Stengel as a Giant.

quick to draw the boundary line. He forbade his Giants to dress in Ruppert's stadium; instead they suited up at the Polo Grounds and took taxicabs across Central Bridge.

Whereupon Casey Stengel, their thirty-three-year-old outfielder, doubled the insult, legging out an inside-the-park home run with two out in the ninth to beat the Yankees, 5–4, in the opener at the Stadium.

His shot to left-center field bounced past Bob Meusel, but the cushion popped out of one of Stengel's shoes as he was rounding second. As he hobbled towards the plate like a spavined old workhorse, Damon Runyon scribbled notes for a timeless lead:

"This is the way old Casey Stengel ran yesterday afternoon, running his home run home. His mouth wide open. His warped old legs bending beneath him at every stride. His arms flying back and forth like those of a man swimming with a crawl stroke. His flanks heaving, his breath whistling, his head far back."

Finally Stengel collapsed atop the plate, his wind done, the game won. He had one more great blow left in him, a home run that won game three, 1–0—and infuriated Ruppert, since Stengel thumbed his nose at the Yankee dugout while rounding the bases.

"When a man wins a World Series game with a home run he should be permitted some exuberance," Landis told Ruppert. "Particularly when his name is Casey Stengel."

And particularly when it was the Giants' last gasp. Ruth, who hit .368 for the Series, had bashed two of his three home runs to give the Yankees game two. "The Ruth is mighty," wrote Heywood Broun, "and shall prevail."

So did his teammates. They cleaned up their former landlords in six games for their first world championship, winning all three at the Polo Grounds. Ruppert buoyantly threw a suitably lavish party at the Commodore downtown. "This is a wonderful occasion," the colonel decreed. "I now have baseball's greatest park, baseball's greatest players and baseball's greatest team."

1924

They were two of baseball's most legendary figures, yet they disliked each other on sight with a bitterness that knew no season. Once at a winter hunting lodge in Georgia, Detroit outfielder Ty Cobb had refused to share a cabin with Babe Ruth, who he felt had black ancestry. "I've never bedded down with a nigger," Cobb growled, "and I'm not going to start now."

In season Cobb had flung a series of epithets at Ruth whenever their paths crossed. Ruth was "an egg on stilts, a beer keg on two straws." Now, on June 13, the league-leading Yankees and second-place Tigers were matched in a critical series at Detroit and tempers were ready to flare.

A few words from Cobb to Ruth ("Do you smell something? Something around here really stinks. Like a polecat."), a 10–6 New York lead in the ninth inning and a "duster" signal from player-manager Cobb to pitcher Leonard "King" Cole provided the spark.

Cole's pitch hit Bob Meusel in the small of the back, Meusel flung his bat at Cole's head and charged the mound, and Cobb ran full-tilt from center to meet Ruth at the plate.

"I rushed at him like a football player trying to knock an opposing man out of the play," Ruth would say. What ensued was a thirty-minute riot that got Cole and Meusel suspended for ten days and lured 40,000 fans to Navin Field the next day, eager for an encore.

The game—and the series—were anticlimactic. There were no further brawls and neither New York nor Detroit won the pennant. Instead, a Washington club with a twenty-seven-year-old manager (Bucky Harris) and a thirty-six-year-old pitcher (Walter Johnson) came from seventh place to win its first American League pennant by two games over the Yankees.

"Washington got hot quicker than almost any club I ever saw," marveled Ruth, whose teammates had hoped to win an unprecedented fourth straight pennant.

Indeed, the Yankees led the league for eight weeks. They won five in a row at Washington in August and 18 of 22 games in September. Yet they lost a critical series at the Stadium at the end of August and the Senators never let them back in the race.

Washington won the series opener, 11–6, despite two Ruth home runs and went on to win three of the four games, bearing off the finale in the tenth inning.

There were still twenty-seven games left in the season but New York never held first place alone again, even though they forced the issue until the final four days.

When the Senators lost the opener of a series at Boston and the Yankees prevailed at Philadelphia, the deficit shrank to a single game. But Washington won the next two to the delight of

Herb Pennock had a 21–9 record.

Boston fans, who still carried a grudge from Ruppert's postwar talent raids. And the Yankees went on to lose two to the Athletics.

So the Senators proceeded to beat the Giants in seven games for their only world championship. And Huggins went home, filled his pipe and philosophized.

"The first pennant is the easiest to win," he told intimates, "no matter how hard the struggle may seem at the time. Then it is all new to your players. Once they have been through it, some of the shine has gone off it."

1925

The "stomachache heard 'round the world" was brought on, legend has it, by a dozen hot dogs and eight bottles of lemon soda. Nobody who knew Babe Ruth found that unusual; his idea of breakfast rarely corresponded to anybody else's. Six eggs, fried potatoes and a porterhouse steak seemed to him a reasonable start, washed down by a pot of coffee and a pint of bourbon mixed with ginger ale.

But on this particular morning, as the Yankees were making their way from Tennessee to North Carolina on their spring barnstorming tour, Ruth was gobbling whatever happened to be available on station platforms as the train was taking on passengers.

He'd been feeling feverish in Chattanooga and slept fitfully the night before. When the club arrived in Asheville, Ruth headed for a taxicab with catcher Steve O'Neill, then pitched headlong.

"Severe grippe and nervous attack," guessed the hotel doctor, but by the next morning Ruth was being loaded onto a Pullman bound for New York with sportswriters filing bedside updates at every station stop. Amateur diagnoses ranged from acute indigestion to venereal disease.

"Every goddamn bone in my body aches," Ruth told them. "But I'll be in the opener anyway. Don't worry."

But the opener came and went with Ruth lying restlessly in St. Vincent's Hospital. London newspapers had already pronounced him dead. Instead, surgeons found an intestinal abscess. The hot dogs and soda had merely been the crowning gustatory indignity to a decade of overindulgence.

From the moment Jack Dunn had brought him to Baltimore's training camp and he'd wolfed down three stacks of wheatcakes and three orders of ham, Ruth had force-fed himself like a Strasbourg goose. His legendary breakfasts were simply preludes to days filled with huge meals, exotic snacks and prodigious quantities of beer.

"You've never seen a man eat the way he did," marveled teammate Waite Hoyt. "If you cut that big slob in half, most of the concessions at Yankee Stadium would come pouring out."

To Ruth a midnight "snack" would include half a dozen club sandwiches, a platter of pigs' knuckles and a pitcher of beer, topped by a fat black cigar. Pickled eels and chocolate ice cream would do between games of a doubleheader. And in St. Louis, his favorite road town, the usual fare would be supplemented by tubs of spare ribs and frogs' legs.

No stomach ailment existed that couldn't be relieved by a fistful of bicarbonate of soda and a loud belch. But now he was flat on his broad back in a Manhattan hospital bed and as Ruth went, so went the Yankees. They were in fourth place at the end of the first week of the season; ironically, it was their best achievement of the year.

By the time Ruth returned to the lineup in June, pale and unsteady on his legs, the club had fallen to seventh while manager Miller Huggins despaired.

"They're through, Ed," he told Barrow after a

particularly abysmal western trip. "I can't even make 'em mad any more. They've just lost the urge to win. They just don't care any more."

"Very well," the general manager replied. "We'll get rid of them and get a new team."

So shortstop Everett Scott, who'd started a major-league record 1,307 games, was benched, then waived. A rookie named Lou Gehrig replaced Wally Pipp at first base, catcher Bennie Bengough took over for slumping Wally Schang. And outfielder Whitey Witt was released.

Still the Yankees remained mired in seventh and Ruth's return only produced further dissension between the club and Huggins, who was grimly trying to restore pride and discipline, particularly on Ruth's part.

His innards healed, Ruth had quickly gone back to his old training regimen—which was no regimen at all. He rarely stayed in the three-dollar hotel rooms the club reserved, opting for $100-a-day suites instead. And he rarely returned from his evening revels before dawn. No novelty there. "Who are you rooming with?" somebody had asked outfielder Ping Bodie during Ruth's first year in New York. "A suitcase," Bodie had replied.

Now, rebukes from Huggins merely provoked a torrent of criticism of managerial strategy from Ruth, who'd labeled the five-foot six-inch Huggins "Little Boy" and "The Flea" and once hung him over the platform railing of a moving train.

A showdown was inevitable and it came, suitably, on August 29 in St. Louis, where Ruth habitually made himself invisible. After two nights of this Huggins phoned Barrow in Manhattan.

"I want to fine that big ape."

"Well, it's all right with me," Barrow responded.

Except for starting pitcher Hoyt, the clubhouse was deserted when Ruth breezed in late for batting practice the third day.

"Sorry I'm late, Hug," he said. "Had some personal business to attend to."

"I know," Huggins told him. "Don't bother to uniform today. You're suspended."

"I'm what? Why you miserable little son of a bitch."

"What's more, you're fined five thousand dollars."

"I'm fined? I'm fined? Like hell I am. I'll see Jake about this. You think Jake will let you get away with this? You're crazy. Five thousand dollars? Why, you little bastard, I'll never play for you again. I'll see Jake. He'll throw you out on your ass."

Huggins shrugged. "That's what I want you to do. And I'd just like to be there when you burst into Ruppert's office carrying that .246 average and telling him I'm picking on you."

So Ruth boarded a train for Chicago, changed for the Twentieth Century Limited and "got indig-

Bob Meusel, homer champ and RBI champ.

While Ruth and Huggins feuded, Ruppert and Ruth meet to resolve Ruth's suspension.

Everett Scott's ironman streak ends.

Benny Bengough, the Yankee catcher.

nant for the benefit of every reporter who interviewed me at station stops."

Huggins is alibiing for his seventh-place effort, Ruth told them. He'd never wear a Yankee uniform as long as Huggins was manager. The choice would be Ruppert's.

Ruth held court briefly at his New York apartment, then led a trail of newspapermen to Ruppert's brewery where the colonel and Barrow read him out for half an hour behind closed doors.

"Gentlemen," Ruppert would tell the press, "I think maybe Root has changed his mind and will continue playing for Mr. Huckins. That's right, isn't it, Root?"

"Yes," Ruth murmured.

"Root is sorry about the whole thing," Ruppert continued. "We are all sorry. But it had to be."

Though the fine stood until Huggins' death four years later, the suspension was lifted when the club went to Boston on September 7 and Ruth brought his average from .246 to .290 over the season's final month. But the season was gone (the Yankees finished 28½ games behind Washington, in seventh place). By the following winter, so was much of the team.

1926

He was thirty-nine years old and he had beaten the Yankees twice in six days and had celebrated with a bottle or two. Now, all Grover Cleveland Alexander wanted was a chance to stretch his legs on the bench and rest.

"I'm going down to the bullpen," the Cardinal pitcher informed player-manager Rogers Hornsby before the seventh game of the World Series. "If you need me, I'll be there."

The call had come with two out in the seventh inning after New York had loaded the bases and sent Tony Lazzeri to the plate. "We're in a tough spot," Hornsby would inform Alexander. "And there's no place to put this guy."

"I'll take care of that," Alexander assured him—and went out to strike out Lazzeri, one of the Yankees' most reliable clutch hitters, on four pitches, in one of baseball's most dramatic moments. Two innings later, after what New York general manager Ed Barrow called "the only dumb play Babe Ruth ever made," the Cardinals had won the day, 3–2, and with it their first world championship.

And Alexander, an epileptic old-timer who'd been picked up for a song from the Cubs early in the season but still had four seasons left in him, was amused by his sudden elevation to demigod.

"You know, you never want to take this hullabaloo and hero stuff too seriously," he told friends afterward. "Yes, I struck out Lazzeri. But suppose that line drive he hit foul had gone fair? Boys, Lazzeri would be the hero tonight and I—well, I'd just be a bum."

Had Lazzeri's drive one pitch earlier passed to the other side of the left-field foul pole New York would have won its second world championship in four years and capped a remarkable season during which the Yankees submerged memories of their seventh-place finish in 1925 and laid the foundation for the greatest team the game had ever known.

Their revival had begun quietly enough amid a number of new faces, a fair amount of confusion at the club's St. Petersburg training quarters, and considerable press skepticism.

Whitey Witt, Wally Schang, Wally Pipp and Everett Scott all had been traded or released since July 1925. One rookie, Mark Koenig, would start at shortstop. Lazzeri, a newcomer from San Francisco, was the new second baseman. And a quiet slugger named Lou Gehrig had become a fixture at first.

Gehrig had joined the lineup virtually unnoticed in June of the previous year when Pipp, a ten-year regular, had complained of a headache after being beaned in batting practice by teammate Charlie Caldwell, who would make a more enduring reputation as Princeton football coach.

"Why don't you take the day off, Wally?" manager Miller Huggins had suggested. "We'll put the kid from Columbia on first today."

Pipp never started another game as a Yankee. Now he and several of his mates were gone and the New York lineup was a patchwork quilt of youngsters and veterans who openly doubted Huggins' competence. "The Yankees are a collection of individuals," Westbrook Pegler wrote from spring training, "who are convinced that their manager is a sap."

Only one New York sportswriter picked the Yankees to win the pennant, yet Huggins, who'd given up the 1925 season for lost after the first western trip, remained curiously optimistic.

"I believe we will win the pennant," he predicted as the club broke camp. "We'll either do that or fall apart. And I don't think we'll fall apart."

As if on cue the Yankees defeated Brooklyn twelve straight times on their barnstorming tour, won eight in a row shortly after returning north and found themselves in first place by the end of April.

Then, after a late-season stumble, they

Mark Koenig, shortstop, and . . . Tony Lazzeri formed the new second base combination for the Yankees.

Urban Shocker, 19–11 record.

clinched their fourth pennant in six years by sweeping a doubleheader from the Browns in St. Louis the day after expectant Cardinal fans had howled and pounded drums outside the Yankees' hotel windows.

St. Louis had never played in a Series and had won the National League race with a .578 percentage, the lowest ever to that point. New York had limped in three games ahead of Cleveland. Yet the two clubs produced a classic, breaking records for attendance (328,000) and gate receipts.

Once Ruth crashed three home runs in game four at Sportsman's Park the Yankees had taken control and returned to the Stadium leading three games to two.

But Alexander, who'd beaten them 6–2 in game two, easily evened the Series with a 10–2 triumph that barely exercised him, then stepped out for a Saturday night on the town. "If you need me tomorrow," he informed Hornsby, "I'll have a little left. This was fairly easy today."

What happened between then and Sunday morning is suspended somewhere between myth and reality. Alexander had an indisputable capacity and liking for hard liquor. With two complete-game Series victories in two starts he had ample reason to indulge.

Some accounts have him struggling in at dawn, breakfasting on a ham sandwich, falling asleep in the bullpen and waking with a vicious hangover and no idea of the score. Others claim he drank moderately, slept well and watched the game alertly.

"I was cold sober the night after I pitched the sixth game," Alexander insisted in later years. "There may have been plenty of times before and since when I wasn't, but I was sober that night."

What is beyond doubt is that the Cardinals brought a 3–2 lead into the bottom of the seventh and that starter Jesse Haines had developed a blood blister from throwing knucklers.

Now, New York's Earle Combs singled and Koenig sacrificed him to second. So Haines walked Ruth intentionally and got Bob Meusel to force him at second. Another walk, this time to Gehrig, loaded the bases with two out. But Haines's blister had burst and blood was dripping from his fingers.

"Can you make it, Jesse?" Hornsby asked him.

Haines grimaced.

"Well, I guess I'll have to relieve you."

So Hornsby motioned to the bullpen and Alexander emerged and began walking toward the infield, working on a chaw and unbuttoning his scarlet sweater jacket.

"We could hardly believe it," Ruth would say, "when the old fellow himself came through the gate."

Since the bullpen was wedged beneath the bleachers Alexander had no idea of the jam that faced him. "All you know," he said, "is what you learn from the voices of the fans overhead. So when I came out I saw the bases filled and Lazzeri standing in the box."

From his station at second base Hornsby met Alexander halfway in, peered into his eyes and found them clear. Or clear enough. "All right, get in there," Hornsby said, slapping Alexander on the back. "You can do it, Pete."

Next to Ruth, Lazzeri was New York's most productive hitter (114 RBI). "I guess there's nothing much to do except give Tony a lot of hell," Alexander decided.

His first pitch, a fastball, missed by inches and Alexander walked down to umpire George Hildebrand, "I've been pitching twenty years," he told him. "You might have given me that one."

The second, a low fastball, was a called strike. Then Lazzeri lashed a drive just inches to the wrong side of the foul pole. "No more of that for you, my lad," Alexander muttered.

Now, where he'd curved him twenty-four hours earlier, Alexander unleashed a fastball across the letters that left the swinging Lazzeri with his legs spread wide, his mouth agape.

There would be one more chance when Ruth walked with two out in the ninth and Meusel and Gehrig were due up. But Ruth, who'd only stolen twelve bases all season, inexplicably took off for second. Catcher Bob O'Farrell's throw beat him by ten feet, ending the game and the Series.

"I'll always remember putting the ball on him," Hornsby would say. "He didn't say a word. He didn't even look around or up at me. He just picked himself off the ground and walked away."

1927

Center fielder Earle Combs, who was leadoff man for this devastating sound-and-light show, called it "five o'clock lightning." When the eighth inning rolled around and New York bats exploded in a thunderstorm of home runs and extra-base hits, victory was a foregone conclusion.

The 1927 Yankees were probably the finest team in baseball history and certainly the most

1927 New York Yankees, World Champions. Generally acknowledged as the best team ever assembled. Front row (l–r) Julie Wera, Mike Gazella, Pat Collins, Eddie Bennett (mascot), Benny Bengough, Ray Morehart, Myles Thomas, Cedric Durst. Middle row (l–r) Urban Shocker, Joe Dugan, Earle Combs, Charlie O'Leary (coach), Miller Huggins (manager), Art Fletcher (coach), Mark Koenig, Dutch Reuther, Johnny Grabowski, George Pipgras. Back row (l–r) Lou Gehrig, Herb Pennock, Tony Lazzeri, Wilcy Moore, Babe Ruth, Don Miller, Bob Meusel, Bob Shawkey, Waite Hoyt, Joe Giard, Ben Paschal, (unknown), Doc Woods (trainer).

Babe Ruth held out for $75,000 and signed for a record $70,000, witnessed by Ruppert and Barrow (standing).

Ruth hitting one of his 60 homers.

September 30, 1927: Ruth hits his 60th homer, breaking his own record of 59 set in 1921.

dramatic. With their Murderer's Row of right fielder Babe Ruth (.356), first baseman Lou Gehrig (.373), second baseman Tony Lazzeri (.309) and left fielder Bob Meusel (.337) at the heart of the lineup, the club won 110 games and led the American League in average (.307), runs (975), home runs (158) and pyrotechnics.

The most productive, stylish and dramatic of them all was Ruth, who chose that year to set the sport's most cherished mark—sixty home runs—a record which stood for thirty-four years, and still stands for a 154-game season.

He was a svelter Ruth in 1927, thanks to an off-season exercise regimen supervised by Arty McGovern in a Manhattan gymnasium that replaced Babe's mostly symbolic Hot Springs boil-offs. And with a new $70,000-a-year contract in his pocket, he was a richer Ruth, too.

The stance and the swing, however, had remained unchanged since he'd set the major-league record of 59 in 1921. Ruth had always dug the knob of his big bat—variously estimated between 42 and 52 ounces—into his right palm and swung from the heels. Choking up was for lesser men. "I never found out whether Babe didn't ever know he had two strikes on him," mused Chicago catcher Moe Berg, "or whether he didn't care."

At any rate, Ruth's swing never varied. "I copied my swing after Joe Jackson's," he'd told writer Grantland Rice. "His is the perfectest. Joe aimed his right shoulder square at the pitcher with his feet about 20 inches apart. But I close my stance to about eight and a half inches or less. I find I pivot better. Once my swing starts, though, I can't change it or pull up. It's all or nothing at all."

For the first two weeks of 1927 Ruth's swing found mostly air; after ten games he'd hit only one homer, that off Philadelphia's Howard Ehmke. Then he crashed one off Rube Walberg, his favorite pigeon that year, which touched off a spree of five in six games.

By the end of May the count was 16, by July 4th, 26. With Gehrig matching him virtually shot for shot Ruth had piled up 43 at the beginning of September and finished the season with a burst, 17 in the final twenty-six games.

In all, Ruth would hit homers off thirty-three pitchers, twenty-three of them righthanders. Though twenty-eight of his shots came inside Yankee Stadium, Ruth had belted one in every American League park by July 24 and eventually hit at least four in every one but Chicago's Comiskey Park.

The record-breaker, a fly ball down the right-field line off a screwball that Ruth golfed from his shoetops, came off Washington lefthander Tom Zachary in the next-to-last game of the season.

For all practical purposes, the season ended on Independence Day when the Yankees shredded the second-place Senators in a doubleheader to the rather incredible tune of 12–1 and 21–1.

"Those fellows not only beat you, they tear your heart out," moaned Washington first baseman Joe Judge. "I wish the season was over."

It was a team without a discernible weakness, from outfielders Combs, Ruth and Meusel to infielders Gehrig and Lazzeri, to a superior pitching staff that led the league in ERA (3.20) and shutouts (11). Every pitcher had a winning record and four of them—Waite Hoyt, Herb Pennock, Urban Shocker and reliever Wilcy Moore—won at least eighteen games.

Five of their starting eight fielders had averages of .309 or better and, on their more inspired afternoons, the Yankees strained credulity. Once, when their train into Detroit was delayed and they had to forgo both batting and fielding practice, the club simply wolfed down a pre-game repast of hot dogs and soda, then went out and beat the

Combs, Ruth and Meusel.

Lou Gehrig.

Tigers, 19–2. The Pirates, who were struggling to win the National League race, hardly seemed a match for them.

"The Yanks will murder 'em," prophesied Brooklyn manager Wilbert Robinson. "They've got the best club that was ever in baseball." Murderer's Row, after all, had knocked in 544 runs; Ruth had hit six more homers than the entire Pirate roster.

When the Yankees arrived at Forbes Field for batting practice prior to the Series, manager Miller Huggins decided to play mind games with his hosts, who had already worked out, dressed and taken seats in the stands.

"See those upper bleachers?" he told his sluggers. "I want to see how many of these nice unblemished baseballs you can drop into those stands." Then, after instructing Hoyt to "lay it in there," Huggins sent Ruth (six foot two, 215 pounds), Gehrig (six feet, 200 pounds) and Meusel (six foot three, 190 pounds) into the cage and watched them smash consecutive home runs.

"You could actually hear them gulp while they watched us," Ruth would say, after belting half a dozen. Gehrig, who'd hit 47 during the season, hit two of his five over the center-field fence, where no National League ball had ever ventured. The ploy had its effect; the Pirates sat stunned.

"I've never seen anything like this before," mused shortstop Glenn Wright. "Do they do this all the time?"

Their reconnaissance done, the Pirates filed out of the park, all but resigned to a sweep. "Boys," manager Donie Bush told them in a team meeting before the opening, "we'll now go over the Yankee lineup and check the weaknesses of each batter."

They found none. "Oh, well, what's the use?" Bush concluded. "Let's go out on the ballfield and hope we all don't get killed."

If it was a killing, it was painless. New York did sweep the Pirates cleanly, but scored only 23 runs and hit only two homers, both by Ruth. Pitching and Pittsburgh errors took care of most of it.

Two walks and two errors gave the Yankees three runs in the opener. George Pipgras scattered seven hits in game two and won, 6–2. Pennock held the Pirates hitless for seven and one-third innings in game three and coasted, 8–1. Then Pittsburgh's Johnny Miljus uncorked two wild pitches in the ninth inning of game four, scoring Combs with the winner and it was over. With barely a trace of lightning.

1928

The play came from the same bag of tricks as the hidden ball and pinch-hitting midgets and it was legal in the National League. A hurler would whip one pitch past a batter, keep his toe on the rubber and quickly deliver another, hoping for a cheap strike.

It would not be allowed in the 1928 World Series, Commissioner Landis told his umpires—but nobody remembered to inform St. Louis manager Bill McKechnie, his Yankee counterpart Miller Huggins, or their clubs.

A minor matter—until Cardinal pitcher Bill Sherdel used the "quick pitch" to strike out Babe Ruth with one out in the seventh inning of game four at Sportsman's Park, touching off one of the most emotional disputes in Series history.

"You can't do that," Ruth howled at Sherdel. Plate umpire Charlie Pfirman, a National Leaguer, agreed with him, reset the count at 0–2 and brushed aside a ten-minute argument by the Cardinals. Ruth, who'd already hit one home run in the fourth and would crash another in the eighth, proceeded to belt the next pitch onto the roof of the right-field pavilion, sending New York on to a 7–3 victory and its second consecutive Series sweep.

Thus ended another vintage season in which the Yankees won their sixth American League pennant in eight seasons, avenged their seven-game loss to St. Louis two years earlier, and got owner Jacob Ruppert to give them the shirt off his back—literally.

Though his club had just completed the most impressive season in baseball history, winning 110 games and ravaging Pittsburgh for the world championship, Ruppert settled in for the winter of 1928 with his wallet all but padlocked.

As the contracts came back predictably unsigned, Ruppert and general manager Ed Barrow resorted to what the players came to term the "Elevated treatment," which involved a financial stone wall at either end and a five-cent rapid-transit ride in between.

When a player turned up at the club offices on 42nd Street to negotiate face-to-face, Barrow would murmur something about soaring operating expenses and shrinking profits and suggest a trip uptown to the colonel's brewery. "It's Ruppert's money," Barrow would shrug. "Go up and see him."

While the player headed for the train Barrow would brief Ruppert by phone and the futile circle would be complete. "I can't understand what has got into you fellows," Ruppert would sigh when the player arrived. "One wants this, another wants that. Root wants $80,000. Gehrig wants more money. Dugan wants more. What do you fellows think I am, a millionaire?"

Ruth settled for the same $70,000, his teammates gradually came to terms and the Yankees went about their customary business of making hash of the pennant race.

Shortly after Independence Day their lead over Philadelphia was 13½ games—yet the club inexplicably came apart down the stretch and was trailing by half a game in early September.

The race came down to a four-game series with the Athletics in the Stadium and New York quickly moved to claim it by sweeping a doubleheader before 80,000 partisans on the first day. George Pipgras won the first game by shutout, Bob Meusel won the nightcap with a grand slam—and the Yankees proceeded to take three of four and eventually win the pennant by 2½ games.

On paper the Series seemed uncompetitive. The Yankees hadn't lost a Series game since Pete Alexander had struck out Tony Lazzeri in the 1926 finale; the Cardinals had struggled to win the National League by two games over the Giants. Yet the Yankees were hobbled. Left fielder Earle Combs had broken a finger, pitcher Herb Pennock was nursing a sore arm. Neither was available. Ruth (sprained ankle and a charley horse), third baseman Joe Dugan (bad knee) and Lazzeri (sore arm) were all playing hurt.

Still, New York won the opener, 4–1, and quickly came to dominate the Series. In game two the Yankees scored eight runs in two and one-third innings off (sweet irony) Alexander. And nothing changed when the Series moved to St. Louis. New York took a 7–3 victory in game three and started talking sweep.

Meanwhile, Ruth was on his way to the finest Series of his career (.625) in stark contrast to 1926 when Cardinal pitchers had walked him 11 times. This time McKechnie told them to challenge him and Ruth merrily hit away.

His leadoff homer over the rightfield pavilion was merely a warning signal in game four; still St. Louis led, 2–1, in the seventh and Sherdel quickly got two strikes on Ruth. Now his "quick pitch" caught Ruth flat-footed and staring. But Pfirman ruled otherwise. "Ruth isn't out," he explained. "Sherdel will have to pitch over to him."

While the Cardinals argued with Pfirman, Ruth laughed as he ducked bottles from the stands, then returned to the batter's box and challenged Sherdel.

"Put one in here again," he shouted, "and I'll knock it out of the park for you." So Ruth did, tying the game and setting off an ovation. Gehrig followed with his fourth homer of the Series to the

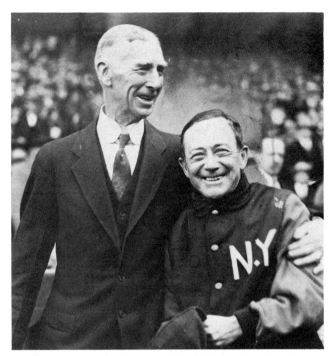

Huggins' sixth Yankee pennant in 1928 equaled Connie Mack's American League record.

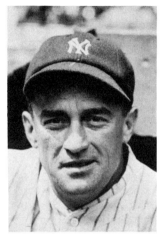

Urban Shocker gets ill early in the season and dies by its end.

Joe Dugan plays his last Yankee season.

Grover Cleveland Alexander (left) of the Cardinals is shown with his opponent, George Pipgras, before they take the mound for the second game of the World Series.

same spot and the Yankees proceeded to send eight men to the plate and score four runs.

For punctuation, Ruth closed out the game and the Series in the ninth with a one-handed grab of a foul ball that he plucked from the lap of a spectator in the leftfield stands. No team had ever swept consecutive World Series. "My boys don't believe in letting these things drag out," Ruppert crowed.

Whereupon the Yankees celebrated all the way back to the Bronx during one of the wildest train rides in memory. At its center was Ruth, naturally, fortified by a fifty-pound basket of choice spare ribs and buckets of beer, and crying, "Is everybody happy?" to the well-wishers that crowded station platforms en route.

Even the reticent, pipe-smoking Huggins got tipsy and spent the following morning searching for his false teeth.

As the night wore on the Yankees organized a raucous parade that snaked through the railroad cars, commandeering pajama tops from passengers on the way and arriving finally at Ruppert's berth to find the door locked.

"This is no night for sleeping," Ruth decided.

"Go away, Root," Ruppert cried.

So Ruth and Gehrig broke down the door, found Ruppert in lavender nightclothes and stripped him to the waist.

"Is this usual, Root?" the colonel protested.

It wasn't—and there would be no more celebrations for four years, until after Huggins was dead and Ruth was in the twilight of his career.

Miller Huggins' health fades, and he dies late in the season.

1929

He'd noticed the blotch with half a month left in the season and had shrugged it off, even after it had grown into a boil and threatened to close an eye.

"Go to a doctor because I've got a red spot on my face?" Miller Huggins scoffed. Five days later, at fifty, the Yankee manager was dead from massive blood poisoning and an era had ended. The passing of Huggins was the grim climax of a season prefaced by personal tragedies when the New York dynasty came crashing down.

The bad omens had actually begun toward the end of the 1928 season when pitcher Urban Shocker died from heart trouble at thirty-eight. Then Helen Ruth, Babe's estranged first wife, was killed in a fire in Boston.

The Yankees, who'd won six pennants in eight years and swept consecutive World Series, never left the ground, winning only 88 games and finishing 18 behind Connie Mack's Philadelphia Athletics.

The 1927 and 1928 clubs had been so dominant, so flawless, that the first strains of what would become a periodic lament had been heard—"Break up the Yankees." But owner Jacob Ruppert, who'd spent fourteen years and several million dollars building them, merely snorted. "I not only have no thought of breaking up the Yankees," he maintained, "but Ed Barrow, Huckins and myself will exert our best efforts to strengthen them."

Yet there was perceptible slippage, even though the meat of the lineup—Ruth, Lou Gehrig, Tony Lazzeri, Earle Combs, Bob Meusel—remained unchanged.

Gehrig wearing No. 4 in a season that sees the Yankees wearing uniform numbers for the first time— the first team to do so regularly.

Tom Zachary had a big year pitching.

Ruth with Leo Durocher.

Bill Dickey is the Yankees' new young catcher.

Ruth remarries a few months after his first wife dies in a fire. They honeymoon in Boston and, encouraged by Ruppert, the second Mrs. Ruth travels the road with Ruth the rest of his career, which caused resentment among Yankee wives who weren't allowed by club rules.

Ruth hits his 500th career homer.

Gehrig's average dropped from .374 to .300, Meusel's from .297 to .261. And a lippy .246 hitter named Leo Durocher, whom Ruth quickly dubbed the "All-American Out," was playing shortstop.

Time and changing chemistry were doing what American League rivals could not, just as Huggins had predicted. "It won't be necessary to break up the Yankees," he'd said prior to the season. "No matter what we do the law of averages will take care of us. We can go on trying to improve this team to the best of our abilities, but the time will come when we will crash."

Although the Yankees were in the 1929 pennant race until August they were never in command after mid-May and would chase the Athletics, who hadn't won a pennant in fifteen years, all summer. Huggins realized that in May. His club had no spark, no hunger.

"I don't think the Yankees are going to catch the Athletics," he told a Cleveland sportswriter. "I don't think these Yankees are going to win any more pennants, certainly not this one. They're getting older and they've become glutted with success. They're getting good salaries and they've taken a great deal of money out of baseball. The Yankees turn to the financial page before the sports page."

Neither was a fruitful pursuit that year. The stock market crashed in October and the Yankees in August, when the fourth-place Browns shut them out three days in a row.

Exasperated, Huggins called a team meeting. "I don't want anybody to leave," he began. "I have something to say to you." What followed was a long managerial tirade that produced no reaction at all.

"They're through, Colonel," Huggins told Ruppert minutes later.

"But we still have a month . . ."

"Forget about it," Huggins said. "Start getting ready for next year. These fellows are through."

"But how do you know?"

"I just finished talking to them. I talked to them twenty minutes. I talked to them calmly, I pleaded with them. Then I abused them. No matter what I said or how I said it, it didn't make the slightest difference. I couldn't make them mad. I couldn't even make them laugh. When I realized that I might as well have been talking to that wall over there, I quit."

Ruppert was mystified. "But why? Why should they be through?"

"I guess they're just tired, Colonel. I'm tired myself. I'm tired out and can't sleep."

Huggins had been molding, teaching, cajoling this team for eleven years, transforming the Yankees from laughable Polo Grounds tenants into the sport's greatest dynasty. Along the way he had endured the derision of one owning partner, and another who never could pronounce his name, had squabbled with his greatest star and brushed aside insults from his players about his five-foot-six-inch height, .265 lifetime batting average, and professional judgment.

Yet his teams had won 1,067 games, six pennants and three world championships. Now neuritis, worry and insomnia were chewing Huggins up. And an ugly red blemish had appeared under his left eye.

"I must have picked up some kind of infection," he told coach Art Fletcher. "I first noticed it last night. I'll have a doctor look at it after the game."

But before the game Huggins turned the team over to Fletcher and walked into the clubhouse to sit beneath a sun lamp. Five days later he was dead.

Eventually, a memorial would be erected in center field at the Stadium. For the moment, grieving players carried his casket out of the Little Church Around the Corner in Manhattan.

Even Ruth, who'd spent a decade shouting at the manager, defying his orders and holding him over the platform railing of moving trains, wept openly. "A great little guy," he concluded, "was Hug."

1930

He had played in this league for sixteen years and worn pinstripes for ten, won 92 games as a left-handed pitcher, then became the greatest slugger in baseball history. And at thirty-five he was older, if not wiser.

And now that Miller Huggins was dead and coach Art Fletcher had turned down the chance to succeed him, Babe Ruth realized that Babe Ruth would be the perfect manager for the Yankees.

He'd mentioned as much to a newspaperman before Huggins's casket was even in the ground. During the off-season he put together an oral résumé and went up to owner Jacob Ruppert's brewery to apply in person.

"I told him that I knew how to handle young pitchers because I had been one myself," Ruth would say. "And I knew how to handle hitters because I was one myself. I told him everything I could think of, but when I had finished he just shook his head, kind of sadly."

Ruth, Ruppert, and Bob Shawkey, the new Yankee manager. Ruth wanted the job.

Ruth signs a two-year contract for $80,000, a season, his career high.

Ruppert welcomes Red Ruffing—another steal from the Red Sox.

"You can't manage yourself, Root," Ruppert concluded. "How do you expect to handle others?"

Only two men had managed the club since Ruppert and Cap Huston had bought it in 1915, yet Ruppert soon found that qualified candidates were scarce.

Fletcher, who'd been Huggins's ablest lieutenant and had taken over command when blood poisoning had killed the Yankee manager eleven games from the end of the 1929 season, had managed the Phillies for four years. Long enough to know, Fletcher realized, that he'd rather remain a third-base coach. "I just turned down the best job in baseball," he told his wife. Next, general manager Ed Barrow approached former Pittsburgh manager Donie Bush—and found that he'd just signed on with the White Sox. And Eddie Collins, who'd managed the White Sox for two years, had consulted Athletics manager Connie Mack and decided that he wasn't quite ready for the most demanding job in baseball.

Finally, Barrow decided on a candidate and phoned Ruppert. "I'm bringing your new manager up to see you."

"Who is it?" Ruppert asked.

"Bob Shawkey."

At first glance it seemed a reasonable compromise. Shawkey had forged a brilliant career as a righthanded pitcher, winning 196 games and playing in five World Series. He had been a Yankee; he knew the standards, the expectations, the players. And from Ruth to the pitching staff the players knew him . . . probably too well.

After a decade of Huggins's reticence and disciplinary tendencies, the Yankees approached Shawkey's ascendancy as a time of indulgence and casually defied his training rules. The blowup came in Philadelphia after Al Simmons had belted a home run off Shawkey's old stablemate Waite Hoyt.

"What did you throw him?" Shawkey asked Hoyt.

"A fastball."

"Well, don't do it again. After this, make him hit your curve ball."

"If I ever threw him my curve ball," Hoyt shouted at Shawkey, "he'd hit it over the stand. Don't tell me how to pitch to Simmons. I'll go on pitching him my way."

"You'll pitch the way I tell you," Shawkey retorted, "or you won't pitch for me at all."

Two weeks later Hoyt and shortstop Mark Koenig were gone, traded to Detroit. Bob Meusel, the left fielder since 1921, had been sent to Cincinnati before the season opened.

In all, thirty-six men wore New York pinstripes that year. Meanwhile, the club was sliding

1931

Lyn Lary was the new Yankee shortstop.

The experiment had lasted for one season and one third-place finish and it had worked fitfully from the beginning. One Yankee, owner Jacob Ruppert and general manager Ed Barrow realized, could not manage his teammates. So Bob Shawkey, who'd been a compromise choice in the first place, was dismissed after the 1930 season and this time Barrow was certain of his man.

The new manager would be well grounded in fundamentals, a gifted handler of personnel and, most important, a stern disciplinarian. Fortunately, he would be immediately available.

Joe McCarthy, who'd brought the Cubs from the National League cellar to the World Series in four years, had just been let go. So Barrow contacted him just prior to the Series opener between the Athletics and St. Louis in Philadelphia and arranged a meeting in Ruppert's New York apartment.

But Ruppert, who was accustomed to personalizing salary negotiations with his world champions, quickly found that McCarthy drove a harder bargain.

"Those are my terms, Colonel," McCarthy insisted when Ruppert balked. "After all, you sent for me. I didn't ask to see you." And McCarthy had departed, with a stunned Ruppert pursuing him down the hallway shouting, "McCardy, McCardy, come back."

The McCarthy approach proved to be equally inflexible—and effective—with players. Though he'd never played a game in the major leagues he'd learned a lifetime's worth of baseball during twenty years in the bushes.

Joe McCarthy had been a fine fielder and a clever tactician during his International League days and had stressed those qualities as a manager. His clubs turned textbook double-plays and absorbed changing game-situations instinctively. It was expected.

"I'm no second-division manager," he told the Yankees from the beginning. "And I won't stand for the second division."

McCarthy thought little of conventional psychology. "Had a pitcher with us this spring who majored in psychology," he once told writers. "Sent him to Newark last week." Yet McCarthy was an adept psychologist with a flair for dramatic symbolism.

He ordered the Yankees' uniforms a half-size larger and had their caps squared off to make them appear bigger. He forbade pre-game

to third, where it would finish the season sixteen games behind Philadelphia.

"The trouble with this club," one veteran concluded after glancing around the clubhouse, "is that there are too many fellows on it who aren't Yankees."

Or that one Yankee was expected to control his former teammates. Though Ruppert and Barrow told Shawkey they were satisfied with his efforts and implied they'd rehire him, they came to realize they needed a dispassionate outsider, and prior to the World Series they approached a tough disciplinarian who'd never played a game in the majors yet had an instinctive feel for managing. His name was Joe McCarthy and he would reestablish a dynasty in the Bronx.

Meanwhile, Shawkey, unaware, turned up at the team offices on 42nd Street hoping to talk contract. "I was heading for Barrow's office when the door opened and McCarthy came walking out," he said. "I took one look and turned around and got out of there. I knew what had happened."

From the start there was mutual loathing between Ruth and Marse Joe McCarthy, the new Yankee manager and, despite the picture, the Bambino never made a secret of his dislike for the man.

Ruth and Gehrig tied for League homers with 46 each, but Gehrig lost the outright title when ...
Lyn Lary ran off base path at game's end, costing Gehrig a 47th homer. Lary, himself, had 107 RBI's this season—the most ever made by a Yankee shortstop.

Lefty Gomez led Yankee pitchers with a 21–9 record, the first of his four 20-win seasons.

Ben Chapman brought color to the Yankees with his spectacular base-stealing—61 that season (trailing only Maisel's 1914 record of 74). Yet, Chapman set another team record—he was caught 23 times.

Earle Combs' 29-game batting streak tied the Yankee record, which stood until DiMaggio's 56 in 1941.

shaving in the clubhouse. And when he discovered a round table in a clubhouse corner when the team arrived for the 1931 opener he immediately summoned attendant Fred Logan.

"What's that?"

"Why, that's the card table," Logan informed him.

"Take it out of here." McCarthy paused. "Wait a minute. Get an axe. Break it up. Now take it out."

Then, turning to the players, he laid down Chapter One of McCarthy's Rules of Order. "This is a clubhouse, not a clubroom. Do your card playing in your homes. When you come in here, I want you to have your minds on baseball."

New York might not catch the Athletics, who would make a triumphant last stand in 1931, but they would play more like the Yankees—with verve, abandon and vigor. For the moment, Ruppert would settle for a stylistic improvement.

"I will stand for you finishing second this year because you are new in this league," the owner had told his manager in spring training. "But I warn you, McCardy. I don't like to finish second."

"Neither do I, Colonel," McCarthy had replied. Ironically, McCarthy's clubs would finish second four times. They would also lay the foundation for the greatest dynasty in baseball history.

1932

Half a century later, no photograph has ever been found. The only testimony beyond newspaper accounts are contradictory memories and an artist's reconstruction that freezes the moment: packed Wrigley Field stands as a backdrop, Cub catcher Gabby Hartnett squatting before impassive umpire Roy Van Graflin and George Herman Ruth with his right index finger pointing to center field. Calling his shot.

Players and managers on both sides disagree on where Ruth pointed or whether he pointed at all. Chicago pitcher Charlie Root, who delivered the ball, swore it never happened and refused to play himself in the Hollywood version of Ruth's life. And seven persons brandished scuffed baseballs outside the park afterward, all claiming they had the genuine article.

But this much is beyond doubt: After taking two strikes from Root, Ruth crashed a prodigious home run over the bleacher screen at the base of the center-field flagpole to break a 4–4 tie in the

Ruth being congratulated by Gehrig after scoring a "called" homer in the fifth inning of the third game of the 1932 World Series in Chicago between the Yankees and the Cubs.

Cub pitcher Charlie Root, who served up Ruth's "called" homer.

Ruth took ill during a snowy April day in Boston, running a fever with "incipient influenza." He was bundled back to New York, lost 12 pounds and, "weak as a cat," still homered in the Yankees' opener.

Joe McCarthy came back to face the Cubs, managed by Charlie Grimm.

Red Ruffing led the League in strikeouts (140), the first of 3 straight years a Yankee pitcher would do so.

Frank Crosetti began his 17-season Yankee career as a player, many more as a coach. He cashed more World Series checks than any other Yankee ever.

Miller Huggins Memorial is dedicated—the first of the famed monuments in center field of Yankee Stadium.

George M. Weiss began his legendary career as general manager with the Yankees in 1932.

fifth inning of the third game to spur the Yankees to a 7–5 victory and a sweep of the 1932 World Series.

It was Ruth's fifteenth—and last—Series homer and, for pure dramatic impact, his most memorable. The Babe had called—and made—other shots: once at the Polo Grounds after an umpire had just ruled one home run an inch foul, another for an ailing boy named Johnny Sylvester, still another to break up a thirteen-inning game and enable the Yankees to make a train.

Yet none of them was predicted and executed with as much flair, or before so hostile an audience. Although the two clubs had never played previously and the Yankees would prevail easily, the encounter was one of the most vitriolic in Series history, marked by bitter bench-jockeying throughout.

To begin with, the Cubs had dismissed Yankee manager Joe McCarthy two years earlier after he'd produced a second-place finish. Then, after former Yankee shortstop Mark Koenig had reemerged from the minors and hit .353 during the last 33 games to insure the 1932 pennant, his Chicago teammates had voted him only a partial share of their winnings.

They were misers, the Yankees decided angrily. Nickel-nursers. When the Cubs filed through the New York dugout on the way to their own before the Series opener at the Stadium, Ruth led a hooting serenade.

"Hey, you lousy bunch of cheapskates," he shouted. "Why do you associate with a bunch of bums like that, Mark?"

And once the Yankees had cleaned up the first two games and the Series shifted to Wrigley, the Ruthian chorus climbed an octave. "Hey, mugs," he called to the Cubs during batting practice before the third game. "You mugs aren't going to see Yankee Stadium any more this year. This is going to be over Sunday afternoon. Four straight."

As punctuation Ruth knocked nine balls into the bleacher seats. "I'd play for half my salary," he informed his hosts, "if I could hit in this dump all my life."

The Cubs responded in kind. Their female fans had jeered and spat on Ruth and his wife as they'd arrived at their hotel. Now, as Ruth came to bat in the first inning, they waved a white towel from the dugout steps. "If I had you on my team," trainer Andy Lotska hollered, "I'd hitch you to a wagon, you big balloon-belly."

Ruth answered with a three-run shot into the right-center-field bleachers. In the fifth, more abuse emanated from the Chicago dugout, augmented by aged fruit and vegetables from the grandstand. Ruth, delighted, flashed the choke sign to the Cub bench and peered out at Root on the mound. "If that bum throws one in here," he advised Hartnett, "I'll hit it over the fence again."

Root's first pitch split the plate. "I raised my hand," Ruth would say, "stuck out one finger and yelled strike one." Root sent another fastball toward the same spot, which Ruth treated the same way. Two fingers. Two strikes.

Kneeling in the on-deck circle Lou Gehrig heard Ruth shout to Root: "I'm going to knock the next pitch down your goddamn throat."

Then, the Babe pointed to deepest center field. Or did he?

"If Ruth had pointed to the center-field stands I'd have knocked him on his fanny with the next pitch, believe me," Root insisted. "He just held up two fingers to show there were only two strikes and he still had one coming."

Other witnesses, including McCarthy and Hartnett, claim Ruth first pointed to off-duty Cub pitcher Guy Bush, who was heckling him from the dugout, and then to the mound, reminding Bush he'd be the next day's victim.

"What happened was this," insisted Zack Taylor, one of the Cubs' substitute catchers. "Our bench was yelling just awful things about Babe's personal life. Anyway, he turned to us. He put up two fingers. Two strikes. Then he put up one finger saying, 'I got one left.' And then he pointed to direct center field. He hit that pitch right into what must have been a sixty-mile-an-hour wind coming off that lake and I don't know how he did it."

As Ruth trotted around the bases on his thirty-seven-year-old legs, the Chicago dugout was dumbstruck. "There they were, all out on the top step and yelling their brains out," center fielder Earle Combs told Ruth afterward. "And then you connected and they watched it and then fell back as if they were being machine-gunned."

Ruth roared with laughter as he rounded the bases. "You lucky bum," he told himself. "Lucky, lucky." He stopped long enough at third to execute a mock-formal bow to his tormentors, then headed home. "That's the first time I ever got the players and the fans going at the same time," he would boast. "I never had so much fun in all my life."

Gehrig whose brilliant Series (.529 with three homers) was overshadowed by Ruth's theatrics, followed with another to right field and the Cubs were finished. The Yankees buried them, 13–6, the next afternoon for their third consecutive Series sweep.

It was the Babe's last hurrah and he willingly let fans and sportswriters embroider it with mythic exaggeration. "I didn't exactly point to any spot like the flagpole," he would confess when pressed. "Anyway, I didn't mean to. I just sorta waved at the whole fence. All I wanted to do was give that thing a ride. Outa the park. Anywhere."

1933

Before April was even played out they suspected that the odds had come back on them, that the Senators were grimly serious this time, that the summer would be long, turbulent and ultimately empty.

In 1933 the Yankees fielded the same lineup that had won the 1932 pennant by 13 games and swept the Cubs for the world championship, but every important hitter had a less inspired season. Lou Gehrig's average dropped from .349 to .334, Babe Ruth's from .341 to .301, Tony Lazzeri's from .300 to .294, Earle Combs's from .321 to .298.

The pitching staff, which had led the American League in complete games and earned-run average, fell off visibly. From the beginning, Washington, rallying around new player-manager Joe Cronin, literally fought them for the pennant.

The bad blood went back to the previous season when New York catcher Bill Dickey had broken Carl Reynolds's jaw with a punch after a collision at the plate. In their first 1933 series at Griffith Stadium, Senator second baseman Buddy Myer set the tone by sliding into first and spiking Gehrig, and Ruth by crashing into shortstop Cronin. Three days later New York outfielder Ben Chapman spiked Myer, who kicked Chapman, which sparked a brawl that emptied both benches and several rows of the grandstand.

And after outfielder Dixie Walker had jumped Myer from behind, Yankee pitcher Lefty Gomez had knocked down a plainclothes policeman with a bat, five spectators had been arrested and Chapman, Myer and Walker had been ejected, the battle flared anew. Washington pitcher Earl Whitehill challenged Chapman as he headed for the showers, Chapman punched Whitehill, and a dozen Senators pursued Chapman and Walker down the dugout stairs.

New York prevailed that day, 16–0, but when hostilities shifted to the Bronx a week later the Yankees stumbled into a bizarre double play that left them mumbling to themselves and convinced the Senators that pinstripes were not necessarily synonymous with infallibility.

With New York trailing 6–4 in the ninth inning, Gehrig and Walker on base and none out, Lazzeri lashed a line drive over Goose Goslin's head in right-center field. Gehrig cautiously hugged second, and Walker, head down, sprinted from first. As Goslin played the ball off the wall both men rounded third only a few feet apart and Washington catcher Luke Sewell braced for a stampede.

"I could see the ball coming in, and out of

Ruth took a $23,000 cut to $52,000. His homer production tumbled from 41 to 34, and his batting average from .341 to .301.

Opening day pitchers Lefty Gomez versus Red Sox' Ivy Andrews. Gomez would lead the League in strikeouts, but his record slid from 24–7 to 16–10.

Ruth pitched an 11-hitter versus the Red Sox in the season finale and homered to win his own game, 6–5.

Lou Gehrig married in the final days of the season. He and his bride were whisked by motorcycle escort to the stadium where, predictably, he hit a homer.

1934

The box score still included his name, as it had daily for more than two decades. He made the All-Star team and by conventional standards his statistics—batting .288, with 22 home runs and 84 RBI's—were impressive enough. But they were no longer Ruthian—and the Babe knew it.

He was thirty-nine years old now, and after 2,349 games and nights filled with overindulgence, his body had come apart from the ground up. "It was becoming more and more difficult for me to drive my legs over the outfield grass," Ruth conceded. He would play in only 125 games in 1934, frequently giving way to pinch runners Sammy Byrd (a.k.a. Babe Ruth's Legs) and Myril Hoag in the late innings, and he would play for less money.

As a concession to Depression economics and his own dropping productivity Ruth had agreed to still another pay cut, this time to $35,000, which was $45,000 less than he'd commanded three years earlier.

On a Yankee roster that included Lou Gehrig and Bill Dickey, both of whom were hitting for better averages and playing every day, Ruth had become a nostalgic period piece, frequently at odds with manager Joe McCarthy, whose job he wanted.

"McCarthy and Ruth barely spoke to one another," said reserve pitcher Burleigh Grimes. "Babe wanted to manage and he didn't particularly care for Joe. There wasn't a hell of a lot Joe could do about Ruth. Christ, the man was an institution."

Yet when a New York columnist polled the team anonymously in June, they unanimously felt that Ruth should be removed from the lineup. It never happened; still, Ruth fretted that he'd blown a golden chance at a new career.

Detroit owner Frank Navin had called about a manager's job the previous fall and Ruth, about to embark on a barnstorming tour of Hawaii, had brushed him off.

"Can't it wait until I get back?"

"No," Navin had replied. "It can't wait. I would like to get this matter settled."

So while Ruth clouted baseballs into the Pacific, Navin bought Athletics catcher Mickey Cochrane and made him player-manager. Late in 1934 Cochrane was managing the Tigers to the first of two consecutive pennants. "One of the great boners of my career," Ruth concluded, and resolved to see owner Jacob Ruppert about the

the corner of my eye caught sight of Gehrig running down the third-base line," Sewell remembered years later. "Maybe Lou didn't think the play was going to be close as he didn't slide, and half broke his stride before he reached the plate."

But Cronin's relay was dead on and Sewell tagged Gehrig standing up. "He hit me hard at the plate and spun me completely around," said Sewell. "But as I spun I caught sight of Walker coming down. I dove down the line, blocking him off from the plate and also tagged him." Dickey grounded to second a moment later and 35,000 New Yorkers sat mystified. "We went downhill from there," Ruth decided.

The Yankees managed to play at a .700 clip until June, then dropped 30 percentage points in eight days as the pitching soured and Ruth slumped. On June 23 Washington took over first place, then swept a symbolic July 4 doubleheader (a year to the day after Reynolds's broken jaw) and stayed in command. In all the Senators won 14 of their 22 games with the Yankees, built a nine-game lead by September 10 and went on to win the pennant by seven.

Meanwhile, back at 161st Street, memories of 1932 had vanished. With home attendance off by nearly a quarter of a million, the Yankees had Ruth, at thirty-eight, pitch the season finale with Boston. He won 6–5 and hit a home run. It had come to that.

Gehrig won the triple crown in 1934 and was named MVP by Sporting News in spite of being KO'd at an exhibition game in Norfolk, Va.

At season's end, Ruth and Gehrig toured Japan while the Yankees mulled Ruth's fate. A feud developed between the two and they never spoke again until Gehrig Day at Yankee Stadium in 1939, when Lou was dying.

Former Fordham star Johnny Murphy was 14–10 as a Yankee rookie. He would convert to relief the next year and lead the League in relief 6 out of 9 years.

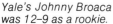

Yale's Johnny Broaca was 12–9 as a rookie.

Rookie Red Rolfe from Dartmouth divided his time between second and third base, but became the regular third baseman the following season for years thereafter.

New York job, just as he had done in 1929 and 1930.

"Well, Root, this is a surprise," Ruppert said when Ruth turned up at the brewery later in the season. "What's on your mind?"

"Are you satisfied with McCarthy as your manager?"

"Why, yes."

"Well, I'm not."

"Root, I know you would like to manage this ball club. Don't think I haven't considered the matter. I have. But this is a big business, Root, and you are unproven as a manager. No one has a greater admiration for you as a player than I have. As a manager . . . I don't know."

Ruppert paused. Perhaps Ruth would consider managing the Yankees' top farm club.

"Would you go to Newark, Root?"

"No. I won't go to Newark or any other minor-league club. Why should I? I'm a big-leaguer. Why should I go to the minors?"

"I think you're being foolish," Ruppert told him.

"Maybe," Ruth replied, "but that's the way I feel about it."

"Then I can do nothing."

The Yankees went on to finish seven games behind the Tigers and Ruth, disgusted, went off to watch the World Series. As he boarded the train leaving St. Louis for Detroit and the final two games, an engineer poked his head out.

"How many home runs you going to hit for the Yankees next year?"

"The hell with the Yankees," Ruth told him. "I wouldn't play with them again if they gave me the club. I'm quitting."

A newspaperman overheard the conversation, printed Ruth's comments, and Ruppert and general manager Ed Barrow read them in New York the next morning. While Ruth was in Japan on another barnstorming tour they decided to unload him.

"They had an interesting contract waiting for me when I returned," Ruth would say. One dollar, Ruppert decreed, unless Ruth proved worthy of more in spring training. So after Ruth had the Boston Braves owner, Judge Emil Fuchs, over for dinner on a Sunday night in February he dropped by Ruppert's office the next morning.

"You're still satisfied with McCarthy as your manager?"

"Yes."

"And there is no chance that you will change your mind?"

"No."

Ruth retreated to the anteroom to fetch Fuchs, who informed Ruppert that he was willing to purchase Ruth and bring him back to Boston, where he'd begun his career in 1914. Whereupon the Colonel handed Ruth a paper containing his unconditional release. Barrow had called every American League club and Ruth had cleared waivers. He was free to go. "I think this is what you want, isn't it, Root?" Ruppert asked him.

"But the price?" Fuchs asked. "What do you want for him?"

"Nothing," Ruppert decided. "Ruth has been a great ballplayer for this club. I am sorry we could not satisfy him now. But I do not wish to stand in his way now to make any profit from his opportunity to better himself."

So Ruth, at forty, returned to Boston and a club that would tumble from fourth to the National League cellar and lose 115 games in 1935. He was to earn $35,000 and a percentage of profits as club vice-president, assistant to manager Bill McKechnie and sometime right fielder. "More titles than an incurable lodge joiner," joked Ruth, but the adventure quickly soured.

There would be no profits. McKechnie hadn't been consulted about an assistant. And Ruth, who'd had trouble in the field for several seasons ("My old dogs just couldn't take it any longer"), could barely make contact at the plate.

"The kids were striking me out or making me pop up on balls I could have hit out of the lot a few years before," Ruth admitted. "It was a rotten feeling."

After 28 games his average had shrunk to .181 and his value as a drawing card—the real reason Fuchs had sought him—had dwindled. "People wouldn't have come out," Ruth said, "to see Saint Peter himself hit .181."

There was one last hurrah in Pittsburgh with Ruth hitting three home runs in a game for the fourth time in his career. It would, he thought, have been a fine note to retire on, but Fuchs, with one eye on the box office, begged him to stay on through the Decoration Day doubleheader with Philadelphia.

"He had advertised me," Ruth shrugged. "But I never should have listened to him." The Babe agreed, reluctantly, played the first few innings of the first game, then limped off with a charley horse. It was the last time, after 2,502 games and 714 home runs, that the name George Herman Ruth ever appeared in a box score. *New York Post* beat man Jerry Mitchell added the epitaph as his lead paragraph the next morning: "He's nobody's Baby now."

1935

The left foot had gone numb one summer night in 1934 while he was crammed into the back of a San Francisco jitney bus, but Joe DiMaggio hadn't realized it.

"I jumped out and my left knee popped like a pistol," he would recall. "I'm sure you could have heard it down the block. I went down as though I'd been shot. The pain was terrific, like a whole set of aching teeth in my knee, and I don't know why I didn't pass out."

Hospital doctors diagnosed sprained tendons and prescribed hot towels and Epsom salts, but those proved useless. DiMaggio's leg gave way again the next morning, and after he was forced to walk around the bases following a home run one day later, he was encased from ankle to thigh in an aluminum splint. Word was quickly relayed from the West Coast to every major league club: The best minor-league player in the country was damaged goods.

Within days, as DiMaggio's market value (which had spiraled to $70,000) diminished, so did scout attendance at San Francisco Seals' games. But the Yankees' Bill Essick, was not a man to jump to conclusions. When DiMaggio returned to the lineup three weeks later Essick carefully inspected his running stride and batting pivot for evidence of strain and found none.

"Don't give up on DiMaggio," he advised New York general manager Ed Barrow by telephone. "Everybody out here thinks I'm crazy, but I'm not. I still think he's all right. Let me watch him for a couple of weeks more and I'll have the final answer on him."

Joe DiMaggio as a San Francisco Seal. He spent 1935 blossoming in California for delivery to the Yankees in 1936.

Johnny Broaca (left) and Vito Tamulis who both won 15 games.

George Selkirk replaced Ruth in right field and wore his No. 3, which the team did not retire for more than 10 years.

Earle Combs returned midseason, never really recovering from a fractured skull suffered the previous season.

Gehrig was KO'd again while playing the Red Sox, but he kept his ironman status alive, reaching 1600 games on August 8, 1935. He "slumped" to a team-high .329 plus 30 homers.

Red Ruffing led the Yankees in victories (16) and batted .339, the highest ever in team history by a regular pitcher.

When Essick's hunch had hardened into conviction he called Barrow again. "Buy DiMaggio. I think you can get him cheap. They're all laughing at me, but I know I'm right."

"What's the name of the best orthopedic man in San Francisco?" Barrow asked.

"Dr. Richard Spencer," Essick replied.

"Have him check the kid's knee," Barrow said. "And tell (Seals' owner Charley) Graham if the doc okays it, we'll talk business with him."

Spencer's prognosis was optimistic and a deal was struck. The Yankees would give Graham $25,000 and five anonymities (outfielder Ted Norbert, first baseman Les Powers, third baseman Ed Farrell and pitchers Jim Densmore and Floyd Newkirk). DiMaggio would stay with the Seals through 1935, take therapy and report to New York's training camp for the 1936 season. If the purchase of Babe Ruth from Boston for $100,000 had been a bargain fifteen years earlier, this was a steal.

DiMaggio would wear pinstripes for thirteen seasons, bat .325 and serve as cornerstone for ten pennant winners and nine world championship clubs. For now, he was merely a nineteen-year-old son of a fisherman with a landlubber's stomach and a natural swing.

Joseph Paul DiMaggio was the eighth of nine children of Sicilian immigrants who felt that baseball was a Sunday thing, hardly secure enough as a profession. While two older brothers had joined their father aboard the family fishing boat, the *Rosalie D,* Joe had dropped out of Galileo High School, worked odd jobs and played shortstop for local sandlot teams.

"*Lagnuso* [lazy]," his father had muttered, but young Joe was entranced. A third brother, Vince, had signed with the Seals. Before long the San Francisco Missions, the Seals' Pacific Coast League rivals, were offering Joe $150 a month. Instead, the Seals grabbed him. He hit safely in 61 straight games during his first full season in 1933, ended up batting .340 with 169 RBI's, and became the league's top drawing card.

And once the knee healed DiMaggio dominated, just as Essick had predicted—.398, 34 home runs and 154 RBI's in 1935.

Meanwhile, the Yankees were finishing three games behind Detroit in the American League race, with a transitional outfield of Jesse Hill, Ben Chapman and George Selkirk. Babe Ruth was gone. Earle Combs, never the same after having fractured his skull in 1934, was playing out his last season as a reserve.

So a job was waiting, along with limousine service, provided by a couple of fellow San Francisco Italians—second baseman Tony Lazzeri and shortstop Frank Crosetti. They delivered DiMaggio to the Yankees' training base at St. Peters-burg where pitcher Red Ruffing stared at him and growled.

"So you're the great DiMaggio."

1936

Giants traveling secretary Eddie Brannick, who worked across the Harlem River from the Yankees but within their range, had dubbed them the Window Breakers—with due respect, of course. For offensive power and balance, not even the 1927 Yankees with their Murderer's Row were a match.

Where Babe Ruth and Lou Gehrig had carried that club, hitting 107 of its 158 home runs, every 1936 regular except center fielder Jake Powell belted at least ten. They led the majors in homers (182), runs (1,065), and slugging average (.483) and the American League defense and pitching.

They controlled the American League pennant race by June, clinched it earlier (September 9) and won it more easily (by 19½ games) than any club in history.

Now Brannick's Giants were seeing the Yankees close-up, in a subway Series for the first time since 1923, and also baffling them—for at least one game. Carl Hubbell, who'd won his last 16 games of the regular season, had uncorked his screwball in the murk and rain of the Polo Grounds and beaten the Yankees 6–1 while allowing only one fly ball, a home run by George Selkirk.

The breakout came in game two, the longest nine-inning Series game ever played (two hours, forty-nine minutes), and it quickly dashed any illusions as the Yankees drummed out a record 18 runs, tattooing five Giant pitchers for 17 hits and setting or equaling six Series records. With President Franklin D. Roosevelt looking on from a box seat, every Yankee starter hit safely and scored a run. And catcher Bill Dickey and second baseman Tony Lazzeri each knocked in five.

By the third inning, when Lazzeri hit the second grand slam in Series history, the Yankees, who had already chased Giant starter Hal Schumacher and reliever Al Smith, were working on Dick Coffman and were leading, 9–1. By the ninth, they were laughing in the dugout as Harry Gumbert, who'd been 11–3 during the season, was being strafed for six more runs, including a three-run shot by Dickey.

Gehrig homering in the All-Star Game. His 49 homers topped the majors, but it would be his last time.

Fellow San Francisco Italians Tony Lazzeri (middle) and Frank Crosetti delivered prize rookie Joe DiMaggio to training camp.

DiMaggio was welcomed by manager McCarthy and Gehrig, who won MVP that season.

The Yankee lineup, labeled the "Window Breakers," powered the team to an easy pennant—its first without Ruth. Pictured (l–r): DiMaggio, Crosetti, Lazzeri, Dickey, Gehrig, Powell, and Selkirk (Rolfe not in shot).

Pat Malone, a 33-year-old former Cub, was the League's top relief pitcher in both saves (9) and victories (8) en route to a 12–4 record.

Led by owner Jake Ruppert, the Yankees celebrate their World Championship.

"Does he ever get anybody out in the National League?" Gehrig asked a teammate. The final was 18–4—"I let 'em score a couple runs to make it close," cracked Yankee starter Lefty Gomez—and the Giants never recovered.

They lost game three in the eighth, 2–1, when a bouncer by Frank Crosetti caromed off pitcher Fred Fitzsimmons's glove. Then Gehrig busted Hubbell with a two-run homer in game four and it was all but over. The Yankees cleaned up the Series back at the Polo Grounds in game six with a seven-run ninth inning, scoring five before the Giants could retire a man, and the Yankees were swilling championship champagne.

It was their first in four years, their first ever without Babe Ruth, and it marked the birth of the greatest dynasty any professional sport had ever known. Under McCarthy, who'd finally shed the "Second Place Joe" label, New York would win the next three world championships with the loss of one game, and six of the next seven American League pennants.

By 1964 the string would stretch to 22 pennants and 16 championships in twenty-eight years. And they would do it with the distinctly crisp and businesslike style that McCarthy had drilled into them.

The roistering, profane behavior of the Ruth era, with its midnight revels and clubhouse brawls, was taboo. McCarthy, a laconic, jut-jawed disciplinarian, had made that clear. In June, with the club crashing its way to the pennant, he'd shipped fielder Ben Chapman, a .302 lifetime hitter, to Washington for Powell because he felt Chapman was temperamental and divisive. Then, when Powell administered a hotfoot to a teammate at a Boston train station during his first road trip, McCarthy led him aside. "You're with the Yankees now," he told Powell. "We don't do those things."

The Yankee way would be three sets of immaculate pinstripes worn half a size large, to make them appear more imposing, and a jacket and necktie off the field at all times. And, as McCarthy had made it plain from the very first, there would be no card playing or pre-game shaving in the clubhouse—the clubhouse was the office, after all, and baseball was a business. No public scenes, no late nights.

The symbols would be Gehrig, the modest workhorse who was named MVP at thirty-three, and rookie Joe DiMaggio, who walked into spring training at age twenty-one, walked out with the left fielder's job and hit .323 with 29 home runs despite missing the first sixteen games with a burned foot. He called the manager Mr. McCarthy and said he'd happily play the sun field in Yankee Stadium.

"Ruth would never play it," he was told.

"I'll play it," DiMaggio decided, "if Mr. McCarthy wants me to."

That was the Yankee way.

1937

With the count 3-and-1 in the fifth inning, a man on first and Black Mike himself crowding the plate, Yankee pitcher Bump Hadley wanted something low on the inside corner. He never thought of a duster. Not at 3-and-1. But somehow his next pitch screeched toward Detroit catcher Mickey Cochrane's head. "The ball sailed," Hadley would say, horrified. "I don't know why. It just did."

And Cochrane, the Tigers' marvelously combative player-manager, lost sight of it six feet from the plate, threw up his hands and tried to duck.

The ball struck with a dull thud just above the right temple and Cochrane fell on his face in the Yankee Stadium dirt. "Good God Almighty," he groaned—and passed out.

For three days Cochrane lay unconscious and near death at New York's St. Elizabeth's Hospital, his skull fractured in three places. "The only time I came to," he would say, "was when they were tapping my spine."

When the danger passed, doctors told Cochrane that at thirty-four his playing days were over. He could manage if he liked, but not for another several weeks. And so, on May 25, the 1937 American League pennant race between New York and Detroit came to a symbolic end.

The Yankees had actually taken the lead two days earlier and with Cochrane, the Tigers' spiritual heart, out of action, Detroit would never seriously challenge again. New York retained the pennant, this time by thirteen games, and prepared to meet the Giants in the World Series for the second straight year, as 3–1 favorites.

The duel was that predictable. In fact, Hearst newspaper columnist Bill Corum said that Giant manager Bill Terry refused to bet him on the outcome. "I'm no sucker," he claimed Terry told him.

From the beginning the Yankees hammered their former landlords and did it ironically for good measure. They pounced on Giant ace Carl Hubbell, who'd dazed them in the 1936 opener, racked him for seven runs in the sixth inning of the first game, and won 8–1 at the Stadium.

The next afternoon the Yankees pummelled three Giant pitchers and posted the same score. "Change your signals," a fan wired Terry, but it was useless. No National League club, no club anywhere, was a match for Joe McCarthy's Yankees that year.

He'd named five of them—first baseman Lou Gehrig, third baseman Red Rolfe, center fielder Joe DiMaggio, catcher Bill Dickey and pitcher

Lefty Gomez, shown with McCarthy, regained his winning ways after two mediocre seasons, leading the League in victories (21), ERA (2.33) and shutouts (6). It was the fourth—and last—time he had won 21 or more games.

Famed Yankee lineup would be broken up at season's end when Lazzeri was peddled to the Cubs to make room for hotshot farmhand Joe Gordon. (L–r: Gehrig, Lazzeri, Crosetti, Rolfe.)

Five Yankees started in the All-Star Game. The three shown here are (l–r) Gehrig, Dickey and DiMaggio along with Red Sox' Joe Cronin.

Yankee Bump Hadley . . . hit Detroit's Mickey Cochrane in one of baseball history's most famous beanings.

Bill Dickey's 133 RBIs are still the most ever by a Yankee catcher.

Fireman Johnny Murphy, shown here with his son, enjoyed his best season—13–4, with 12 of those wins in relief, along with 10 saves.

Rival World Series managers Joe McCarthy of the Yankees and Bill Terry of the Giants meet before the renewal of the "Subway Series."

Lefty Gomez—to the starting All-Star team that July and they'd beaten the National League, 8–3, by themselves. Gehrig had knocked in four runs, Rolfe had tripled home the winner and Gomez wound up with the victory.

So deep was their roster and so confident were they of the talent ripening on their minor-league vines that the Yankees would willingly let second baseman Tony Lazzeri go to the Cubs after the season for the waiver price after hitting .400 in the 1937 Series, capping a dozen years in pinstripes. He was thirty-four, after all, and they had "a kid in Newark" named Joe Gordon who seemed ready. Gordon would play seven years in a New York uniform before the Yankees traded him to Cleveland for Allie Reynolds, who'd pitch in six Series for them. There would always be "a kid in Newark," thanks to the farming instincts of general managers Ed Barrow and George Weiss.

"I read the papers every day to see how Tommy Henrich and Red Rolfe were doing down in Triple-A ball," outfielder George Selkirk had admitted several years before. "If they had gone four for four, you'd better believe it made me try harder."

Meanwhile, New York still had five Hall of Famers in Gehrig, DiMaggio, Dickey, Gomez and Red Ruffing, and when they went back across the Harlem River for game three there were thousands of empty seats in the unreserved sections of the Polo Grounds.

Only 37,385 people watched the Yankees rub out the Giants, 5–1, on a Saturday afternoon. It was a Series virtually devoid of suspense and the Yankees closed it out in five games with

Gomez, a .147 lifetime hitter, driving in the winning run.

The only Giant outburst had come in the second inning of game four when they scored six runs on seven singles and an error. It proved to be their swan song; after three National League pennants in five years, the Giants wouldn't win another until Bobby Thomson's "shot heard 'round the world" sank the Dodgers in the 1951 playoff. There was no longer any question as to who owned New York.

Jacob Ruppert, sick in bed, heard the news from McCarthy.

"Colonel, you're the champion again," his manager told him.

"Fine, fine, McCardy," Ruppert nodded. "Do it again next year."

The mandate was that simple, that inflexible. "Those were the only orders I ever got from him after each World Series," McCarthy would muse. "Do it again next year. And generally we did. You've got to follow orders, right?"

1938

For seven years he'd fed them nothing but haze from his seamless three-quarter overhand delivery. "I just rare back and fog 'er through," Dizzy Dean would say.

But the fastball had fled after a freakish afternoon at the 1937 All-Star Game when Cleveland outfielder Earl Averill had smashed the big toe of Dean's planted left foot with a line drive through the box. "Fractured, hell," Dean groaned to teammates. "It's broke."

Doctors told him it was foolish to hurry back into action—the Cardinals were a fourth-place club that year—but Dean had shrugged. He would favor the toe, develop a jerky unbalanced delivery and throw sidearm.

"Don't, Jerome, don't," advised Braves manager Bill McKechnie when St. Louis came to Boston. "You'll hurt your arm." As predicted Dean felt something snap in his right arm late in the game and watched it fall limp. "You've done it, Jerome," moaned McKechnie, who was coaching third base. "You've done it."

Jay Hanna Dean (a.k.a. Jerome), who'd won 102 games in four years and led the Cardinals' Gashouse Gang to the 1934 world championship, won only one more game in 1937. When

Ruth and DiMaggio finally meet, introduced by sports writer
Bill Corum.

Joe Gordon as a rookie
second baseman who would
become a Yankee fixture.

Monte Pearson threw a no-hitter for the
Yankees.

Future Hall of Famer and League president
Joe Cronin of the Red Sox brawled with the
entire Yankee team during a May doubleheader
at Yankee Stadium that set an attendance
record.

Dizzy Dean of the Cubs meets Mrs. Babe Ruth during the third game of the World Series.

Tony Lazzeri came back as a Cub in the World Series, pictured here with Joe "Flash" Gordon, who succeeded him as Yankees second baseman.

doctors found a frightening assortment of inflamed muscles in his back and shoulder during the off-season, they told him he'd never again throw normally. No more fastballs. No more fog.

Still the Cubs gave the Cardinals a club-record $185,000 and three players for Dean in the spring of 1938. "We got Dizzy's spirit, courage and enthusiasm in addition to his arm," reasoned owner Philip Wrigley.

Chicago also wrung seven critical victories from Dean's new repertoire of soft junk, curves and "nuthin' balls," and came from the middle of the National League pack to overtake Pittsburgh for the pennant in the final week.

While the Yankees had won the American League race by 9½ games over Boston, the Cubs had struggled, firing manager Charlie Grimm in midseason. They needed a ten-game winning streak and player-manager Gabby Hartnett's miracle home run "in the gloaming" to beat Pittsburgh, which had already ordered Series press badges and built a new press box atop the Forbes Field roof.

Still, National League President Ford Frick had told the players that the Yankees could be taken. They'd had a slow start (probably because of Joe DiMaggio, who'd held out for $40,000, signed for $25,000 and missed nine games), hadn't taken over first place until July 12 and lost eleven of their final fifteen after clinching the pennant.

"They've let down," Frick insisted, "and it'll be difficult for them to get back." Yet only one of the Cubs, former Yankee second baseman Tony Lazzeri, seemed to believe it. "We're as good as they are," he growled. "We'll beat their brains out."

Most of his teammates weren't as certain. "How do you figure this Series?" they asked New York sportswriters. "Do you think we can win?"

Now the Cubs were down a game to the Yankees in the World Series and Hartnett had decided to go with Dean, a twenty-seven year old with a sixty-five-year-old arm. For seven innings Dean had New York batters—"DiMaggio, Dickey, all those fellas"—popping up his goofballs and grinding them into the dirt of Wrigley Field.

"My arm was about to kill me," he'd admit. "At times it felt as if the bone was sticking out of the flesh. I had nothing on the ball. I was making a big motion, a big windmill motion and then throwing off-speed balls."

But for a crazy second-inning pratfall, when third baseman Stan Hack and shortstop Billy Jurges had cracked heads chasing Joe Gordon's dribbler through the hole, Dean would have been leading 3–0. Instead it was 3–2 and Dean was hanging in gamely.

He got Gordon and Myril Hoag to hit into force plays in the eighth, then watched shortstop

Frank Crosetti, New York's weakest bat, step into the box. Dean worked him to 2–2, then slipped a curve past for a third strike—but the umpire disagreed.

Thus reprieved, Crosetti whacked the next pitch into the left-field bleachers, scoring Hoag ahead of him. "That was the lowest moment of my life," Dean would say. "I knowed my arm was gone. I couldn't break a pane of glass. But Crosetti never was a powerful hitter so I figured I had a chance."

Instead Dean, scowling and cursing, watched Crosetti circle the bases, a .245 lifetime hitter celebrating his only Series homer. "You couldn't a done that five years ago," Dean shouted at him. "I know, Diz," Crosetti admitted. "I know."

End of game, end of Dean, end of Series—for practical purposes, at least. Not that the Cubs had expected much more. New York had swept them six years earlier when Babe Ruth had called his shot.

Now Crosetti had them down two games to none and the Series was shifting to Yankee Stadium, where the Cubs had never won. The result was predictable—5–2 and 8–3 victories for New York, who worked over nine Cub pitchers—and a grim train ride back to Chicago, with Hartnett muttering that he'd be happy to unload the entire roster during the off-season.

Hartnett was half as good as his word—four starters and two regular pitchers were shipped out—and the Cubs didn't contend again until 1945. Dean, his arm consigned to the grave, won only nine more games, thus rewriting a basic rule of anatomy. The toebone was connected to the armbone.

1939

Nobody wanted to leave the dressing room. Nobody wanted to talk. The Yankees pulled on their uniforms silently that afternoon, stalling for time at their lockers. Then coach Art Fletcher walked slowly over to Ellsworth Dahlgren and whispered a sentence no Yankee but Lou Gehrig had heard in fourteen years—"Babe," Fletcher said, "you're playing first base today."

Dahlgren, stunned, felt his teammates patting his back and wishing him good luck as he headed down the ramp to the dugout at Detroit's Briggs Stadium and came face to face with Gehrig.

"There were tears in our eyes as we looked at each other," Dahlgren said. "Then I heard myself saying: 'Come on, Lou, you better get out there. You've put me in a terrible spot.'"

"Go on, get out there," Gehrig urged him, "and knock in some runs." Then Henry Louis Gehrig walked out to home plate as New York's captain and handed over the lineup card to umpire Steve Basil without a word. Basil glanced at it casually—Crosetti, Rolfe, DiMaggio, Yankee names never seemed to change—then looked up abruptly.

"Dahlgren, first base?" he noticed. "Hey, what's this, Lou?" Then he realized that Gehrig was weeping. After 2,130 consecutive games, all of them in Yankee pinstripes, the Iron Horse was benching himself.

His legs had turned to lead. His arms had lost their power, his hands their deftness. Gehrig had slogged through 1938—his worst season since his rookie days—hitting .295 with only 29 home runs and managing only four singles in a World Series where his teammates had feasted on Cub pitching.

The malaise had continued during spring training, where he was slow afield and powerless at the plate, even though he was making contact. "He tried to go from first to third on a single in a game at Clearwater," teammate Tommy Henrich noticed. "And when he went around second it looked like he was trying to run uphill at a 45-degree angle."

Maybe it was his age, his peers guessed. Gehrig was thirty-six and never had been a gifted athlete; his strength, determination and hard work had made him a Hall of Famer. "These big guys, they go fast," Detroit's Ty Cobb had remarked. "When they fall apart it's like the one-hoss shay."

Gehrig had voluntarily taken a $5,000 salary cut. But the job, manager Joe McCarthy said, was his. "The kid stays in," McCarthy told all inquisitors, "until he takes himself out."

Now, on May 2, eight games into the 1939 season, his batting average had tumbled to .143 with one run batted in. When pitcher Johnny Murphy congratulated him for making an easy game-ending putout against the second-division Senators, Gehrig had made up his mind.

"That's when I decided to quit," he said. "It was an ordinary routine play and I should have been on the bag waiting for the throw. When they start feeling sorry for you, it's time to hang up your glove."

So when McCarthy arrived at the hotel in Detroit before the next series Gehrig was waiting for him.

"I'm benching myself, Joe."

"Why?"

"For the good of the team. I just can't seem

Gehrig ends his "Ironman" streak and sits out for the first time in Detroit.

to get going and nobody has to tell me how bad I've been and how much of a drawback I've been to the team. I've been thinking—the time has come for me to quit."

McCarthy sighed. "All right, Lou. Take a rest. I'll put Babe Dahlgren on first base today. But remember, that's your position and whenever you want it back just walk out and take it."

But Lou Gehrig never played another game. Seven weeks later the Mayo Clinic informed him he was suffering from amyotrophic lateral sclerosis, a form of infantile paralysis. As his spine was hardening, his central nervous system was deteriorating. There was no known cure, doctors told him, and no chance of playing again. At best, he had a fifty-fifty chance to live.

Still, Gehrig was the captain and as long as he could pull on a uniform and walk he would carry out his duties. So while his teammates cruised to a record fourth straight American League pennant that summer, leaving Boston seventeen games behind, Gehrig limped out to deliver the lineup card that included Dahlgren's name and watched the games from the dugout.

He was, after all, "The Pride of the Yankees," the club's most enduring symbol, repository of all the virtues—class, dignity, confidence, discipline— that McCarthy and Jacob Ruppert had tried to drill into the franchise.

Yet his most dominant quality had been his durability. From the moment he pinch-hit for shortstop Pee Wee Wanninger on June 1, 1925, Gehrig hadn't missed a game. Manager Miller Huggins had given him a starting assignment the next afternoon when regular Wally Pipp complained of a headache after having been beaned in batting practice.

"Why don't you take the day off?" Huggins had suggested. "We'll put the kid from Columbia on first today." The kid from Columbia was actually a dropout, the only child of German immigrants, who'd grown up on Manhattan's Upper East Side, rode the trolley to high school and waited tables at a fraternity house.

Yankee scout Paul Krichell had spotted him at a Columbia-Rutgers game in New Brunswick and immediately phoned general manager Ed Barrow.

"I've just seen the next Babe Ruth," Krichell announced.

"Go home and sleep it off," Barrow advised him, "and tell me about it in the morning."

Gehrig was a powerfully built sophomore with thick legs who was studying to be an accountant. But his father needed surgery and the Yankees were offering a $1,500 bonus. So Gehrig signed and set about mastering his craft. "Lou didn't learn quickly but he learned thoroughly," Pipp noticed. "He sweated out each detail, step by step, until he had mastered it."

Gehrig would come to the plate 8,001 times, bat .340 lifetime with 1,990 runs batted in and 493 home runs, and easily made the Hall of Fame.

Yet he never earned more than $37,000 in a season and was overshadowed for a decade by a roistering, profane teammate with an affinity for late nights, home brew and camel's-hair caps.

"I'm not a headline guy," Gehrig shrugged. "I'm just the guy who follows Babe Ruth in the batting order." He'd followed Ruth's "called shot" blast in the 1932 Series with a home run of his own—yet nobody seemed to remember. And when he'd crashed four home runs in Philadelphia that year ("Keed, that was the greatest I ever seen," Ruth told him), the feat was given secondary play in the next morning's newspapers. Giants manager John McGraw had chosen that day to resign.

Yet Gehrig was the sole constant through three generations of Yankees. He'd played on the 1927 club, perhaps the most dominant in baseball history, as one of its Murderer's Row. He had been the cornerstone for three second-place teams in the mid-thirties when McCarthy was retooling the franchise, then earned three more Series rings as the dynasty was reborn. And his 2,130 consecutive games had set an unapproachable standard.

Gehrig had played through bumps, split

Lou wipes away a tear on Gehrig Day at Yankee Stadium.

*Gehrig receives a special presentation
from manager Joe McCarthy on July 4, 1939—
a token of friendship from his teammates.*

*Babe Ruth embraces Gehrig during the tribute—the first
time they'd spoken in years.*

Babe Dahlgren succeeded Gehrig as Yankee
first baseman.

Joe DiMaggio was the major leagues' batting champion at
.381, his career high and the second best average in Yankee
history behind Babe Ruth's .393 in 1923. Joe also was the
League's MVP and Sporting News' choice as "Major
League Player of the Year."

Red Rolfe led the majors in hits with 213, and his .329 average
is still the highest ever by a Yankee third baseman.

Yankee pitchers (l–r)—Back row: Charles (Red) Ruffing, Oral Hildebrand, Johnny Murphy, Atley Donald, Steve Sundra, Monte Pearson. Front row: Vernon (Lefty) Gomez, Marius Russo, Spurgeon (Spud) Chandler, Irving (Bump) Hadley.

Opposing managers Joe McCarthy and Joe Cronin were on the same side in the All-Star Game, when McCarthy stirred controversy by starting six Yankees. Later in the season, they were angry foes during a game of "stall ball" in Boston forfeited to the Yankees (a ruling rescinded by the League).

Ruppert died and manager Joe McCarthy and Mayor LaGuardia watched as a plaque was dedicated at Yankee Stadium.

fingers, lumbago, illness and a 1934 beaning that produced a concussion. Gehrig had merely borrowed one of Ruth's oversized caps, sliced it open to accommodate his swollen skull and rapped out three triples the next day.

Now, married for only five years, he was dying, and the Yankees quickly made arrangements for a July 4 tribute at the Stadium, summoning back Gehrig's 1927 teammates.

"For the past two weeks you have been reading about what a bad break I got," Gehrig told a capacity crowd that was blinking back tears along with him. "Yet today I consider myself the luckiest man on the face of the earth."

He had worked for Ruppert and Barrow, Huggins and McCarthy, and played alongside nine Hall of Famers, from Ruth to Joe DiMaggio. He had worn one uniform and had a hand in seven world championships. "I might have had a tough break," he concluded, "but I have an awful lot to live for."

His name would never appear in another box score, but Gehrig was in uniform when the Yankees met Cincinnati in the World Series. As expected it was another foregone conclusion.

New York won the first three games (as righthander Monte Pearson pitched a no-hitter for seven and a third innings in game two) then closed out the Redlegs, 7–4, in the tenth inning of game four at Crosley Field as Cincinnati catcher Ernie Lombardi "swooned" when a throw from right fielder Ival Goodman hit him in the protective cup. New York's Charlie Keller knocked Lombardi down coming in from third and three Yankees scored.

On the train ride back to Manhattan, which McCarthy wanted kept subdued, Gehrig played an agonizing game of bridge, his shaking hands unable to deal, his fingers mangling the cards. The signs, his teammates realized, had been visible in spring training.

Gehrig, pitcher Wes Ferrell remembered, had inexplicably fallen to the clubhouse floor. "He lay there for a second, frowning," Ferrell noticed. "Like he couldn't understand what was happening."

In two years, Gehrig would be dead and an era would die with him.

1940

After four unprecedented championship seasons in a row they had struck bottom after one month and had stayed there for two weeks. It had taken the Yankees three more months to inch as high as fifth place in the American League and a .500 record.

Now, after winning sixteen of nineteen games during the last three weeks of August, New York was only half a game behind first-place Detroit and had two rested pitchers ready for a September 11 doubleheader with dissension-torn Cleveland in Municipal Stadium.

These were the fabled "Crybaby Indians," so dubbed because they'd tried to persuade club president Alva Bradley to fire manager Oscar Vitt (whom they found excessively critical), then went public with their complaints.

In three weeks, during late August and early September, the Indians had blown a 5½-game lead and surrendered first place to the Tigers. They seemed ripe for a sweep, and after the Yankees knocked 27-game winner Bob Feller out of the box in the fourth inning to take the opener, it seemed inevitable.

Word had come from Detroit that Boston had beaten the Tigers in their first game; New York had taken over the league lead. And Yankee ace Red Ruffing would pitch the second game.

But storm clouds settled in over Lake Erie, literally and figuratively, before the nightcap. The Yankees lost their early lead after first baseman Babe Dahlgren muffed a routine throw from shortstop Frank Crosetti in the sixth inning. Then, as the heavens opened over the stadium, the Bossard brothers, who'd been the Indians' groundskeepers for years, realized they'd "mislaid" the infield tarpaulin.

Rain quickly turned the dirt to muck, play was called and Cleveland declared the victor. Meanwhile, Detroit defeated the Red Sox in the second game and New York never saw first place again.

A miserable western swing—Detroit, St. Louis and Chicago passed for the West in those days—finished the Yankees off and they ended up third, two games behind the pennant-winning Tigers.

It was a forgettable end to New York's worst season (88–66) since 1930—pockmarked by gloomy individual performances throughout. Crosetti (.194), catcher Bill Dickey (.247) and third baseman Red Rolfe (.250) all had their poorest years simultaneously. Lefty Gomez's sore arm limited him to nine appearances. And Ruffing,

Joe and his brother Dominic of the Red Sox in training. Joe would hit .352 to win his second consecutive batting championship.

Charlie Keller hit 3 homers in a game and led the League in walks, but his batting average fell to .286 from the .334 he hit as a rookie the year before.

Joe Gordon, shown sliding home in a Yankee–Cleveland game, hit 30 homers, still the most ever by a Yankee second baseman.

with four straight 20-victory seasons behind him, ended up 15–12.

The only .300 hitter was the likely one, center fielder Joe DiMaggio, who'd inherited the slugger's mantle from retired Lou Gehrig. After an unremarkable start he put together a 23-game hitting streak in July that led to a final .352 average and DiMaggio's second straight American League batting title (following his career-high .381 of 1939). The streak was merely an appetizer for another more than twice as long in 1941 that would make him a baseball immortal.

Brooklyn-born Marius Russo was 14–8 in his second big-league season. He and Red Ruffing (who had his fourth straight 20-victory season in 1939—the only Yankee pitcher ever to do so) were the only Yankee pitchers with 10 or more victories.

Yankee outfield: DiMaggio, Keller, and Selkirk.

1941

The way it started, with a first-inning single off a mediocre Chicago pitcher named Edgar Smith in a game the Yankees would lose 3–1, was eminently forgettable.

Joe DiMaggio didn't realize what he was up to for another three weeks, when a few New York newspapermen rummaged in the record books and informed him that his 24-game hitting streak was only five short of the club record.

"That's when I became conscious of the streak," DiMaggio would say. "When the writers started talking about the records I could break. But at that stage I didn't think too much about it."

Hitting streaks were no novelty to him, after all. He'd strung 61 games together as a minor-leaguer in 1933 and 23 games as a Yankee in 1940. Yet this one seemed touched by magic.

His teammates had been stumbling along in fourth place on May 15, 5½ games behind Cleveland, their bats sound asleep. They'd lost four in a row and seven of nine. "YANK ATTACK WEAKEST IN YEARS," groaned the New York *Journal-American* after the 13–1 collapse to the White Sox, and manager Joe McCarthy had immediately reshuffled his lineup.

And DiMaggio had slipped to .306, 46 points lower than his previous year's batting title figure. But as he stacked one game atop another the Yankees rose out of the slough and became contenders. By June when DiMaggio's streak reached 24 games, New York had won eight straight.

When it ended, 32 games later in Cleveland, DiMaggio had crafted baseball's most enduring record and New York was on its way to an absurdly easy pennant.

DiMaggio's 56-game hitting streak captured the nation's attention, overshadowing Ted Williams' .406 season and earning him the MVP Award.

He breaks Sisler's League record at 42, equals, and then breaks Wee Willie Keeler's major league record, before the streak ends at Cleveland in July.

It took two superb fielding plays by Indian third baseman Ken Keltner to snap DiMaggio's spell at 56 games; otherwise the streak would have run on to an astounding 73 games, nearly half a season.

As it was the feat consumed more than a third of the 154-game schedule and overshadowed Ted Williams's .406 season for the Red Sox, the last .400 year by a major leaguer.

When the streak ended with DiMaggio grounding into a ninth-inning double play he had rapped out 91 hits (including 16 doubles, four triples and 15 home runs) in 223 at-bats for a .408 average, had knocked in 55 runs and struck out only seven times.

More impressively he had maintained his grace and composure throughout. "I never saw a guy so calm," marveled roommate Lefty Gomez. "I wound up with the upset stomachs."

Indeed, the streak was halfway along before DiMaggio realized that he might be making history. At 30 games he broke the club record shared by Roger Peckinpaugh and Earle Combs; still ahead loomed the 41-game American League mark set by St. Louis's George Sisler two decades earlier.

Meanwhile, the task grew progressively more difficult—official scorers, conscious of their critical role, scrutinized each ground ball like Talmudic scholars. And pitchers bore down even harder.

Yet everyone seemed imbued with a sense of history and propriety. In the thirty-sixth game, with Yankees on second and third, two out and DiMaggio hitting in the ninth, St. Louis manager Luke Sewell forbade pitcher Bob Muncrief to deliver the obvious intentional walk. "He means too much to baseball to be cheated out of his chance at a record through a technicality," Sewell declared.

So Muncrief, who agreed with Sewell, pitched to DiMaggio—and watched him single. "It wouldn't have been fair to walk him," Muncrief realized. "Not to him or to me. Hell, he's the greatest player I ever saw."

Others—specifically Athletics pitcher Johnny Babich—weren't quite as altruistic. Babich, a certified Yankee-killer who'd beaten them five times in 1940, had vowed that DiMaggio wouldn't reach base.

So Babich walked him the first time, then threw him three wide pitches the next. DiMaggio, desperate, glanced at third-base coach Art Fletcher, was delighted to see his flashing the 'hit' sign, and lashed the next pitch through Babich's legs for a double and his 40th straight.

"After I took my turn at first I looked at him," DiMaggio would recall with pleasure. "His face was white as a sheet."

By now the pressure had built to a peak. "In those last twenty days," DiMaggio admitted, "I went to bat with my palms wet." With one good week he could pass not only Sisler but Wee Willie Keeler, who'd set the major league record of 44 in 1897. A herd of newspapermen followed the Yankees everywhere and fans mobbed DiMaggio any time he appeared in public. He had to turn over his fan mail to the front office to answer. The world had closed in.

"I was able to control myself," he would say. "But that doesn't mean I wasn't dying inside. I had no tomorrows. It was either do it today or fail."

He tied Sisler's record with a two-base hit at Washington in the first game of a doubleheader, then went to the bat rack between games and found that someone had stolen his lucky bat, which he had sanded and oiled and heated until it had turned black.

But momentum overcame superstition. DiMaggio borrowed a bat from Tommy Henrich and ripped a single into left field in the seventh inning of the nightcap.

So Sisler was behind him. Three days later he took Keeler by crashing a high inside fastball off Boston's Dick Newsome into the left-field stands at Yankee Stadium. Only 8,682 spectators saw it; the temperature that day was 100 degrees on the field.

With the pressure eased, The Bat returned. An anonymous caller from Newark said that a friend had filched it as a prank; it would be returned to the Stadium for game 45 of what was now a national obsession. Newspapers held their late afternoon editions for word.

Les Brown and His Band of Renown memorialized him with a song ("Joltin' Joe DiMaggio, we want you on our side"). Opposing clubs ran three-column advertisements announcing his presence. The streak reached 50, the All-Star break came and went. DiMaggio was chasing DiMaggio, nobody else. "I did want to keep on going," he mused. "I wanted it to go on forever."

Then, on the evening of July 17, he and Gomez walked out of the Hotel Cleveland and climbed into a taxi for Municipal Stadium, where 67,468 spectators—the largest crowd ever to watch a night game to that time—were waiting.

"I got a feeling if you don't get a hit the first time up," the driver told DiMaggio, "they're going to stop you tonight."

Gomez exploded. "What the hell is this? What are you trying to do, jinx him?" DiMaggio shrugged and tipped the driver anyway. "Well," he philosophized, "if it is, it is."

It didn't seem likely that the Indians would stop him, not in the series opener, anyway. Though Cleveland ace Bob Feller would pitch the second game, Al Smith, who'd end up 12–13 that year, was on the mound.

In the first inning DiMaggio ripped one of his pitches on the ground just inside the bag at third. But Keltner, backhanding the ball neatly, made the play from foul territory. In the New York dugout Gomez cursed. "That lousy cabdriver."

Smith walked DiMaggio in the fourth, then got him to bounce another ball to Keltner in the seventh. "Keltner's two plays down the line," DiMaggio would reminisce years later. "I remember that like it was yesterday."

There would be one more chance in the ninth, but by then Jim Bagby had relieved Smith. DiMaggio had faced Bagby once during the streak and had homered in game 28.

This time DiMaggio waited out two balls and a strike, then lashed a fastball "as hard as I ever hit any ground ball" at shortstop Lou Boudreau. The ball bounced off Boudreau's shoulder, but he managed to pluck it out of the air and turn a double play. DiMaggio rounded first, retrieved his glove and jogged to center field without a trace of emotion.

"Well, that's over," DiMaggio said softly, reaching for a cigarette in the clubhouse. But the Yankees swept on. They'd won 41 games during DiMaggio's streak and would take 14 of their next 16 and leave the Red Sox 17 games behind, clinching the pennant on September 4. Along the way they found time to have a silver cigar humidor engraved at Tiffany's for the man who spurred them on.

Meanwhile, across the East River, the Dodgers were pulling off a feat of their own, winning their first National League pennant in twenty-one years. When they arrived home after clinching the pennant hundreds of fans jammed Grand Central Station to greet them. The Yankees were forgotten conquerors, their achievement old news.

"It ain't fair," cracked former (and future) Dodger utility man Frenchy Bordagaray, now a Yankee reserve. "There wasn't anybody there to meet us when we came back with the pennant. I couldn't even find a redcap to carry my bag."

The idea of the Yankees in a World Series was no novelty. They'd won four of the previous five and were riding a streak of nine straight victories in Series games.

But where the Giants, Cubs and Redlegs had been compliant, the Yankees' Brooklyn neighbors proved stubborn. After stranding the lead runs in the ninth inning of the opener the Dodgers rubbed out a 2–0 deficit and won game two. Then, with forty-year-old Fred Fitzsimmons (the oldest pitcher ever to start a Series game) performing heroically, Brooklyn held the Yankees scoreless through the seventh inning of the third

A dying Lou Gehrig.

After Lou's death, the Gehrig plaque becomes the second of the famed monuments in centerfield at Yankee stadium.

game. Then they watched New York pitcher Marius Russo chip Fitzsimmons's kneecap with a line drive. That knocked out Fitzsimmons and the Dodgers followed in the eighth.

But in the ninth inning of game four at Ebbets Field they finally had the Yankees in a hammerlock, one out from a 4–3 victory that would tie the Series.

Reliever Hugh Casey had gotten first baseman Johnny Sturm and third baseman Red Rolfe to hit easy grounders. Now he had a full count on right fielder Tommy Henrich, who'd been hitless all afternoon, and decided to go for the spitter. Or did he? "Everybody says it was a spitter but I don't buy that," Henrich insisted. "Casey didn't have a great curve but that ball exploded. It was the best one he threw all afternoon and it had me fooled completely. I'll admit that."

Henrich lunged—and missed. Unfortunately for the Dodgers, catcher Mickey Owen missed it as well. The ball dropped abruptly and skidded past Owen. "Even as I was trying to hold up I was thinking that the ball had broken so fast that Owen might have trouble with it too," Henrich figured. "When I saw that little white jackrabbit bouncing I said, 'Let's go.' It rolled all the way to the fence. I could have walked to first."

With umpire Larry Goetz's right arm still raised, Owen, one of the finest defensive catchers in the game, chased the ball all the way to the backstop. "It was all my fault," he said. "It was a great breaking curve and I should have had it. It got away from me and by the time I got hold of it near the corner of the dugout I couldn't have thrown anyone out at first."

So the Yankees, resigned to defeat, found themselves reborn. "When Henrich swung and missed we all got up and started toward the runway that led out of the dugout," shortstop Phil Rizzuto said. "Some of us were already in it. I know I was."

The Dodgers merely sat stunned—particularly manager Leo Durocher. "For the first time in my life I was shell-shocked," he conceded. "I should have gotten off the bench and gone out to the mound to talk to my pitcher. Instead, I just sat on my ass."

And let a badly shaken Casey (who would shoot himself ten years later) face six more batters as the Yankees staged the most dramatic uprising since the Athletics' ten-run seventh inning against the Cubs, in the 1929 Series.

"All hell broke loose after that," said Yankee pitcher Spud Chandler. "Base hits like thunder." DiMaggio ripped an 0–2 slider into left field for a single. Left fielder Charlie Keller fouled off half a dozen balls at 0–2, then blasted a fastball off the right-field wall that scored Henrich and DiMaggio. Then catcher Bill Dickey walked, second base-

The Yankee pitching staff allowed the fewest runs, yet no single hurler won more than 15 games. Shown with McCarthy (l–r): Chandler, Donald, Breuer, Gomez, Ruffing, Peek, Bonham, Murphy, Branch and Stanceau.

man Joe Gordon doubled him home behind Keller and it was 7–4. "Well," DiMaggio laughed, "they say everything happens in Brooklyn."

After the Dodgers went down in order in their half, Owen and club President Larry MacPhail wept in the clubhouse. Why did fate always favor pinstripes? "They haven't beaten you a blasted game yet," MacPhail told his men. But it was over. You never gave the Yankees a second life.

Brooklyn fans gave Owen a sympathetic ovation the next afternoon—"they stood and cheered," said Rizzuto, "and it rocked old Ebbets Field." But New York buried the Dodgers, 3–1, as pitcher Tiny Bonham retired twenty of the last twenty-two batters he faced.

"WAIT 'TIL NEXT YEAR," groused an eight-column headline in the next day's Brooklyn *Eagle*. It was the first chorus of what would be a fourteen-year refrain.

Ernie Bonham was the Yankees' top pitcher (21–5), leading the League in pct. (.808), complete games (22) and shutouts (6). He was second in ERA (2.27).

Pinch-runner Tuck Stainback was thrown out at third by Enos Slaughter's bullseye from right field in the turning point of the Series.

1942

For more than a decade St. Louis had been a pleasant oasis for them, offering a fine view of the Mississippi, delicious spare ribs, yeasty beer and easy victories over the Browns, who'd managed one first-division finish since 1929.

"Somehow I can't seem to get it through my head that we're going out there to play the Series," catcher Bill Dickey mused as the train headed west. "It seemed just like any other trip to St. Louis."

Yankee clubs rarely played for world championships there and rarely lost them anywhere. Since 1927, when they'd swept Pittsburgh, New York had won all eight of their Series appearances with the loss of only four games. This time they'd cruised to another American League pennant by nine games over Boston and twiddled their thumbs while the Cardinals edged Brooklyn for the National League title on the final day. Even in St. Louis, fans wanted odds on Series bets with New York partisans.

No St. Louis club had won a pennant since the 1934 Gashouse Gang, and this one had to erase a ten-game Dodger lead on August 6. They were young (no starters over thirty) and unproven, the fruit of Branch Rickey's farm system.

And now, as predicted, the Yankees were murdering them in their own park in the opener. Pitcher Red Ruffing, who'd had a no-hitter brewing

Sophomore shortstop Phil Rizzuto, 5'6", welcomed 6'4" rookie pitcher Johnny Lindell.

Red Ruffing (with opposing pitcher Johnny Beazley) started the series opener, as he had the two previous seasons, and, for the third straight time, he won it.

Buddy Hassett, the Yankees' third regular first baseman in as many seasons, hit .284 in season and .333 in the World Series before going into the service.

DiMaggio was thinking Army in 1942, and entered at season's end, being replaced in the outfield by converted pitcher Lindell.

Veteran catcher Rollie Hemsley joined the Yankees as their backup catcher for the next 2½ seasons.

until the eighth inning, was breezing behind a 7–0 lead with two outs and one man on base in the ninth. All that remained was rookie Ray Sanders, pinch-hitting for rookie Whitey Kurowski.

But Ruffing walked him—and never got another out. Marty Marion tripled, scoring Walker Cooper and Sanders. Four singles produced two more runs, chased Ruffing and brought up rookie Stan Musial. The Cardinals had batted around.

Yankee reliever Spud Chandler put an end to it by getting Musial to ground out to first, but the point had been made. The Cardinals could score on these people. "We went into the clubhouse and said, well, we gave them one hell of a scare," said right fielder Enos Slaughter.

The Yankees *were* vulnerable, even seven runs ahead and one out from victory. "That was just the shot in the arm our boys needed," crowed former St. Louis pitcher Dizzy Dean. "We'll never stop now."

The grinding pennant race with the Dodgers they now regarded as a boon. "We'll go out and beat the Yankees the same way," insisted manager Billy Southworth. "One thing this young club isn't afraid of is reputations."

The Cardinals had performed beautifully down the stretch, winning 43 of their last 52 games, and 106 in all, the most by a National League champion since 1909. Since most of them had come up hungry from Southern mill towns or dirt farms, a $6,000 winner's share seemed like a fortune.

They were confident, enthusiastic and aggressive on the base paths. "They might not be so hot at the plate," Braves manager Casey Stengel conceded. "But they sure got a lot of strength in their ankles."

Once New York showed signs of uncertainty, the Cardinals were convinced they could win it. In the most dramatic reversal of Series form since the 1915 Red Sox, St. Louis lost the opener and then swept the Phillies, leaving the Yankees disbelieving, arguing with umpires and on the defensive. Very un-Yankeelike.

The Cardinals, Dickey and his mates learned, were not at all like the Browns. They relished tight squeezes in late innings and seemed to enjoy squandering leads because it was so much fun regaining them.

Game two was typical. After the Yankees had climbed out of a three-run hole to tie the score in the eighth inning, Slaughter doubled and Musial singled him home to put St. Louis ahead, 4–3. Then with one out in the ninth Slaughter threw out pinch runner Tucker Stainback at third base from right field.

"Some fellows like to say that throw of mine cut the hearts out of the Yankees," Slaughter said. Possibly. Whatever, New York was never the same. The Cardinals saved their masterpiece for the Stadium and game three. Everything that had distinguished their play during the season— inspired pitching, fundamental offense, timely defense—was put on display.

St. Louis scored one run on a walk, a bunt, a sacrifice and an infield out, the other on two singles and an error. In the late innings, center fielder Terry Moore robbed Joe DiMaggio of a triple, Musial dove into the left-field boxes to filch a home run from Joe Gordon and Slaughter scaled the right-field wall to haul down a Charlie Keller drive. And Cardinal pitcher Ernie White scattered six hits to shut out New York in a Series game for the first time in sixteen years.

The Yankees, barely pressed during the season, were now unraveling like a nickel baseball. Losing 6–1 in game four, they groused to the umpires, came back to score five runs in the sixth, then lost it 9–6, once a wild and unnecessary throw to second by Dickey after a walk opened the floodgates.

Now it was a matter of pride, of not becoming the first American League team to lose all three games at home. As incentive, club officials posted a notice on the clubhouse blackboard: TRAIN FOR ST. LOUIS LEAVES 8 PM TONIGHT. GRAND CENTRAL TERMINAL. BRING YOUR HAND LUGGAGE WITH YOU.

The fifth game went down to the ninth inning tied at 2–2. Then Kurowski, who would never hit another Series homer, belted a two-run blast to left field just inside the foul pole. "There it goes," shouted Moore as ball met bat. "There it goes."

And so went the Yankees, amid a flurry of second-guessing, as the Cardinals sang "Pass the Biscuits, Mirandy," their theme song down the stretch.

"What's the matter?" growled Yankee manager Joe McCarthy. "Have they forgotten that this ball club had won eight World Series in a row? What do you have to do, win all the time?"

1943

It was a suitable year for a Last Hurrah. With Europe and the South Pacific in flames, half of their lineup in the armed forces and the game itself more of a home-front diversion than the national pastime, the Yankees chose 1943 to tack one final championship onto the Joe McCarthy

Spring training was held at Asbury Park, NJ because of wartime travel restrictions.

Spud Chandler was the League's MVP with a 20–4 record and a 1.64 ERA, the best ever by a Yankee pitcher.

Typical of the parade of players entering service, Red Ruffing passed his physical and was inducted, kissing his baseball bat farewell.

Kate Smith took time out from singing "God Bless America" to team up with George Selkirk.

era and settle a World Series score with St. Louis.

The Yankees' regular first baseman, short-stop and two outfielders were gone. Catcher Bill Dickey, at thirty-six, was the only starter who would hit .300. Yet New York won the American League pennant by 13½ games over Washington and cleaned up the Cardinals in five.

After seven pennants in eight years it would be the Yankees' last summer atop the league until 1947, when their roster would have undergone a transformation. It was also the last year that major league baseball would be truly major until 1946; by the spring of 1944 most of its regulars would belong to military rosters.

As it was, war had already engulfed the world and baseball seemed frivolous by comparison. In fact, before the 1942 season, Commissioner Kenesaw Mountain Landis had offered to "close down for the duration of the war" if the President deemed it necessary.

Franklin D. Roosevelt hadn't. In a "Green Light Letter," he told Landis that while individual players would be expected to serve just as any American of draft age, the game was a "definite

recreational asset" to the country and thus was worthwhile.

Even so, baseball made practical concessions to a wartime economy. Bowing to travel restrictions most clubs conducted spring training close to home under sandlot conditions. The Yankees forsook St. Petersburg for Asbury Park, a seaside resort on the Jersey shore where salt water taffy was provided them gratis and temperatures hovered around 45 degress. They worked out, shivering, on the local high school diamond, then retreated to the clubhouse where scout Paul Krichell kept a potbellied stove burning wood all day.

Meanwhile, McCarthy tried to fill in his lineup card. First baseman Buddy Hassett, shortstop Phil Rizzuto, center fielder Joe DiMaggio, right fielder Tommy Henrich and pitcher Red Ruffing had all been called to active duty. So McCarthy put Nick Etten, who'd been acquired from the Phillies for two minor-leaguers and $10,000 during the winter, at first base. Frank Crosetti was shifted to short and replaced at third base by rookie Billy Johnson. Rookie Bud Metheny filled in for Henrich. A converted pitcher, Johnny Lindell, took up for DiMaggio.

Yet there were enough old and proven faces for McCarthy to mold a contender. Joe Gordon still turned crisp double plays at second. Crosetti was a twelve-year veteran, Charlie Keller a fixture in left, Dickey a Hall of Famer. And the nucleus of the league's best pitching staff—Spud Chandler, Tiny Bonham, Hank Borowy and Atley Donald—was still on hand.

The Yankees coalesced into an easy pennant winner as Chandler (20–4, 1.64) was named league MVP, Etten knocked in 107 runs and Keller muscled 31 home runs. Now the Yankees wanted to correct history.

They'd stumbled badly before the Cardinals in the 1942 Series, losing four straight games after winning the opener. As destiny would have it, St. Louis won the National League race by 18 games over Cincinnati, yet the war had played havoc with the Cardinal roster, too.

Enos Slaughter and Terry Moore, two thirds of St. Louis's fine defensive outfield, had been snapped up. So had pitcher Johnny Beazley, who'd beaten New York twice in 1942.

But thanks to deep farm systems—and New York and St. Louis boasted the best—the rosters were still of Series caliber. And after the Yankees won the opener, 4–2, at the Stadium, the Cardinals took it as a positive omen.

They'd lost the 1942 opener and it had galvanized them. Again they came back to win the second game, 4–3, as batterymates Mort and Walker Cooper dedicated the victory to their father, who'd died the night before.

Yankee sluggers (l–r): Gordon, Etten, Dickey and Keller—only Dickey would hit .300.

Rookie Bud Metheny replaced Tommy Henrich in the Yankee outfield.

Stan Musial of the Cardinals and Charlie Keller pose before the Series opener.

Rookie Billy Johnson won the third base job, becoming a Yankee fixture throughout the 40s.

The similarity ended there. As another concession to travel restrictions Landis had ordered that the first three games be played in New York; the Yankees would have the advantage of an extra home game before the Series shifted parks. The Yankees used a giddy eighth-inning burst to rub out a 2–1 Cardinal lead in game three and break the pattern.

It began with a bobbled ball by St. Louis center fielder Harry Walker and a dropped tag by third baseman Whitey Kurowski. That put Yankees on first and third with none out. After Crosetti was intentionally walked, Johnson tripled between left and center, clearing the bases and sparking a five-run rally. The Cardinals, who committed four errors (and ten in all during the Series), were never the same.

After a two-day break and a train ride West, McCarthy sent out Marius Russo, a sore-armed lefthander who'd been 5–10 during the season, to face Max Lanier. Russo would never win another game, but he limited the Cardinals to seven hits, doubled twice and scored the winner in a 2–1 game in the eighth.

The next day Chandler, capping the finest year of his career, went out to face Cooper and end it. So confident were the Yankees that they wouldn't have to stay for a sixth game that they'd packed their bags and checked out of the hotel. "I wasn't what you'd call brilliant even though I shut them out," Chandler admitted. "I gave up ten base hits and a couple of walks but they left eleven men on base."

The turning point came in the fourth inning after Chandler yielded a single to Kurowski, walked Ray Sanders on four pitches, then went 3–0 to Johnny Hopp. That brought Dickey out to the mound.

"What's the matter?" the catcher asked Chandler.

"Nothing."

"Then get the ball over the plate."

Chandler proceeded to strike out Hopp on three pitches, the last an outside fastball, and escaped from the inning.

"Fellows," Chandler informed his mates, "there's no way I can lose today."

It was left to Dickey, the last link to the club's Glory Era of the twenties, to apply the crusher in the sixth. With two out Keller had singled. Now Dickey, who'd been one of the five batters Cooper had struck out consecutively to begin the game, stepped into the box hoping for a fastball.

"Well, I got it," he said, "and hit it good, but not hard. At least I didn't think so. But when I was running to first I saw the ball heading for the roof, and [coach] Earle Combs yelled at me: 'You got one, Bill!' Then I saw Art Fletcher at third waving his cap and I knew it was a home run."

It was Dickey's 37th—and final—Series hit and it clinched New York's tenth world championship, the seventh and last for McCarthy. Less than an hour later the Yankees were singing "The Sidewalks of New York" under the showers.

They would accept 10 percent of their $6,100 winner's share in war bonds, and their caps—along with those of their rivals—would be shipped to the South Pacific, where they'd be awarded to American pilots who shot down Japanese Zeroes. There was, after all, a war on.

1944

The question seemed traditional enough. Spring training had just begun, the Yankees were coming off their seventh American League pennant in eight years and manager Joe McCarthy was being asked to speculate on his opening-day lineup. But these were not traditional times.

"How could I possibly do that?" McCarthy replied. "Why, I couldn't tell you who will be here next Tuesday." He paused, and riffled through his mental file. "Well, I could give you an infield," McCarthy allowed. "Neun could play first. I could cover second. Schulte on short, Fletcher on third, Krichell catching and Schreiber pitching. And some of you writers could fill in, too."

Johnny Neun, John Schulte and Art Fletcher were McCarthy's coaches, Paul Krichell a scout. And Paul Schreiber was a batting-practice pitcher who eventually *would* be activated in 1945, at age forty-two, and pitch four innings after a twenty-two-year layoff. This was wartime baseball; the caliber, *Time* magazine guessed, "was between AA and A, but still baseball."

Just barely. Most of what happened in 1944 had never been seen before or since in the major leagues. With rubber needed for military use, Spalding developed a ball with a core of cork and balata (from South American tree sap) that was deader than Jacob Marley. Yankee first baseman Nick Etten managed to hit twenty-two of them for home runs and led the league with the lowest total in twenty-six years.

And the St. Louis Browns, who'd seen the first division only once since 1929, won their first and only pennant—without a 20-game winner and with only one hitter above .295. Their secret? Eighteen 4-F specimens with creaky ankles, bad backs and missing fingers—unfit for military duty but sound enough to flesh out a roster.

Nick Etten led the League in homers with 22.

Outfielder Lindell blossomed, hitting .300, leading the
League in total bases (297), and placing third in homers (18),
RBI's (103), and slugging (.500).

Second baseman George Stirnweiss led the majors in hits
(205), stolen bases (55).

Atley Donald and . . .
Walt Dubiel won 13 games each.

Jim Turner, at age 41, was among the League's top relievers with 3 wins and 7 saves.

Paul Waner, former Pirate and future Hall of Famer, was picked up from Brooklyn on waivers in September.

With 470 major leaguers on active military service by the end of the season, the Browns represented the best of the worst. The Yankees, who'd won the 1943 pennant by 13½ games and beaten the Cardinals in five, had been decimated.

Buddy Hassett, Phil Rizzuto, Joe DiMaggio, Tommy Henrich and Red Ruffing had been drafted before the 1943 season; now second baseman Joe Gordon, third baseman Billy Johnson, left fielder Charlie Keller, catcher Bill Dickey and their best pitcher, Spud Chandler, had been claimed. Not one of the eight regulars from the 1942 club remained; anonymous faces appeared at most positions.

"McCarthy will really have to go to work this season," mused White Sox manager Jimmy Dykes. "He won't be able to sit back the way he did in other years and simply push buttons."

This time the buttons were named Snuffy Stirnweiss, Mollie Milosevich, Oscar Grimes, Hersh Martin and Mike Garback. Yet McCarthy managed to mold a contender out of them. The Yankees held first place as late as mid-September and had a mathematical chance at the pennant until the final weekend, when the Browns swept four games from them and edged Detroit by a game. New York would finish third, its 83 victories the fewest since 1925.

It was a year when anyone might have worn pinstripes—even forty-one-year-old Paul Waner, who'd played for the Pirates against Ruth, Gehrig & Co. in 1927. "How come you're in the outfield with the Yankees?" called a voice from the bleachers one afternoon.

"Because Joe DiMaggio's in the Army," Waner replied.

1945

The Colonel had been dead for six years, yet his franchise and its tradition had continued to flourish. Jacob, who'd signed the paycheck of every Yankee from Home Run Baker to Joe DiMaggio, had passed away during the winter of 1939 while the club was still in mid-Renaissance.

New York had won a fourth straight pennant that fall and would claim three more before the war siphoned off the entire lineup. Some things—the farm system, the pinstripes, general manager Ed Barrow, field manager Joe McCarthy—remained constant.

George Stirnweiss (with Oscar Grimes on the right) led the League in batting and other departments too.

New co-owners Del Webb (l) and Larry McPhail (r) join veteran GM Ed Barrow (center).

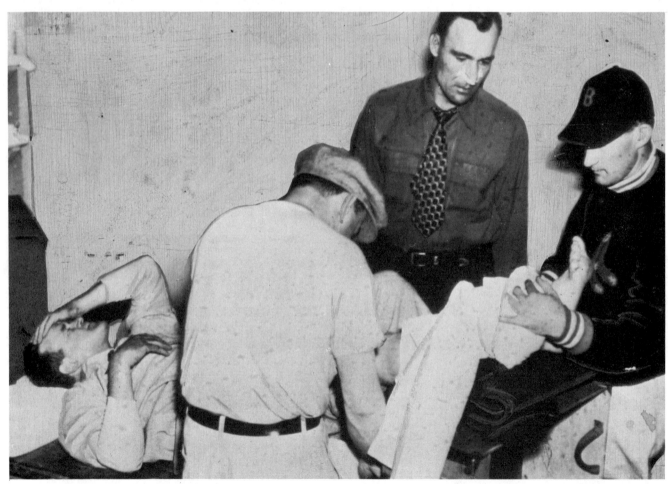

Future Hall of Famer Joe Cronin, the Red Sox' player–manager and Yankee nemesis, ended his playing career during an April game in Yankee Stadium, breaking his leg as he caught his spikes on second base.

Catcher Bob Garback tags out a runner.

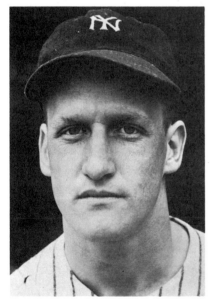

Controversially, star pitcher Hank Borowy was sold to the Cubs for $97,000 and helped Chicago to a pennant.

McCarthy returns after taking off 3 weeks because of nerves. He is greeted by (l–r) coach Art Fletcher, pitcher Red Ruffing, and coach Johnny Schulte.

The Yankees sign pledges supporting the War Fund.

Joe Page (r) blossomed in his second season (2.82 ERA)—his first winning season (6–3 record). Shown with fellow pitcher Steve Roser.

Red Ruffing said goodbye to the Army and rejoined the Yankees in time to notch a 7–3 record.

Tuck Stainback hit .257 in his final Yankee season.

Yet, as the turmoil in Europe and the Pacific built to a climax in the winter of 1945, the Yankees were heading for a crossroads. Their worst finish in twenty years lay ahead. The Stadium, scouting system and minor-league structure were showing signs of decline. And an imaginative promoter named Larry MacPhail was pondering getting up a syndicate to buy all of it.

He was a colonel, too, a staff officer for the undersecretary of war, but MacPhail had nothing in common with Ruppert, certainly not a Rhenish castle on the Hudson and several million dollars. MacPhail was audacious and flamboyant—he'd tried to capture Kaiser Wilhelm II shortly after the World War I armistice was signed, and ended up with a House of Hohenzollern ashtray.

Where Ruppert had been a patrician sportsman who regarded a baseball franchise as a diversion, MacPhail was a natural general manager with a flair for marketing. He'd introduced night baseball to the major leagues a decade earlier when he was at Cincinnati, and laid the foundation for two pennants there. Then he'd revived a flagging Brooklyn team in a bandbox of a ballpark and watched it win its first pennant in two decades.

Now MacPhail approached millionaire Dan Topping and construction magnate Del Webb with a plan to buy the Yankees from the Ruppert estate, which had been willed to Ruppert's two nieces and a lady friend. The price was $2.8 million and it included everything—the club, the Stadium, minor-league parks in Newark and Kansas City, and the whole farm system. The deal was cut in January over the objections of Barrow, who'd been general manager since 1920 and who viewed MacPhail as something between a hustler and a charlatan.

"Only over my dead body will MacPhail buy the Yankees," Barrow had vowed, but now MacPhail was president and Barrow was working for him. Barrow's role—chairman of the board—was largely ceremonial. MacPhail was running the enterprise and things changed quickly. He set about retooling the scouting and farm systems, devised a Stadium Club and moved the club offices crosstown from 42nd Street to the more fashionable Fifth Avenue and 57th.

For the time being, though, the lineup remained relatively unchanged and relentlessly mediocre. The war was still on and the heart of the club—Joe DiMaggio, Joe Gordon, Phil Rizzuto, Tommy Henrich, Charlie Keller, Spud Chandler—was still involved in it. The Yankees were Nick Etten, Snuffy Stirnweiss, Oscar Grimes, Mike Garbark, Tucker Stainback—and they were destined for a fourth-place finish and an 81–71 record in 1945, their worst in twenty years.

In July an exasperated MacPhail told a New

York sportswriter that a number of the players were going through the motions, that Etten (despite a league-leading 111 RBI's) wasn't earning his salary, that two of the pitchers were useless. Then he dropped a bomb—Hank Borowy, the best pitcher on New York's marginal staff, had been waived and then traded to the Cubs for $97,000. Borowy, explained MacPhail, aware of his ace's 10–5 record, rarely pitched well during the second half of the season; but Borowy went 11–2 from there and the Cubs won the pennant.

The deal ran counter to Yankee tradition; the club rarely sold its stars. Besides, New York was only four games out of first place.

McCarthy, saying his nerves were acting up, went back to his Buffalo farm, stayed there for three weeks and offered to resign. Thirty-five games into the 1946 season he would do so. Barrow was already gone by then—"no ship can have two captains," he said.

The Ruppert era had vanished.

Co-owner Larry McPhail (r) named Yankee great Bill Dickey manager, but he wouldn't last the season.

1946

The warning flag had been hoisted midway through the 1945 season when president Larry MacPhail had sold his best pitcher to the Cubs and Joe McCarthy responded with his three-week sabbatical. When he returned McCarthy had offered his resignation, which MacPhail had refused.

Now it was late May of 1946 and McCarthy, his gallbladder acting up again, was packing his bags in a Detroit hotel and planning to board a plane for Buffalo—and retirement. He had been feeling poorly as the club had departed for its first western swing and had missed three games. "He was in bad shape," Joe DiMaggio had noticed. "He was drinking too much and he wasn't eating right and he was worried about the team because it was playing so lousy." After fifteen years as New York's manager and twenty years in baseball, McCarthy believed the pressures were damaging his health. This time he would go home to Buffalo and stay there.

The next morning when the Yankees arrived in Boston, MacPhail was waiting for them with a telegram. "My doctor advised me that my health will be seriously jeopardized if I continue," McCarthy had cabled. "This is the sole reason for my decision which, as you know, is entirely voluntary on my part. I have enjoyed our pleasant relations . . ."

At 39, fireman Johnny Murphy was back for a final Yankee season—coming out of the bullpen 27 times to collect 4 wins, 2 losses, and 7 saves.

Phil Rizzuto was back from the war, greeted by fellow infielder Snuffy Stirnweiss.

*The Yankee outfield is reunited:
Henrich, DiMaggio and Keller.*

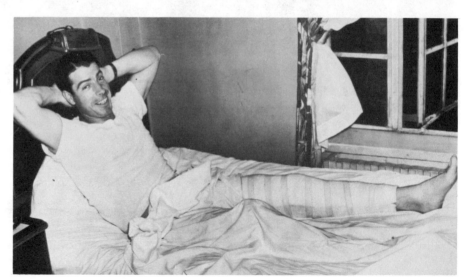

*Joe DiMaggio battled post-war
injuries all season—first a knee, then
a sore arm.*

Yogi Berra made his Yankee debut late in the season when summoned from the minors.

Bill Bevens was the Yankees' No. 2 pitcher, winning 16, as noted by teammate Billy Johnson.

The Red Sox won the pennant but the Yankees stopped their 15-game winning streak with Ernie Bonham (l) pitching a 2-hitter and Tommy Henrich driving in both runs of a 2–0 win.

Yet it was clear to most observers that McCarthy had enjoyed it less since the arrival of MacPhail, an impetuous promoter with an active hand. McCarthy was used to a passive owner in Jacob Ruppert, and to a general manager, in Ed Barrow, who backed him. Since MacPhail had taken over the club presidency in the winter of 1945 he had neither.

Though the heart of New York's prewar championship lineup had returned from military service the atmosphere was hardly the same. MacPhail had established two training camps, in St. Petersburg and Bradenton, which irked McCarthy, who wanted his people in one place. Press conferences were being called to announce anything MacPhail found promotable. McCarthy's declining health was a factor in his leaving, but so was front-office interference.

So, thirty-five games into the season, McCarthy had walked away from it, and the era of Marse Joe, which had produced eight pennants and seven world championships, had come to an end. And while the majority of the championship 1943 regulars were back in pinstripes—second baseman Joe Gordon, shortstop Phil Rizzuto, outfielders Tommy Henrich, Charlie Keller and Joe DiMaggio, pitchers Spud Chandler and Johnny Murphy—what they returned to was unlike anything they'd known.

The team offices had been moved from 42nd Street to 57th and Fifth Avenue. Arc lights had been rigged for night games (the first would be played five days after McCarthy's resignation). And MacPhail, ever the huckster, would stage promotion after promotion to fill the Stadium. He held archery contests and footraces. He arranged fashion shows to lure female customers and passed out nylons. Attendance, coincidentally or not, soared from 880,000 to 2.2 million, nearly double the franchise's best previous year.

Yet the on-field mediocrity that had marked their wartime clubs dogged the Yankees still. New York held first place for one day (in April) and finished third, 17 games behind a Red Sox club that hadn't won a pennant in twenty-eight years. By the end of the season a New York club that hadn't changed managers in midseason since 1914 (except when Miller Huggins died in 1929) had had three—McCarthy, former catcher Bill Dickey (who lasted 105 games, then resigned when MacPhail wouldn't make a longer commitment) and coach Johnny Neun.

"It grows more and more un-Yankeelike." Will Wedge wrote in the New York Sun.

1947

He was an unspectacular right-handed pitcher who'd lost twice as many games as he'd won during the season and would play only one more day in the major leagues. Yet, for one afternoon, Floyd (Bill) Bevens had found magic amid his wildness and now was only one out from immortality in Cooperstown.

This was the ninth inning of the fourth game of the 1947 World Series and no Dodger player had hit safely. Nine of them had walked, though, and now Carl Furillo stood on first with pitcher Hugh Casey due up. Instead, Dodger manager Burt Shotton made two strategic moves. Al Gionfriddo, a rarely used outfielder with sprinter's speed, would run for Furillo. And Pete Reiser would bat for Casey.

One stolen base, an intentional walk, a pinch runner and a pinch double later, Bevens was trudging through a jubilant mob to the Ebbets Field showers, the only man ever to pitch a Series one-hitter and lose.

It was the crowning oddity to probably the most emotional and dramatic October to that time, whose two most memorable games were won by the Series loser and whose most memorable participants—Bevens, Gionfriddo and Dodger veteran Cookie Lavagetto—never played another major league season.

This was the year when the Yankee dynasty was revived for the second time under a new manager, when Joe DiMaggio returned to his prewar form, when a new pitching staff signed on and president Larry MacPhail tearfully announced his farewell at the end.

Most of all it was the season when the Yankees rediscovered the stability and confidence that had brought them seven pennants in eight years prior to World War II.

After three managers—Joe McCarthy, Bill Dickey and Johnny Neun—had held the reins, in 1946 MacPhail had hired Bucky Harris, whose Washington clubs had beaten New York out of pennants in 1924 and 1925. Harris hadn't managed since an abortive stint with the seventh-place Phillies in 1943, yet he quickly restored a calm, professional ambience to the Yankee clubhouse.

And although the club had nobody among the league's top five in batting average or home runs, New York won 19 straight in midseason and left Detroit a dozen games behind. The ingredients were basic—a .315 season by DiMaggio, who'd undergone heel surgery, fine defense and the

Bucky Harris was named Yankee manager.

Rookie Frank Shea, a Connecticut product, was No. 2 starter at 14–5.

President Harry S. Truman tossed out the first ball on Opening Day at Washington.

DiMaggio underwent heel surgery during the off-season and then returned to his pre-war form and won his third League MVP.

Yankee infield of (top, clockwise): George Stirnweiss, George McQuinn, Phil Rizzuto, and Billy Johnson.

Joe Page was the majors' top reliever with 14 victories, 17 saves, 2.15 ERA.

league's best pitching, served up by a superb new rotation.

Only Spud Chandler remained from the pre-war staff. Allie Reynolds, obtained from Cleveland for second baseman Joe Gordon the previous fall, was the new Yankee ace—he'd win 19 games. Rookie Spec Shea won 14. And lighthearted Joe Page, DiMaggio's roommate, had developed into the league's best reliever with 14 victories and 17 saves.

Yet after two Series games with their borough rivals, observers wondered whether the Yankees needed any staff at all. They landed on Brooklyn's Ralph Branca for five runs in the fifth inning of the Stadium opener and coasted, 5–3. Then they riddled four Dodger pitchers for 15 hits in game two and won, 10–3. During the entire Series no Brooklyn starter would survive the fifth inning. This was a world championship worth televising for the first time?

"The worst we've ever seen," decided New York *Daily News* columnist Jimmy Powers. "It took exactly four minutes short of five dismal hours to play the first two alleged games."

But once the clubs crossed the Brooklyn Bridge for game three the roles switched and the clock ran on. The Dodgers pounced on Bobo Newsom and Vic Raschi for six runs in the second inning and kept five New York pitchers busy for three hours and five minutes of a 9–8 Brooklyn triumph, the longest Series game to that point.

Yet the next day Bevens, who'd been 7–13 during the season, either baffled or walked every Dodger he faced. Control was his only problem; in the fifth inning, two walks, a sacrifice and a fielder's choice cost Bevens a shutout. His mates had already dug up two runs for him. The victory—and the no-hitter—were still within his grasp.

When left fielder Johnny Lindell went back against the wall to haul down Bruce Edwards's leadoff drive in the ninth, it seemed possible. After Furillo walked, Bevens got Spider Jorgensen to foul out to first baseman George McQuinn, and the Dodgers were down to their last out and the bottom of their batting order.

So Shotton sent in Gionfriddo to run for Furillo. And Reiser, who'd busted his ankle breaking up a double play the day before but had sworn the team doctor to secrecy, limped out to hit for Casey.

Harris let Bevens throw Reiser two balls and a strike. Then Gionfriddo stole second base on his belly, and with the count 3–1 Harris ordered Bevens to walk Reiser. Second baseman Eddie Stanky, a strict single-hitter, was on deck; the percentages seemed better.

"Reiser had power and could hit a home run," Harris would explain to second-guessers who chided him for putting the winning run on

base. "I knew that Stanky would be easier to pitch to and that they were out of lefthanded hitters. I'd do it again tomorrow."

Reiser, who could not have run out a ground ball, shrugged and hobbled to first when he was replaced by pinch runner Eddie Miksis. "DiMaggio told me years later that Harris knew I had a broken ankle," Reiser would say, "but that he still didn't want to pitch to me. 'He'll still swing, ankle or no ankle,' Harris said. That was a nice tribute, but it cost him."

Instead of Stanky, Shotton chose Lavagetto, a thirty-four-year-old journeyman infielder who'd played in only forty-one games that season and was one-for-twelve lifetime in Series play. "The scouting sheets said to throw hard to Lavagetto and away from him," Bevens remembered. But the sheets were wrong. Inside fastballs were problems for Lavagetto, but he could handle something outside.

Bevens's first pitch, a fastball high and away, got Lavagetto to fan. But Lavagetto ripped the second, in the same spot, to the opposite field and presented rightfielder Tommy Henrich with a tough judgment.

"I knew it was creamed," Henrich said. "At least to the wall. But fifteen feet high or seven? That was the dilemma. If I get away from the wall to play the carom and it's only six feet high I've given away a no-hitter. If I go to the wall and it's too high, I've given away the game. Those are five seconds I could have lived without."

As it was the ball cleared Henrich's head by six feet and bounced off the wall. Lavagetto, rounding first on his way to a double, glanced at the third-base line. "I turned and saw the two runs scoring and that's all there was to it," he said. "You can throw everything else out. That's the top thrill of my life. Nothing else can happen."

Gionfriddo scored easily. Then Bevens, backing up the plate, watched Miksis slide across, grinning. Umpire Larry Goetz bent over to dust off the plate, then caught himself. "What am I doing?" he murmured. "The game is over."

It was Brooklyn 3, New York 2 and the Series was tied. Casey, who'd thrown one pitch in the eighth inning, was the winner. As Dodger fans celebrated, Bevens walked unnoticed to the clubhouse. Behind him, a movie advertisement loomed large on the wall for "The Secret Life of Walter Mitty."

The next afternoon with the score again 2–1 in New York's favor, a Dodger on base and two out in the ninth, Lavagetto emerged from the Dodger dugout once more, this time batting for Casey with a chance to force the Yankees to the brink. In the outfield, DiMaggio and Henrich stared at each other. "For Christ's sake," DiMaggio told Henrich, "say a prayer."

Dying Babe Ruth was given a "Day" at Yankee Stadium.

Ralph Houk (middle), with Berra and Aaron
Robinson, was a rookie catcher. Yogi was in his first full
season, and they would both go on to carve niches
in Yankee history.

Rizzuto slides safely into second during the Yankee–St. Louis
game. That's Brown second baseman Johnny Berardino
receiving—now a star of the TV soap, "General Hospital."

Al Gionfriddo makes a spectacular catch to rob DiMaggio in game 6 with two Yanks on base. It
made series history.

Joe DiMaggio, with his son, edged rival Ted Williams by one point for the League's MVP even though Ted won the batting title and hit 28 points higher than DiMag.

Larry McPhail stuns the baseball world by resigning as Yankee president in the victorious locker room celebration following game 7. With him are Del Webb (c) and Dan Topping (r).

This time Lavagetto struck out. Now Brooklyn, down three games to two, had been cornered, with the Series shifting back to the Stadium. The Dodgers piled up a 4–0 lead in the third inning of game six, chasing Reynolds, but New York tied it on a double, a wild pitch, an error and five straight singles, then took the lead in the fourth.

But the Dodgers pounded Page for four runs in the sixth and went ahead, 8–5. Whereupon the Yankees put two men on in the bottom of the inning and got DiMaggio to the plate with two out. Gionfriddo, meanwhile, had replaced Miksis in left for defensive purposes. "Shotton said play DiMaggio to pull," Gionfriddo said. "Keep him from getting an extra-base hit."

So DiMaggio, whose homer had won game five, crashed one toward the left-field bullpen, just to the left of the 415-foot marker and just above the waist-high fence.

Gionfriddo turned, chased, lost his cap and, just as reserve Dodger catcher Bobby Bragan was about to catch the ball inside the bullpen, grabbed it after it had cleared the rail. "My butt hit the bullpen fence," the five-foot-six outfielder said.

As Yankee partisans gasped, Gionfriddo's teammates whooped. "I have seen many, many greater plays," said Brooklyn shortstop Pee Wee Reese, "but I did not expect that one to be made."

Neither did DiMaggio. Six years earlier he had watched Cleveland third baseman Ken Keltner snap his 56-game hitting streak and hadn't shown a trace of emotion. Now, he was furious.

"In all the years I played with Joe I think I only saw him get mad once," said New York shortstop Phil Rizzuto. "Joe was at second when Gionfriddo caught it and Joe knocked the base loose from its hinges and kicked some dirt free. He was really steamed."

The Yankees would load the bases with one out in the ninth, but Casey got out of it with only one run's damage and Brooklyn prevailed, 8–6.

The Dodgers would make one last charge in the final game the next afternoon, knocking out Shea in the second and taking a 2–0 lead. But they'd used a dozen pitchers in three days. The Yankees got rid of Hal Gregg in the fourth, took a 3–2 lead, added two more for good measure and let Page (who appeared in four games) clean up. He allowed only one Dodger to reach first base in five innings and the Yankees had won their first championship since 1943.

In a raucous Stadium clubhouse MacPhail waved a beer bottle and announced his resignation. "I'm through, I'm through," he cried. "My heart won't stand it."

1948

He had been gone since 1934 but they had never gotten around to retiring his number. George Herman Ruth had finished his career as a Boston Brave and limped off into the shadows, finished at forty. The Yankees had seen him occasionally since, as a raspy-voiced spectator. And in 1947 they'd held a day for him at the Stadium, yet didn't retire his number.

Now it was 1948 and there might not be another chance. Ruth was fifty-three and cancer had ravaged his throat. He'd realized it during the winter and told friends that he was not going to waste away in a hospital bed.

So Ruth turned up at spring training for a last turn with his game, and on June 13 the Yankees said goodbye with the formality and dignity the man deserved. Twenty-five years had passed since the Stadium, the House That Ruth Built, had opened. So the front office brought back Ruth's teammates for a retirement ceremony, staged a brief exhibition with the current club and installed Ruth as the old-timers' manager for a day.

He did not—could not—play. His old pin-striped uniform, with its number 3, hung loosely on shoulders and a torso that had once perched atop spindly legs like a beer barrel on stilts, as Ty Cobb had said.

So Ruth sat in the dugout in uniform, a camel's-hair coat buttoned around his tender throat to keep out the damp air, and his teammates approached him for his autograph.

"They took a good many years to retire your number, Babe," joked pitcher Waite Hoyt. "They retired mine in 1930—damn quick, too. And without notice."

Ruth had had fourteen years' notice. When he walked out to make a final appearance as a Yankee, nearly 50,000 spectators blinked back tears. His voice a hoarse whisper now, Ruth told them how wonderful it was to be back and how proud he was to have hit the first homer in the Stadium. Then he was gone, and the Yankees of 1948 went on to defeat Cleveland, 5–3, and stay in a pennant race that the Indians and Boston had been threatening to decide between themselves.

The Yankees would remain in contention until the final two days of the season, when the Red Sox would eliminate them and go on to play—and lose—a one-game playoff with the Indians for the pennant.

But Ruth would not be there to see it. On

Governor Tom Dewey threw out the Opening Day pitch. DiMaggio received one award ('47 MVP) and presented another to Babe Ruth who . . .

. . . dressed for the last time in a Yankee uniform at the Ruth Farewell in June at Yankee Stadium.

Yankees acquired veteran pitchers Ed Lopat (l) from Chicago and Red Embree from Cleveland. Lopat was 17–11, No. 2 on staff behind Vic Raschi's 19–8, and went on to an outstanding Yankee career.

Tom Henrich ripped 4 grand slams during the season, tying Lou Gehrig's record of 1934—still the Yankee record.

Rookie Bobby Brown was an off-season medical student. Playing mostly third base, he hit .300 in 69 games in 1947 and .300 in 113 games in 1948.

Catcher Charlie Silvera blocks the plate and sends Washington runner Eddie Yost (an NYU product) sprawling in Yankee Stadium action.

August 16 the cancer had taken him, stilling the voice that had guffawed through railroad dining cars and ballpark clubhouses for two decades.

"Game called by darkness—let the curtain fall," Grantland Rice wrote. "No more remembered thunder sweeps the field. No more the ancient echoes hear the call to one who wore so well both sword and shield. The Big Guy's left us with the night to face, and there is no one who can take his place."

There had never been another like Ruth. Thousands of fans passed his remains as they lay in state at the Stadium and jammed the streets outside St. Patrick's Cathedral for his funeral. They buried him on a brutally hot day as his former teammates sweltered by his casket.

"Lord, I'd give my right arm for an ice-cold beer right now," Joe Dugan whispered as he helped carry the heavy coffin out of the cathedral and into the sweltering heat. Fellow pallbearer Waite Hoyt grunted. "So would the Babe," he said.

1949

He was a clown. Always had been. Charles Dillon Stengel had played for five National League clubs in fourteen years and hadn't been serious for a moment. As a Giant, he won a World Series game with a home run and thumbed his nose at the Yankees as he rounded the bases. He lifted his cap to greet his old friends in Brooklyn as he stepped into the batter's box at Ebbets Field and a sparrow flew out. He spoke in a roundabout version of English called Stengelese that contained a thread of indisputable logic—somewhere.

Stengel had managed one winning major league club in nine years. The seventh-place Dodgers actually paid him not to manage in 1937; six years later, when a Boston cabdriver knocked Stengel down and broke his leg and he missed two months as Braves manager, a Boston sports columnist voted the driver "the man who did the most for Boston baseball in 1943."

Stengel hadn't held a major league job since, but now Yankee management had chosen him, at age fifty-eight, to run a club that had just won 94 games and lost the pennant on the next-to-last day of the season.

Observers who were stunned when general manager George Weiss dismissed Bucky Harris

Joe DiMaggio signs baseball's first $100,000 contract. Dan Topping, seated, and George Weiss, general manager, standing.

the day after the 1948 season ended ("It was like being socked in the head with a steel pipe," admitted Harris, 1947 Manager of the Year) were equally surprised when Stengel was plucked from the minor league Oakland Oaks, where he'd just won the Pacific Coast League pennant.

"They don't hand out jobs like this just because they like your company," Stengel reasoned. "I got this job because these people think I can produce for them."

Weiss had liked what Stengel had done with the Yankees' farm club in Kansas City in 1945. At Oakland, the pennant was its first in twenty-seven years.

Beneath the verbal haze of his Stengelese whirred a mind that believed firmly in fundamentals and had a shrewd command of tactics. If Stengel's teams at Brooklyn and Boston had been relentlessly mediocre, Weiss reasoned, it was only because his material was, too. With a lineup stocked with DiMaggios, Henriches and fine pitchers, Stengel would produce contenders.

Skeptical sportswriters picked the Yankees for third—which delighted Stengel, who was accustomed to trudging wearily through the second division. "Third ain't so bad," he figured. "I never finished third before. That's pretty high up."

So he set to work in spring training and drilled basics into a club that was thought to be beyond them. "It will look new and baffling," Stengel conceded, but the approach paid off immediately. The Yankees won 16 of their first 21 games and grabbed first place in a hammerlock, even without Joe DiMaggio. Winter surgery on

Weiss hired Casey Stengel as manager. He got a spray of flowers opening day as Governor Dewey and Mrs. Babe Ruth looked on.

Star fireman Joe Page with Yankee GM George Weiss was the majors' top reliever, winning 10 and adding 27 saves, but his off-field antics caused Weiss headaches.

The Yankees had a new second base combination—rookie Jerry Coleman joining veteran shortstop Phil Rizzuto, shown flipping to Coleman on a double play over the Indians' Jim Hegan.

Boston's Johnny Pesky slides safely under Ralph Houk, according to Umpire Bill Grieve, on Bobby Doerr's squeeze bunt. The run gave Boston the game and a temporary lead over New York in the season's final week.

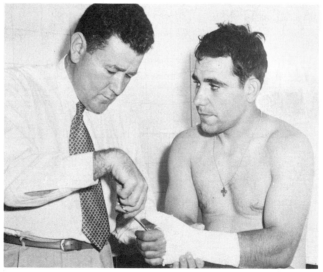

Yankees were plagued with more than 40 assorted injuries, including Berra's broken thumb and Henrich's cracked ribs.

DiMag had off-season heel surgery that sidelined him 3 months and watched the opening day from the sidelines.

DiMag and mother on "DiMaggio Day" during the crucial final weekend of the series with the Red Sox. Brother Dom is at left.

Red Sox Manager, Joe McCarthy congratulates Yankee Manager Casey Stengel, with Mel Allen describing the Yankee victory celebration to fans listening on the ratio.

Big and little Joe DiMaggio go up the runway to the Yankee lockers at Ebbets Field after the Yankees won the Series.

Casey celebrates his first championship as manager with GM George Weiss, co-owners Dan Topping and Del Webb.

his aching right heel hadn't eased the pain that had bothered him since the end of the war. "Fellas," Stengel told his club in spring training, "Joe won't be with us for a while."

Meaning three months. When DiMaggio returned at the end of June he rejoined a New York team that was facing a three-game series with the Red Sox in Fenway Park and clinging gamely to the league lead.

He was hardly in playing shape and hadn't seen a ball thrown by a rival in an official game in nine months, but DiMaggio was no longer in pain, which was enough to make him buoyantly optimistic in the clubhouse before what he would afterward label "the greatest series of my career."

The heel had held up nicely in an exhibition with the Giants the day before. "I might be ready for the series with Boston," DiMaggio had informed Stengel. "You're the boss," Stengel told him.

DiMaggio had lunched with Manhattan restaurateur Toots Shor that afternoon, still uncertain. "Night game tonight, eh?" Shor said. "Who's going for the Sox?"

"McDermott," DiMaggio replied. "Tough boy under the lights." Thus the challenge. And so before 36,000 spectators, the largest night crowd in Fenway history to that time, the limping, thirty-four-year-old DiMaggio made a classic reentry, his tender heel encased in a cushioned spiked shoe. DiMaggio's two-run homer in the third provided the winning runs and his catch of Ted Williams's long fly ball with two out in the ninth insured them.

The next afternoon, with the Yankees trailing 7–1 in the fifth, DiMaggio belted a three-run homer to drag them back into the game, then won it with a blast over the left-field wall with two out in the eighth.

During batting practice the next day, a biplane circled packed Fenway trailing a banner: *The Great DiMaggio!* And he delivered the coup de grace in that finale, a mammoth three-run shot that hit the light tower in left, about eighty feet above the field. Boston fans, who'd never borne any love for anybody in pinstripes except the great Ruth, instinctively stood and applauded what amounted to a sweep of their home team by one man.

They could afford to be magnanimous. As the Yankees lost DiMaggio (viral infection), first baseman Johnny Mize (sprained shoulder) and catcher Yogi Berra (broken thumb) and used outfielder Tommy Henrich despite his cracked ribs, Boston won 59 and lost 19 over the second half of the season and claimed first place with five games to play.

With two games left and a one-game lead the Red Sox came to the Stadium, and Stengel spent a sleepless night scribbling down lineups, tossing them away and scribbling more. Could DiMaggio play, having lost fifteen pounds? Could Berra, his fractured thumb still sore, catch Allie Reynolds's fastballs?

The real question, it turned out, was whether Reynolds could find the plate. After he'd walked three straight batters, thrown a wild pitch and allowed three singles and two runs in three innings, Stengel yanked him and sent in reliever Joe Page. But Page immediately walked in two more runs as Stengel, distraught, paced and cursed in the dugout.

Furious at himself, Page yielded only one single the rest of the way, and his mates tied the game, 4–4, by the bottom of the fifth. When outfielder Johnny Lindell, who hadn't hit a homer since July and only five all season, poled one down the left-field line with two out in the eighth for a 5–4 victory, Stengel winked. "I think we've got 'em," he said. "I can feel it in my bones."

So, once again, a season had come down to one game, but this time the Yankees were playing in it. With Williams blinded by the sun in left field, shortstop Phil Rizzuto dumped a triple twenty feet from him and scored on an infield out by Henrich in the first inning. A Henrich homer and a bloop double by rookie second baseman Jerry Coleman with the bases loaded and two out added four more runs in the eighth.

But New York righthander Vic Raschi, three outs from the pennant, relaxed perceptibly and a triple by Bobby Doerr past a stumbling DiMaggio led to three quick Boston runs. With two out, and the tying run at the plate in Birdie Tebbetts, Berra walked out to calm Raschi down—or fire him up.

"Give me the goddamn ball," Raschi growled, "and get the hell out of here." Moments later Henrich would settle under a pop foul, squeezing it near the first-base stands, and New York celebrated its second pennant in three years—its first under a clown.

For purposes of poetic justice, the World Series opponent would be the Dodgers, who'd traded Stengel in 1917 and fired him in 1936. Brooklyn, too, had won its pennant on the final day of the season, beating Philadelphia in extra innings to finish a game ahead of fading St. Louis.

Emotionally drained, the two clubs sleepwalked through the first eight innings of the Stadium opener scoreless, blinded by Reynolds on one side and Don Newcombe on the other. Finally, Henrich, who'd carried the Yankees in the early season when their entire outfield was sidelined, poked a home run into the lower right-field stands to end it.

Brooklyn returned the favor the next afternoon as Preacher Roe shut out New York on six hits and bore off a victory by the same 1–0 score.

So the duel shifted to Ebbets Field, and the Series turned on a two-out, bases-loaded single in the ninth by Yankee Johnny Mize, who would make a habit of October pinch hits. This one gave the Yankees a 4–3 victory that survived homers by Luis Olmo and Roy Campanella in the bottom of the inning and put New York in command.

Newcombe, who would never be able to beat New York in a Series game despite a brilliant career, came back the next day and was chased with three runs in the fourth. Then replacement Joe Hatten loaded the bases in the fifth and let Bobby Brown clear them with a triple.

Four Dodger runs off Ed Lopat in the sixth merely brought out Reynolds and inspired him to throw shutout stuff the rest of the way. Its pitching exhausted, Brooklyn died peacefully the following afternoon before loved ones, New York rattled three pitchers for ten runs in six innings, forced Dodger manager Burt Shotton to trot out three more, and prevailed, 10–6. The Yankees would not lose another Series until 1955, when Stengel had already established himself alongside Miller Huggins and Joe McCarthy.

"I am the same kind of manager I always was," he would say, drinking his first official champagne since 1923. "But nowadays I seem to get a little more assistance from my help."

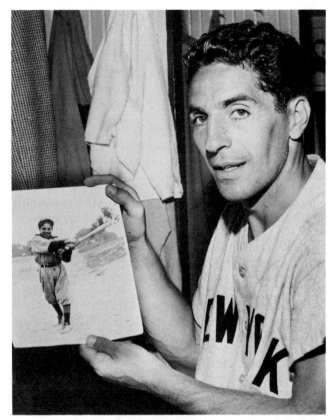

Phil Rizzuto was the League's MVP and Sporting News' "Major League Player of the Year." His .324 still ranks the highest by a Yankee shortstop.

1950

He was born on East 66th Street and grew up in Queens, a cocky blond city kid who grew up throwing a Spalding rubber ball against the wall of a trolley garage and saw no reason why he couldn't pitch for the Yankees. Eddie Ford had telephoned scout Paul Krichell after Binghamton, his minor league team, had finished its 1949 season and asked him to have manager Casey Stengel bring him up for the Yankees' pennant drive.

"You may think I'm cocky," Ford had conceded, "but I can win for you. I've learned everything I can learn in the minor leagues."

The offer was politely refused but now it was July of 1950. Ford was pitching well for a hopeless Kansas City affiliate in the American Association and the Yankees were embroiled in a four-way pennant race. So one morning at six o'clock Ford was aroused by a call from Kansas City manager Joe Kuhel. "The Yankees want you to get up to Boston," Kuhel told him. "As soon as you can."

Rookie Whitey Ford

Rookie Billy Martin.

Vic Raschi was 21–8 for a League-leading .724 pct. It was his second of three-straight 21-victory seasons.

Injuries continued to hurt Henrich and he retired at season's end after 73 games, concluding his career with 1284 games, now the nineteenth most in Yankee history.

DiMag's replacement in center field was 18-year-old Mickey Mantle who was hitting .383 while playing shortstop for Class C Joplin. He'd be starting in the outfield next to DiMag in 1951.

After his recall from Korea, Gen. MacArthur attended a Yankee game with his wife.

Rookie Jackie Jensen hits a homer. He'd become the only man ever to play in the Rose Bowl (as a University of California star), East-West football game, the World Series, and the baseball All-Star game. Stengel traded him away, and he would come back to haunt the Yankees as MVP.

Ford's debut, relieving in an 11–2 lost cause, was eminently forgettable. Five runs, seven hits, six walks and a wild pitch—all the while tipping off his pitches. "I think we ended up losing 17–4," Ford would recall. "Something tidy like that."

But Stengel liked Ford's deceptive fastball, his breaking pitch and his attitude, and began starting him against second-division clubs. By the end of the season he'd gone 9–1, with the only earned-run average under 3.00 on the New York staff, and the Yankees had won the pennant by three games over Detroit.

Now it was the fourth game of the World Series and the Yankees were looking for a sweep from a Philadelphia Phillies club that was playing for a championship for the first time since 1915.

So Stengel looked to a twenty-one-year-old city kid who wouldn't mind walking out to the Yankee Stadium mound and facing a desperate opponent before 68,000 people. "Hell," Ford figured. "Half of them were my relatives anyway."

For eight and two-thirds innings he baffled the Phillies, scattering six hits. Now with two men on base and one out from a Series shutout, Ford got Andy Seminick to lift a fly toward Gene Woodling in left field.

But sun and haze from cigarette smoke obscured Woodling's vision; the ball glanced off his leg, allowing Puddinhead Jones and Ken Johnson to score. When Mike Goliat followed with a single Stengel came out, concerned about a lead

that had suddenly shrunk to 5–2, replaced Ford with Allie Reynolds, and listened to Ford's relatives—all 34,000 of them—boo.

"I'll never forget Reynolds coming in," Ford would say. "He was the meanest-looking pitcher I ever saw. Allie just came in and blew three fastballs past Stan Lopata and that was the Series."

It was the first of a Series record ten victories for Ford, the Yankees' third championship in four years and their sixth sweep, which they achieved by scoring a grand total of 11 runs. The reason was pitching, a solid rotation that was the backbone of a club that didn't overwhelm anybody yet managed to win every vital series.

All season long they'd been scuffling with Detroit, Cleveland and Boston, losing their grip on first place in mid-June and not regaining it until September. But when the crunch came New York had taken two of three from the Tigers at Detroit (with Ford winning the decisive game) and two from the Red Sox at Yankee Stadium.

They'd clinched the pennant on the next-to-last day of the season but instead of the defending National League champion Dodgers, the Yankees found themselves facing Philadelphia's "Whiz Kids," who'd beaten Brooklyn on Dick Sisler's tenth-inning home run in the season finale.

Phillies manager Eddie Sawyer found himself in a quandary. His number-two starter, Curt Simmons, had been claimed by the military late in the season. His ace, Robin Roberts, had pitched in three of their final five games. Stengel was opening with 20-game winner Vic Raschi.

So Sawyer tapped Jim Konstanty, who was the best reliever in either league (16–7, 22 saves in 74 appearances) but hadn't started a game in four years. Thus began three of the best consecutive pitcher's duels in Series annals.

Konstanty, who would pitch in all but one game, yielded only four hits and one run. But Raschi, a hulking righthander who always took the mound unshaven, and who uncorked rising fastballs as a substitute for conversation, allowed only two hits, no runs and nothing at all after the fifth inning.

A double by Bobby Brown and two sacrifice flies provided the only run Raschi needed. When Sawyer came up with Roberts the next afternoon, Stengel countered with Reynolds, who was riding a streak of twelve consecutive scoreless Series innings, and the string of zeroes continued.

The Yankees nicked Roberts for a run in the second on a walk and two singles; the Phillies retaliated in the fifth inning with their own on two singles and a sacrifice. So it went until the top of the tenth.

Reynolds, who'd just gotten out of a jam when Phil Rizzuto and Jerry Coleman had turned a double play behind him, had ducked into the

The Yankees added veteran Tom Ferrick (l) to the pitching staff (8 victories and 9 saves out of the bullpen) and . . .
first baseman–outfielder–pinchhitter Johnny Hopp (.333), seen with Johnny Mize on left.

DiMag joined the exclusive 2000-hit club, and NY writers honored him, Keller and Henrich as "the greatest ever" Yankee outfield.

Jerry Coleman won the Babe Ruth Award as the World Series' MVP.

clubhouse for a quick cigarette. Suddenly he heard a muffled roar from the stands. Roberts had tried to slip a fastball past Joe DiMaggio, who'd deposited it in Shibe Park's upper left-field stands. New York 2, Philadelphia 1. "If it was a speck off," marveled Seminick, the Phillies catcher, "DiMaggio could put it in the seats for you."

So the Series shifted to Yankee Stadium—and little changed. Sawyer was down to lefthander Ken Heintzelman, who'd been 3–9 during the season. Stengel still had a horse in reserve in Ed Lopat, who'd won 18 games with a deft assortment of junk.

The Phillies led 2–1 with two out in the eighth, but Heintzelman, tiring, grew wild. He walked Coleman, Yogi Berra and DiMaggio in a row and was yanked for Konstanty, who got Brown to ground to Granny Hamner at short. "I can still see it," Seminick would say. "Granny took his eyes off the ball for an instant and that's all you have to do. If he had made the play we would have been alive."

Instead, Coleman came home with the tying run and with two out in the ninth Woodling, Rizzuto and Coleman all singled to end it. The Phillies had allowed New York six runs and were trailing three games to none; taken with their four losses in 1915 they had now lost seven straight Series games by one run.

So Stengel sent out his youngest, brashest pitcher to finish them off the next day. As Ford shut down Philadelphia inning after inning, his teammates chased Bob Miller in the first and piled up a 5–0 lead after six.

The only question was whether a rookie from the East Side could nail down a shutout in his Series debut and limit the Phillies to three runs total, the lowest since that made by the 1905 Athletics. Seminick's fly ball was the crowning touch—or so it seemed.

"It wasn't an easy fly ball," Ford mused. "It was sort of a line drive and I could see it was trouble the way Gene was going after it, trying to flip his sunglasses down so he could see it."

Woodling never did. So it ended 5–2, and Ford shrugged and consoled Woodling afterward. "I went over to let him know I wasn't mad," Ford said. "Especially a guy like Woodling, the way he used to put out."

No harm done. The Yankees were still world champions, the dynasty well on its way. "In another five years," decided general manager George Weiss, "they'll appreciate how good this club really is."

1951

For more than a month Brooklyn scout Andy High had followed the Yankees during their stretch drive, scribbling down his impressions of everything, particularly their aging center fielder. His report was blunt and dead on, but when the Dodgers blew a 13½-game lead and lost a playoff to the Giants it was useless—at least to Brooklyn.

So in the spirit of National League fraternity, High had turned over his notes to the Giants and now, after they'd stunned the Yankees in the 1951 World Series opener, Giant manager Leo Durocher was exultant. "It's great," he told reporters. "I never saw a report like it."

Neither had the Yankee center fielder. "He can't stop quickly or throw hard," High had written about Joe DiMaggio. "You can take the extra base on him ... He can't run and won't bunt ... His reflexes are very slow and he can't pull a good fastball."

DiMaggio had known it before anybody. He'd told sportswriters during spring training that the upcoming season would be his last. He was not yet thirty-seven but his legs hurt every day. He'd had surgery on both heels, his right knee had bothered him for several years, his throwing shoulder was arthritic. "It was agony for him just getting in and out of a taxicab," shortstop Phil Rizzuto noticed.

Most of all it was agony for DiMaggio to play below his own demanding standards. As 1951 wore on it was obvious he was headed for his worst season at the plate—.263 with only 71 RBI's and 12 homers. He simply couldn't get around on pitches any more. "Certain pitchers were getting Joe out with the slider," teammate Ed Lopat would say, "and he felt bad about it. He knew he just couldn't handle the pitch."

As the summer continued DiMaggio drew more and more within himself. He became moody, spoke rarely, brooded. In July manager Casey Stengel yanked him after he'd misplayed a ball in the first inning. Yet when the Series began DiMaggio was still in center field—but hitting miserably. And the Yankees, who'd swept the Phillies for their third world championship in four years in 1950, were suddenly in trouble.

The Giants hadn't won a pennant since 1937. Now, after Bobby Thomson's "shot heard 'round the world" had given them a dramatic playoff victory over the Dodgers, they'd used that momentum to take two of the first three games from their crosstown rivals.

His pitching staff exhausted, Durocher had

The Yankees trained in Phoenix, swapping bases for one year with the Giants. Yogi must have liked the climate because he went on to win the League MVP Award that season.

Mantle's first homer in NY was in a preseason game at Ebbets Field. He is wearing No. 6; No. 7 was acquired late in the season when Mapes was traded. A switch-hitter, he could power a ball from both sides of the plate, play defense, and run bases with speed.

Sophomore Billy Martin instructs rookies Mickey Mantle and Gil McDougald (r), who still sport their "N" (for Newark) farm team caps. McDougald won Rookie of the Year.

After retiring as Red Sox manager, Joe McCarthy returned to Yankee Stadium and was feted with a "day."

Allie Reynolds pitched 2 no-hitters, but . . .
Joe Page, shackled by arm trouble, said goodbye to the
Yankees, farmed out to KC to resurface briefly with the
Pirates in 1954.

Ed Lopat (21–9) had the
Yankees' best winning pct.
and his only 20-victory season.

Johnny Sain was acquired
from the Braves in June. He
went 2–1 with 1 save, pitched
effective relief, and spot
started 3 more years for the
Yankees.

The Yankees clinched the pennant behind Vic Raschi,
en route to his 21–10 record.

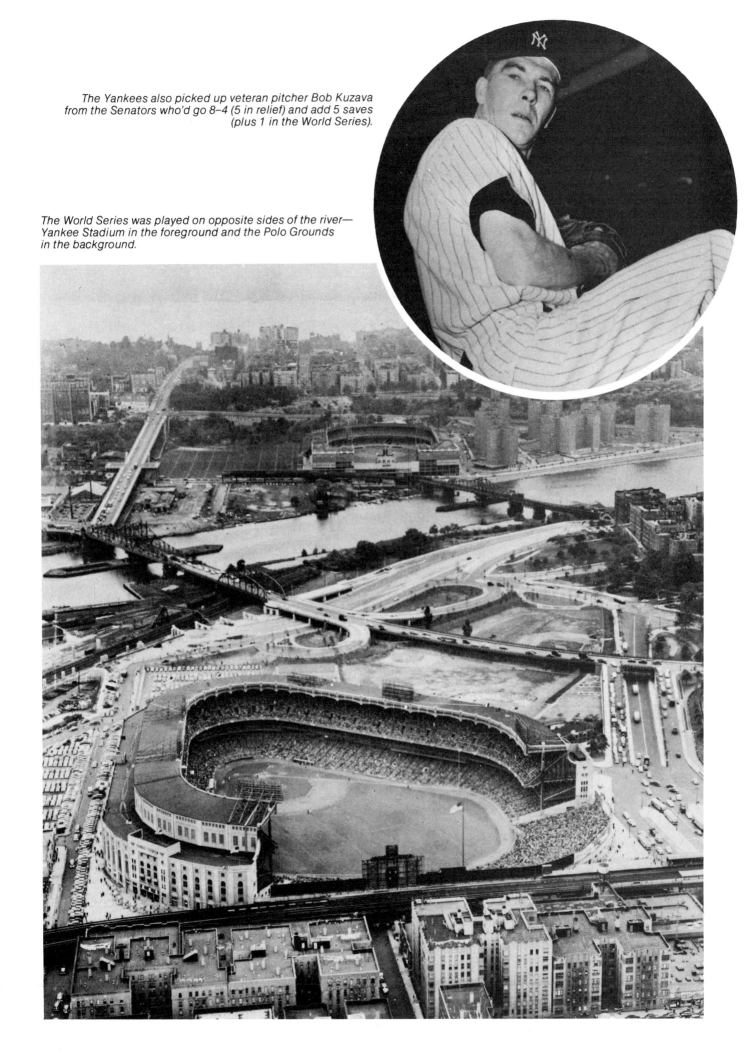

The Yankees also picked up veteran pitcher Bob Kuzava from the Senators who'd go 8–4 (5 in relief) and add 5 saves (plus 1 in the World Series).

The World Series was played on opposite sides of the river— Yankee Stadium in the foreground and the Polo Grounds in the background.

DiMag's final World Series homer.

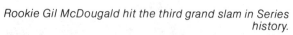

Rookie Gil McDougald hit the third grand slam in Series history.

Phil Rizzuto, MVP of the World Series, kicks up his heels, as Hank Bauer turns to watch.

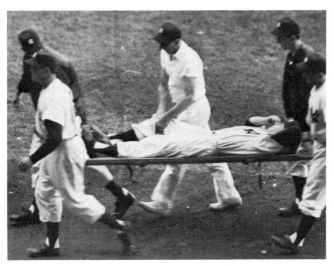

Mickey Mantle injured his knee in game 2. His dad hurt his back helping Mickey into a cab on the way to the hospital, where it was discovered that the elder Mantle had a fatal illness.

Hank Bauer was the hero of game 6 with a bases-loaded triple. Vic Raschi was the winning pitcher.

Giants Manager Leo Durocher congratulates Casey Stengel after the final game.

DiMaggio wipes away a tear as he formally announces his retirement at age 37.

gone with journeyman lefthander Dave Koslo in the opener at the Stadium—and Koslo had mastered the Yankees, 5–1, on seven hits, their first loss in a Series opener since 1936.

The Yankees had won the second game, 3–1, but had lost rookie Mickey Mantle with torn knee ligaments. Then second baseman Eddie Stanky had kicked the ball out of Rizzuto's glove on an aborted hit-and-run attempt and the Giants had scored five runs in an inning to grab game three.

Alarmed, Stengel had held a team meeting before the fourth game. "Fellas, I just want to mention one thing to you," he said. "You are not playing these guys twenty-two games. You only have four or five to play. What the hell are you going to do, let them run you out of the ball park? Let's go."

Duly chastened, the Yankees rubbed out the Giants in three straight and closed out the Series.

DiMaggio hit a two-run homer, the last of his career, to help even it. Then a grand slam by second baseman Gil McDougald touched off a 13–1 cakewalk. Finally, right fielder Hank Bauer tripled home three runs in the sixth inning of game six and speared a Sal Yvars liner on his knees in the ninth to end it.

Afterward, in a jammed Yankee clubhouse, Stengel sought out DiMaggio, who'd doubled in the eighth and trotted out to center field to a five-minute ovation before his final inning. "If it wasn't for you, we wouldn't have done it," Stengel told him. "Joe, this is your title. Yours alone. You did it."

It was one to quit on and DiMaggio vowed he would. "I have played my final game," he murmured, popping open a beer at his locker. Babe Ruth had been a pathetic figure at the end, playing out his final year as a Boston Brave after the Yankees had offered him a one-dollar contract. Lou Gehrig had slowed to a limp, his arms powerless when he retired, just two years before a nerve disease killed him. DiMaggio would not hang on past his time.

He'd told a New York Times photographer that the retirement was imminent: "Because I don't want them to remember me struggling." The entire season had been a struggle. There were flashes of brilliance, but they were largely obscured by pain that engendered mediocrity. "I don't want your pity," DiMaggio told writers who crowded around him after he'd beaten seventh-place Washington with a triple and a home run. "I have not asked anything from anybody."

Above all the man would not be patronized. As the pennant race built to a climax, league-leading Cleveland came to the Stadium for their final meeting of the season. After he tripled home two runs to knock out pitcher Bob Feller and

insure a victory, DiMaggio arrived at his locker to find a stack of congratulatory cables. "Now when I get a hit," he winced, "they send me telegrams."

He would knock in five runs in the Series and win one game but nothing would change DiMaggio's mind. Shortly after the Series, *Life* magazine printed excerpts from High's scouting report; if there were any doubts lingering, that probably ended them. Before long DiMaggio met with club owners Dan Topping and Del Webb.

"I'm never going to put that goddamn uniform on again," he told them. "Nobody knows how much pain I've been in. I'm finished. I can't play any more."

"Take some time to think about it," Topping advised him. Webb nodded. "Don't worry about the money. You can have the same $100,000 next year. We'll get the contact drawn up and sent it to you."

DiMaggio shook his head. "It's not the money," he replied. "It's me. I don't want to play baseball like this."

A few months later he called Topping and Webb again and told them to set a date for a press conference. And on December 12 he walked into the club office where Yankee publicist Red Patterson was handing a printed release to a roomful of reporters. "Joe DiMaggio," it announced, "today announced his retirement as an active player."

He had worn pinstripes for thirteen years, had batted .325 lifetime, knocked in 1,537 runs, hit 361 homers. He had played in 1,736 games (despite missing three war years) and ten Series, and the Yankees had won nine of them. He had been to the Yankees of his generation what Gehrig had been to the previous one, the embodiment of endurance, productivity and class. Now it was time to go.

"Why?" he was asked.

"Because I no longer have it," DiMaggio said simply. "I once made a solemn promise to myself that I wouldn't try to hang on once the end is in sight. I've seen too many beat-up players struggle to stay up there and it was always a sad spectacle.

"You all know that I've had more than my share of injuries and setbacks during my career. Lately they've been too frequent and too serious to laugh off. And when baseball is no longer fun, it is no longer a game. So I've played my last game of ball."

In another corner of the room Stengel was asked about 1952 and his new center fielder. "The kid," he decided. "Mickey Mantle."

1952

Joe Collins, the Yankee first baseman, never saw the ball. It was late afternoon in Ebbets Field, the sun had flooded the right side of the infield and now Dodger second baseman Jackie Robinson skied a pop fly between the mound and first base. Catcher Yogi Berra called for Collins to take the ball but Collins, blinded, never moved.

This was the seventh inning of the seventh game of the 1952 World Series and Brooklyn had loaded the bases with two out. If the ball fell in, the Yankees' 4–2 lead—and possibly the game and the championship—were gone. So New York second baseman Billy Martin, stationed almost on the outfield grass, glanced over at Collins and decided to take matters into his own bare hand.

"I could see that he didn't know where the ball was," Martin would say, "and I knew if he didn't get it the ball would drop and two, probably three runs would score. I took off."

Three Yankees—Collins, Berra and pitcher Bob Kuzava—had formed a loose triangle around the ball. Into the vortex rushed Martin as the Dodgers were racing around the bases.

"I could tell the wind was taking it toward home plate," Martin said. "And I was thinking about Yogi. I was afraid he'd be coming out for the ball and sometimes when he did he kept his mask on. I heard nothing, no one yelling, no one calling me off the ball. But I knew I might knock into somebody. I didn't realize how long a run I had to make until I watched the play on the motion pictures."

Martin was past the mound and heading toward the plate when he gloved the ball two feet from the ground. Carl Furillo had already crossed the plate and Billy Cox was on his way home with the tying run. Martin, still worried about a collision, pulled the ball out of his glove and squeezed it in his bare hand. If he was knocked cold, he thought, he'd subconsciously grip the ball better that way.

"But I didn't run into anybody," Martin said, "and I didn't think the play was so much until I got to the dugout and they were all slapping me on the back and saying, great play."

It was the play of the Series. Kuzava shut out Brooklyn for the final two innings and the Yankees had won their fifth world championship in six years. And the hero was a fiery twenty-four-year-old named Alfred Manuel Martin, who had a knack for pulling out tough games, particularly in October.

He'd grown up poor and combative in West

Jerry Coleman was recalled as a Marine pilot during the Korean conflict.

Allie Reynolds was the Yankees' top pitcher: 20–8 with 2.06 ERA—his best career marks—and he added 2–1 and 1.77 in the World Series.

With DiMag retired the new Yankee outfield had Mantle in center, Hank Bauer in left, and Gene Woodling in right field.

Mantle shooting a game of snookers in hometown pool room in Commerce, OK.

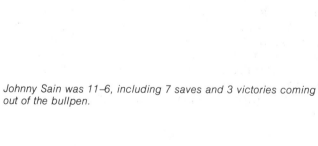

Near fight between A's and Yankees, with catcher Ralph Houk protecting Tom Morgan, the Yankee pitcher.

Johnny Sain was 11–6, including 7 saves and 3 victories coming out of the bullpen.

The Yankee's World Series lineup against the Brooklyn Dodgers (l–r):
Mize, Collins, Woodling, McDougald, Bauer, Rizzuto, Martin, Noren, Berra, Mantle.

Johnny Sain called out by Umpire Art Passarella at first during game 5, despite Sain's foot on the bag while the ball is still airborne. That's Dodger Gil Hodges and Yankee coach Bill Dickey with Sain and Passarella.

Hustling Billy Martin saved the Series with clutch catch.

Bob Kuzava was the Yankee pitching hero of game 7.

Berkeley, California, and while he claimed he never started a fight, he never backed away from one. Yankee general manager George Weiss and most opponents considered him brassy and obnoxious—"that fresh kid" was the usual description. But manager Casey Stengel, who'd managed Martin at Oakland in the Pacific Coast League, loved him.

"It should wake my other tigers up," Stengel mused after Martin had bloodied the face of Red Sox rookie Jimmy Piersall in a pre-game fistfight at Fenway Park. "It's about time they realize they gotta fight harder this year. I just hope that some of the kid's fire spreads to some of the others."

This was a new era and Stengel wasn't quite sure how to approach it. Joe DiMaggio had retired during the winter. "Who's gonna hit the fence this year?" Stengel wondered aloud in spring training. "Who's gonna make home runs now that DiMaggio is gone?"

He had four candidates—Bob Cerv, Irv Noren, Jackie Jensen and a fresh-faced twenty-year-old miner's son from Commerce, Oklahoma, named Mickey Charles Mantle. Just two years earlier Mantle had been a promising shortstop in Class C ball. By the middle of 1952 Stengel was calling him the best switch-hitter he'd ever seen.

In between Stengel had noticed him at his 1951 "instructual" camp in Phoenix. "Kiddo, I think we'll try you in the outfield," Stengel suggested. "What do you think of it?"

On opening day Mantle was playing alongside DiMaggio in right field. He would go to the Yankees' Kansas City farm club for forty games of seasoning and never spend another day in the minors. When New York met the Giants in the 1951 Series, Mantle was starting again—for two games. Chasing a fly ball with DiMaggio, Mantle caught a cleat in a Yankee Stadium sprinkler and damaged his right knee.

It was the first of what would be a series of leg ailments that bothered Mantle daily and which he later felt cut short his career. But, by May 1952, he was in center field as DiMaggio's permanent replacement. The team that Stengel had inherited in 1949 was undergoing a metamorphosis.

Tommy Henrich, the last link to the thirties, had given way to Collins at first base. Martin had taken over for service-bound Jerry Coleman at second. Gil McDougald, the 1951 Rookie of the Year, had inherited third. Yet the core of three championship clubs was still there—Phil Rizzuto at short, Gene Woodling and Hank Bauer in the outfield, and Berra catching a pitching staff anchored by Vic Raschi, Allie Reynolds and Ed Lopat.

Again the main contender was Cleveland, which would be the Yankees' chief barrier every season until 1957. The pennant race came down to the last game of the two teams' season series, at Municipal Stadium, on September 14, with New York leading by 1½ games. Indian manager Al Lopez, who'd decided he'd use 20-game winners Mike Garcia, Early Wynn and Bob Lemon exclusively down the stretch, chose Garcia since he was 4–0 against New York that summer.

"What do you think of Lopez's plan?" Stengel was asked.

"I always heard it couldn't be done," he replied, "but sometimes it don't always work."

Whatever—the Yankees pounced on Garcia who'd pitched 30 scoreless innings for four runs in the third inning and ended up with seven. Lopat and Reynolds, in their turn, held the Indians to one run. That was the turning point; the New York lead was now 2½ games with eleven to play. Though Cleveland won nine of its next ten, New York took eight of nine and won the pennant by two games.

"They said we couldn't win in 1949," said Berra. "They said we weren't good enough in 1950. They gave us a chance in 1951. In 1952 all the experts said Cleveland was going to win. We won again. And we will keep winning."

Meanwhile, the Dodgers, who'd blown a 13½-game lead and a playoff to the Giants in 1951, had won the National League pennant by 4½ games this time and smelled destiny.

As Philadelphia manager Eddie Sawyer had done two years before, Brooklyn's Chuck Dressen gave the opening assignment to his best reliever, Joe Black, and watched him scatter six hits. Pee Wee Reese, Duke Snider and Robinson, who loved the intimate dimensions of their Ebbets bandbox, poked home runs and the Dodgers prevailed, 4–2.

Behind Raschi's three-hitter and a three-run homer by Martin, the Yankees grabbed the second game and confidently crossed the bridges to the

Bronx. Three days later they returned to Brooklyn, shaken. A double steal and a passed ball by Berra had given the Dodgers game three in the ninth inning; Snider had won game five with an eleventh-inning double.

Now, trailing three games to two and facing extinction before a Brooklyn crowd that thoroughly despised them, the Yankees fell behind in the sixth, 1–0. It took homers by Berra and Mantle to force a seventh game.

Mantle put New York ahead 3–2 with a sixth-inning homer in the finale and added another run with a single in the seventh. Then Stengel, who'd replaced Lopat with Reynolds and Reynolds with Raschi, sent for Kuzava, who'd locked up the 1951 championship with some ninth-inning relief. Yankee fans gulped.

Brooklyn had loaded the bases on Raschi. Kuzava, a lefthander, was pitching in a park with a ten-foot left-field barrier. But Kuzava got Snider to pop to third. Two out. Now Robinson approached the plate and "he hit the lousiest popup I ever seen in a World Series," Stengel would say. Except that nobody was moving to catch it except Martin, who'd broken his ankle in two places in spring training while making a film on sliding techniques for DiMaggio's television show.

"I got it just as it reached knee level," Martin said. "Kuzava held them the rest of the way and we were champs again."

And all of Brooklyn sighed. Six straight Series lost, four in a row to New York. As the Yankees uncorked champagne, Dodger organist Gladys Gooding played "This Nearly Was Mine" and New York *Herald Tribune* writer Roger Kahn typed a Brooklyn lament in the press box. "Every year," he began, "is next year for the New York Yankees."

1953

Why should this year, this World Series have been any different? "The Dodgers are the Dodgers," Yankee second baseman Billy Martin crowed after the final out at the Stadium. "If they had eight Babe Ruths they couldn't beat us."

Another October had come and gone and the tableau was unchanged. Jubilent men in pinstripes were rubbing champagne into each other's hair, celebrating an unprecedented fifth straight world championship. And their Brooklyn counter-

parts, heads in hands, were staring into their lockers. Series losers for the seventh straight time.

Once again it had been Martin, the brashest Yankee of them all, who had delivered the crushing blow. In 1952 he'd come racing in from the edge of the outfield to grab a Jackie Robinson pop fly that first baseman Joe Collins had lost in the sun, and saved a 4–2 New York victory with the bases full in the seventh inning of the seventh game.

This time his grinning face had poked through virtually every game, right from the Series opener at the Stadium. With the bases full in the first inning Martin had hit Carl Erskine's breaking ball over Robinson's head in left field for a triple and a 4–0 New York lead that led to a 9–5 victory. In the second game, with the Yankees trailing 2–1 in the seventh, he'd deposited a Preacher Roe screwball into the left-field seats to tie the score and set up a 4–2 triumph.

He'd tried to save a lost cause in game four by sprinting from second on Mickey Mantle's single to left with two out in the ninth, but Dodger catcher Roy Campanella had tagged him between the eyes and knocked him sprawling, providing a lovely photograph of Martin airborne for the next day's tabloids.

He'd hit a two-run homer in the seventh inning of game five to put a 6–2 New York lead beyond question and force the Dodgers to the brink. And now he'd broken their hearts again, knocking in one run in the first inning of game six and the winner with one out in the ninth, lashing a single to center that scored Hank Bauer from second.

In all, Martin had gone 12 for 24, with a double, two triples, two home runs and eight runs batted in. His twelve hits had tied a Series record. Only Ruth in 1928 had enjoyed a more prolific October; fittingly, Martin walked off with the Babe Ruth Award for the Series MVP. "That's the worst thing that coulda happened to Martin," manager Casey Stengel would sigh. "I ain't gonna be able to live with that little sonovabitch next year."

Actually, Stengel loved Martin's intensity and scrap, which had a way of sparking a Yankee club that might otherwise have become complacent. They'd dominated the American League every year but one since 1947, winning the Series each time. In 1953 they'd assumed the pennant almost by divine right, winning 11 of 14 in April and picking up 18 straight victories in late May and early June for a 10½-game lead over Cleveland.

Then they'd gone into a puzzling and dramatic tailspin, losing nine straight at home at the end of June. Stengel, who'd been patient throughout, grew annoyed at persistent probing by newspapermen and closed his clubhouse to them. After New York finally beat Boston in the ninth inning, he held a team meeting and chewed out

Johnny Mize notched his 2000th career hit during his final Yankee season.

Bauer, Berra, Martin, and Joe Collins starred in the opener. Each had 2 hits in the 9–5 victory, including homers by Berra and Collins, triples by Bauer and Martin.

Sophie Tucker greets rival managers Stengel and Dressen of the Dodgers at the World Series opener.

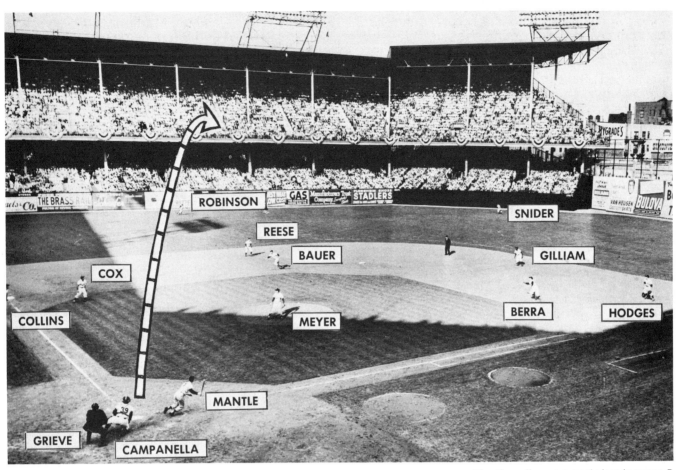

Mantle wallops a grand slam in game 5.

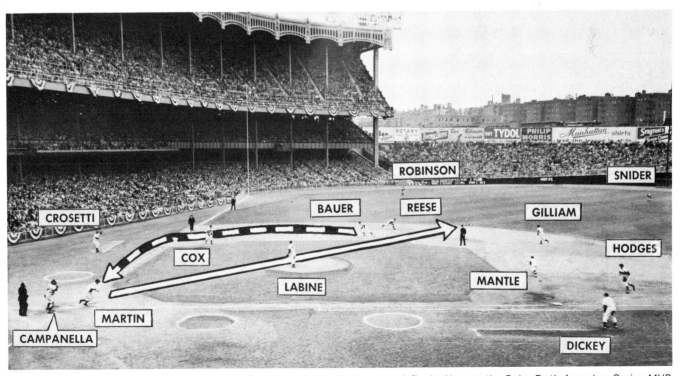

Martin gets a winning hit in game 6 finale. He won the Babe Ruth Award as Series MVP.

his players. The result was a breakout that kept the Yankees in control of the race until the end.

Only two barriers might have stopped them. One was a low railroad trestle in Philadelphia that ripped off the roof of their bus and sent glass and Yankees flying after a night game with the Athletics. Yet only pitcher Allie Reynolds, who arose the next morning with back pains, was injured; he never pitched as effectively again.

The other roadblock was a four-game Stadium series in August with Chicago, which had replaced the Indians as the primary challenger. The Yankees and White Sox thoroughly disliked each other, and Stengel took particular delight in deflating counterpart Paul Richards, who'd said he'd discovered a hidden flaw in the New York machine.

"If he's so smart," Stengel cracked, "why can't he beat Philadelphia?"

Whatever the flaw might have been the White Sox never came close to unveiling it; Stengel buried them with lefthanders. Ed Lopat stifled them 6–1 in the opener as Martin, Mantle and Yogi Berra crashed home runs. Then Stengel sent out Whitey Ford and Bob Kuzava for a doubleheader and chuckled as Ford won 1–0 and Kuzava spun a no-hitter for 8⅓ innings of a 3–0 victory.

Chicago won the finale but left the Bronx seven games out. The race was over; the Yankees would finish 8½ games ahead of Cleveland. They were truly in mid-dynasty now, as Stengel had predicted in spring training. "They better catch us this year," he'd warned, "because with the rookies we have coming up it may be difficult for quite some time."

Not even the best Dodger team in history, the Boys of Summer in full flower, could stop them. Brooklyn had won 105 games, the most in either league since the 1944 Cardinals, and had finished 13 games ahead of Milwaukee. There would never, they thought, be a better chance to bring down the Yankees.

Instead, the Dodgers found themselves gasping for air throughout the Series. After losing the first two games in the Bronx ("EGAD, MEN, WAKE UP," the Brooklyn *Eagle* urged them), they needed a Series record 14 strikeouts from Erskine and an eighth-inning homer from Campanella to save game three and Campanella's tag of Martin to choke off a New York rally in game four.

There was a final chance in game six once Carl Furillo ripped a two-run homer into the Stadium stands in right field in the ninth to tie the game at 3–3. But Hank Bauer walked and Mantle singled him to second. With one out Martin walked to the plate. "This fella," Stengel told shortstop Phil Rizzuto in the dugout, "is gonna break up the game."

With the count 1–1, Brooklyn pitcher Clem

Labine fired a fastball, Martin laced it on a line into center field and Bauer came pounding home. Fielding the ball hopelessly, Duke Snider merely stuffed the ball into his pocket and jogged in; Bauer was only a few feet from home. Why bother? "I should have thrown," Snider realized much later. "Suppose Bauer had fallen down?"

No chance. The Yankees were the Yankees, just as the Dodgers always seemed to remain the Dodgers. And Martin was Martin, whipping himself to glory in the Series. "My career average may only have been .257," he admitted, "but my one-for-four would kill you. In October, my one-for-three would kill you."

1954

It was the Year the Yankees Lost the Pennant after a five-year reign—or more precisely the year Cleveland tore it away. The Yankees, after all, won 103 games in 1954, their best record since 1942. Yet they still finished eight games behind the Indians, whom Casey Stengel had been regarding with alarm for two years.

"I better watch that fella," he said of Cleveland manager Al Lopez, who had been a Brooklyn Dodger and a Boston Brave under Stengel. "He was a pretty good catcher for me and he knows what it's all about."

Lopez also knew he had one of the finest pitching staffs in baseball history, built around righthanded starters Early Wynn (23–11), Bob Lemon (23–7) and Mike García (19–8) and a bullpen of Don Mossi, Ray Narleski and Hal Newhouser. His fourth and fifth starters, Art Houtteman and Bob Feller, won 28 games between them. And his starting lineup, including a Jew (Al Rosen), a Latin (Bobby Avila) and two blacks (Larry Doby and Al Smith), was a true melting pot of ambition and drive.

They held first place for all but a few hours of the season and cut the heart out of the Yankees in a September doubleheader at Municipal Stadium before the largest crowd (86,563) ever to witness a non-Series game. When the Indians blew the World Series in four straight to a Giant club that would have finished fourteen games behind them in the American League, people found it inconceivable.

Particularly the Yankees, who'd been having trouble with Cleveland since 1948, when the

Casey Stengel helps hoist the Yankees' fifth straight pennant on Opening Day.

Vic Raschi and George Weiss usually weren't smiling at each other. Following another contract dispute, Weiss shipped the veteran pitcher to the Cardinals after carving a 120–50 record over 8 Yankee seasons.

Pitcher Bob Grim (20–6) was the League's Rookie of the Year.

Former Series foe Enos Slaughter joined the Yanks with reluctance after 13 Cardinal seasons. He'd play parts of 6 seasons and 3 World Series as a Yankee.

Shown with Bill Dickey, Bill Skowron was another pretty fair rookie, the hard-hitting first baseman adding his big bat to the Yankee arsenal.

Stengel, often frustrated, failed to win the flag for the first time in his 6 seasons as manager despite winning 103 games (the most by Yankees since 1932). Yet they finished 8 games behind Cleveland.

Veteran reserve catcher Ralph Houk became a Yankee coach.

Indians had dethroned them as league champions.

Cleveland had been second for three years now, and when August became September the Indians arrived in New York 4½ games in front for a three-game series. The Indians had thumped the Yankees there in July, irking Stengel, who respected Lopez but considered his players a "bunch of plumbers."

"They ain't gonna beat me, neither," he vowed. Wynn managed to win the opener, but Ed Lopat limited Cleveland to one run in the second game. And Whitey Ford's pitching, a homer by Mickey Mantle and a lovely catch by left fielder Irv Noren that cost Hank Majeski a two-run homer won the third. The gap was now 3½ games. "We're back in business," Stengel proclaimed afterward, putting his feet up on his clubhouse desk.

But ten days later the Cleveland lead had ballooned to 6½ games; losing a doubleheader by Lake Erie would virtually put New York out of the race. The Yankees had to have both and

Stengel knew it. "We're six behind," he calculated, "and we go in there tomorra and we win two and we're only four behind and we go from there."

Instead, New York took a double-dunking, their first since the middle of 1953. Lopez had rested Lemon and Wynn, his two aces. Stengel had Ford for the opener but in the nightcap had to use Tommy Byrne, a thirty-four-year-old former Yankee lefthander who'd been purchased from the minors. It might not have made a shred of difference. Lemon threw a six-hitter to smother the Yankees, 4–1. Then Wynn shrugged off a two-run Yogi Berra homer in the first inning, gave New York only a bunt single by Hank Bauer the rest of the way, and won 3–2. The Cleveland lead was now 8½ games, the magic number three.

"Until after the last two games I didn't expect to lose it," Stengel would admit. "The fault was carelessness in all parts including myself. I kept saying, 'We'll catch 'em next week.'"

Instead, the dynasty burped; a fledgling magazine called *Sports Illustrated* dubbed it "The Twilight of the Gods." Yet the twilight was brief. Between 1955 and 1964 New York would only lose one pennant. The Indians haven't won another since.

1955

They danced all night in the streets, from Flatbush to Bay Ridge. Church bells bonged, motorcades snaked along, strangers embraced, confetti fell everywhere.

"There was one guy who kept telling me he'd been waiting for this since 1916," said Dodger pitcher Johnny Podres, the Series MVP. "Can you imagine waiting thirty-nine years for something? I don't know how late the party went on or if it ended at all."

After half a century and seven straight losses in World Series, five of them to the Yankees, *this* was the long-awaited "next year" in Brooklyn. When shortstop Pee Wee Reese scooped up Elston Howard's grounder and flipped the ball to Gil Hodges at first base, the Dodgers had come from two games down to shut out the Yankees in the finale, 2–0, and there was a championship to celebrate.

The hero was a happy-go-lucky Cuban named Sandy Amoros, whom manager Walter Alston had installed in left field for defensive pur-

Pitching coach Jim Turner welcomes Bob Turley, obtained in a trade with the Orioles. He struck out 210, which still ranks as the most by a Yankee pitcher.

Elston Howard became the first black player on the Yankees.

Don Larsen was another pitcher from the Orioles.

Tommy Byrne was 16–5 after being recycled from the minors the previous September.

Whitey Ford pitched consecutive one-hitters en route to 18–7 record, sharing the League lead in victories with Bob Lemon of Cleveland, and earning the League's Pitcher of the Year nomination by Sporting News.

Billy Hunter, acquired from the Orioles, became the new Yankee shortstop. Rizzuto still played plenty, but Hunter saw more action.

Stengel welcomed Billy Martin back from the Army in August. Martin got 2 hits in his first game back, played in 20, and earned his full share when the Yanks won the pennant.

Yogi won his second straight MVP Award, shown here tagging out Boston's Billy Klaus as the Yanks beat the Sox in a crucial game late in September.

The Yankees' bullpen punch: Jim Konstanty (7–2, 11 saves in 45 relief appearances) and (r) Tom Morgan (7–3, 10 saves in 40 games).

Hank Bauer is embraced by Berra and Rizzuto after game 6 of the World Series, as the Yanks evened the Series against the Dodgers 3–3. Bauer was the Series' top hitter with .429.

poses in the sixth inning. Within moments, with two Yankees on and none out, Amoros had raced to the left-field corner, speared Yogi Berra's slicing fly ball and doubled Gil McDougald off first.

But it was really a victory for the aging Boys of Summer—Jackie Robinson, Carl Furillo and Reese—who'd been losing Octobers to the Yankees since 1947. And it was a galling defeat for New York, which had retooled its pitching staff, regained the American League pennant and taken a victory over the Dodgers for granted.

There'd never been any reason to do otherwise; the Yankees had snuffed out Brooklyn in 1941, 1947, 1949, 1952 and 1953. "Don't worry," Casey Stengel assured inquisitors. "The Yankees always take care of the Series."

They hadn't lost one since 1942, when the Cardinals had come from a game down to win four straight. And after losing the 1954 pennant to Cleveland in the final two weeks, New York had rebuilt an aging pitching staff largely through one seventeen-player trade with Baltimore in November. Essentially, for the price of thirty-two-year-old outfielder Gene Woodling, the Yankees picked up righthanders Bob Turley and Don Larsen and infielder Billy Hunter. Turley would win seventeen games, Larsen nine, and Hunter would play regularly at shortstop.

When Billy Martin returned from the Army on September 2, the Yankees trailed the Indians by half a game. That day, in celebration of their friend's return, Whitey Ford pitched a one-hitter and Mickey Mantle hit a game-winning three-run homer. Martin, the Yankees felt, would provide the same prod he always had to their autumnal ambitions. "The fresh little bastard," Stengel would say fondly. "How I love him."

But with eleven games remaining Cleveland still led by half a game and the fourth-place Red Sox had arrived at Yankee Stadium for a three-game series. "I had three cars when I went into the Army," Martin told his mates, "and now I don't even have one. I'm broke and you're playing as though you're trying to lose. We gotta get into the Series. We gotta."

Yet by the ninth inning of the opener prospects looked bleak. Mantle had torn a thigh muscle running out a bunt in the second inning. Moose Skowron, furious at having struck out, kicked a dugout water cooler and broke a toe. With two of his top hitters gone and Boston's top reliever, Ellis Kinder, on the mound, Stengel looked to Hank Bauer, who crashed the tying home run. Berra followed with another. New York 5, Boston 4.

The Yankees never lost the league lead again and took their seventh pennant in nine years by three games over Cleveland. The Indians' management, which had already sold $3 million worth of Series tickets, mailed back refunds with the words "We're Sorry" on the envelope.

Meanwhile, the Dodgers had won the National League in a breeze over Milwaukee. After setting a major league record by sweeping their first ten games, Brooklyn had dropped two to the Giants then won eleven more. The Dodgers went on to win 25 of their first 29 and had a 9½-game lead by mid-May, a 15½ game advantage by August 4. The final margin was 13½ games and the stage was set. The Yankees were still missing Mantle. Perhaps it was an omen.

Yet when the Series began in the Bronx (it was no longer a nickel series; the fare was now fifteen cents) all the ghosts came flooding back. The Yankees rocked Don Newcombe, Brooklyn's only 20-game winner, for three home runs in the first six innings, two by first baseman Joe Collins, and won 6–5.

Then Tommy Byrne, a former Yankee who'd bounced from the Browns to the White Sox to the Senators to the minors before the Yankees had brought him back, twirled a five-hitter in game two. New York scored all four runs (two by Byrne) after two were out in the fourth, on four singles, a walk and a hit batsman. Was destiny always to be so for New York?

"We gotta win this one," Robinson told the Dodgers before game three. "If we lose again they'll be calling us choke-up guys for the rest of our lives. Do we want that?"

No club had ever won a Series after losing the first two games, but Brooklyn took the first step the next afternoon by relying on an unlikely source, twenty-three-year-old left-hander Johnny Podres, who'd won nine and lost ten during the season.

Podres had failed to finish his previous thirteen starts, but this time—as the Dodgers got him two runs in the first, second, fourth and seventh innings—he went the distance. Then, in game four, homers by Roy Campanella, Duke Snider and Hodges turned a 3–1 New York lead into what became an 8–5 Dodger victory and the Series was tied.

One gamble—with Podres—had paid off, so Alston now tried another. Where custom dictated he come back with Newcombe, Alston selected rookie Roger Craig and Brooklyn bats made it work at Ebbets Field. Amoros hit a two-run shot in the second inning, Snider added two more homers (he had four in the Series) and the Yankees had not only been beaten, 5–3, but, incredibly, nudged to the brink. "I'll be glad to get out of this rat trap," muttered Bauer.

The Dodgers, surprisingly enough, now had breathing room, so Alston gambled again and started twenty-four-year-old Karl Spooner. He

lasted one third of an inning and never pitched another game in the majors; New York pounded him for five runs, including a three-run homer by Skowron, cruised 5–1 and forced a seventh game.

Not since 1926 had the Yankees lost a Series that had gone the distance. Newcombe, who'd lost three of his last five outings after boasting an 18–2 record, had never beaten the Yankees in three Series attempts. So Alston went back to Podres and watched him go the route again, scattering eight hits. Suddenly a Series that had produced a record seventeen home runs in six games lost its thunder.

Brooklyn scratched for one run in the fourth on a Campanella double and a Hodges single. A Reese single, two sacrifice bunts and a sacrifice fly squeezed out another in the sixth. But Alston, trying to capitalize on loaded bases, had batted George Shuba for light-hitting second baseman Don Zimmer and watched him ground out.

So Junior Gilliam, a gifted utility man, was moved to second and Amoros trotted out to left. Martin and McDougald, the tying runs, were on base with none out when Berra, a lefthander who hit with power, banged a long fly to the opposite field with the Dodgers shifted toward right.

"The ball seemed to hang up in the air forever," said Podres, "and Amoros is still running. I started to think: Is he going to get it? I'll tell you, that's a helpless goddamned feeling, standing on the mound at a moment like that."

Amoros ran full tilt toward the left-field line and with his right arm fully extended gloved the ball, spun, and caught McDougald too. In the dugout, Yankees cursed. Amoros had cheated on the shift and had actually been out of position, playing closer to the left-field line than he should have. "We couldn't believe it," said Ford. "Only a lefthanded fielder could have made that catch at all. No fielder should have made it, period."

New York would threaten once more, placing men on first and third with one out in the eighth. But Berra flied to right and Bauer struck out. Podres got the Yankees in order in the ninth and Brooklyn released three generations' worth of bottled emotion in one all-night whoosh.

Amoros, who spoke almost no English, grinned broadly at sportswriters who literally couldn't interview him. In the Yankee clubhouse Martin, who'd saved the 1952 Series with a running catch and won the 1953 championship with a ninth-inning single, sobbed and pounded his hands bloody against the wall. "I still thought we were going to win," he said.

But that night belonged to the people on the other side of the bridge.

"The champagne was really pouring," said Podres, recalling the victory party at a Brooklyn hotel. "All you had to do was hold out your glass and somebody would fill it up. The streets were filled with people and every so often I had to go out and wave to them, then go back inside again to the handshakes, the pats on the back, the champagne. Boy, the champagne"

This year, finally, a championship tree had grown in Brooklyn that no Yankee was going to chop down. None would ever grow again.

1956

He'd had the worst record in the American League just two years earlier, a 21-game loser who tipped off his pitches and never did have much respect for a convention called spring training. Three days earlier he'd walked four Dodgers in less than two innings and had been removed.

Now Don Larsen was one out from a kind of flawlessness no pitcher had ever known, a World Series perfect game. He had thrown 92 pitches and retired 26 Brooklyn batters. Only Dale Mitchell, pinch-hitting for pitcher Sal Maglie, remained.

"I was so weak in the knees I thought I was going to faint," Larsen would say. "When Mitchell came up I was so nervous I almost fell down. My legs were rubbery and my fingers didn't feel like they were on my hand. I said to myself, 'Please help me, somebody.' "

Umpire Babe Pinelli, calling his last game, would not. If Larsen was going to Cooperstown, he would have to make it on his own. "Refusing Larsen anything he didn't earn 100 percent was the hardest thing I've ever done in baseball," Pinelli admitted.

Five pitches later Larsen had carved himself out a piece of immortality with a rising fastball that caught Mitchell looking and baseball history had been made. Since then reality and myth have blurred together.

It was neither the Series opener nor clincher, as some believe. Larsen's 2–0 victory gave the Yankees a 3–2 edge in the 1956 Series, but it didn't turn the tide; the next afternoon Brooklyn's Clem Labine shut out New York in ten innings and forced a suspenseless finale at Ebbets Field that the Yankees won 9–0 to regain the world championship the Dodgers had filched the year before.

One moment remains frozen in a timeless photograph—Larsen's right arm in mid-action, second baseman Billy Martin behind him, hands on knees, and a string of zeroes behind Martin on the Yankee Stadium scoreboard. Perfection.

"People have asked me what I did in the game," catcher Yogi Berra said much later. "I had to look it up because I couldn't remember. I don't remember what any of us did. I just remember Larsen."

Yet few knew him then as anything beyond another face in the New York rotation. Larsen was a tall twenty-seven-year-old who'd spent only four years in the majors. The St. Louis Browns, for whom he'd won seven and lost twelve in 1953, had wanted to make an outfielder of him. He'd come to New York in the fall of 1954 as one body in a seventeen-man trade with Baltimore that Yankee general manager George Weiss hoped would rebuild his aging pitching staff.

With a contending team behind him and Casey Stengel tutoring him, Larsen had been 9–2 in 1955 and seemed promising, providing he would take the game seriously.

Larsen liked parties and late hours. "Let the good times roll, baby doll," was his credo. "The only thing Don fears," quipped Oriole manager Jimmy Dykes, "is sleep." Teammates dubbed him "Gooneybird," and after Larsen wrapped a car around a St. Petersburg light pole in the spring of 1956 Stengel had shrugged, "He went out to mail a letter." At four in the morning.

Yet there was a gift there somewhere ("He should be good, but he ain't," Stengel would sigh before trading Larsen three years later). Larsen had a deceptive curve that he could throw at varying speeds. After Stengel urged him to deliver the ball without a windup early that season— the better to disguise his pitches—Larsen won eleven and lost five.

Still, he labored unnoticed through the summer, obscured by three stablemates with better records in Whitey Ford, Johnny Kucks and Tom Sturdivant, by a club that was running away with the pennant, and by center fielder Mickey Mantle, who had burst into full flower at twenty-four.

Mantle had crashed two long home runs at Washington on opening day. By the end of May he'd hit 20 and despite a gimpy knee was in pursuit of Babe Ruth's season record of 60. By August 25 the total had reached 44. On September 18 he slammed number 50 so decisively into the upper deck at Chicago's Comiskey Park that Stengel swore "seats were flyin' around for five minutes."

Mantle finished the season with 52, added a .353 average and 130 runs batted in for the Triple Crown, and walked off with the American League MVP Award. The pennant, New York's eighth in ten years, was a foregone conclusion; the Yankees led by 10½ games in July and eventually won the race by nine games over Cleveland.

Again, for the sixth time since 1947, the Series opponent was Brooklyn, which had clinched the pennant on the season's final day. But where the Dodgers had lost the first two games in 1955 they swept both at home this time and dumped the Yankees into an early ditch.

Johnny Podres, who'd won two of the 1955 Series games for Brooklyn, including the seventh, had been claimed by the Navy. Yet the Dodgers had found another Yankee-killer in thirty-nine-year-old Sal "The Barber" Maglie, whose unshaven scowl and right arm they'd purchased from the Indians in May.

Maglie yielded a two-run homer to Mantle in the first inning of the opener but recovered to go the distance, and homers by Jackie Robinson and Gil Hodges did the rest.

Spurred by a Berra grand slam the Yankees unloaded on their favorite Series pigeon, Dodger pitcher Don Newcombe, for five runs in the second inning of the second game, took a 6–0 lead and sent him, furious, to the showers.

"You never can win the big ones," a parking lot attendant taunted Newcombe outside. "You're a choke." Newcombe, who'd won twenty-seven games that season plus the Cy Young Award, bristled and punched his tormentor in the face. Back inside Ebbets Field, though, his teammates were rallying manfully. Two singles, two walks, an error, a sacrifice and a three-run homer by Duke Snider produced six runs in the bottom half of the inning and the Dodgers went on to a 13–8 triumph. "YANKEES MOIDERED," crowed a Brooklyn newspaper headline the next morning.

Once the Series crossed over to the Bronx, though, the momentum reversed. Enos Slaughter, the hero of the 1946 Series, had been disgusted when the Cardinals had traded him at age thirty-eight to New York two years earlier. "I feel sick all over," he'd said. Now he clouted a three-run homer in the sixth inning of game three and the Yankees had finally drawn blood.

The next day Sturdivant went the distance, Hank Bauer boomed a two-run shot in the seventh to assure a 6–2 breeze, tie the Series and clear the decks for Larsen. A New York loss would force the Yankees to the edge of the pit when the Series returned to Brooklyn, yet Larsen was unruffled.

He ate pizza and drank beer the night before, telling New York sportswriter Art Richman, "I might even pitch a no-hitter."

From the first batter he faced, the control that had deserted Larsen three days earlier was back in force. "Oh-oh, Larsen's got it today," Pinelli realized as he struck out Dodger leadoff batter Junior Gilliam with a breaking ball.

But for six innings neither Larsen nor anybody else thought much about what was happening. As it was he'd needed a combination of

President Eisenhower became a Yankee follower who was caught up with the nation, as Mantle chased Ruth's homer record en route to the Triple Crown.

The final pitch of Larsen's perfect game.

Berra leaps into Larsen's arms after the final out of the perfect game.

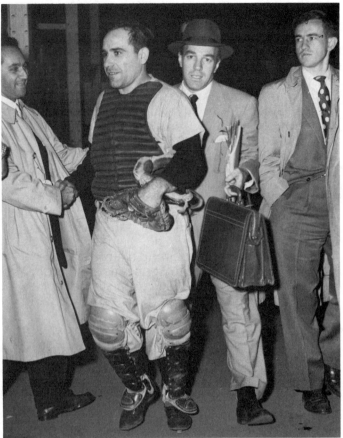

Berra wades through the media after his 2 homers in game 7 and catching Kuck's 3-hitter.

Johnny Kucks is surrounded by teammates Skowron and Berra after pitching a 3-hit shutout, as the Yanks rolled to a 9–0 victory in Game 7. Kucks, a 23-year-old sophomore, was 18–9 in the regular season.

Mantle won the Triple Crown, leading the majors in hitting (.353) and homers (52) and was the MVP.

luck and circumstance to keep Dodgers off base and runs off the board.

A Robinson bouncer in the second inning had skipped off third baseman Andy Carey's glove but the ball had caromed to shortstop Gil McDougald, who'd thrown out Robinson, thirty-seven and heavy-legged, by half a step. In the fourth a long drive down the right-field line by Snider just veered foul; in the fifth Mantle tracked down a smash to left-center field by Hodges, and a Sandy Amoros drive turned foul by inches.

Meanwhile, Mantle had poled a homer in the fourth and the Yankees had pushed across a second run with two singles and a sacrifice in the sixth. After Larsen had retired the side in the seventh he stepped into the dugout runway for a cigarette. "Do you think I'll make it?" he murmured to Mantle. But Mantle passed by, stone faced; you did not mention a no-hitter in progress for fear of jinxing it.

As Larsen took the mound for the eighth to face the middle of the Brooklyn order, the enormity of it all struck him. Four men had pitched one-hitters in Series games. One of them, Yankee Bill Bevens, had lost his no-hitter and the game on a pinch double with two outs in the ninth in 1947. "I hope what happened to him doesn't happen to me," Larsen thought.

He got Robinson to ground back to him, Hodges to line to third and Amoros to fly to center, then returned to the dugout to a standing ovation. When Larsen emerged to lead off the New York half he received another.

Now only Carl Furillo, Roy Campanella and Maglie stood between Larsen and immortality. Voices shouted advice from the Yankee dugout. "Everybody suddenly got scared we weren't playing the outfield right," Stengel said. "I never seen so many managers." Martin had already called Carey, McDougald and first baseman Joe Collins together. "Nothing gets through," he told them.

Furillo fouled off four pitches, then flied to Bauer in right. Campanella grounded limply to Martin, who gave the ball an extra squeeze before firing it to Collins. So Alston sent Mitchell, a thirty-five-year-old lefthanded hitter, to bat for Maglie.

The Dodgers had bought Mitchell from Cleveland, where he'd spent a decade as an outfielder, and he had gone six-for-fourteen as a pinch hitter for them down the stretch. "I was afraid he might get one of those nice big hoppers or a line drive somewhere," Larsen fretted.

Which was Mitchell's only goal—to reach base. He watched Larsen's first offering break high for a ball. The second caught him looking, the third swinging. Then Mitchell fouled off the fourth. Still, one ball and two strikes. Berra sig-

naled for the fastball and it came in rising. Mitchell moved to it—then let it go by. "We all stood frozen," Pinelli said. Then the umpire's right hand went up. "The third strike," he proclaimed. "And out!"

Perfect bedlam. Larsen came woodenly off the mound, dazed. Berra dashed out to meet him and leaped into his arms. In the press box sportswriter Shirley Povich tapped out a suitable lead: "The million-to-one shot came in. Hell froze over. A month of Sundays hit the calendar."

It would be nice to report that Larsen turned one flawless day into a magnificent career and that the Yankeess proceeded to sweep the Dodgers away the next afternoon at Ebbets Field and claimed the championship. Neither happened.

Larsen turned in essentially the same record in 1957. By 1959 he was a losing pitcher again; in 1960 he would be 1–10 for Kansas City. By the time Larsen retired in 1967 he would have labored for the Athletics, White Sox, Giants, Astros, Orioles and Cubs and finished with a lifetime record of 81–91.

His perfect day brought him lasting fame and a standing invitation to Yankee Old-Timers Days, but hardly riches; ironically, while he was on the mound that day his estranged wife was in court trying to attach his $8,715 Series share.

And the Yankees found themselves shut out by Clem Labine in ten innings in game six, 1–0, despite a four-hitter by Bob Turley, Larsen's former stablemate in Baltimore. "Kid, just hold 'em for seven innings and you got it made," advised Collins, the veteran of six Series. "Because the shadows will come in and you'll win."

Through the ninth Turley had conceded Brooklyn no runs—in the tenth on a walk, a sacrifice and Robinson's game-ending single beat him. "Hey, Joe, the damn shadows are out in right field," Turley had yelled to Collins in exasperation. "Where are my runs?"

Being held in reserve for Newcombe in game seven, of course. Alston had avoided using him since his game-two shelling; now he had no option. Stengel spent a sleepless night in deliberation then chose Kucks, whose sinker was more likely to be grounded into the Ebbets Field dirt than popped over the fence.

Kucks responded by tossing a three-hit shutout and Berra, who'd chased Newcombe with a slam in the second game, tagged him for a two-run homer right away.

Then, after Campanella had dropped a foul tip that would have ended the third inning, Berra crashed another. "It was a good pitch, Newk," Berra called in consolation as he rounded the bases, and Newcombe nodded in frustration. "I couldn't be any more ready than I am now,"

Newcombe had said before the game. "I want to beat them more than anything else in my life. I won't rest until I do."

Now it was 4–0 and Brooklyn fans, always quick to label Newcombe "gutless" in the Big One, hooted. "I feel sorry for him," Yankee pitcher Whitey Ford would say. "It was awful the way the fans booed him." Then Elston Howard led off the fourth with another homer and Alston came out to replace Newcombe with Don Bessent.

Humiliated, Newcombe showered, dressed and drove home weeping. He would be 149–90 lifetime but 0–4 against Yankees. There was no greater sin in Flatbush. "I'm sorry, Ma," Newcombe told his mother half an hour later. "What's to be sorry?" she shrugged.

Back at Ebbets, Moose Skowron had bashed a slam off Roger Craig in the seventh; the Yankees would win 9–0 and bear off their seventh championship in ten years. No Brooklyn team would ever see another one. "Aargh," grumbled Dodger fans, "wait till *last* year."

1957

For the price of a shine a Series was lost. The Yankees had a two-to-one edge in games and a 5–4 lead in the tenth inning of game four. Milwaukee pinch hitter Nippy Jones had one pair of highly polished shoes and wits enough to demand that plate umpire Augie Donatelli examine the ball after Yankee reliever Tommy Byrne had hit him on the foot with a low pitch.

When the ball showed a telltale black smudge Jones was awarded first base and the gears reversed in the Braves' direction. Jones was replaced by pinch runner Felix Mantilla, who was sacrificed to second. Then shortstop Johnny Logan doubled Mantilla home to tie the score and third baseman Eddie Mathews deposited a home run over the rightfield fence for a 7–5 victory.

Thus turned what was dubbed the Shinola Series. Reprieved, the Braves turned to ex-Yankee pitcher Burdette twice in the final three games for his wicked assortment of screwballs, sinkers, sliders and alleged spitters, and came out of it with their first championship since 1914.

For the Braves, who'd changed from a seventh-place club into a contender as soon as owner Lou Pieri moved them from Boston in 1953, it was a stunning achievement. For the Yankees, a

Mantle signed contract next to Babe's portrait and would repeat his 1956 MVP honor despite a foot injury and shin splints.

Stengel welcomed 2 veteran pitchers in a KC trade: Art Ditmar (l) would go 8–3 with 6 saves, and Bobby Shantz 11–5, leading the majors with 2.45 ERA.

By June, Stengel traded
Martin to KC, replacing him
with Bobby Richardson.
Martin had been teaming with
shortstop Gil McDougald (r).

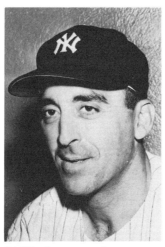

Old Yankee nemesis
Sal Maglie was acquired
September 1.

Phil Rizzuto (l) joined the Yankee broadcasting team of
Mel Allen (c) and Red Barber (r).

Tony Kubek (r) won the Dawson Award
as top rookie in training camp, going on
to become the League's Rookie of
the Year with a .297 batting average.
Sophomore Jerry Lumpe (l) would hit
.346 in 40 games.

Nippy Jones shows shoe polish
on the ball to the umpire.

Bauer, pitcher Bob Turley and Yogi Berra celebrate game 6's victory that tied the Series. Turley tossed a 4-hitter, striking out 8; Berra hit a 2-run homer; and Bauer snapped the 2–2 score with the game-winning homer.

Jerry Coleman retired in November after hitting .364 in the Series, having played all 7 games at second.

baffling setback. They had been odds-on favorites to win their ninth pennant in eleven years and had done so, by eight games over Chicago. Yet in some ways it had been an ill-starred season from the first, pocked by bad omens.

"I don't think it's gonna be a runaway," Casey Stengel told reporters at spring training. "Because that fella in center field can get hurt." He meant Mickey Mantle, who'd been bothered by a series of knee and leg injuries since he'd broken in six years earlier. Before training camp was done Stengel had been proven prophetic.

While playing demolition derby with electric carts at a golf course teammate Billy Martin knocked over Mantle's cart, pinning Mantle's foot underneath and spraining ligaments. Mantle, consigned to crutches, missed the first month of the season and later developed shin splints (after gashing his leg with a golf putter) that hampered him throughout the Series.

Then Martin hurt his own foot, came down with tonsilitis, was beaned and wound up losing his position to twenty-two-year-old Bobby Richardson. And the Third Musketeer, Whitey Ford, hurt his arm in the opening-day cold and missed two months.

So it went. On May 7 Gil McDougald caught Cleveland pitcher Herb Score full in the face with a line drive, shattering his nose and damaging his right eye. "If anything happens to his eye," McDougald vowed, "I will quit baseball."

As it turned out neither was the same player again. Score, who'd won twenty games the year before and had drawn a $1-million offer from Boston, never had another winning season. McDougald, the league's best shortstop, was out of baseball by the end of 1960.

A week later, in the wake of an incident at New York's Copacabana nightclub, where Hank Bauer was accused of breaking a drunken bowler's nose, general manager George Weiss fined Mantle, Martin, Bauer, Ford and Yogi Berra $1,000 apiece, and traded Martin, whom he had never liked, to Kansas City a month later.

All of which had begun turning up in the American League standings, where the Yankees trailed the White Sox by six games in early June. It took a full-tilt brawl at Comiskey Park that same week to turn the season around.

A duster thrown by New York's Art Ditmar at Larry Doby touched it off; giant White Sox first baseman Walt Dropo finished it by shredding Enos Slaughter's jersey and undershirt. Enlivened, the Yankees won their next nine games and assumed the league lead. Before long they were brandishing the kind of late-inning threat that revived memories of the 1927 club and its "5 o'clock lightning."

"Please warn the fans that they are not to leave until the last man is out," Stengel advised reporters after Mantle's bases-loaded triple in the ninth had beaten Chicago one day. "Not to sit there worryin' about the traffic."

The White Sox were dispatched during the final week in August with a three-game sweep at Comiskey that inflated New York's lead to 6½ games. Meanwhile, the Braves, whom New York had never played in a World Series, were winning their first National League pennant since 1948 by eight games over St. Louis.

Though the Yankees had two regulars hurt—Mantle with his shin splints and first baseman Moose Skowron with a bad back—they were still solid favorites to retain the world championship, and Ford disposed of Milwaukee with a crisp four-hitter in the opener.

Then the Braves unveiled Burdette, a tall thirty-year-old righthander whom the Yankees had last seen when they traded him plus $50,000 for Johnny Sain in 1951, when they'd needed a proven pitcher for the stretch run. Along with Warren Spahn, the last link from the 1948 pennant winners, Burdette had developed into a certified ace with a spitter that was widely respected yet never detected.

He shut out New York for the final six innings of the second game as the Braves won, 4–2, and brought the Series back to a Milwaukee populace that had never witnessed one.

What they saw was a third game that slipped totally away from the Braves after Stengel summoned Don Larsen in relief to retire Henry Aaron with two outs and the bases loaded in the second. The Yankees, who'd grabbed a three-run lead in the first, went on to score two more in the third, two in the fourth and five in the seventh on Tony Kubek's second home run for a jarring 12–3 final score with a three-run homer by Elston Howard.

New York erased a 4–1 deficit that was greeted with total silence with two out in the ninth inning of game four. When the Yankees took the lead in the tenth, the Braves were staring at a 3–1 gap in games and the prospect of extinction at home the next day.

So Milwaukee manager Fred Haney sent up Jones, a thirty-two-year-old journeyman playing his last year in the majors who was 12-for-52 lifetime as a pinch hitter, to bat for Spahn. A Byrne curve glanced off his right foot, skipped to the grandstand barrier, rebounded and rolled back to the plate.

Donatelli, assuming the ball had just gotten away from Berra, called Jones back. While the Braves argued that Jones had been hit, Byrne tried to signal Berra to retrieve the ball for alterations. Too late. Milwaukee third base coach Connie Ryan brought it back to Donatelli and Jones pointed out the evidence: "Polish from my shoe."

So Donatelli waved him on and moments later the Series was tied. The next afternoon Burdette spun a seven-hitter, allowing no Yankee past second base. Three singles in the sixth got him the only run he needed and left fielder Wes Covington, spearing McDougald's drive in the fourth as it was going over the fence, stifled New York's best chance.

Now it was the Yankees who were teetering on the edge, and Stengel looked for Bob Turley's fastball to even the Series.

Turley yielded homers to Aaron and Frank Torre but Berra, playing in a record-breaking 53rd Series game, had already poked a two-run shot in the third and Bauer would win it, 3–2, with a blast into the left-field stands.

So for the third straight year the world championship would be decided in a seventh game. Stengel chose Larsen, who'd yielded up perfection a year earlier. Haney looked, again, to Burdette, who had shut out the Yankees for fifteen straight innings. With the help of bad Yankee base-running (Bauer and Enos Slaughter both ended up on second in the first inning) Burdette extended the string to twenty-four. Only Giant pitcher Christy Mathewson, tossing three shutouts at Philadelphia in 1905, had ever done more to win a Series.

The Yankees, who'd always peaked in October, found themselves bereft of heroes. Skowron, whose grand slam had buried Brooklyn in the 1956 Series, had hobbled to the sidelines with a bad back in the opener. Mantle, whose shin splints had cost him a second straight Triple Crown, had torn shoulder ligaments in game four during a base-path tumble and was clearly subpar. And Martin, who'd saved the 1952 Series and won it in 1953, had been traded.

Now Milwaukee jumped on Larsen for three of their four runs in the third, helped by one of three Yankee errors, and forced Stengel to go to his bullpen four times. When it was done the Braves had taken the game, 5–0, and the championship—and were eager for a rematch.

"We'd like to play them again next year," Burdette said. "I'm sure we're going to win the pennant. But I'm not sure about them." The Yankees read that remark—and burned silently all winter.

1958

Warren Spahn's remark had been made in the hilarity of the champions' dressing room after the 1957 World Series but the Yankees had remembered it all winter.

"The Yankees couldn't finish fifth in the National League," proclaimed the Milwaukee pitcher. His stablemate, Lew Burdette, said he wasn't sure New York would qualify for a rematch the following year. The Yankees had set out to prove both of them wrong.

The American League pennant was a foregone conclusion, a ten-game cakewalk over Chicago that was all but decided by Memorial Day. What New York wanted was revenge for a squandered championship the year before. No revenge ever came tougher, yet few tasted sweeter.

Trailing the Braves three games to one and playing their last game in the Stadium, the Yankees rose from the grave to beat down Milwaukee in seven, sending the Braves fans they despised silently into the Wisconsin twilight.

The man most responsible was a burly right-hander named Bob Turley who, after being shelled in the second game, came back to win the fifth, save the sixth and win the seventh in relief. He was the only 20-game winner on a staff where only one other pitcher, lefthander Whitey Ford, won more than nine—yet it was the best staff for earned run average (3.22) in the league.

And though the lineup included only one man with a batting average over .300 (Mickey Mantle at .304), New York so dominated the league that their rivals essentially gave up the chase before midseason.

"In this league there are no pennant contenders," sighed Cleveland manager Joe Gordon, a former Yankee himself. "There is just the Yankees and no one to challenge them."

Late in May their record was 25–6, their lead on pursuers a full nine games. By the end of July New York had lengthened it to fifteen games, by August 2 to seventeen, the largest ever crafted that early in the season. The Yankees were young, deep and confident. The rest of the league was collapsing under them.

While rival fans hooted and sporting columnists condemned their monopoly, Stengel chafed. "Why is everyone mad at us?" he growled. "What do they expect us to do, roll over and play dead?"

As it happened, injuries would level the Yankees out. Ford won fourteen games by early August, strained his arm and didn't win another for the rest of the season. Bobby Shantz's spikes pierced Tom Sturdivant's heel while the two pitchers were fooling in the outfield before a game; Sturdivant ended up on the disabled list. Johnny Kucks went 1–5 during the last two months, Art Ditmar 2–6.

The miseries spread into the field as well. Second baseman Gil McDougald's back went into spasms; he batted .207 down the stretch. Shortstop Tony Kubek lost twenty pounds with an impacted tooth, then pulled a thigh muscle. First baseman Moose Skowron's back had been bad to begin with.

Hardly coincidentally, the club skidded through August and September, losing 28 of their last 51 games and limping home like a lame miler who'd already lapped the field.

When they finally clinched the pennant in Kansas City on September 14, the Yankees let loose with a whoosh of relief and swilled champagne on the train to Detroit. While the steam was being blown off, pitcher Ryne Duren, well into his cups, challenged coach Ralph Houk to a fistfight, tried to shove Houk's lighted cigar down his throat and ended up kicking pitcher Don Larsen in the mouth.

When the club arrived in Detroit George Weiss hired private detectives to tail a number of his players. It was an old Yankee tradition—Jacob Ruppert had done it to Babe Ruth & Co. in the twenties, Larry MacPhail had done the same to Joe Page and friends in the forties.

So one pair of detectives shadowed Mantle, Ford and catcher Darrell Johnson—and lost them in a Catholic church. Others followed Bobby Richardson, Kubek, Shantz and Kucks to a YMCA and watched them play Ping-Pong. Maybe the Yankees really were "milk drinkers," to use Stengel's terminology.

At any rate they had retentive memories and once the Braves had retained the National League pennant (with the same 92–62 record as New York's) the rematch was joined. Yet from the start Spahn and Burdette seemed bent on proving their prophecies.

As Spahn went the distance at County Stadium, Milwaukee came from behind to tie the opener in the eighth inning and win it in the tenth. Center fielder Billy Bruton, who'd missed the entire 1957 Series with a bad knee, ripped a single between center and right to score Joe Adcock from second as Mantle and Bauer, disgusted, let the ball roll all the way to the fence.

Then, after the Yankees managed only one run with the bases loaded in the first inning of the second game, the Braves mauled Turley for four of their seven runs in the bottom half. Bruton led off with a homer into the right-field bleachers; by

Turley won the Cy Young Award as the Yank's only 20-game victor. In the World Series he won game 5, saved game 6 and won game 7 in relief.

Relief pitcher Ryne Duren was The Sporting News' Rookie of the Year, sharing the lead in saves (20), along with 6 wins.

Hank Aaron was the top hitter in 1957's Series and Bauer the top homer hitter in the 1958 Series as the Yanks and Braves faced each other both years.

Elston Howard makes a crucial catch to turn the World Series around in game 5. He would be voted the Series' MVP.

the time his teammates had batted around, Milwaukee had chased both Turley and reliever Duke Maas, lashed out a double and two singles and watched Burdette, a lifetime .183 hitter, crunch a three-run homer.

The final was 13–5 and New York needed two home runs in the ninth to make it even that respectable. Back in the comparative sanity of Yankee Stadium, Larsen pitched shutout ball for seven innings of game three, Bauer knocked in all four runs with a single and a 400-foot homer and Duren wrapped up a 4–0 victory that got New York breathing again. For one day.

Spahn came back the following afternoon with a two-hitter, yielding only a triple in the fourth to Mantle (who died on third with one out) and a single to Skowron in the seventh. Yankee leftfielder Norm Siebern lost two balls in the sun, the Braves exploited them for two runs and New York was suddenly faced with the prospect of losing successive Series at home.

It wouldn't be necessary, Spahn predicted, to return to County Stadium. After all, Burdette, who'd beaten the Yankees four straight times, would be on the mound the next day. No club since the 1925 Pirates had ever come back from a 3–1 deficit to win a championship, and for five innings of game five it seemed unlikely that the Yankees would do the same.

McDougald had poled a homer in the third, but Bruton had singled over Kubek's head to lead off the sixth. Now Braves second baseman Red Schoendienst looped a fly toward Elston Howard in left field that seemed certain to advance Bruton to third. Instead, Howard dove and saved the ball just before it touched the grass and doubled up Bruton. Eddie Mathews proceeded to single, giving birth to a number of what-ifs.

"To tell you the truth I thought it was going to fall in," Howard admitted, "and so did Bruton. He was already around second when I caught it."

Thus reprieved, the Yankees batted around in the bottom half of the seventh and hung six runs on Burdette, who would never win another Series game. Turley went on to shut out the Braves, 7–0, on five hits and the Yankees packed their bags with a vengeance.

Milwaukee would come back with Spahn at home, New York would sent out Ford. But Ford loaded the bases with one out in the second and the Yankees behind 2–1 and was yanked for Ditmar, who eventually gave way to Duren.

Two singles, a Bruton error and a sacrifice enabled the Yankees to tie it in the sixth and with Spahn, at thirty-seven, still working, the game went into extra innings.

McDougald immediately tagged Spahn for a homer, and three New York singles—the third

off reliever Don McMahon—shook down another run. If Duren could hold the top of the Milwaukee order, there would be a seventh game. But a walk and two singles later it was 4–3 and Stengel was motioning for Turley. He got Frank Torre to line sharply to McDougald on the fringe of the outfield and it was over. For the fourth consecutive year the Series would go to the limit.

The Braves would ride with Burdette. Stengel kept his choice secret until an hour before the game, then chose Larsen. Milwaukee touched him for a run within minutes and put two men on base with one out in the third. With New York leading 2–1 (two errors by Torre on routine 3–1 grounders in the second led to both runs) Stengel was taking no chances. Turley strolled out from the bullpen.

He was Bullet Bob, a fastball addict in the Allie Reynolds tradition. He'd come from Baltimore with Larsen four years earlier when Weiss had retooled an aging pitching staff and had developed, over time, into the Yankee's righthanded ace.

Turley drank milk, read real estate books and did not appear to need a private detective to chronicle his comings and goings. He would give the Braves one run, a homer by Del Crandall, to tie the score in the sixth but nothing else until two were out in the ninth. By then the Yankees had pummelled Burdette for four more runs in the eighth, three of them from the bat of Skowron, who'd missed virtually the entire 1957 Series.

As Skowron rounded the bases, a 6–2 victory on ice, County Stadium emptied quickly. A few minutes later the Yankees were champions again, the way they'd wanted to be. They'd beaten Spahn and Burdette in their own yard to complete the best Series comeback in thirty-three years. On the flight back to LaGuardia they drained champagne bottles, burned the corks and arrived in blackface.

"I guess," Stengel decided, a large dollar sign scribbled onto his face, "that we could play in the National League after all."

1959

Nothing like this had happened in nineteen years. The Yankees, long accustomed to being booed on the road, were hearing catcalls every day in Yankee Stadium. Everybody from the White

At .301 Bobby Richardson was the Yankees' only .300 hitter as the club averaged .260.

The Yankees obtained outfielder-third baseman Hector Lopez and pitcher Ralph Terry (l) from KC in a trade for Tom Sturdivant, Johnny Kucks and Jerry Lumpe.

Casey Stengel juggled his lineup, but nothing could prevent the leanest Yankee season since 1925— third place, 15 games off the top.

Sox to their favorite farm team, the Athletics, were teeing off on them.

There were injuries on the field, sore arms in the bullpen and doubt in the front office. On May 20 they all came together in a stark headline over a photograph showing a disconsolate Mickey Mantle, his head down. "The Day the Yankees Hit the Bottom," it read.

The standings told the tale—for the first time since May 1940 New York could be found in last place in the American League, 8½ games behind Cleveland. Detroit righthander Frank Lary, the foremost Yankee-killer of his day, had beaten them 13–6 in the Stadium that day and Mantle, who would struggle through his most painful and dismal year yet, had been hooted even while circling the bases after a two-run homer.

When it was done and the Yankees were filing silently into the clubhouse, the front office set a restraining line for photographers fifty feet from the players' path. "The Yankee players," decreed a club official, "are not to be humiliated."

They had been world champions just seven months before and technically still were. They could pull themselves back into the pennant race and did, within two weeks. But this was destined to be New York's leanest season since 1925. The Yankees would finish with a 79–75 record, in third place fifteen games behind a Chicago club that hadn't won a pennant in forty years.

It was the beginning of the end for manager Casey Stengel, who'd won nine pennants and seven championships but would eventually be cashiered for one he didn't win. "This bad season was an emergency to our owners," Stengel said wryly. "They thought the manager was slipping. They thought the coaches were slipping. They thought the players were slipping. But maybe the people in the front office didn't have such a good year themselves."

The problems had begun during the off-season when owner Dan Topping did away with Stengel's beloved "instructual" schools (where he'd discovered Mantle) and ordered general manager George Weiss to take a hard line on contracts even though the club had staged the greatest Series resurrection in thirty-three years by coming from a 3–1 deficit to beat Milwaukee in 1958.

Not that it was any novelty. The New York front office traditionally managed to turn a championship season into a disadvantage at signing time, explaining that since pennants were automatic in the Bronx, Series shares should be considered part of the salary.

So Mantle and pitcher Whitey Ford were both unsigned when spring training began and many of their teammates were grumbling.

From the beginning the season turned sour. Bob Turley, who'd won two Series games and saved a third the previous autumn, went blah, his fastball gone, his record sliding from 21–7 to 8–11. Two starting pitchers, Don Larsen and Tom Sturdivant, turned up with sore arms. Third baseman Andy Carey developed an infected hand. Utility infielder Gil McDougald was hit on the hands by Boston pitcher Bill Monbouquette and missed two weeks. Hank Bauer slipped from .268 to .238 with only 39 runs batted in. Mantle strained his throwing shoulder, broke an index finger in the batting cage, then, along with four teammates, was leveled by the flu.

In less than two months the league had turned upside down on the Yankees. Then they mounted an offensive, led by Mantle (who raised his average 50 points in eleven days), a briefly healthy Moose Skowron, Kansas City refugee Hector Lopez, and Ryne Duren, who pitched 36 consecutive shutout innings over 18 games.

Within two weeks New York had closed to within 2½ games of the Indians. Then they went to Chicago, where new owner Bill Veeck was putting his promotional genius to work. Amid skyrockets from an exploding scoreboard and Handel's *Messiah,* the Yankees lost three of four in 100-degree heat to a crew of White Sox that couldn't hit but never stopped running. Their battle song, Veeck said, was "Bobbles, Bingles and Bunts."

A few days later Mantle hurt an ankle and hobbled through the balance of the season. The summer came undone permanently during the second week of July, when the Yankees lost five of six at Boston and fell to fifth, 7½ games out.

From there it was a Midsummer's Nightmare. McDougald and Tony Kubek collided chasing a popup and ended up dazed. Skowron, whose back hadn't been right for two years, broke an arm in a base-path collision with Detroit's Coot Veal. Lopez banged an elbow and Carey, his replacement, contracted hepatitis. Finally, Duren, running from the bullpen to the dugout after a game at Boston, tripped over two fans and broke a wrist.

"We're having a lot of trouble with everything," Stengel concluded. "You got nine guys not hitting and the pitching not so hot either and what are you going to do?"

1960

Bill Virdon cursed the moment he watched the ball leave his bat and bounce toward Yankee shortstop Tony Kubek. Routine grounder, classic double-play ball, he thought. Kubek would get Gino Cimoli at second, Virdon would be nipped at first and the Pirates' eighth-inning rally would die aborning. And New York, leading 7–4 in the seventh game at Pittsburgh, would go on to claim the world championship.

But the ball was never gloved, the throw never made. Instead, Virdon arrived at first base and discovered Kubek on the ground near second, his hand clutching his Adam's apple. The grounder had ricocheted off a pebble, a clot of dirt, a rut . . . something . . . and angled up sharply. Everybody was safe and Kubek, breathless and hurt, was on his way to a hospital.

From there unraveled a championship the Yankees had won, lost and won again—depending upon the day of the week—and finally would lose. The double play that wasn't led to five Pirate runs and after the Yankees had scored twice in their half of the ninth to tie the score, a miner's son named Bill Mazeroski hit the most dramatic home run in Series history to push Pittsburgh to a 10–9 triumph and its first world championship since 1925.

The Yankees had set Series records for runs (55), hits (91), extra-base hits (27) and batting average (.338). They had drubbed the Pirates 16–3, 10–0 and 12–0. They did everything possible in a Series—except win it.

"I can't believe it," moaned left fielder Yogi Berra.

"I'll never believe it," decided Yankee pinch hitter Dale Long, a former Pirate.

Neither would the Yankee front office, which had fidgeted through the club's worst season in thirty-four years in 1959, and had expected nothing less than a return to championship form in 1960. So, two days after the cheering had died down in Pittsburgh, owner Dan Topping and general manager George Weiss identified their scapegoat, seventy-year-old manager Casey Stengel, and dismissed him. The term they used was resignation, but it was a euphemism.

"You're goddamn right I was fired," Stengel growled at his farewell press conference. Thus ended the most successful span in franchise history, a twelve-year stretch during which Stengel managed the Yankees to ten pennants and seven championships and built a dynasty that would win four more American League flags before the talent ran out in 1965.

"Competence has ceased to be the measuring rod in the Yankee scheme of things," wrote *New York Times* columnist Arthur Daley. "It can be overruled and negated by the date on a man's birth certificate."

Stengel had seen the end coming well before. He'd squabbled with the front office for much of the disappointing 1959 season. "They would have liked to get rid of a lot of people, including the manager and most of the coaches," he realized. If management hadn't been reluctant to swallow a full year of Stengel's salary, they might have released him then. As it was, Topping had offered the job to Al Lopez, who'd just managed the White Sox to their first pennant in forty years. Lopez had refused, but the front office's intentions were obvious.

Meanwhile, Weiss cleaned as much of his personnel house as he could. Pitcher Don Larsen (he of the 1956 Series perfect game), outfielders Norm Siebern and Hank Bauer, and first baseman Marv Throneberry were shipped to Kansas City, the Yankees' favorite junkyard. In return they received shortstop Joe DeMaestri, first baseman Kent Hadley and a promising outfielder named Roger Maris.

Still, the Yankees slogged through spring training and, after Stengel was hospitalized with a virus, the club fell six games behind Baltimore by the end of May. Both team and manager recovered nicely.

"They examined all my organs," Stengel said proudly. "Some of them are quite remarkable and others are not so good. A lot of museums are bidding for them." Upon his return the Yankees won 14 of 15, sweeping four from the White Sox at Chicago, and took over first place.

Yet poor pitching kept New York from pulling away. When the staff returned to form, thanks to the infusion of rookie Bill Stafford and recycled National Leaguer Luis Arroyo, the Yankees won their final fifteen games and finished eight ahead of the Orioles. Waiting for the Yankees this time was not the Milwaukee club they'd struggled with in 1957 and 1958 but the Pirates, who hadn't won the National League pennant since Babe Ruth and his colleagues had swept them in 1927.

Stengel wanted to use Stafford, whom the Yankees considered their best prospect since Whitey Ford, in the first game. Coaches Ralph Houk and Frank Crosetti disagreed; a rookie, they believed, shouldn't start a World Series opener. So righthander Art Ditmar, a seven-year veteran who'd pitched in three previous Series games in relief, was chosen and the Pirates evicted him with three runs in the first inning en route to a 6–4 victory.

Stengel in last training camp with his last coaching staff (l–r): Lopat, Crosetti, Houk, Dickey.

Roger Maris was obtained from KC for Hank Bauer and won the RBI title and MVP Award. Mantle hit 40 homers to capture the home run title for the fourth time in 6 years; together they totaled 79 homers.

The Yanks had firepower with (l–r) Mantle, Berra, Skowron, McDougald, Howard and Maris. But only Skowron hit over .284, hitting .309 including 26 homers after being sidelined much of 1959 with an aching back.

With Coates, Ford, Turley, Ditmar and Maas as starting pitchers, Ditmar emerged with the most victories (15–9), but he was shelled in games 1 and 5 (0–2, 21.60 ERA in 1.2 innings).

Then, on the verge of erasing a 3–1 Yankee lead in the fourth inning of the second game, Pittsburgh manager Danny Murtaugh gambled, pinch-hit for pitcher Bob Friend and watched New York blow the game apart.

The Yankees easily retired pinch hitter Gene Baker and Virdon to snuff out the embryonic rally, then cannonaded five Pirate relievers (including old Dodger acquaintance Clem Labine) for 13 runs and a 16–3 victory, the most one-sided Series game since 1936. Seven of the runs came in the sixth when New York sent a dozen batters to the plate. And only two came on home runs, both by Mickey Mantle. The second, a 475-foot, three-run blast, cleared the center-field wall. No right-handed hitter had ever done that at Forbes Field.

The Pirates, with ghosts of 1927 and Murderer's Row dancing in their heads, were easy prey at Yankee Stadium two days later. Yankee second baseman Bobby Richardson, who'd hit only one home run during the season but would set a Series record with 12 runs batted in, smashed a two-strike grand slam off Labine to complete a six-run first inning that ended the afternoon early. New York added four more in the fourth on a two-run single by Richardson and a homer by Mantle and it was 10–0; Ford's sparkling four-hitter was delightfully unnecessary.

Yet Pittsburgh, which should have been put to rout by now, fought back in game four and tied the Series with a 3–2 victory. Then the Pirates shelled Ditmar again, scoring three runs in the second, grabbed game five, 5–2, and turned the Series completely around. Masters of their fate just two days earlier, the Yankees now needed to win the final two games at Forbes Field and beat Pittsburgh's two aces, Friend and Vernon Law, in the process.

As Ford held the Pirates at bay, the Yankees tattooed Friend for two runs with a double and two singles before a man was out in the third and nicked reliever Tom Cheney for three more. So it was 6–0 and the Yankees added half a dozen more before the day was done to garland Ford's seven-hit shutout, 12–0, and tie the Series.

Law loomed as a tougher proposition; he'd won 20 games during the season, plus Series games one and four. Now, through four innings, he'd allowed only two singles. And Bob Turley, whom Stengel had chosen just before the game after originally awarding the assignment to Stafford and changing his mind, had lasted just 20 pitches. With two out in the first inning Pirate first baseman Rocky Nelson swung at a bad pitch for a two-run homer.

"It was cap-high and a foot wide," Turley said. "Yet he pulled it over the fence in right field." But logic had long since fled from this Series. So Stengel went back to Stafford, whom he'd now by-passed as a starter in two games, and watched the Pirates extract two more runs from him with two out in the second inning.

Now it was 4–0 for Pittsburgh and slipping away rapidly. But Moose Skowron greeted Law with a home run into the lower right-field stands in the fifth and the momentum shifted abruptly toward New York. When Richardson led off the sixth with a single and Kubek walked, Murtaugh replaced Law with ace reliever Elroy Face—which was exactly what the Yankees had been hoping for.

Face had saved all three Pittsburgh victories and had popped off about it (to New York minds, anyway) in the newspaper. "If we can get Law out and Face in," Berra had predicted, "we'll win."

After Mantle had singled home Richardson, Berra poked a three-run homer into the upper right-field stands and it was 5–4. When Murtaugh let Face continue, New York rattled him for two more in the eighth after two were out. So it was 7–4 and Stengel was six outs from his eighth championship. Cimoli, pinch-hitting for Face, led off with a single. But Bobby Shantz, who'd held the Pirates scoreless since relieving in the third, got Virdon to hit the ball on the ground.

Moments later Kubek was sprawling, choking, and Stengel was running out of the dugout rasping, "Give him room, he'll be all right, he'll play."

But Kubek couldn't play, and the Yankees began coming unstuck. Dick Groat, hitless all day and 5 for 27 in the Series, lashed a single into left to score Cimoli. So Shantz left for reliever Jim Coates, who nailed two quick outs and got Roberto Clemente to chop a grounder toward Skowron at first. It seemed an easy 3–1 play but Coates, assuming Skowron would make it alone, held up. So Clemente reached base and Virdon scored. New York 7, Pittsburgh 6.

After the Series loss to the Pirates, a frustrated Stengel was let go, to be replaced by Ralph Houk.

A month later, George Weiss said goodbye after 29 years and was replaced by Roy Haney.

Still Coates needed only to retire reserve catcher Hal Smith, a former Yankee farmhand who had played five years for the Orioles and Athletics. Coates worked Smith to 3–2 then watched, disgusted, as Smith put the next pitch over the left-field wall for a three-run homer and a 9–7 Pirate lead. Coates threw his glove high into the air; before it came down Stengel had replaced him with Ralph Terry, his fourth reliever of the day.

Terry got Don Hoak to fly to Berra in left, so the Series had come down to one inning and the top of the Yankee order was waiting to unload on Friend, whom Murtaugh was using for the second day in a row.

When Richardson and Long dinged Friend for singles, Murtaugh sent out Harvey Haddix. But Mantle singled Richardson home and Gil Mc-Dougald, running for Long, came home on an infield out.

New York 9, Pittsburgh 9 now, but the Pirates had made a season out of ninth-inning resurrections. They'd won 23 games in the final time at bat, 12 of them with two out. Did it matter that Mazeroski, the number-eight hitter, was at bat?

"One to go home," Murtaugh yelled to him. Terry's first pitch, a slider, sailed high. The second—"the wrong one," Terry would say glumly—was a high fastball. "I came to bat intending to go for the long ball," Mazeroski said, and it was unlikely he'd see a better offering. "I caught it on the fat of my bat. I knew immediately it was a well-hit ball. I watched it sail over the fence as I rounded the bases. I touched every one."

Berra, in left field, never moved. No need to. As joyous Pirate fans escorted Mazeroski home and Mantle wept in the clubhouse, Terry cursed, "Casey," he told his manager, "I hate to have it end this way."

"How were you operatin'?" Stengel asked him. "What were you tryin' to throw him?"

"I was trying to keep it low," Terry replied.

"As long as you were trying to pitch him the right way, I'm gonna sleep easy at night," Stengel assured him. Not so the Yankee front office. When the club returned to New York Topping called a press conference and had his lawyer prepare a statement for Stengel to read.

Stengel was retiring because of age and the Yankees, grateful for more than a decade of championship baseball, were going to give him $160,000. It was something less than true. Stengel was being dismissed and he'd earned the $160,000 as part of a profit-sharing program. The prepared statement came apart under questioning moments after it was read.

"I couldn't be a yes-man," Stengel said. "I never was and I never will be." He could have continued, Stengel believed, and would have liked to. "But they have a program which should run into an old-age program," Stengel said, "and I am positive they are the owners of the ball club. Mr. Webb is of the same opinion as Mr. Topping as regarding the age limit and Mr. Topping runs the ball club. I was told my services were no longer desired."

Ralph Houk, who'd coached under Stengel for five years and had taken over when Stengel had been hospitalized early in the season, would be the new manager. Stengel, who didn't need the money anyway, would be hired two seasons later to preside over the birth of the Mets, New York's new National League franchise. He was young enough to work in the Polo Grounds, a battered relic of a ballyard, but not in Yankee Stadium. "I'll never make the mistake," Casey grumbled, "of being seventy again."

1961

He was twenty-six years old and he was losing his crew cut in clumps. "Look at this," Roger Maris showed manager Ralph Houk. "My goddamn hair is coming out. Did your hair ever fall out from playing baseball?"

No, Houk conceded, it hadn't. But then,

Houk had played eight years with the Yankees and never hit a home run. In one season Maris was already somewhere between 50 and 61, chasing a dead man and being haunted by him.

It had been thirty-four years since George Herman Ruth had set the major league record of 60 in one season. Now Maris, New York's right fielder, was on the verge and realizing that neither the commissioner of baseball, nor Yankee management, nor a fair number of sportswriters, nor most rival fans, nor the grandstand spectators behind him at Yankee Stadium wanted him to.

"Do you really want to break Babe Ruth's record?" one reporter asked in Chicago.

"Damn right."

"What I mean is, Ruth was a great man."

"Maybe I'm not a great man," Maris replied. "But I damn well want to break the record."

Commissioner Ford Frick, who'd been friendly with Ruth as a New York sportswriter, wanted that record kept intact. In July, when it was apparent that Maris had a chance at 61, Frick announced that he would have to hit them in 154 games, the length of the season in Ruth's day. If the record had to fall, the New York front office preferred that Mickey Mantle, who had hit 52 in 1956 and was matching Maris almost blast for blast, would be the man.

"They favored Mickey to break it," Maris said years later. "I was never the fair-haired boy over there." To begin with, he had not been bred to be a Yankee. Maris had been discovered and signed by the Cleveland organization and had played one year as a regular before being traded to Kansas City for Vic Power.

When the Yankees made another in a series of raids on the Athletics roster in 1959 (between 1953 and 1961 New York and Kansas City would deal with each other seventeen times), Maris arrived unheralded in a seven-player deal designed to rejuvenate the New York outfield.

Though he was hardly a power hitter in the Ruth or Mantle mold, Maris was a fine fielder with a reliable arm who had a knack for pulling any ball within the strike zone. Manager Casey Stengel loved him and Maris made an immediate impact, winning the American League MVP Award as the Yankees regained the pennant in 1960.

He had hit only 39 homers that year and batted an unspectacular .283 (his career best, as it turned out), yet in camp prior to the 1961 season Stengel conceded that Maris could eclipse Ruth's mark. "Why shouldn't he break it?" Stengel mused. "He's got more power than Staleen."

Or at least more productive power. "If I hit a ball just right," Maris figured, "it goes about 450 feet. But they don't give you two home runs for hitting one 800 feet, do they?"

For the first ten games Maris didn't hit any.

Ralph Houk succeeded Casey Stengel. Behind Houk (l–r): Co-owners Del Webb, Dan Topping, and the new general manager, Roy Hamey, who succeeded George Weiss.

These four Yankee sluggers went on to total 165 homers in 1961: (l–r) Mickey Mantle 54, Roger Maris 61, Bill Skowron 28 and Yogi Berra 22.

Whitey Ford and Luis Arroyo (r) were a top 1–2 pitching punch: Ford had his first 20-victory season (24–5) and won the Cy Young Award. Arroyo was 15–5, leading the majors with 29 saves in 65 appearances to be Fireman of the Year.

Maris and Mantle both chased Ruth's record until
Mantle fell by the wayside with a career-high 54.

Maris' sixtieth homer that tied Ruth's record on
September 26, 1961, on a curve thrown by Orioles'
Jack Fisher.

By May 2, sixteen games into the season, he'd hit only one. His fourth, in the twenty-ninth game, didn't come until May 17. Ruth had already hit nine by that date.

But, as May turned into June, the shots came in bunches—two on Memorial Day at Boston, then nearly one a day for the next two weeks. By June 22 Maris had piled up 27, found himself twelve games ahead of Ruth's pace, and began hearing The Question for the first time. "Do you think you can break Ruth's record?" a New York writer asked. "How the hell do I know?" Maris shrugged.

But pushed by Mantle, who was rarely more than one or two behind, Maris continued in his rhythm through July. He hit four off four different Chicago pitchers (including ex-Yankee Don Larsen) on July 25 to reach 40, with Mantle still only two behind him. By now, reporters were laying siege to him daily and Frick had cranked the pressure a few notches higher by announcing a week earlier that Maris had to break the record by the 154th game. Beyond that, an asterisk would accompany his achievement in the record book.

Maris bristled. "Frick should have said that all records made during the new schedule would have an asterisk," he would reflect years later. "And he should have said it before the season, if he said it at all. But he decided on the asterisk when it looked like I'd break the record."

Gradually it struck Maris that despite the crowds that jammed ball parks to watch him and the publicity that threatened to engulf him, a great number of people did not want him to break the record. "I guess I came along and did something that evidently was sacred," he mused. "Something that nobody was supposed to do, especially me."

Comparisons to Ruth, in which Maris invariably suffered, were inevitable. He was not the gregarious man Ruth was, had nowhere near the capacity for food, drink, women and late hours, and neither sought adulation nor relished it. "It would have been a hell of a lot more fun to play the game under one mask and then leave the park wearing another," Maris said. "Some guys loved the life of a celebrity. Some of them would have walked down Fifth Avenue in their Yankee uniforms if they could have. But all it brought me was headaches. You can't eat glamour."

By August Maris found he could barely eat at all, at least not in public. His favorite breakfast was bologna and eggs at the Stage Delicatessen. He had to avoid the place after fans began descending on him. The only place where he retained a shred of privacy, Maris concluded gloomily, was in the bathroom. "They even ask for autographs at Mass," he sighed.

And the clubhouse provided no escape.

Maris began arriving earlier and earlier before games, then realized that he couldn't duck the crush of inquisitors or the multitude or grinding sameness of their questions.

Some were irrelevant. "Who's your favorite female singer?"

"I don't have a favorite female singer," Maris replied.

"Well, is it all right if I wrote down Doris Day?"

Others were outrageously personal. "Do you play around on the road?"

"I'm a married man," Maris said.

"I'm married myself," the questioner continued, "but I play around on the road."

"That's your business."

The rest were either ludicrous (Would you rather bat .300 or hit sixty home runs?) or simply the same. Are you excited? ... Can you? ... Will you? A Japanese sports editor wired a list of eighteen questions he wanted answered to the Associated Press. After half a dozen Maris threw up his hands. "This is driving me nuts," he said. "That's my next question," the AP man nodded. "They want to know how you're reacting to all this."

Directly, often bluntly. That was Maris's way. "You've got to be an idiot," he told a man who asked him what a .260 hitter was doing hitting all those home runs. As the summer wore on Maris began to be described as surly, uncooperative, unworthy. How dare he?

"Throw the first two inside and make him foul them," Hall of Famer Rogers Hornsby advised prospective pitchers. "Then come outside so he can't pull. It would be a shame if Ruth's record got beaten by a .270 hitter."

Yet Maris stayed well ahead of Ruth's pace. By August 22, 125 games into the season, he had reached 50, thirteen games before Ruth had. The horde of camp followers increased, finally reaching six dozen reporters, grilling him every day.

"Mick, it's driving me nuts, I'm telling you," he confessed to Mantle. "And I'm telling you," Mantle responded, "you've got to get used to it."

Meanwhile, the flood of homers slowed to a trickle. After hitting his fifty-first Maris went a week without belting another. After his fifty-sixth, on September 9, he went another week without one. While pitchers were throwing him balls and marginal strikes, Maris was going 6 for 50.

With four games left before Frick's deadline and his total at 56, Maris now stood alone. Mantle had been knocked out of the race by an infection that developed after a penicillin shot. He would finish with 54, happy to play Lou Gehrig to Maris's Ruth. In 1927, Gehrig, batting behind Ruth, had hit 47 and pushed him toward immortality. Mantle

Maris' sixty-first homer, breaking Ruth's record on October 1 off Red Sox righthander Tracy Stallard—360 feet into the lower right field stands at Yankee Stadium.

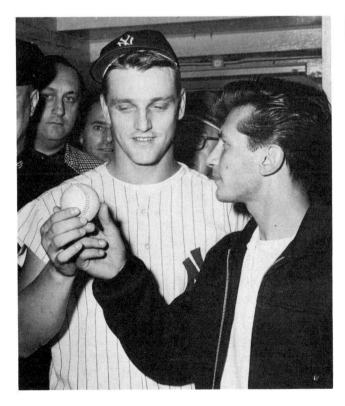

A special crown is awarded Maris "Sultan of Swat."

Fan Sal Durate returns the historic sixty-first home run ball to Maris after the game.

The Yanks clinch the pennant at Baltimore (l–r): Arroyo, Maris, Houk and Ford.

Reds manager Fred Hutchinson wears a rueful smile as he congratulates Houk on the Series win for the Yanks.

hit behind Maris, forcing most pitchers to deal with Maris. "Well, I got my man," Mantle told Maris, joking, after he'd passed Gehrig's total. "The pressure's off me."

It would never leave Maris, not even after the 154th game came and went. He was stuck at 58 as the Yankees arrived in Baltimore. Oriole manager Paul Richards was pitching fastballer Milt Pappas with a strong wind, the residue of Hurricane Esther, blowing from right field. Maris, distraught, went to Houk's office before the deadline game, the opener of a doubleheader.

"I need help," he told the manager, weeping. "I can't handle this. They keep asking the same questions. It never lets up."

"You've got to handle this all by yourself," Houk told him. "Just get your hits and everything will take care of itself."

Maris had never asked for the comparison. Beating Ruth's record did not tarnish the Babe's memory. "Why can't they understand?" Maris would repeat. "I don't want to be Babe Ruth. He was a great ballplayer. I'm not trying to replace him. The record is there and damn right I want to break it. But that isn't replacing him."

Maris left Houk's office and went out to chase a ghost in Ruth's hometown. Pappas got him to fly to right field in the first inning, but Maris dumped a rising ball into the bleachers in the third for No. 59. He had passed Jimmie Foxx and Hank Greenberg. Only Ruth remained.

But there would be no record—not according to Frick, anyway. In the ninth Hoyt Wilhelm, arguably the finest reliever in baseball history, got Maris to ground harmlessly down the first-base line. "If you throw him anything but knuckleballs," Richards had warned Wilhelm, "it will cost you five thousand dollars."

The Yankees had clinched the pennant that day but their celebration was overlooked. Reporters surrounded Maris. "I tried," he said. "I tried." Yet the pressure only slightly abated. A season was still a season. Nine games remained, the last five at home.

In game 158, with Baltimore pitcher Jack Fisher on the Stadium mound and fewer than 22,000 spectators in the stands, Maris equaled the record. One of Fisher's curves landed in the upper deck in right field. "The minute I threw it I said to myself, that does it," Fisher said. "That's number sixty."

Maris leaned on his bat at the plate, watched the ball disappear, then trotted around the bases. He would take the next day off. Then the sixth-place Red Sox shut him down two days in a row. Now game 162, the season finale, loomed at the Stadium. Boston rookie Tracy Stallard could make history either way. He got Maris to fly out in the first. Then in the fourth, after he let an outside fastball and an inside curve go by for balls, Maris clubbed a waist-high fastball over Lu Clinton's head into the lower right-field stands for the game's only run.

A young Coney Island truck driver named Sal Durante came up with the ball, thus earning a $5,000 reward and a free trip to the Seattle World's Fair. Maris was forced to make four curtain calls. "If I never hit another home run," he said, "this is one they can never take away from me."

Maris would win the MVP Award again and the Yankees would nearly double his salary to $72,000. Meanwhile, a championship season had been somewhat obscured. Houk, replacing Casey Stengel, had led the Yankees to the pennant by eight games over Detroit in his first season. Pitcher Whitey Ford had enjoyed his best season (25–4), backed by one of the finest staffs in club history.

The World Series, against a Cincinnati team that had won its first pennant in twenty-one years, was anticlimactic. The Yankees grabbed it in five games, relying on reserves. Ford shut out the Reds, 2–0, in the opener at the Stadium and went on to wipe out Ruth's Series pitching record of 29⅔ consecutive scoreless innings until an ankle injury in the fifth inning of game four stopped him.

Mantle, with blood from a thigh abscess soaking through his uniform, had been yanked an inning earlier. Yogi Berra, who'd played in sixty-five Series games, sat down with a bad shoulder for the finale but it barely mattered.

John Blanchard crashed a two-run homer in the first inning that led to a 5–0 lead. Hector Lopez, filling in in left field, proceeded to knock in five more runs and the Yankees laughed their way to a 13–5 clincher. "The Reds," someone joked, "didn't even look good throwing the ball back to the pitcher."

1962

He had begun to wonder if this was his destiny, always to be undone by October. Ralph Terry had served up the waist-high fastball that Pittsburgh's Bill Mazeroski powdered in the ninth inning of the seventh game of the 1960 World Series and stole a championship away from the Yankees. The next fall New York lost one game in a giggler of a Series with Cincinnati. Ralph Terry was the losing pitcher.

Now in the 1962 Series the Giants had beaten him in game two and forced him to the brink in game five before teammate Tom Tresh had saved the day with a three-run homer in the eighth inning. Now, again, it was the ninth inning of a seventh game, with the Yankees leading by one run. Thoughts of Mazeroski and a fastball vanishing above an ivy-covered wall came flashing back.

San Francisco's Matty Alou, batting for pitcher Billy O'Dell, had led off by beating out a bunt. Terry, bearing down, had struck out Alou's brother Felipe and Chuck Hiller. But Willie Mays had doubled and only a perfect throw from right fielder Roger Maris and a crisp relay from second baseman Bobby Richardson had held Alou at third.

Which brought Willie McCovey, who'd hit a towering homer off Terry in the second game, into the box. One bloop single, with both Alou and Mays running, would give the Giants their first championship over the Yankees since 1922.

Instead, seconds later Richardson had snared McCovey's line smash and Terry was being borne off the Candlestick Park infield on his teammates' shoulders. Later, as Terry was guzzling champagne at his locker, Joe DiMaggio spotted him. "You can forget that Pittsburgh thing now, Ralph," he shouted. Terry nodded.

"I want to thank God for a second opportunity," he would say. "You don't often get a second chance to prove yourself, in baseball or in life."

For Terry and his teammates the championship was a reaffirmation that Terry, who'd won 39 games in two years, was one of the finest right-handers in the game. And that the Yankees dynasty, interrupted by Chicago in 1959 and by Pittsburgh in 1960, had been fully restored.

The lineup was strong and deep again, the pitching flexible and well-stocked. And in Ralph Houk, the only manager to win world championships in his first two years on the job, New York had discovered a worthy replacement for Casey Stengel.

Where Stengel had been the master manipulator, platooning regulars, juggling staffs, cajoling, growling, pushing, Houk was a combative optimist. He picked one lineup and one rotation and stayed with it, praised his players daily and always thought the pennant was not only possible but likely.

After all, Houk had survived the Battle of the Bulge at Bastogne, winning the Silver and Bronze Stars as well as a Purple Heart, emerging from World War II as a major. He'd played eight years in a Yankee uniform (most of them as a rarely used catcher) and earned six Series rings. He'd managed the Yankees' farm club in Denver and

Stengel came back wearing a strange uniform as a new National League team was born in New York—the Metropolitans. They met the Yankees for the first time in spring training, where the old professor had a reunion with his former prize pupil, Ralph Houk, Stengel's successor as Yankee manager.

Maris received his second straight MVP and Luis Arroyo the Fireman of the Year Award—achievements neither would reach again. Maris fell from 61 to 33 homers, and Arroyo tumbled from 15–5 and 29 saves to 1–3 and 7 saves.

Tom Tresh, here with his father, the former longtime White Sox catcher Mike Tresh, won Rookie of the Year. Tresh stepped in for Kubek (on Army duty) and hit .286, plus 20 homers while playing 111 games at shortstop and 43 more in the outfield.

The Yanks slumped early when Mantle tore a thigh muscle in May and missed 30 games, but he bounced back to win his third MVP.

Ralph Terry was the Yankees' ace at 23–12 despite giving up 40 homers, the most ever by a Yankee pitcher in one season.

Berra marked a new plateau, playing his 2000th game.

coached under Stengel. Now the job was his and even as the 1962 season showed signs of coming apart early, Houk saw silver linings everywhere.

Within four days in mid-May Mickey Mantle tore a thigh muscle (he missed 40 games), top reliever Luis Arroyo blew out his arm and wound up on the disabled list and lefthander Whitey Ford, who'd won 25 games in 1961, strained his arm.

With Mantle unavailable enemy hurlers gleefully pitched around Maris, who went 21 for 110 during Mantle's absence. As spectators hooted and press criticism grew in intensity, Maris fretted. "Sometimes," he brooded, "I wish I never hit those sixty home runs." Meanwhile, as the Yankees went 15–15 during the next month, they slipped to fourth place in the American League, four games behind leader Cleveland. Through it all, Houk displayed his what-me-worry? grin. "When Whitey and Mickey return," he told all doubters, "we will win."

And so they did. In early July Mantle and Maris each hit six homers in four games and Mantle went on to bat .321. Ford came back to win 17 games with a 2.90 earned-run average. The Yankees won ten straight games almost immediately, took a three-game lead over the Angels and proceeded to win the pennant by five games over the Twins.

Meanwhile, the Yankees watched with a mounting sense of deja vu as the Dodgers lost ten of their final thirteen games, blew a four-game lead in the final week and ended up losing a playoff to the Giants in the last inning of the final game by walking home the winning run.

This was 1951 all over again . . . except that only Mays remained from that roster and that the Giants and Yankees were no longer a subway ride away from each other.

The IRT didn't reach San Francisco, where owner Horace Stoneham had moved his club four years earlier. And the Polo Grounds had never seen the kind of clouds that seemed permanently suspended above Candlestick Park.

This was the longest Series ever, consuming thirteen days and split by four days of rain between games five and six as the Yankees, leading three games to two, waited anxiously to close it out.

They'd alternated victories throughout—the Yankees winning the odd-numbered games, the Giants the evens. Now, as the clubs warmed up before game seven, clubhouse attendants placed a bottle of Mumm's Extra Dry champagne in every Giant locker. But Terry, gratified that Houk was entrusting him with the finale, was feeling buoyant. He'd won $300 from Mr. Berra, the team's lucky charm, the night before on one poker hand. "I beat Yogi, I beat Yogi," he crowed. "It's an omen."

Perhaps it was. For nearly six innings, until San Francisco pitcher Jack Sanford singled, Terry spun a perfect game. Until the eighth inning, he never threw two called balls in a row. A forty-mile-an-hour wind, a souvenir of Typhoon Frieda, whistled in from the outfield.

Finally, in the seventh, the Giants began hitting Terry. Mays lashed a line drive to the left-field corner that Tresh just managed to run down and take backhanded, out of sight of the New York dugout. Then McCovey tripled over Mantle's head to the center field fence. On another day, in another park, it might have gone out. "I can't say what would have happened if the wind wasn't blowing," McCovey shrugged. "Because the wind was blowing and it's always blowing."

So Terry struck out Orlando Cepeda and finally it came down to the ninth. New York had pushed one run in the fifth when Tony Kubek had hit into a double play with the bases loaded. Now, once Matty Alou had bunted his way on, the top of the San Francisco order loomed.

But Terry got Felipe Alou and Hiller. Only Mays remained and Mays was looking for the fences. "I was going for the bomb," he admitted. "We needed a home run. I was going for it. But I was a little behind the pitch."

Instead of a soaring shot he skidded a sizzler across the grass to the corner in right. As Alou rounded second and raced for third Maris simultaneously came up with the ball and pegged it to Richardson, who relayed it to Elston Howard at the plate. Third-base coach Whitey Lockman, computing angles and player placement, had held Alou on third as Mays pulled up with a double. Later, second-guessers would castigate Lockman, but no Giant did.

"Wouldn't that have been a hell of a way to end the season?" mused reserve catcher Ed Bailey. "McCovey coming up and the tying run thrown out at the plate by fifteen feet."

As McCovey approached the plate Houk went out to chat with Terry. "I really don't know what the hell I'm doing out here," Houk admitted. "But I thought I'd better come out and talk with you anyway. What I'm getting at is, do you want to pitch to this guy or walk him?"

Terry decided he'd rather pitch to McCovey. "Let's give him good stuff just outside the strike zone and hope he'll fish for it," he told Houk. Houk returned to the dugout and motioned to Richardson to move over, but Richardson decided to stay where he was.

"Some strange sense told me to play him more toward the first-base side," Richardson said. "I guess I was really out of position. A yard to one side or the other and I couldn't have had a chance at that ball."

Terry's first pitch was a slow curve outside.

Mantle became the seventh major leaguer to hit 400 or more homers.

Mantle slammed 4 consecutive homers in a 2-day span—one of four to do it in Yankee history.

Jack Reed (center) hit his only big league homer in the Yankees' 9–7 victory in the longest game in club history—a 7-hour, 22-inning marathon in Detroit on June 24. Rookie Jim Bouton pitched 7 shutout innings of relief to get the victory.

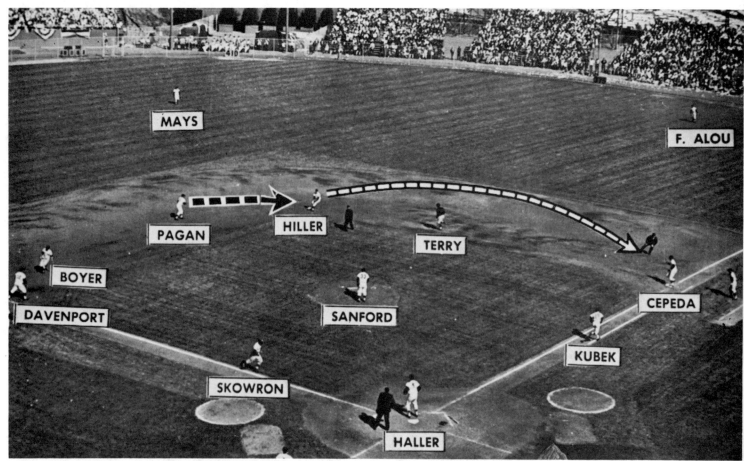

MAYS

F. ALOU

PAGAN

HILLER

TERRY

BOYER

SANFORD

CEPEDA

DAVENPORT

KUBEK

SKOWRON

HALLER

The only run of the seventh game finale scores, as Tony Kubek hits into a fifth-inning double play.

Teammates carry Ralph Terry off the field after his 4-hit, 1–0 victory. He was voted the Babe Ruth Award as Series MVP.

McCovey pushed it down the right-field line and the wind blew it foul. The second pitch was an inside fastball that McCovey ripped chest-high right at Richardson. It was, McCovey would tell Richardson a decade later, the hardest ball he ever hit. Richardson gloved it without moving, then dropped to one knee to make sure.

"I was running toward third when I looked and saw Richardson catch the ball," said Mays. "And I thought, oh geez, there goes three-four thousand dollars."

Terry threw his glove, then his cap in the air. The Giants' champagne remained unopened.

1963

The devastation was so quick, so complete, so unquestionable that they had to laugh. Four games, four runs scored—and out. After Los Angeles pitcher Sandy Koufax got Hector Lopez to ground harmlessly to shortstop Maury Wills and put an end to a five-day World Series, the Yankees sat stunned in their clubhouse at Dodger Stadium.

First baseman Joe Pepitone, who'd missed a routine throw from third baseman Clete Boyer that had led to the winning run in the seventh inning, was in tears. Then pitcher Whitey Ford, who'd lost a two-hitter, walked over to Pepitone. "You really blew that sonovabitch," he cracked, "didn't you, kid?" Pepitone, Ford and Mickey Mantle broke up and the gloom lifted. "Okay," shouted manager Ralph Houk. "Let's get the hell out of here."

There was nothing else to do, and despite the humor of the moment, the loss burned. No Yankee club since 1922 had ever been swept in a Series. And by the Dodgers, yet, who had been one-for-seven lifetime against New York in October.

"There are only two ways you can come out of a Series," Mantle would say. "You can come out of it feeling great or feeling like we are. That was the worst beating I'd ever seen the Yankees take."

They had batted .171 as a team, the lowest in Series history. They had scored only two runs in the final three games. They had never led in any game.

Was this the same club that was gunning for a third consecutive world championship? That had suffered injuries to so many regulars that it didn't have its normal lineup together once from June until the final week of September and still won the American League pennant by 10½ games over the White Sox?

"We're better than we were last year," Houk had decided in spring training. Deeper, younger where it counted, with an impeccable pitching staff. In June the Yankees lost shortstop Tony Kubek for two weeks with leg and neck injuries, replacement Phil Linz with torn knee ligaments, right fielder Roger Maris with a bruised ankle—and Mantle with a fractured foot and torn ankle tendons. He had enmeshed his spikes in a chain-link fence chasing a Brooks Robinson fly at Baltimore. "It's broke," he told teammates. "I know it's broke."

Yet New York went on to win ten of its next eleven without Mantle, passed the Orioles and White Sox and took over first place by the middle of the month.

Between the first of July and the first of August the Yankees increased their lead from 2½ games over the White Sox to eight games. Then Mantle returned, after missing sixty-one games, crashed a pinch-hit home run in his first at-bat and Yankee pitching took it from there. The rotation of Ford (24–7), Jim Bouton (21–7), Ralph Terry (17–15) and rookie Al Downing (13–5) was unsurpassed: in early August they completed eleven of thirteen starts and at one point allowed only three earned runs in sixty innings.

"It's good to see some good young players coming into the league," mused former well-traveled manager Jimmy Dykes. "But why do they always have to be wearing the Yankee uniform?"

By September the lead was 11 games, then 14. The Series was assumed; it would open in Yankee Stadium against the same Dodger club that had blown the National League pennant to the Giants in the last inning of the final game of a playoff the year before. New York was a clear 8–5 favorite and its ace, Ford, would be starting the opener in his favorite ball park, dueling a left-hander in Koufax, who'd won 25 games, 11 by shutout, and struck out 306 batters.

Rested and emotionally pumped, Koufax took the mound and struck out the first five men he faced, the cream of the New York order—Kubek, Bobby Richardson, Tresh, Mantle and Maris. Koufax had grown up in Brooklyn when the Yankees were ruining Dodger seasons every autumn. This was symbolic for him.

"I felt I had to show myself and my team and the Yankees, too, that the Yankees were just a team of baseball players and not a pride of supermen," he figured.

Nobody since the Cardinals' Mort Cooper in 1943 had fanned the first five batters in a Series game; the key was getting Richardson, who'd struck out only 22 times in 630 at-bats

Joe Pepitone replaced the traded Bill Skowron at first base, teaming in the infield with (l–r) Clete Boyer (third), Tony Kubek (shortstop) and Bobby Richardson (second base).

Pepitone got off to a powerful start, slugging 2 homers on Opening Day, and went on to establish himself as one of the more memorable characters in Yankee history.

(L–r) Rookie Al Downing (13–5) helped give the Yanks an impressive pitching staff, joining Whitey Ford (24–7), Ralph Terry (17–14), Stan Williams (9–8) and Jim Bouton (21–7).

Mantle nearly slammed a fair ball out of Yankee Stadium on May 22 when his game-winning homer off A's' Bill Fischer struck the facade 6 feet from the top.

Who's on third? Lopez changes his mind after breaking for the plate on a grounder, sliding back to third to find Clete Boyer on the bag from second. Red Sox players Frank Malzone (#11), Bob Tillman (#10), and Ed Bressoud (facing lens) tagged every pinstripe in sight. Lopez was called out.

Clete Boyer, one of the best third basemen in Yankee history, played the hot corner brilliantly.

Bouton's off-balance finish to his deliveries left him vulnerable to line drives, and one off the bat of Oriole Jackie Brandt smashed into Bouton's face one night in Baltimore.

Mickey Mantle, who had fractured a foot and torn ankle tendons in early June, returned to tie DiMaggio's 1736 games played. Here he is seen as a live fourth monument in deep centerfield at Yankee Stadium.

Bouton, Ford and Downing couldn't prevent a Dodgers Series sweep—the first time a Yankee team had been swept since 1922.

Ralph Houk enjoyed his cigar and his third pennant in as many years as manager.

during the season. "One of the Yankees told me that when he saw Richardson go down swinging on a high fastball he had a feeling they were in trouble," Koufax said.

The procession of K's continued. Six of seven, ten of thirteen. Until two were out in the fifth Koufax was working on a perfect game. By then, thanks to catcher John Roseboro's three-run homer into the upper right-field deck, he also had a 5–0 lead as a base.

"I threw nice and easy," Koufax said, "and I knew I had great stuff. Not good stuff. Great stuff." In the fifth, with the bases full, he struck out pinch hitter Lopez to end the inning.

Koufax would only waver twice. In the sixth, tiring slightly, he walked Richardson and Tresh in a row and got a visit from Roseboro.

"What's the matter?" his catcher wondered.

"My elbow's a little tight," Koufax replied. "I'm having trouble throwing the curve."

"Just throw the fastball," Roseboro said. So he did—and Mantle and Maris popped two of them up to end the inning.

Then with two out in the eighth Tresh nicked Koufax for a two-run homer into the left-field stands. But that was all. Moments before that, Koufax had struck out Richardson for the third time. "There's no use me even going up there," Richardson muttered to Mantle while passing the on-deck circle.

As Los Angeles carried its 5–2 lead into the ninth inning the only question was whether Koufax could break the Series record of 14 strikeouts set by Dodger Carl Erskine against the Yankees—ten years earlier to the day. Koufax already had 13, but the middle of the New York order was due up. Elston Howard, whom Koufax had struck out in the seventh, lined to Dick Tracewski at second. Then Pepitone singled and Boyer, the only New York starter who hadn't whiffed, flied to center. Now Harry Bright, pinch-hitting for Yankee reliever Steve Hamilton, stepped in. Koufax got him swinging and went down to the clubhouse to accept Erskine's congratulations.

"When it got to fourteen I thought that was enough," Koufax told him. "But you saw how it was. I had to get the last man."

It was the kind of Series performance that comes along once a decade. The Yankees shrugged and planned to unload on Johnny Podres, who'd beaten them twice in 1955, the only time New York had ever lost a championship to the Dodgers. Instead, Podres hummed a six-hitter and his teammates extracted two runs from Downing before a man was out.

Leadoff man Wills had singled, then had been trapped off first. But Pepitone's throw to Richardson at second was high and Wills made it

safely on his belly. "The team that didn't beat itself," Koufax realized, "had handed us another opening."

So Junior Gilliam singled and a double by Willie Davis scored two runs. Then Moose Skowron, whom the Yankees had unloaded over the winter for pitcher Stan Williams, homered in the fourth and the Yankees were finished. The final score was 4–1, New York's only run coming with one out in the ninth, and the Dodgers gleefully boarded a plane for the Coast.

This time they would use righthander Don Drysdale, who felt compelled to live up to his colleagues' newly established standard.

After Los Angeles scratched Bouton for a run in the first on a walk, a wild pitch and a grounder that bounced off the mound and Richardson's shin, Drysdale blanked New York on three hits, striking Bouton out with the bases full in the second, and fanning Mantle to strand Kubek on third base in the sixth.

"We're not hitting," sighed Houk, but denied that a sweep was likely. "They still got twenty-seven more men to get out," he growled. "It's not the end."

It might as well have been. Koufax continued where he'd left off. He struck out Kubek and Tresh in the first, Pepitone and Boyer in the third. He had a no-hitter boiling until center fielder Willie Davis lost a Richardson double in the sun in the fourth inning.

But this time Ford was also pitching beautifully. Except for Frank Howard's booming home run into the second deck of the left-field stands in the fifth, he didn't make a mistake. "Later they even painted the seat that Howard hit a different color," Ford marveled. "As though it was some kind of landmark."

Mantle made up for it with a 380-foot blast into the left center-field pavilion in the seventh and it was tied. Ford, realizing that a cheap run would probably mean a sweep, bore down. "I threw mostly mud balls or cut balls the whole game," he admitted years later. "I used enough mud that day to build a dam but not enough to hold back the Dodgers."

Ford's fragile dam came apart in the bottom half of the inning. Gilliam hit a routine grounder to Boyer but Pepitone lost his throw in a sea of white shirts behind third base. Then Gilliam, who ended up on third as the ball bounced to the grandstand, came home on Willie Davis's sacrifice.

So it was 2–1 going into the ninth, and when Richardson led off with a single with Tresh on deck and Mantle following, the Yankees still breathed. But Koufax caught Tresh looking. Then, with two strikes on Mantle, Koufax looked in and saw Roseboro wiggling two fingers. Changeup curve. It caught Mantle looking, too, and the Dodgers were one out from their first championship since 1955 and their first sweep ever.

But Tracewski, the second baseman, boggled a force that would have nailed Richardson at second. One last chance now, with Lopez at bat. This time Koufax got him to ground to short and it was over. Five days, four games. "It worked out just about the way I thought," chuckled Los Angeles manager Walter Alston. "Although maybe a little faster."

1964

It was their Last Hurrah before the darkest hours the franchise had ever known, eleven years without a pennant, three straight seasons in the second division, fewer fans than the National League's last-place Mets.

The Yankees limped through a tortured summer, retained the American League pennant by a single game over Chicago, then lost the World Series in the seventh game to a St. Louis club that won its pennant only because Philadelphia squandered a 6½-game lead with two weeks to play.

Then, the day after the Series finale, the front office fired manager Yogi Berra.

That was the final curious scene in a complicated backstage drama during which Berra was "fired" in July and "replaced" by Cardinal manager Johnny Keane, who'd secretly agreed to take the New York job even before he'd beaten the Yankees in the Series.

Lame duck managers were no novelty around the Stadium by now. Even before the 1963 season Yankee manager Ralph Houk, who'd already agreed to move into the front office as general manager after the season, had summoned Berra, who was finishing an eighteen-year Hall of Fame stint as a Yankee.

Houk said he would manage out the year, but after that the job was Berra's. The agreement was kept quiet all season, and after the Dodgers had swept New York in the Series the shift took place, with Houk replacing retiring general manager Roy Hamey. "It was the best-kept secret I ever heard," said ex-Yankee and team broadcaster Phil Rizzuto, a close companion of Berra.

Yet it seemed a reasonable move. Berra had been a Yankee ever since the 1946 season, had

Yogi Berra signs his contract as the new Yankee manager, witnessed by co-owner Dan Topping (standing) and Ralph Houk, who moved up from manager to general manager.

set a major league record for home runs by a catcher (313) and set Series records for appearances (14), hits (71), games played (75) and championship rings (10). He was earthy, humorous and well liked, a welcome change from the Yankees' chilly corporate image and hopefully an antidote for the charm that Casey Stengel and his Mets were working on New York's paying customers.

Only two problems loomed. Berra had never managed, and he would be supervising players who knew him as a peer, not an authority figure. "You?" son Larry puzzled when Berra broke the news at home. "The Yankee manager?"

"What will be your biggest problem next season, Yogi?" he'd been asked at the ritual press conference. "If I can manage," he'd replied.

From the beginning the experiment was rocky. Houk had won three pennants in three years. "The players had liked Ralph so much that they weren't able to accept anybody else," pitcher Jim Bouton said. "And we were never able to accept Yogi."

With a sympathetic Houk sitting in the front office, players quickly found a willing shoulder to cry on. Yogi's in over his head, they told him. He can't handle pitchers. We wish we had you back.

The club lost its first three games in extra innings. Early on Mickey Mantle, Roger Maris and Tom Tresh all pulled hamstring muscles; the

Pete Mikkelsen listens to a watch he received as winner of the Dawson Award. He went on to become the team's top reliever—7 victories plus 9 saves for 16 points.

Co-owner Del Webb presents a floral good luck piece to Yogi on Opening Day. By July, he had decided with Dan Topping that Yogi would go after the season.

Elston Howard was twice honored, receiving the League's MVP Award and being honored with a "Day" at the Stadium. Shown, his wife, Arlene; mother, Mrs. Wayman Hill, and Elston, Jr. and Cheryl.

Jim Bouton doing his "Crazy Guggenheim" bit to the delight of rookie pitcher Mel Stottelmyre, but not to the delight of Yankee management who often considered his behavior undignified.

Above: Berra, being interviewed by former teammate Jerry Coleman, clinched the pennant. The Yankees wouldn't win another for 12 years.

Left: Al Downing, going 13–8, led the League in strikeouts with 217, still the third most strikeouts in Yankee history.

As criticism of Berra mounted, Phil Linz (seen stealing home against the Twins' catcher Jerry Zimmerman) got into an argument with Yogi over an harmonica.

Jim Bouton won his first of 2 Series victories.

In the Series, Elston Howard leaps high for Mantle's overthrow as the Yanks lost the opener, 9–5.

The Yanks stunned baseball by naming Johnny Keane, whose Cardinals had beaten the Yankees in the Series, as the new manager, replacing Yogi Berra.

Mantle won Game 3 with a homer on reliever Barney Schultz' first pitch in the ninth inning. It was Mantle's sixteenth series homer—a record.

New York outfield now featured ex-third baseman Hector Lopez, rookie Pedro Gonzalez and ex-catcher John Blanchard. Then starters Al Downing and Bouton came up hurt and before mid-June the Yankees were lodged behind Chicago and Baltimore, 6½ games off the pace.

When the injuries cleared up, though, the club went on a tear, swept five from the White Sox, then swept them again and took over first place. Then they blew a game to the Orioles (after leading 7–2 in the seventh) and had to chase Baltimore through the dog days while criticism of Berra mounted.

Finally, after losing 10 of 15 games and four straight at Chicago the tension swelled and burst on August 20. An amateurish harmonica rendition of "Mary Had a Little Lamb" by shortstop Phil Linz had irked Berra as the team bus was stuck in steamy traffic en route to O'Hare Airport. Berra told Linz to "shove that thing." "Do it yourself," Linz told Berra and flipped him the harmonica, cutting Joe Pepitone's leg in the process.

While Berra and Linz argued, Mantle, reaching for the instrument, called over to pitcher Whitey Ford. "It looks like I'm going to be managing this ball club pretty soon," Mantle told him. "You can be my third-base coach and this is what we'll do. One toot—that's a bunt. Two toots—that's hit and run."

Though the club went on to lose its next two in Boston the incident broke the malaise and the Yankees came from six games back to regain first place on September 17 as Chicago and Baltimore both reverted to .500 baseball.

The Yankees went on to win 11 in a row and 31 of their final 40, and clinched their ninth pennant in ten years with three games to play. But Berra's fate was already sealed. Dan Topping, Del Webb and Houk had met in July and determined that no matter what the outcome of the season, Berra would be dismissed.

Meanwhile Keane, whose Cardinals had beaten the Mets on the final day to win their first pennant since 1946, had already tendered his resignation to owner Augie Busch, annoyed by repeated rumors during the season that Leo Durocher was being considered to replace him. The resignation had not been accepted, but Keane had already arranged through an intermediary to take the New York job after the Series.

For the better part of four games the Yankees made their front office's judgment look awful. After losing a 4–2 lead and the opener, 9–5, at St. Louis, New York grabbed the second (8–3) and third (2–1) games and chased Cardinal starter Ray Sadecki with three runs in the first inning of game four.

But with one blow, a grand slam off Downing in the sixth by Ken Boyer, Clete's older brother, St.

Louis turned the Series around. Bob Gibson struck out thirteen Yankees the next afternoon, catcher Tim McCarver delivered a three-run homer in the tenth to win it, 5–2, and New York was perched on the brink.

St. Louis led the sixth game, 1–0, for four innings. Then Maris and Mantle brought back a taste of 1961 by poking back-to-back homers to right field in the sixth to give New York the lead. Pepitone applied the coup de grâce with two out in the eighth, greeting reliever Gordie Richardson with a grand slam that ended it, 8–3.

That was the dynasty's last gasp, the final Series victory until October 11, 1977. The next day in the finale Gibson picked up the thread he'd spun two games earlier, striking out nine more Yankees for a Series total of thirty-one. And his teammates pounced on New York for a 6–0 lead after five innings.

The unraveling began subtly in the fourth—a single, a walk, a blown double play, another single, a double steal and a third single scored three runs. A leadoff homer by Lou Brock paved the way for three more in the fifth. Gibson conceded Mantle's 18th and final Series homer in the sixth, a three-run shot, and two more to Linz and Boyer in the ninth. But it wasn't nearly enough. The Cardinals prevailed, 7–5, and another era in New York had ended.

"We'll get 'em next year," Berra promised in the clubhouse. But on the flight back to New York Houk gave a message to Berra. "Mr. Topping wants to see you in his office," Berra was told. "Tomorrow morning at ten."

Berra naturally assumed he'd be rehired; he'd already asked Ford to stay on as player-coach. Instead, he was dismissed. No reason given. The press conference was set for that afternoon.

"Who's going to replace him?" a reporter asked Houk.

"We have two or three men under consideration."

"Is Keane one of them?"

He was—Keane had resigned from the Cards an hour earlier. And he and Houk had already reached an agreement. As Berra took a coaching job under Stengel with the Mets, so ended an eighteen-year reign that produced fifteen pennants and ten world championships—history's most complete domination of one professional sport by one team.

1965

He was a religious man who'd been born in St. Louis and had once considered becoming a priest. And what Johnny Keane saw in his 1965 spring training camp appalled him.

The Yankees—his Yankees now—were spending their nights at Fort Lauderdale watering holes and their days losing exhibition games. They had been doing both and then proceeding to win pennants for years, but Keane had been in St. Louis then.

He had seen the Yankees up close once, the year before, and his Cardinals had beaten them in seven games for the world championship. He was managing them now and their "careless habits" bothered him.

Keane began calling team meetings and lecturing his players, and each time his list of transgressors grew larger. "By the last meeting the number of guys who had gotten careless had increased to twenty-three," said pitcher Jim Bouton. "Bobby Richardson and Tony Kubek were the only ones on the club who weren't careless."

So the Yankees began snickering at Keane and before long they were complaining to general manager Ralph Houk about him, just as they had complained about Berra during the previous season. They nicknamed Keane "Squeaky" and compared stories about him, which Keane eventually realized. "Good afternoon," Keane would greet a cluster of his men in a hotel lobby, "gentlemen of the jury."

This was the new era and its first year was New York's grimmest since 1925. The dynasty had come crashing down in the seventh game of the 1964 Series after the Yankees had blown a 2–1 edge in games and a 3–0 lead in game four. The final pennant, the fifteenth in eighteen years, had been an anachronism; Houk and owners Dan Topping and Del Webb had decided in July that Berra would be dismissed, willy-nilly, at the end of the season.

Now mediocrity was in full flower around the Stadium and the championship roster, both regulars and reserves, was beginning to come apart. Kubek, the starting shortstop for nine seasons, would struggle through his worst year (.218) with an aching back and would retire at twenty-nine. Right fielder Roger Maris broke his hand and hurt his hamstring during the season and catcher Elston Howard injured his arm. Left-hander Whitey Ford, the staff ace since the early fifties, had felt his arm go dead in the sixth inning of the 1964 Series opener.

Yogi visited his old team in training camp wearing the uniform of a Met coach. Bobby Richardson (l) and Elston Howard (r) check out the different insignia.

Whitey Ford concentrated on strengthening his shoulder after off-season surgery. He would go on to win 16 games but lose 13. His ERA swelled to a career-high of 3.24 in what was to be the 36-year-old southpaw's last season.

Mantle (with DiMaggio at training) wasn't smiling long as he struggled with a nightmarish season: His batting averaged skidded from .303 to .255, his RBIs from 111 to 46, his homers from 35 to 19—all in 122 games.

Mel Stottlemyre emerged as the Yanks' big winner, going 20–9. He led the League in completed games (18) and innings (291)—the silver lining to a dismal season.

It was a bad year, too, for Howard and backup catcher Johnny Blanchard. An aching elbow limited Howard to 110 games, and his batting average plunged 80 points to .233. Blanchard was traded to the As.

And Maris pulled a hamstring muscle while making a running catch in April.

Mantle pulled a hamstring trying to score from second
on a passed ball in a game against the A's in June.

Symbolic of the Yanks' futile season, rookie Ross Moschitto
kicks up a cloud of dust pursuing a Harmon Killebrew triple.

Manager Johnny Keane had to go to the bullpen frequently.
The reliever he pointed to most was Pedro Ramos—65
times, which tied him with Luis Arroyo for most appearances
in one season. He totaled 5 victories plus 19 saves.

Mantle, his wife Merlyn and Mickey, Jr. at "Mantle Day"
in Yankee Stadium.

"It just went limp," Ford said. "No blood was getting down from the shoulder. The artery was blocked. The blood was just coming down through the little capillaries and I didn't have a pulse for a year." Winter surgery had repaired his circulation and Ford would win 16 games in 1965, but he would also lose 13, his most ever, and post his highest earned-run average—3.24.

And Mickey Mantle, his legs gone at thirty-three, was suffering through a frightful year. "I began to feel that I was truly headed downhill," he said. "My shoulder, which I thought had pretty well healed, began to bother me more and more, and no amount of treatment seemed to ease it. I just couldn't uncork those long throws any more."

Then in June Mantle tore a hamstring trying to score on a passed ball. His final statistics—a .255 average (down from .303), 46 RBIs (down from 111) and 19 home runs (down from 35)—represented his worst full year yet in the majors. With the scouting system in disrepair and the farm teams barren there were few replacements.

"About twelve guys got old one day," Bouton realized. Suddenly the team that had made only two trades in two years, made four before May. Pitcher Stan Williams, who'd been obtained for Moose Skowron two years earlier, was sold to Cleveland for cash. Reserve catcher John Blanchard, the ultimate Yankee who'd once said he'd rather rot on the bench as a Yankee than play regularly elsewhere, was dealt to the Athletics with pitcher Rollie Sheldon.

Sheldon wept. "I'm going to Kansas City," Blanchard told Richardson. "Great," Richardson told him. "You'll get a chance to play every day." Blanchard shook his head. "I don't want to play every day. I want to stay here."

As a Yankee. But Blanchard's Yankees were vanishing. By the end of the season New York had plunged to sixth place with a 77–85 record, 10 games out of fifth and 25 behind champion Minnesota. It was their worst effort in forty years—yet one season later it would seem decent by comparison.

1966

It was the Year They Fired the Messenger, the season the franchise fell totally apart, the summer the Yankees owned the cellar. It began with 16 losses in their first 20 games and ended in tenth place, the first time New York had viewed the American League from the bottom since 1912, when they were called the Highlanders.

In between, the front office fired manager Johnny Keane and radio announcer Red Barber and resolved to trade virtually every regular who wasn't going to retire. It was a season with few victories (70) and less laughter. "It was an extremely unhappy clubhouse that year," pitcher Jim Bouton would say. "Everybody was in a bad mood. I can't remember laughing and smiling and joking like we used to. Everybody was rubbing each other the wrong way."

Yet the lineup, in name at least, had changed little from that of the 1964 championship club. Joe Pepitone, Bobby Richardson and Clete Boyer still patrolled the infield, Tom Tresh, Mickey Mantle and Roger Maris the outfield. Elston Howard still caught much of the same pitching staff—Whitey Ford, Al Downing, Mel Stottlemyre, Hal Reniff, Steve Hamilton, Bouton. Only shortstop Tony Kubek was missing, replaced by Horace Clarke.

But the chemistry had gone bad. "These were very powerful people—Whitey, Mickey, Maris, Boyer, myself—used to having control of destinies, controlling all situations," Bouton theorized. "But when you put us all together in a losing situation, it's like taking rats and putting them in a tight situation where they can't get out and turning up the electricity. You can imagine what they would do to each other. And that was what was happening to us at the end."

Keane, who'd presided over a sixth-place finish in 1965, had been dismissed well before that. When the record reached, 4–16, general manager Ralph Houk, who'd won pennants in 1961, 1962 and 1963, fired Keane and assumed both jobs.

"It surely was not the fault of Johnny Keane that we hit the chutes when we did," Mantle felt. "We may have subconsciously felt that Ralph was the real boss and that anybody else was an interloper. But after Ralph came back we kept right on sliding downhill until we could go no further."

The statistics told it all. Only one starter, Fritz Peterson, won more games than he lost. Stottlemyre, the club's only 20–game winner in 1965, now lost 20 games. Only one regular, Mantle, hit above .270. Meanwhile, attendance sagged to fewer than 1.2 million for the first time since World War II.

It was the bitter fruit of age, injury, and a minor-league system that had long since stopped sending up championship-caliber prospects. The institution of the draft and the Yankees' unwillingness to pay large bonuses had taken their toll.

George Weiss, as he was being shooed from the general manager's office after the 1960 season, had predicted the decline with dismal accuracy.

Keane was fired after the Yanks lost 16 of their first 20 games and Ralph Houk (here interviewed by Howard Cosell) came back from the front office to replace him.

Maris signed his last Yankee contract, shipped to the Cardinals after the season, hitting a career-low .233 and 13 homers in 119 games.

Beset with arm troubles, Whitey Ford neared the end of his notable career, pitching only 73 innings and encountering his first losing record—2–5.

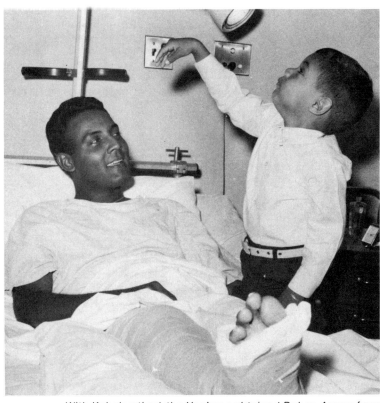

With Kubek retired, the Yankees obtained Ruben Amaro from Philadelphia, but he tore knee ligaments in a mid-April collision with teammate Tom Tresh, so... rookie Howard Clarke became Yankee shortstop.

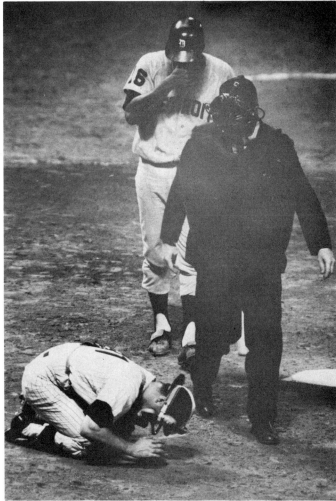

The bullpen was kept busy. Jack Hamilton (shown with catcher Howard) relieved in 41 games (7–2 with 3 saves), Hal Reniff in 56 games (3–7 with 9 saves) and Pedro Ramos in 51 games (3–9 with 13 saves).

Jake Gibbs became Howard's backup, but he too was sidelined in the season's final weeks in a freak accident—his hand fractured by the backlash of Tiger Earl Wilson's bat.

Manager Houk was frustrated all season as the Yankees fell apart and finished last for the first time since 1912.

Rookie Fritz Peterson was the only Yank, at 12–11, who won more than he lost while Mel Stottlemyre went from a 20-game winner in '65 to a 20-game loser (12–20) in '66.

Michael Burke on his first day as Yankee president for the new owners, CBS, sat among the more than 60,000 empty seats. Broadcaster Red Barber reported the smallest crowd in Stadium history and was fired after 13 years at the Yankee microphone.

"The Yankees have five more years at the most under the new management," he said. "Five more years at the most."

Unable to confront reality, management finally decided to avoid it. They had dumped one announcer, Mel Allen, after the 1964 season. Now Barber, who'd spent thirteen years at a Yankee microphone after two decades at Cincinnati and Brooklyn, was marked for extinction. Two weeks from the end of 1965 his unwavering honesty sealed his fate.

It had rained for two days. The field was sticky with mud, the seats wet, the air foggy. On Michael Burke's first day as club president Barber was supposed to do a telecast that would inevitably show the most empty seats since the Stadium had opened in 1923. Burke was sitting alone in the stands among 412 other diehards.

The pennant race was over. The story was more than 60,000 empty seats. Barber asked for a camera shot of the empty grandstands and bleachers. "No shot," he was told. Perry Smith, the club's vice-president for radio and television, had refused. So no cameras followed foul balls, none panned the sidelines. But Barber, an old radio man, would not lie.

"I don't know what the paid attendance is today," he told his audience, "but whatever it is, it is the smallest crowd in the history of the stadium. And that smallest crowd is the story, not the ball game."

The Boston Red Sox, on a bus en route from LaGuardia Airport for the next day's game, laughed when they heard the simulcast on the radio. "Old Red will sure catch hell for saying that," they agreed. Four days later Burke informed Barber that his contract would not be renewed.

And so the Yankee front office, standing amid the ruins of an empire, had reverted to ancient days. They had disposed of the messenger who brought bad news. CBS, which had bought the club two years earlier because it was "compatible with the entertainment and information business," was now providing neither.

Lee McPhail, the son of former Yankee owner Larry McPhail, returned as general manager. CBS boss William Paley (center) visited spring training as the network took 100% ownership.

1967

They'd waited until the summer's leaves had fallen and then the front office had begun its purge. A championship season in 1964 had been followed by the worst since 1925, which had been followed

Houk greeted Bill Robinson, a young outfielder acquired from Atlanta for Clete Boyer.

His legs gone, Mantle became first baseman, trading positions with Joe Pepitone.

Horace Clarke was the only returning starter in the infield, playing a different position (second base) with Ruben Amaro moving to shortstop. That's Clarke in rear and Amaro relaying in foreground, as Pete Ward is forced out.

Charlie Smith was the new third baseman, acquired from St. Louis for Roger Maris.

His pitching arm gone, Whitey Ford retired, staying on as a scout.

Dooley Womack's 65 appearances (5 victories, 17 saves) tied Luis Arroyo (1961) and Pedro Ramos (1965) for most games ever by a Yankee pitcher.

Red Sox pitcher Jose Santiago and his teammates trudge off the field after the Yankees beat them in the twentieth inning at 1:57 A.M. (note scoreboard) when Clarke delivered the winning hit to end the 6-hour, 9-minute marathon.

by the worst—tenth place—since the team had been known as the Yankees. Management had fired Johnny Keane 20 games into the 1966 season (he died of heart failure a year later) and broadcaster Red Barber at the end of it. Now, they put their hand to the roster.

On October 19 Hector Lopez, who'd played in five World Series as the game's foremost utility man, was released. A month later third baseman Clete Boyer, an eight-year Yankee, was shipped to Atlanta for outfielder Bill Robinson, whom management labeled as its next Mickey Mantle. (He proved to be something less.)

Then Roger Maris, who'd broken Babe Ruth's season home run record only five years earlier, was ferried to St. Louis for third baseman Charlie Smith. Second baseman Bobby Richardson had the foresight to retire at thirty-one after a dozen years in pinstripes. The leavetakings, in Boyer's and Maris's case, left scars.

"I loved the organization so much," Boyer would say. "I had tried to put out for them and play all the time. Richardson and Kubek quit and I was the best infielder they had. I was really the only one. And then they trade me. I didn't deserve to be traded."

Maris had helped the Yankees to their final pennant in 1964 with a brilliant burst of late-season hitting. In the summer of 1965, playing with a pulled hamstring, he dislocated two fingers on an umpire's cleat sliding into home, then broke the hand a few days later. In 1966, as his average slid to .233, his runs batted in to 43, he was booed steadily.

Then management insulted him by trading him even up to the Cardinals for Smith, a journeyman who'd played for five clubs in six years. Maris responded by immediately helping St. Louis to two pennants. Smith faded into oblivion.

Old Yankees like John Blanchard were disgusted. "CBS shouldn't have bought the Yankees," he said. "How the hell can you go from first place to tenth place? Only Jackie Gleason could have made some of those trades. Or Imogene Coca. Art Carney maybe was in on some of those trades."

The 1967 lineup, not to be confused with a CBS situation comedy, was a patchwork quilt of hacks, youngsters and great names playing out the final year or two of their careers.

Mantle, his throwing shoulder and legs already in the grave, had been shifted from the outfield to first base, where his lack of mobility was less obvious. Shortstop Horace Clarke, who'd played only twenty-three games at second base in his two-year career, was now the regular there, and Smith was at third.

Ruben Amaro, an ex-Phillie with a bum knee, was assigned to shortstop. Tom Tresh, whose career would be cut short by injury two years later,

was still in left but Joe Pepitone, a natural first baseman, had to fill in for Mantle in center field. Steve Whitaker, with 31 games of major league experience, was installed in right. Elston Howard, who'd played in nine Series, most of them as catcher, would be traded to Boston in August and replaced by a former Mississippi quarterback named Jake Gibbs.

Ironically, it was an improvement, if moving from tenth to ninth can be considered an improvement. The Red Sox, who'd been ninth in 1966, actually won the pennant. New York was the same .400 team. Only the Stadium exterior, painted blue and white during the winter, had changed.

1968

His father had died at thirty-nine, eaten up with Hodgkin's disease after a life spent in an Oklahoma mine, and Mickey Mantle was convinced that he was marked for the same fate. "When we were roommates I was into player relations and pensions," former Yankee second baseman Jerry Coleman would say. "But he'd say, 'I'll never get one. I won't live long enough.' "

As it was Mantle was visited with a different curse, which snuffed out his professional life several years early—a pair of legs that came apart on him piece by piece across two decades.

After he was kicked in the shin during a high school football game he'd developed osteomyelitis, a degenerative bone disease that was serious enough to keep Mantle out of the military. Everything else was done to him by baseball, beginning with a Yankee Stadium water sprinkler that hooked a cleat during the 1951 World Series.

"I twisted my knee and got torn ligaments," Mantle would reminisce. "That was the start of my knee operations. I had four. You start out with two sets of cartilage in each knee; now I've got only one set left. Once they operated on my shoulder and tied the tendons together. I had a cyst cut out of my right knee another time."

He also broke a foot, tore hamstrings and suffered through abscesses that would turn his uniform pants scarlet with blood. Finally, after 2,400 games, almost 250 more than club iron man Lou Gehrig, the body would not accept any more. So, when the 1968 season came to an end, Mantle went reluctantly into retirement at thirty-six, his teeth clenched.

He had been the last link to the fifties, when

*Mantle slammed his 521st homer lefthanded against Detroit . . .
. . . and his 522nd homer righthanded against Cleveland.*

*The Yankees finished in the second division for
the fourth straight year, but the fans appreciated the
improvement from ninth to fifth place. The Yanks
nudged over the .500 mark (83–70, .512), for the
first time since 1964.*

Mel Stottlemyre was 21–12, the Yanks' first 20-game winner since 1965 when Stottlemyre was 20–9.

Jim Bouton was in his final Yankee season, departing to Seattle and taking a 53–51 Yankee record with him— and notebooks that would become his bestseller.

world championships were assumed, the fourth figure—with Gehrig, Babe Ruth and Joe DiMaggio —in the Yankees' Mount Rushmore.

Later he would have nightmares. "I'm in a cab trying to get to Yankee Stadium," he'd say. "Casey is calling my name and I hear it announced on the public address. But I can't get out of the cab. Something's holding me back."

Mantle had landed in New York in 1951 as an innocent from Oklahoma—the Commerce Comet—with only a few years of minor-league experience behind him. "He was a real country boy, all shy and embarrassed," remembered Whitey Ford, his running mate throughout his career. "He arrived with a straw suitcase, two pairs of slacks and one blue sports jacket that probably cost about eight dollars."

Yet Casey Stengel installed him in right field next to DiMaggio. When the Yankees sent him down for a while that summer for seasoning and his confidence wilted, Mantle's father chewed him out ("Hell, you ain't got no guts. I thought I raised a man. You're nothing but a goddamned baby.") and turned him around.

That fall Mantle started in the World Series before being injured in the Stadium outfield. When he went back to Oklahoma for the off-season a con man representing the "Will Rogers Insurance Company" fleeced him out of his World Series check. Mantle was no financier; he was a ballplayer. "He was fairly amazin'," Stengel would testify, "in several respects."

Though his legs were never the same after he tore up his right knee that first year, he was probably the best all-around player the franchise had seen. He could field, throw, run (three seconds to first base) and hit from either side of the plate.

Mantle hit .298 lifetime with 1,509 runs batted in and 536 home runs. He even joked about his bases on balls and strikeouts, a combined total of 3,400. "I mustn't have been so hot," Mantle would wink. "I spent seven years without even hitting the ball."

Injuries cost him the better part of the 1963 season and at least 25 games in four others. But unless the muscles were torn or bones broken it was impossible to keep him out of the lineup. "Well, I guess I gotta keep you out today," Stengel would growl, watching Mantle hobble into the clubhouse. "Goddammit, Case," Mantle would protest. "Put me in."

He would bind screaming muscles and tendons in tape, stuff open abscesses with bandages and head out for a doubleheader in August heat. Once Cleveland third baseman Al Rosen, trying to shame a sore-limbed teammate into playing the Yankees, used Mantle as a standard. "Look at Mantle," Rosen chided him. "He plays on a worse leg than yours every day."

Mantle's legs, both of them, had been ground into mincemeat. "Sometimes we'd be sitting and talking or having dinner and he'd be there sort of rubbing his knees with his hand," Ford remembered. "Then when it came time to get up and leave he'd take a long, long while just lifting up out of his chair, like it was killing him to put all that weight on those bad knees. I think he was in pain all the time I knew him."

By 1965 it had all but ruined Mantle. First baseman Joe Pepitone, who'd replace him in center field, remembered how he found a slumping Mantle weeping in the dugout bathroom because the club was destined for sixth place and he couldn't help them.

His throwing shoulder hurt so badly that Mantle could no longer fire a ball from the outfield; he would flip it to left fielder Tom Tresh. The legs that once covered the distance from home to first in 3.1 seconds (3.0 as a lefty) could no longer move.

The Yankees shifted him to first base for his final two seasons, but by 1968 Mantle's average had slumped to .237. As DiMaggio had decided in 1951 and Gehrig in 1939 (both of them also at thirty-six), Mantle realized it was time to go.

The players he'd won championships with— Billy Martin, Yogi Berra, Tony Kubek, Bobby Richardson—had all retired. Ford, his arm gone, had called it quits the year before at thirty-nine. Mantle's teammates now were named Bobby Cox, Roy White, Jake Gibbs, Bill Robinson.

As a final tribute, Detroit pitcher Denny McLain grooved one for Mantle in the waning days of the season. It was a harmless gesture— the Tigers had clinched their first pennant in twenty-three years the night before, the Yankees were consigned to fifth. As Mantle crushed it for home run No. 535 to pass Jimmie Foxx, McLain saluted him. "He was my idol," McLain explained. The next June they would retire Mantle's number, 7, at the Stadium, then bear him along the base lines in a golf cart. It was the only game left to him.

1969

They had pulled him up from Richmond for the last few months of the 1964 season and the final pennant drive a dynasty could muster. Mel Stottlemyre had been twenty-two that summer and after

Mantle announced his retirement after giving it one final try at spring training.

Yankee Bobby Murcer and Seattle Pilot Ray Oyler are at the bottom of this pile during a brawl in May—one of many that season.

Mantle was honored at a retirement day.

After two years in the Army, Bobby Murcer was converted to the outfield and played well there. He led the team in extra-base hits (54), including 26 homers—one less than team leader Joe Pepitone.

Jack Aker was obtained from Seattle for Fred Talbot and became the Yankees' top reliever: 8 victories, 11 saves and a team-leading 2.05 ERA.

he won nine games in seven weeks he found himself a permanent member of the best pitching rotation in baseball, starting regularly with Whitey Ford, Jim Bouton and Al Downing.

When the World Series began manager Yogi Berra twice paired him against St. Louis ace Bob Gibson and Stottlemyre came in with one 8–3 victory and a seven-inning nondecision that a reliever lost in the tenth.

Finally, Berra had had to start him in the seventh game on two days' rest, and after the Cardinals whacked him for three runs in the fourth inning, Stottlemyre blamed himself for losing the Series. Catcher Elston Howard wouldn't hear it. "You did a hell of a job," Howard told him.

Stottlemyre was going to be the cornerstone of a staff that would have to carry the Yankees through the sixties while the rest of the lineup was rejuvenated. After he won 20 games in 1965, there was no doubt.

"I figured with Stottlemyre, myself and Downing, that we were never going to get beat," Bouton mused. "That we were going to go on forever."

Instead, the club had collapsed around him. In 1966, when New York finished last in the American League, Stottlemyre lost 20 games yet still equalled Fritz Peterson for most victories on the staff with 12. Then maverick Bouton was dispatched to Seattle. Downing, with only 10 victories in two years, would be shipped to Oakland at the end of 1969.

By then all that remained was Stottlemyre and The Kids. Attendance had slipped to barely more than a million, the lowest total since 1945. The club was still slogging along in fifth place while manager Ralph Houk tried to nurture young talent. The roster had become a revolving door. In 1969 the front office would make a dozen trades and all but complete the housecleaning that had begun in 1966.

Tom Tresh, Joe Pepitone and Downing were unloaded before the year was out. At its start, the Yankee lineup featured an infield of Joe Pepitone, Horace Clarke, Gene Michael and Jerry Kenney, an outfield of Roy White, Bill Robinson and Bobby Murcer, and a promising young catcher named Thurman Munson who'd be named Rookie of the Year.

The only constant since 1964 had been Stottlemyre. He'd won 21 games for a fifth-place club in 1968. Now, as the Yankees treaded water in the same spot, he won 20.

When the guard changed in 1974 and new owner George Steinbrenner was installing a championship foundation, Stottlemyre was the last relic of the mid-sixties. Only Ford and Red Ruffing had pitched more innings than his 2,662, only Ford more shutouts than Stottlemyre's 40. His 164 victories placed him fifth in club history.

The Yankees brought up a young catcher named Thurman Munson, who received an award his second day in uniform from ex-Yankee Gene Woodling, who signed him.

After ending his career with two seasons in Boston, Elston Howard returned to the Yankees as coach. Here he is greeted by McPhail and former teammate Ford.

But when his right arm gave out, it happened quickly, irrevocably. A shoulder rotator cuff gave way against the Angels on a June evening; except for one August relief appearance, Stottlemyre never pitched again. In the spring of 1975, after he was told to prepare at his own pace, the Yankees released him.

"In all the years I knew him I never knew Mel to speak a bad word against anybody," Munson would say. "But this time he was furious. He felt he had been lied to. So the incident left a bad taste with everyone."

1970

He had been a Yankee ever since he returned from World War II with a chestful of medals for valor. For eight years Ralph Houk buckled on shinguards whenever Yogi Berra or Charlie Silvera couldn't make it. For six more he'd labored in the system, managing New York's minor league affiliate in Denver and serving as a Yankee coach under manager Casey Stengel.

When Stengel came down with a virus in the middle of the 1960 pennant race, it was Houk that management chose to mind the store for a few weeks. And when Stengel was dismissed after the World Series that year, it was Houk who was named to preside over the dynasty.

It wasn't that they loved Stengel less, owner Del Webb explained, but that the front office had decided that they either had to promote Houk or risk losing him. What had made Houk a model major also made him a desirable manager—loyalty to the troops, a drive to win, and boundless optimism. All of those qualities were designed to inspire devotion from a club that had listened to Stengel's raspy growl for over a decade. "I thought Ralph Houk was the greatest sonovabitch ever to wear spikes," third baseman Clete Boyer would say, and most of his colleagues agreed.

Houk invariably began and ended each day with a huge grin that was impervious to slumps, injuries, summer heat or the shadow of the Minnesota Twins a few games behind and gaining. The pennant was never out of reach, the championship just a matter of faith. More important, Houk got his players believing it.

"They enjoy playing for Houk because he tells them where they stand, he alibis for their mistakes, he's continually building confidence by

Houk was named Manager of the Year as the Yankees finished second in their division. Houk was popular with his players—a two-fisted manager who often fought for them.

Munson led the regulars in hitting .302 and was named League Rookie of the Year in 1970.

Bobby Murcer hit 4 consecutive homers in a doubleheader on June 24—joining Gehrig, Blanchard and Mantle.

Fritz Peterson led Yankee starters with a 20–11 record— his only 20-victory season in the majors.

Horace Clarke stands on first after his ninth-inning single broke Joe Niekro's no-hitter at Detroit. It was the third time in a month Clarke spoiled no-hitters in the ninth.

Lindy McDaniel had the Yankees' lowest ERA at 2.01 while coming out of the bullpen and pitching in 62 games. He won 9, lost 5 and saved 29—tying the Yankee record set by Luis Arroyo in 1961. Those 29 saves still rank as third most in Yankee history.

Versatile Danny Cater, obtained from the A's, hit .301 in his first season while playing first base (131 games), third base (42 games) and outfield (7 games).

Yankee pitcher Stan Bahnsen covers plate and tags out Cleveland's Vada Pinson, who resents the position of the tag and . . .

Munson (far left) grabs Pinson, Gene Michaels joins in, and both benches are soon empty.

. . . decks Bahnsen.

Two great former Yankee outfielders were honored when plaques were dedicated in the outfield at Yankee Stadium.

The Yankees popped champagne to celebrate their second-place finish.

blowing that smoke and he doesn't have a curfew," said pitcher Jim Bouton. "That's why he was the best manager I ever had."

And that's why the Yankee front office reinstalled Houk in the dugout in 1966 after two years as general manager and stuck with him through the darkest days in franchise history.

Houk had been part of the dynasty ever since it was revived in 1947. He won three pennants in his first three years as manager and was the first man ever to win world championships in his first two seasons. Like the military man he was (his baseball nickname, naturally, was The Major), he never lost sight of his objective. "You take the hill, you smash the gun emplacement, you win the pennant, there's solid accomplishment," said White Sox owner Bill Veeck. "There's something you can plan and blueprint and come to grips with."

Houk was the perfect man for a tunnel that had only the merest flicker of light at its end. The Yankees' fall from grace had been immediate and final; in two years they plunged from the top of the American League to the bottom. Their climb upward would take twelve years and Houk would be in Detroit when it was complete.

But by 1970, the fifth year of his resurrection ("The Horace Clarke Era," as some New York sportswriters dubbed it), Houk could finally smell a pennant chase.

He had a Rookie of the Year in catcher Thurman Munson, three reliable starting pitchers in Mel Stottlemyre, Stan Bahnsen and 20-game winner Fritz Peterson, and a bullpen anchored by thirty-four-year-old Lindy McDaniel, a religious sort who mailed out a newsletter called "Pitching for the Master."

After losing 12 of their first 21 games the Yankees won seven of their first eight in May, were 46–39 by the All-Star break and finished second in their division with their best record since 1964. The title had been out of reach for most of the season; Baltimore would win it by 15 games and go on to capture their second championship in five years.

But after two years of fifth-place finishes, runner-up money was an achievement for the Yankees. When his people clinched it Houk ordered a champagne party in the clubhouse. "We were whooping it up as though we'd won the pennant," Munson said. "I know old Yankee purists must have been thinking that celebrating second place was really bush, but we enjoyed it."

After all, the record was 93–69; only Baltimore, Cincinnati and Minnesota had posted better ones. Only five Yankee clubs had ever surpassed it without winning the pennant. Miller Huggins might not have been popping corks over it, but Ralph Houk would. He would also be named American League Manager of the Year. For his tunnel vision.

1971

They had gone so long without a pennant—seven years, by far the longest drought since 1920—that they'd taken to celebrating even marginally significant milestones. Now, as the franchise's gray days continued, they were willing to accept charity from a 63–96 team to finish above .500, an achievement that their predecessors had once taken for granted.

The 1971 Yankees struggled to keep their heads above water all summer; the end of every month found them with a losing record, despite interim bursts of good fortune. When the final day arrived, they'd lost six of their last eight games and had slipped to 81–80, with only a night date against the Senators at Robert F. Kennedy Stadium remaining.

But Washington owner Robert Short had inadvertently done them a favor. Claiming mounting pools of red ink and eyeing greener pastures in Texas, Short had announced he'd be moving the club to the Dallas area. Ten days earlier, his fellow owners had voted to let him do so.

Senators fans, who had lost one team in 1960 but had never gone without a major league franchise in seven decades, were furious. As the season wound down they draped "Short Stinks" banners from the upper deck. Now, with their club leading its final game, 7–5, with two out in the top of the ninth inning, much of the crowd of nearly 20,000 (including an estimated 4,000 gate crashers) poured onto the diamond to bear off souvenirs. Home plate was ripped from its moorings, letters were stripped from the scoreboard. Unable to clear the field and restore order, the umpires simply declared a forfeit—the first in the major leagues since 1954—and awarded the game (9–0) and a winning season to the Yankees.

Yet it was simply one more incomplete achievement in a season that had been filled with them. Outfielder Bobby Murcer hit .331, the best average of his career, yet lost the batting title by six percentage points to Minnesota's Tony Oliva.

The starting rotation of Mel Stottlemyre, Fritz Peterson, Stan Bahnsen, Steve Kline and Mike Kekich completed 67 games, the best effort by a New York staff since 1952. The reason? A dismal bullpen that produced only a dozen saves, by far the league's poorest effort.

And catcher Thurman Munson was named to the American League All-Star team—then proceeded to hit .251 for the season, a drop of 51 points from his rookie year. His fielding, however, was impeccable—or nearly so. He handled 614 chances perfectly, but was charged with an error

Veteran Felipe Alou was acquired from Oakland as an outfielder–first baseman and contributed a .289 batting average and 8 homers.

Munson's defense was superb, but he was frustrated offensively. His batting average plunged 51 points to .251, and he was called out here in this resounding collision-to-be with Angel catcher Johnny Stephenson.

Bobby Murcer hit .331, his career best.

Houk recalled Ron Blomberg (r) from Syracuse and obtained Met Ron Swoboda (l) from Montreal. Blomberg would hit .322 in 64 games, Swoboda .261 in 54 games.

when Oriole Andy Etchebarren knocked him cold at the plate in June. All it cost him was the Yankee record for a catcher and the chance to become the only man besides Athletic Buddy Rosar in 1946 to field a perfect season behind the plate.

So it went. In a season that was every bit as unspectacular as the several that had preceded it, the Yankees sought their consolation prizes where they could. Even if it meant taking a gift from the deathbed of a franchise.

1972

The television people had bought the club as a way of "broadening the base" in the autumn of 1964, seduced by another pennant freshly won and the great names—Mantle, Maris, Ford, Kubek, Richardson, Howard—still on the roster.

CBS was merely a cab ride away from the Stadium and the Yankees seemed like a fine corporate acquisition—a proud tradition, world-wide visibility, a dash of chic, a touch of class. Both employer and employee even wore pinstriped suits. It was a business, network executive Michael Burke said, "that we would enjoy being in."

Instead, there had been seven Bad Years at Black Rock (the media nickname for the network's ebony granite headquarters on West 52nd Street). The farm clubs and scouting system that had nurtured Yankee success for decades had gone to seed. The names were aging and injury-prone, playing out the string. When the championship feeling evaporated with a sixth-place finish the following season, so did the fans.

Attendance had dipped by 100,000 immediately, then sagged by another 100,000 when New York sank to the American League cellar in 1966. Now, in 1972, it had slid to 966,328, the first time it had been under a million since 1945, even though the product had improved.

The Yankees had finished second to Baltimore in 1970 and also had a winning season the following year. In 1972, studded with promising young talent, they would contend for the divisional championship until the final few weeks. Yet the Mets, their once laughable National League neighbors from Queens, would draw more than twice as many paying customers. The difference was stylistic, the difference between pistachio and vanilla ice cream.

The Yankees, to put it bluntly, were boring.

National League veteran Johnny Callison joined the Yankees, hitting .258 as a regular outfielder.

Murcer hit for the cycle—the twelfth and last Yankee to do so. He led the League in total bases with 314, batting at .294 while smacking a career-high 33 homers.

Celerino Sanchez was summoned from Syracuse and plugged a void at third base.

Sparky Lyle, obtained from the Red Sox, was used as the relief pitcher often: 59 times, leading the Yankee pitchers in ERA (1.92) while gathering 9 saves and a League-leading 35 saves with 44 points—still the most in one season in Yankee history.

Felipe Alou lashes his 2000th career hit.

"Yankees like nothing in nature," *The New Yorker*'s Roger Angell scribbled in his notebook. "Most sedative BB team in memory, so uninspired as to suggest bestowal of new sobriquet: Bronx Sashweights? CBS Plastercasts?"

As the season wore on and New York remained in the thick of the race, the club struck sparks. In a span of three days the Yankees banged out 60 hits in doubleheaders against Kansas City and Texas. By the end of August they found themselves only a game and a half behind divisional leader Baltimore and watching the out-of-town scoreboard nightly.

They'd also developed a late-inning ritual, based on the appearance of flamboyant Sparky Lyle who'd been obtained from Boston during spring training for first baseman Danny Cater and shortstop Mario Guerrero. With men on base and New York clinging to a slender lead, manager Ralph Houk would raise his left arm and a pinstriped white automobile would bear Lyle and his hard lefthanded slider to the mound while the Stadium organist played "Pomp and Circumstance." Lyle would toss his jacket to a batboy, chomp down on a wad of tobacco and nail down a save frequently enough to keep the Yankees in the race.

When they came apart it happened all at once, in late September; New York lost its final five games and finished fourth again, three games above .500. During the winter the CBS brass decided they'd seen one summer rerun too many and opted to cancel.

They would sell the club for $10 million, a loss of more than $3 million, to a man from Cleveland who built ships and had borne nostalgic memories of the Yankees since childhood. "When the Yankees came to town it was like Barnum and Bailey coming to town," George Steinbrenner would say. "The excitement."

For eight years, that feeling had been sorely missing in the Bronx.

1973

He was a millionaire shipbuilder from Cleveland who knew little about baseball or the Bronx and he promised to keep a respectable distance from his new pinstriped plaything. "I won't be active in the day-to-day operations of the club at all," announced George Steinbrenner III the day he

CBS sold the Yankees in January to a group headed by George Steinbrenner. He told the press he wouldn't "be active in the day-to-day operations of the club at all." But, by Opening Day, he was telling Houk which Yankees needed haircuts.

Mrs. Babe Ruth was among fans attending Opening Day, the fiftieth anniversary of the Stadium's opening. She is holding a replica of the 1923 souvenir program.

The Yankees had a new 1–2 power punch in Bobby Murcer (l) and Graig Nettles (r), who was obtained from Cleveland. They shared the home-run lead with 22 each. Murcer, .304, Nettles .234.

Blomberg made history on April 6 at Boston when he stepped to the plate as the League's first designated hitter under a new rule. He went 1-for-3 for the game, hit .329 for the season in 100 games, including 55 as DH. More often, Jim Ray Hart was in the DH slot with 106 games.

Rookie righthander Doc Medich (shown here with baseball clown Max Patkin) had the best ERA (2.91) and winning percentage (.609) in the Yankee rotation, while fashioning a 14–9 record.

A home-plate smashup between Munson and Boston catcher Carlton Fisk sparked a free-for-all at Fenway Park that delayed the game 25 minutes.

The team collapsed in late season, and the fans got on the Yankees, particularly Houk. "It pained me when Ralph was forced to come out and make a pitching change," Munson said. "He got a terrible booing and walked back to the dugout like a beaten man."

Veteran fireballer Sam McDowell was purchased from San Francisco and went 5–8 for the Yankees.

bought the Yankees during the winter of 1973. "I can't spread myself so thin. I've got enough headaches with my shipping company."

Yet on opening day, as the National Anthem was playing, here was Steinbrenner scribbling down the numbers of several of his players. "He was developing his famous Yankee haircut policy, catcher Thurman Munson realized, "about ten years behind the times."

Afterward, manager Ralph Houk relayed the message to his team: "I want numbers 19, 47 and 28 to cut their hair." The reign of George The Third had begun, and its first year was as unpredictable and unstructured as any in franchise history.

The goofiness began in spring training when pitchers Fritz Peterson and Mike Kekich announced that they were exchanging families, a "life swap" that included wives, children and household pets. Six feet beneath a tasteful headstone, former owner Jacob Ruppert presumably whirled.

Then the Yankees proceeded to lose their first four games, three of them in Boston. By mid-May they would be involved in the thick of the division race—but so would everybody else. All six teams in the American League East were separated by one game—and none of them had winning records.

But, by the end of June, spurred by trades that fetched starting pitchers Sam McDowell from San Francisco and Pat Dobson from Atlanta, the Yankees had taken over first place for the first time since 1964. They had already acquired a solid shortstop in Fred Stanley and a superb third baseman in Graig Nettles. Molded around a nucleus of Horace Clarke, Gene Michael, Bobby Murcer, Roy White, Munson and the Alou brothers (Felipe and Matty), it made for a contender.

From May 20 until July 4 New York won 30 of 45 games, including a stretch of 14 in 15 at home, yet attendance was slow to catch up. The Mets, on their way to the National League pennant, were still moving more bodies through turnstiles. *The New Yorker*'s Roger Angell, who'd described the club as "sedative" a year earlier, was puzzled. "I think," he wrote, "the problem is ghosts."

The Yankees of Decades Past still haunted. Steinbrenner, who'd been fascinated by "the Yankees when he watched them play the Indians at Municipal Stadium as a child, was determined to recreate the past.

The hair policy, his locker inspections, his grooming tips, were not all that different from manager Joe McCarthy's attitude in the thirties and forties. "I want to develop pride in the players as Yankees," Steinbrenner explained. "The Yankee system isn't what it used to be and we've got to get it back to what it was."

And the American League standings back to what *they* were. New York held the divisional lead until August. Then the club broke apart with astonishing speed, losing 18 of its next 27 games and dropping into fourth. The Yankees would finish two games below .500 and 17 behind the Orioles.

"The final month was one of the worst I've lived through," Munson would say. "The fans were on us every day, especially on Ralph. They were never worse than they were during the last game. It pained me when Ralph was forced to come out and make a pitching change late in the game. He got a terrible booing and walked back to the dugout like a beaten man."

Houk, who'd won three pennants in his first three seasons, then came back to preside over the club's long reconstruction, resigned after the finale. That night, as the club made plans to share Shea Stadium with the Mets, they closed up Yankee Stadium for a two-year renovation.

To exorcise ghosts, among other things.

1974

The players called it the Friday Night Massacre and eventually they grew to accept it as merely another facet of Life With George. It was the 26th of April, the Yankees were only half a game out of first place in the American League East and they'd just beaten the Rangers in Texas.

When they emerged from the showers they learned that four of the club's eight pitchers—Fritz Peterson, Fred Beene, Steve Kline and Tom Buskey—had been traded to the Indians for first baseman Chris Chambliss and pitchers Dick Tidrow and Cecil Upshaw.

"Half the pitching staff was gone," marveled catcher Thurman Munson. "Just like that. And here came [general manager] Gabe Paul, a big smile on his face, right into the clubhouse."

The players were both furious and suspicious. Half a dozen Yankees were former Indians as it was. Both Paul and owner George Steinbrenner were from Cleveland. "The connection bothered us," Munson admitted. "It seems as though they were bringing the whole Indian team here."

Coincidentally or not, New York toppled from first to last place within two months. Chaos had become routine—yet the confusion had rarely abated since Steinbrenner had bought the club from CBS the year before.

Dick Williams was announced as the new manager and appeared in pinstripes at a December press conference, but A's owner Charlie Finley refused to release him and League President Joe Cronin ruled in Finley's favor.

In January Bill Virdon was named manager and welcomed by coaches Whitey Ford (l) and Elston Howard (r).

It was the spring of 1974 and the Yankees were playing in a borrowed ball park in Queens with a manager they hadn't really wanted and an owner under indictment. Stability was not in their vocabulary.

They'd known about the shift in stadia; Yankee Stadium was undergoing a two-year remodeling, so the club was prepared to share Shea Stadium with their National League brethren, the Mets. And Ralph Houk had resigned after the final game of the 1973 season, so the players were prepared for a change. But not for Bill Virdon.

Steinbrenner had wanted to hire Dick Williams, who'd just managed Oakland to its second straight world championship. When A's owner Charles Finley refused to release Williams from his contract without two minor leaguers as compensation, the dispute was appealed to outgoing American League president Joe Cronin, who ruled in Finley's favor.

So the Yankees had hired Virdon, who'd been dismissed in midseason by Pittsburgh; ironically, it had been Virdon's grounder that had caught New York shortstop Tony Kubek in the throat in the final game of the 1960 World Series and led to Bill Mazeroski's home run and the championship.

But where Houk had been a rump-slapper and a communicator, Virdon was a quiet man who was used to power hitting at Pittsburgh. "I don't know squat about pitching," he admitted. He had a bad stomach (Yankee players quickly dubbed him Mr. Milkshake) and an aversion to lengthy or frequent conversations. He often sent coach Dick Howser to home plate with the starting lineup.

"He could go weeks without speaking to you," Munson realized, "for no other reason than he had nothing to say."

Then Steinbrenner had been informed on opening day that he was under indictment for having made illegal contributions to the Nixon campaign during the 1972 presidential election.

Meanwhile, the Yankee roster had become a revolving door; before the season was done forty-four players, including nineteen pitchers, would wear pinstripes. The Friday Night Massacre was only one of twelve trades or acquisitions the front office would make by New Year's Eve, yet it proved to be the turning point. "That was the start of everything," Paul would say much later. "It broke up the country club. There was great camaraderie on those losing ballclubs."

By September 5, New York had claimed first place by winning 12 of 14 games to overtake slumping Boston. Then Baltimore won 10 straight, sweeping the Yankees on consecutive complete games by Jim Palmer, Mike Cuellar and Dave McNally, and grabbed the lead back.

The Yankees would repossess it briefly, but

After 25 years in pinstripes, Ralph Houk came back wearing the uniform of the Detroit Tigers.

Lyle's 66 appearances were the most in a season by a Yankee pitcher—until eclipsed by his 72 in 1977. He finished the season with a team-low ERA of 1.66 along with a record of 9–3 plus 15 saves.

Outfielder Lou Pinella was obtained from KC for Lindy McDaniel and hit .305 to lead the Yankee regulars in batting.

Elliott Maddox was purchased from Texas and hit .303 while playing spectacularly in center field and totalling a second-in-League 18 assists.

Walt "No-Neck" Williams was gotten from Cleveland and the outfielder quickly proved a popular Yankee, although hitting only .113 in 43 games.

Chris Chambliss was the new first baseman, acquired from Cleveland. His bat came alive in the pennant drive—his 18–game streak was the longest since Kubek's 19 in 1961.

when the Red Sox cleaned out New York in a twi-night doubleheader at Shea on the 24th, pennant prospects looked dim. Luis Tiant, Boston's thirty-three-year-old righthander, had rhumbaed his way to a six-hit shutout in the first game; two New York errors and a Bobby Murcer spill on the base paths botched the nightcap.

A furious crowd of 46,000 littered the diamond with firecrackers and tennis balls and brawled among themselves. "I don't blame 'em," said a frustrated Murcer. "Tonight I wanted to get up there and whale with 'em."

So the gap was one game with five to play but the Yankees made a final stand in Cleveland, sweeping three while Steinbrenner celebrated in the stands. The Orioles, though, were also winning. New York flew to Milwaukee for the final two games, still one game out.

Whereupon the dizziness that had pursued the club all year continued. Murcer, trying to break up a fistfight in the hotel lobby between reserve catchers Rick Dempsey and Bill Sudakis, was injured and missed the game. Possibly, he might have caught the fly ball that Elliott Maddox and Lou Piniella misplayed in the eighth, enabling the Brewers to tie the score, win in extra innings and eliminate the Yankees from their best chance at a pennant in a decade.

"Tomorrow is one of the biggest games of the year," Steinbrenner told his players at a party held that night. "You go out and show 'em that you can win tomorrow and that way you'll get your minds off losing the pennant. Go out there and kick their asses."

The players raised their eyebrows, puzzled. "Everyone kinda said, The season's over and he wants us to kick their ass tomorrow," said reliever Sparky Lyle.

But orders were orders in Steinbrenner's shop so Lyle's teammates went out, beat Milwaukee by a run and finished two games behind Baltimore. By the time spring training convened in 1975 Steinbrenner would be communicating with his club by tape recorders and third parties. He was convicted in August and fined $15,000 in lieu of a six-year jail sentence on the illegal campaign contribution charges.

After the 1974 season Commissioner Bowie Kuhn, invoking the game's good name, banned Steinbrenner from operating the franchise for two years. After less than that long in power, George the Third had involuntarily abdicated.

1975

They had packed him off into exile in 1957. Kansas City was a synonym for exile in those days and Billy Martin had been singled out, fairly or not, as the instigator of a fistfight with a drunken bowler at New York's Copacabana nightclub. So the Yankees—specifically general manager George Weiss, who'd never liked Martin from his first days with the club—had traded him in a seven-player package in June and Martin had gone on to play for the Tigers, Indians, Reds, Braves and Twins before retiring four years later.

He'd been a frequent visitor to the Stadium since, managing three American League clubs with the same street-smart aggressiveness that had marked his playing days. Alfred Manuel Martin had taken unsettled teams, won divisional titles with them, squabbled with management, been fired and moved on to do the same thing elsewhere.

He'd gone through that cycle at Minnesota and Detroit and now, despite an unexpected second-place effort, he had been dismissed at Texas in the middle of the 1975 season and had gone off to Colorado to fish, his 1976 salary already guaranteed.

Back in the Bronx as July turned into August, Yankee owner George Steinbrenner was fidgeting in exile. His Yankees had lost their grip on first place in the American League East and had fallen ten games behind Boston.

Bill Virdon had been named 1974 Manager of the Year for maneuvering New York to a second-place finish, but Steinbrenner thought he lacked panache. His own players called him Mr. Milkshake. Billy Martin hadn't frequented a soda fountain in years.

"Your temperaments aren't compatible," President Gabe Paul told Steinbrenner. "There are going to be problems." Steinbrenner shrugged and sent Paul and scout Birdie Tebbetts to find Martin and get him interested. The deal was no better than what he'd had with the Rangers—$72,000 a year. But it was the Yankee job. Once a Yankee . . . .

Yet the terms of the contract bothered Martin. He had to "personally conduct yourself at all times so as to represent the best interest of the New York Yankees and to adhere to all club policies." He could not criticize management. He had to be available to consult with the front office. Breach any of the above and management could fire him with no liability for his salary.

"They hadn't even hired me and here the people were talking about firing me," Martin would

Catfish Hunter joined the Yankees as the first free agent, signing a five-year contract for a reported $3.2 million. The Yanks also acquired Bobby Bonds (l) from San Francisco in a stunning trade for Murcer.

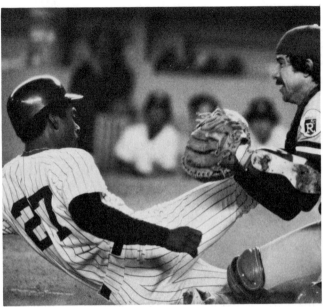

Maddox twisted a knee here but damaged it far worse in June when he tore a cartilage. Hitting .307, he would not play again in 1975 and never returned to his '74 form.

Despite various injuries, Bonds managed to hit 32 homers and steal 30 bases—the first player to have three 30–30 seasons. He would be dealt away after the season.

Chambliss' batting average climbed more than 60 points, his .304 tied for eighth best in the League.

say. "I had to be out of my mind to sign that contract."

But he did and suddenly found himself being introduced as the new manager at the Yankees Old Timers' Day, a celebration to which he hadn't even been invited originally. Virdon had quietly cleaned out his desk several hours earlier.

Martin had fretted about working for Steinbrenner, particularly under those terms. "I was putting myself in a position where he could handcuff me and I didn't know him very well," Martin would say. "I had heard he was wild and erratic."

And this year Steinbrenner was at a distance. After Steinbrenner's conviction for illegal contributions to the 1972 Nixon presidential campaign, baseball Commissioner Bowie Kuhn had suspended him for two years. He could not frequent the team offices or the clubhouse, yet Steinbrenner was not a man to sit idle.

"Gather round here and listen," Virdon had instructed his club one day, then flicked on a tape recorder.

"I'll be a sonovabitch if I'm going to sit up here and sign these paychecks and watch us get our asses kicked by a bunch of rummies," barked a recorded voice.

"It was George," reliever Sparky Lyle realized.

George would always be there, at least figuratively, cajoling, ordering, overseeing. But until Kuhn's suspension was lifted in March 1976 Martin was running the club, at least from the dugout, and the players responded to him immediately.

Like them, Martin had been a Yankee. He had won two World Series personally, one with his glove, one with his bat. He had seen the inside of a cocktail lounge. "He remembers what it was like to be a player," Lyle said. "Everybody on the team really loved him. We were excited about having Billy as a manager because he'd make a move, pinch-hit or steal or bunt and he'd walk up and down the dugout and explain why he did what he did."

Energized, the Yankees won six of their next eight before leveling off and finishing third, 12 games behind the Red Sox. But Martin had already begun planning for 1976, pruning the roster in his mind and molding a nucleus.

He had watched the club closely from the day he'd arrived, but kept his own counsel. "I wanted to see who were the clubhouse lawyers, alibiers and complainers and get rid of them," Martin reasoned. "You can't keep those types and still have a winning team."

Pitcher Pat Dobson had mentioned to a reporter that the players probably wouldn't heed Martin. "I made a little note to myself that he'd be the first guy we'd get rid of at the end of the season," Martin decided. Another pitcher, Doc

Doc Medich was 16–16 in his final Yankee season, traded away in December.

Medich, blamed the outfielders for his losses. Medich was shipped out in December to Pittsburgh. Outfielder Bobby Bonds wanted to stay out of the lineup near the end of the season and tend to a sore leg while Martin was trying to pile up victories for psychological purposes. Bonds went to the Angels the same day Medich was jettisoned.

Finally, thanks to Steinbrenner's munificence, there was enough talent on hand to rebuild to Martin's liking. Pitcher Catfish Hunter had already been scooped up from the free-agent table for more than $3 million in salary, bonuses and extras during the winter of 1975, and had won 23 games. The Dobson, Bonds and Medich trades brought three proven pitchers (Ed Figueroa, Dock Ellis and Ken Brett), and three starters in designated hitter Oscar Gamble, second baseman Willie Randolph and centerfielder Mickey Rivers.

"I felt we were going to win," Martin said. "I couldn't wait to get to camp."

1976

He couldn't find home plate. Or third base for that matter. Yankee fans, pennant-starved after a dozen years of mediocrity or worse, had swarmed onto the Stadium diamond as soon as they saw the ball drop into the right-field stands.

They met first baseman Chris Chambliss midway between second and third and buried him with delight. Chambliss's home run off Kansas City reliever Mark Littell had just given the Yankees a 7–6 victory over the Royals and the American League pennant in the ninth inning of the final game of their playoff series.

For the first time since 1964, when the Yankees had won their last pennant by a single game over Chicago, there was something to celebrate in the Bronx.

The franchise had come full cycle since then—a different owner, a new manager, a remodeled Stadium and a club stocked with young talent that had largely been obtained elsewhere.

For decades the Yankee had rebuilt their roster by dipping into a teeming farm system; now President Gabe Paul's horse-trading instincts and owner George Steinbrenner's cash had forged a more direct path to success. Only four men on the twenty-five-player roster had come up through the system; only catcher Thurman Munson and outfielder Roy White remained from the 1970 season, when the Yankees, resigned to runner-up status,

had popped champagne corks to celebrate second place.

The Yankees were an amalgam of capable refugees from Cleveland, from Pittsburgh, from California. Three of their regulars—Chambliss, third baseman Graig Nettles and outfielder Oscar Gamble—had been Indians. Center fielder Mickey Rivers and pitchers Rudy May and Ed Figueroa were former Angels. Second baseman Willie Randolph and pitcher Dock Ellis were ex-Pirates.

The only similarities between the 1964 club and this one were the name, the pinstripes and former catchers Yogi Berra and Elston Howard, both now Yankee coaches. When the Yankees arrived at spring training they were introduced to new ground rules and a new workout philosophy. What manager Billy Martin had found, taking over from Bill Virdon in August of 1975, had annoyed him.

"It wasn't the Yankee clubhouse the way I remembered it," Martin said. "Anyone who wanted to was running around the clubhouse. It wasn't a professional way of doing things and the lack of professionalism was reflected in the way the team was playing. The execution was weak, the players were not doing the basic things on the field like hitting the cutoff man or advancing the runner and too many of the players weren't being aggressive enough on the field."

All of that would change. Martin abolished the traditionally leisurely double sessions at Fort Lauderdale and instituted one three-hour workout on two diamonds that kept everyone in perpetual motion, working on fundamentals.

But Steinbrenner was troubled by the shorter, if more productive working day. "You burn them up down here," Martin countered, "and by the end of the season they have nothing left."

When Martin took his people north for opening day inside a totally refurbished Yankee Stadium, they were crisp, confident and well conditioned.

They came from four runs down to drub Minnesota in the opener with Joe DiMaggio, Mickey Mantle and the widows of Babe Ruth and Lou Gehrig looking on, and went on to win 15 of their first 20 games. The race in the American League East, as in all four divisions that season, was over by the first week in June. "It was the happiest ball club I think I ever managed," Martin felt. "The guys were just having fun playing hard, aggressive baseball."

On May 20 the aggression had spilled over into a bench-clearing brawl at the Stadium, where New York was entertaining defending league champion Boston in a three-game series. Red Sox right fielder Dwight Evans had cut down Yankee counterpart Lou Piniella at the plate, but Piniella had bowled over catcher Carlton Fisk, knees into chest, in an effort to jar the ball loose.

The rebuilt Yankee Stadium.

Willie Randolph was obtained from Pittsburgh with Dock Ellis and Ken Brett for Doc Medich. He won the Dawson Award and hit .267 while playing a steady second base.

Berra is welcomed back by fellow-coach Elston Howard (l) and Yankee president Gabe Paul (r). No. 8 was reactivated for the new coach.

Pitcher Ed Figueroa (above) and . . .
. . . outfielder Mickey River (right) were acquired from
the Angels for Bobby Bonds. Figueroa became the
winningest starter with 19 victories and had the
lowest ERA with 3.01, while Rivers led the
hitters at .312.

Billy Martin didn't like the Baltimore trade in mid-June, but
owner George Steinbrenner assured him,
"This trade just won you the pennant."

Munson was named MVP—the Yankees' first since Elston
Howard in 1963. A Gibraltar behind the plate, he batted .302.

What ensued was a free-for-all between two old rivals that cost Boston its only lefthanded starter, Bill Lee, when Nettles dislocated the pitcher's shoulder.

Though the Red Sox, infuriated, scored eight runs in the next three innings and trounced New York, they were never again the same club. They dropped the final two games of the series, ended up firing 1975 Manager of the Year Darrell Johnson in July and finished third. When owner Tom Yawkey died the same summer, it marked the beginning of the dissolution of a ball club.

For several years the Red Sox, loaded with home-grown talent, had been shaping up as the club of the late seventies and early eighties; now the Yankees were replacing them with an imported lineup that was pennant caliber.

Chambliss, Randolph, Nettles and former Indian shortstop Fred Stanley formed their infield, White, Rivers and Gamble the outfield. Piniella, a former Royal, was designated hitter. Munson was catching an entire pitching staff that had been raised on other farms.

And Steinbrenner wasn't done yet. Hours before the trading deadline on June 15 he put together a ten-player deal with Baltimore that involved seven pitchers and two catchers and reaped him left-hander Ken Holtzman, a 20-game winner.

"This trade just won you a pennant," Martin recalls Steinbrenner saying. "You now have the best team on paper and now you're a push-button manager." But Martin was appalled. "It was one of the most ridiculous trades I had ever seen or heard of," he decided.

Three of the departed Yankees were lefthanders, a must in the Stadium. Steinbrenner had given up a promising young catcher in Rick Dempsey for a lesser one in Elrod Hendricks. Still, New York immediately won eight straight games and opened a 15-game lead in July.

When the inevitable slippage occurred—six out of seven in August—Steinbrenner was shocked. Martin had turned down his request to have a recorded Steinbrenner fight-talk played to his club in spring training. Now the owner wanted to pep up his pitchers and dropped by before a game to give them a speech. Martin recalls the scene vividly.

"You guys don't want it bad enough," Steinbrenner told them. "You're not giving one hundred percent. You guys are Yankees and you have to play like Yankees." The pitchers listened, straight-faced, then laughed at Steinbrenner after he left, according to the manager. "They didn't pay any attention," Martin said. "He thought they did, but they didn't."

The slump ended in due time and by the end of August New York's lead had swollen to 11½

games. Even a blown four-game Stadium series to the Orioles, the only challenger left, proved harmless. The Yankees clinched the divisional title in a Detroit restaurant while listening to Baltimore lose by phone, then squirted champagne on each other.

A best-of-five playoff (another novelty since 1964) still loomed with the Royals, though, and it began with bad feeling between Martin and two Kansas City players.

The Yankees had traded George Brett's brother Ken to Chicago and pitcher Larry Gura to the Royals two days apart that spring. "Brett told reporters I had lied to his brother and Gura said I had lied to him," Martin said. "He said I had promised him a starting job."

As Martin watched, delighted, Brett threw wildly to first trying to complete a bases-loaded double play to give the Yankees two first-inning runs, and New York went on to drill Gura (while Martin heckled him) for 12 hits and win the opener, 4–1, at Kansas City.

But the ease of the victory was deceptive. The Yankees made five errors in the second game, failed to hold a 3–2 lead in the sixth and lost, 7–3. In game three they had to rally from a 3–0 first inning deficit to win, 5–3. And in game four, despite Nettles's two home runs, the Royals roughed up Catfish Hunter for five runs on five hits in three innings, won 7–4 and forced the issue to the limit.

When John Mayberry rocked a two-run homer off Figueroa in the first inning, the Yankees found themselves in deep trouble. By the eighth inning, though, New York had chased not only starter Dennis Leonard but relievers Paul Splittorff, Marty Pattin and Andy Hassler and established a 6–3 lead.

But Figueroa, tiring, put two Royals on base in the eighth, with Brett due up, and Martin replaced him with Grant Jackson, one of the more anonymous journeymen in the league until he'd gone 8–0 for the Orioles in 1973 after eight years of mediocrity. Moments later it was tied, 6–6, after Brett had pounded a ball over the right-field fence.

"The whole scene," Martin said, "came down to who could score one run first." So it went to the bottom of the ninth with Chambliss leading off and the clock showing after eleven p.m.

Littell, Kansas City's fifth pitcher, served up a fastball that Chambliss, after blasting it on a line to right field, stood at the plate and watched rise. He saw Royals outfielders Al Cowens and Hal McRae stare at the ball, then watched McRae leap for it and come down with glove empty.

"By the time Chambliss was on third all hope of reaching the plate was gone," said Munson, who'd still been in full catching gear when Cham-

Chambliss jumps for joy as he watches his home run disappear into the stands, giving the team their first pennant since 1964.

"People say it was a great year, but how can it be great when you lose 4 straight," Martin asked. "But next year, we're going to go all the way."

bliss swung and had jumped, ecstatic, from the dugout. "He never did make it."

At least not until much later. Accompanied by two policemen, Chambliss finally emerged from the clubhouse and touched home plate, just to make it official. Inside, his teammates partied until two a.m., then returned seven hours later to board a bus for LaGuardia Airport and a flight to Cincinnati—and both a World Series and a group of Reds that were unlike any the Yankees had ever seen.

To begin with, the Series was mostly at night, the air so cold that portable heaters had to be rigged in the dugouts. "When are we going to stop letting TV tell us when we are going to play?" griped Martin, who'd once saved a Series after his first baseman had lost a ball in the sun. "This is asinine, playing night games in October. It's damn near freezing out there."

And the Reds were hardly the compliant chumps that the Yankees had dispatched in four straight in 1939 and five games in 1961. This was the Big Red Machine of Pete Rose, Johnny Bench, Tony Perez and Joe Morgan that had beaten the Red Sox in a dramatic 1975 Series, retained their divisional title by ten games and swept Eastern leader Philadelphia for the pennant.

The Reds were rested, had a 20-game winner ready in lefthander Don Gullett (whom the Yankees were to sign as a free agent in November) and were playing at home. The Yankees, with only one day between the playoff and Series games, were down to their number five starter, Doyle Alexander, whom Martin considered marginal.

Morgan blasted a two-out homer off Alexander in the first inning, Gullett held New York to five hits and the Reds ruled, 5–1. The second game, which New York had struggled gamely to tie after Cincinnati had jumped on Hunter for three runs in the second inning, came unglued with two outs in the ninth after Reds outfielder Ken Griffey had hit what appeared to be an inning-ending grounder to Stanley at shortstop. But Stanley threw the ball into the Reds' dugout, Griffey wound up on second and Perez singled him home with a line drive. Steinbrenner, irate, forbade Martin to ever start Stanley again. "I'll get rid of him, Billy," Martin recalls Steinbrenner warning, "if you play him."

Back in the Bronx, nothing changed. Cincinnati ripped Ellis for three runs in the second inning of game three, banged out 13 hits and won, 6–2. For the second time in three Series, the Yankees were facing a sweep and seemed helpless to prevent one.

They would take the lead for the only time in the first inning of game four, when Munson singled with two out, but Bench hit one three-run homer in the fourth and another in the ninth to rout New York, 7–2. While Martin wept in the trainer's room

Cincinnati manager Sparky Anderson was insulting the Yankee MVP at the post-game press conference. "Munson is an outstanding player and he would hit .300 in the National League," Anderson said. "But don't ever embarrass nobody by comparing them to Johnny Bench."

Meanwhile, Steinbrenner sought out Martin in the clubhouse. "If daggers could have come out of the man's eyes they would have," Martin said. "He was looking at me like, 'How can you do this to me?'—as if I had lost the Series in four straight on purpose, like he was embarrassed. Who the hell wasn't embarrassed?

"The Reds outplayed us. It was then that George decided he was going to make some changes, that he was really going to get into things, because he wasn't going to be embarrassed like that again."

1977

It was a feat that was Ruthian in its dimensions, but Babe Ruth had never done it. No baseball player had. Three home runs on three consecutive swings of the bat were unlikely enough, but to produce them in the final game of the World Series was stuff for Cooperstown.

"Nothing can top this," Reggie Jackson concluded, after his three homers had brought the Yankees an 8–4 victory over Los Angeles and their first world championship since 1962. "Who in hell's ever going to hit three home runs in a deciding World Series game? I won't. Babe Ruth, Hank Aaron, Joe DiMaggio ... at least I was with them for one night."

In statistical fact Jackson had surpassed them. He not only hit the first pitch into the Yankee Stadium seats in his final three at-bats, but also set a Series record for most homers (five), all of them coming in his last nine at-bats, the last four on consecutive swings in the final two games.

Even the Dodgers, realizing that each blow was sealing their fate more irrevocably, were moved. "I must admit when he hit the third one, and I was sure nobody was looking, I applauded into my glove," said first baseman Steve Garvey.

It was a stunning climax to one of the most turbulent seasons in Yankee history, during which the owner argued with his manager, the manager with Jackson, and Jackson with virtually all of his teammates.

New York had won 100 games, retained the pennant and won a Series for the first time in fifteen years (by far the longest drought in Yankee history), yet the consuming issue from November through October had been Reggie.

He had played on two world championship clubs at Oakland and built a career out of the long ball (no American Leaguer hit more during the seventies) and clutch hitting in October, when it counted most. After A's owner Charles Finley had traded him to Baltimore after the 1975 season Jackson had played out his option and declared himself a free agent.

Owner George Steinbrenner wooed Jackson personally during the month following the 1976 Series, dining with him at the "21" Club and flying to Chicago to meet him for Thanksgiving breakfast. Four clubs sought Reggie after he'd announced his displeasure with the Orioles, but Jackson had gone with the Yankees.

"Steinbrenner took it on his own to hunt me down," Jackson said. "He's like me. He's a little crazy but he's a hustler. It was like trying to hustle a girl in a bar. Some clubs offered several hundred thousand dollars more, possibly seven figures more, but the reason I'm a Yankee is that George Steinbrenner outhustled everybody else."

The terms of the contract were staggering— a $2.6-million package over five years. Only pitcher Catfish Hunter had ever reaped more from New York management, but Hunter hadn't arrived in the Bronx brimming with Jackson's confident oratory. Both the money and the oratory were resented by a number of Jackson's new teammates —particularly captain Thurman Munson, who'd been assured by Steinbrenner, when he'd foresworn free agency and signed a four-year contract the previous March, that only Hunter would draw a higher wage.

Munson was one of the few Yankees who'd come up through the club's farm system and had endured the fourth- and fifth-place finishes of the late sixties and early seventies. He was the constant, the gruff team leader holding the club together from behind the plate as its first captain since Lou Gehrig. Now came Jackson, more highly paid (if you counted the deferred money and bonuses) and taking on the role as franchise savior. Their relationship, marginally cordial to begin with, was ruptured permanently when *Sport* magazine's May issue hit the stands with comments Jackson had reportedly made in spring training.

"It all flows from me," Jackson was quoted as saying. "I've got to keep it all going. I'm the straw that stirs the drink ... Munson thinks he can be the straw that stirs the drink, but he can only stir it bad."

Munson, who'd led the Yankees to their first pennant in a dozen years in 1976, fumed. "He

Reggie Jackson arrived in New York, signed as a free agent for a $2.6-million package over 5 years.

Ron Guidry won his first Yankee game and added 15 more for a 16–7 record, tying with Figueroa (16–11).

Sparky Lyle won the Cy Young Award, with 72 relief appearances and a 13–5 record, 26 saves and 2.17 ERA.

Mike Torrez was obtained from Oakland in April in a trade that sent Dock Ellis to the A's.

Billy Martin and Reggie Jackson had an angry confrontation in Boston. The manager pulled the outfielder during an inning and accused him of loafing in the field.

The new Yankee shortstop was Bucky Dent, obtained from the White Sox in a deal for Oscar Gamble.

Graig Nettles was no slouch at bat, either. His career-high 37 homers and 107 RBIs are both the most ever by a Yankee third baseman.

Torrez pitched 2 complete Series game victories, including the game 6 finale—his last game as a Yankee, defecting to the Red Sox as a free agent in November.

Reggie ripped three homers on three consecutive pitches in the game 6 finale.

Mayor Beame, Steinbrenner and Martin celebrate the first Yankee World Championship since 1962 in a rain-soaked parade in New York.

made it clear he would never forgive Reggie for it," said Billy Martin, "and I don't think he ever did. It always stuck in his craw."

Meanwhile, relations between Jackson and Martin were decidedly cool. Jackson had been pursued, won and signed by Steinbrenner and it was to Steinbrenner he felt he owed his allegiance.

"He said there would be no problems: 'George and I see eye to eye on everything'," Martin would say, irritated. "He forgot one guy—Billy Martin."

Martin had managed a club that won the pennant by 10½ games without Jackson; Jackson would be only one man among twenty-five in the Bronx.

So Martin ignored Steinbrenner's suggestions to bat Jackson in the cleanup spot in the order, preferring first baseman Chris Chambliss. "Who was it who hit the home run off Mark Littell to win the pennant?" Martin said. "George didn't remember that."

Jackson would bat fifth, and occasionally, when Martin figured the percentages weren't good, he benched Jackson against certain pitchers. A confrontation was inevitable and it came on national television in Boston during a weekend series in June.

The Yankees had lost Friday's game and were trailing 7–4 in the sixth on Saturday afternoon, thanks to five Red Sox home runs. Then Boston's Jim Rice lofted a long fly ball toward Jackson in right.

"He jogged toward the ball," Martin fumed, "fielded it on about the fiftieth hop, took his sweet time throwing it in and made a weak throw in the general direction of the pitcher's mound."

So Rice wound up on second and Martin sent out Paul Blair to replace Jackson. Moments later a network audience that included Steinbrenner watched Martin and Jackson shout at each other in the dugout.

"You showed me up," Jackson yelled. "You showed me up. How could you do it to me on television?" Curses followed. "I tried to get him," Martin said. "I went right after him and Elston Howard tried to stop me and I threw him out of the way."

Finally, coach Yogi Berra restrained Martin, and Jackson showered and left the park. The next day President Gabe Paul got Martin and Jackson together in his room for breakfast and an armistice. Instead, the dispute flared anew.

"Nobody's restraining me now," Martin told Jackson. "You wanted to fight me yesterday. How about now? Right now." Tempers cooled, but when the club arrived in Detroit Steinbrenner was waiting for Martin.

"How could you have done a thing like that?" Steinbrenner asked. If it were up to him,

Steinbrenner said, Martin would be fired, but he would leave the decision to Paul. Steinbrenner had already talked with Jackson and reserve catcher/peacemaker Fran Healy, who'd persuaded him not to dismiss Martin over one incident.

Still, Martin walked a tightrope. He'd signed a contract that allowed management to fire him if they felt his conduct was unworthy, if he criticized the front office or wasn't available daily at the ball park for consultation.

Steinbrenner had already fined Martin $2,500 in May for ripping management decisions. By July, with the club in first place, the owner-manager relationship reached a crisis point. Finally, Munson and outfielder Lou Piniella went to Steinbrenner's hotel room in Milwaukee.

"You've got to get off Billy's back," Munson would recall they told him. "You're driving him crazy. If you're going to fire him, fire him. If you're not, leave him alone and let him manage."

Steinbrenner agreed to remove the irksome provisos from Martin's contract, but he wanted some answers. For his manager's benefit he scribbled the batting averages of the New York, Boston and Baltimore lineups on a blackboard and compared them. "Well, what's wrong with the team?" he asked Martin.

"You, George, you're what's wrong with the team," Martin says he told him. "You're meddling all the time, you're creating problems leaking out stories to the newspapers. You're the problem. That isn't like the New York Yankees. We don't leak stories or do things like that. That's unlike any Yankee I ever saw in my life."

The stability and consistency that had always been a franchise hallmark had vanished. Within two weeks word filtered back to Martin that Steinbrenner had been asking around about Los Angeles manager Walter Alston, that he had offered Yankee coach Dick Howser Martin's job. Several days later Steinbrenner released his "Seven Commandments" by which Martin would henceforth be judged.

- Does he win?
- Does he work hard enough?
- Is he emotionally equipped to lead the men under him?
- Is he organized?
- Is he prepared?
- Does he understand human nature?
- Is he honorable?

Then, shortly thereafter, Steinbrenner told Martin he was doing a "great job," raised his salary to $90,000 and gave him a two-year contract. So it went.

The Yankees overhauled Boston down the stretch, Jackson hit a grand slam in the clinching game, and New York prepared to meet Kansas City again for the pennant playoff.

Once again it would go to the full five games and in the finale Martin would take a gamble—knowing his job was on the line by doing so—and bench Jackson against Royals lefthander Paul Splittorff, who'd always given him problems.

Once Splittorff had been replaced by right-hander Doug Bird in the eighth, Jackson singled home a run as a pinch hitter that helped New York erase a 3–1 deficit and win the game, 5–3, and the pennant. Afterward, Martin doused Steinbrenner with champagne. "That's for trying to fire me," Martin crowed. Steinbrenner was not amused. "What do you mean 'try'?" he replied. "If I want to fire you, I'll fire you."

So it continued, as New York met Los Angeles in the World Series. "After Kansas City," Martin felt, "the Dodgers were a piece of cake." New York won three of the first four games to take total control. Even after the Dodgers siphoned off game five, the championship seemed secure enough for Steinbrenner to give Martin a large bonus that included a Lincoln Continental, say he'd pay for Martin's apartment and agree to keep him on for 1978.

That night, as the Series returned to New York in game six, Jackson made it secure. With the Yankees trailing 3–2 in the fourth he ripped a low inside fastball on a line 370 feet into the right-field seats for two runs.

That disposed of starter Burt Hooten. In the fifth Jackson hit the same pitch to the same spot, again with a man on, to make it 7–3 and chase reliever Elias Sosa. Then in the eighth inning he demolished a Charlie Hough knuckler, sending the ball 500 feet into the bleachers in dead center. Three swings, three homers.

"Twenty or thirty years ago you might have made a movie like this," third baseman Graig Nettles said. "Today people would never believe it."

For the first time since 1962, when second baseman Bobby Richardson gloved a Willie McCovey line drive in Candlestick Park, the Yankees were world champions. Martin's job was guaranteed, Jackson's salary justified (a candy bar would even be named after him, just as he'd wanted). And Steinbrenner, who'd once lost a quarter of a million dollars on a forgettable basketball team called the Cleveland Pipers, was standing atop his world.

"I was happy for George," Martin would admit. "Because George wanted it so bad. I said to myself, 'Now he can really have fun at the "21" Club. He'll go around and give rings out to his friends and he'll be able to talk about this one as long as he lives.' "

1978

Boston pitcher Mike Torrez had already left the mound, certain that the fly ball to left field was routine, that the seventh inning was over and he still had his 2–0 lead and his four-hitter and his former teammates well under control.

"Then I looked over my shoulder on the way to the dugout, and I couldn't believe it," Torrez said. "Yaz is backing to the wall, popping his glove, looking up. I said, 'What's this? What the . . .' "

The routine fly, lofted by a Yankee shortstop named Bucky Dent who'd hit only .140 in his last 20 games and just fouled a ball off his own ankle, had dropped weakly into the netting above the Green Monster, Fenway Park's tantalizingly close wall.

" 'Goddam,' I was saying to myself," Torrez remembered later. " 'Goddam, how could that happen?' It's still hard to believe. I've seen the replays on television, Carlton Fisk calling for the fastball inside. It went exactly where I wanted it but Bucky hit it just hard enough to get out of the park with that breeze."

And Chris Chambliss, Roy White and Dent had all trotted joyously around the bases, wiping out Boston's lead and setting the stage for a Reggie Jackson homer in the eighth that would cap the most stirring comeback in league history.

The Yankees, trailing the Red Sox by 14 games on July 19, had come from the dead to grab first place on September 13, had lost sole possession on the final day of the season and had won only the second playoff in American League history to get it back.

From there the Yankees would wipe out Kansas City for their third straight pennant and make World Series history by losing the first two games to the Dodgers then sweeping the next four.

Along the way they'd accepted manager Billy Martin's tearful resignation, rehired him five days later for the 1980 season and finished out the summer with Bob Lemon, who'd been dismissed by the White Sox in June. Given all that, Dent's flukish homer moments after changing bats merely fit into the grand pattern.

From the beginning it had been an unsettled season, reflected in the standings, the clubhouse, and newspaper headlines. Five players, including captain Thurman Munson, were fined for missing the Welcome Home luncheon on opening day. "After six games and one week of false serenity," Jack Wilkinson wrote in the New York

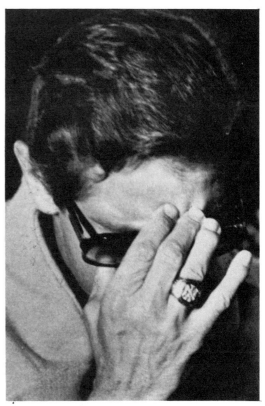

Lou Pinella batted .314, the Yankees' only .300 hitter.

Bob Lemon succeeded Martin as manager.

The season's first half was filled with tension and pressure, as the Yankees fell 14 games behind the Red Sox. Tearfully, Billy Martin resigned in late July.

Rich Gossage was signed as a free agent and was named Fireman of the Year with 27 saves and 10 victories, while relieving 63 times.

Martin stole the show at Old Timers' Day when it was announced he would manage the team again in 1980.

Rich Gossage leaps into Thurman Munson's arms as the Yankees eliminate the Royals to win the pennant.

Thurman Munson's season wasn't without frustration despite hitting .297, the team's second-best average, snapping his streak of three straight years over .300.

Reggie Jackson extends his hand to Yankee president
Al Rosen and owner George Steinbrenner after slamming an
eighth-inning homer that proved the title-deciding run
in the one-game playoff at Boston.

Bucky Dent won the Series MVP. He hit .417 and accounted
for more than a quarter of the Yankees' 36-run total, driving
in 7 and scoring 3, as the Yankees defeated the Dodgers for
the World Championship.

Daily News, "life is back to normal with the Yankees."

They were defending world champions, thought Graig Nettles, not a Rotary group. "If they're looking for somebody to play 160 games at third base," he said, "I'm their man. If they're looking for somebody to attend luncheons, let them hire Georgie Jessel."

The club didn't rise above the .500 mark until April 28, lost seven out of eight on the West Coast in early June and fell eight games behind Boston on June 18. By July 8 the gap had grown to 11½ games, then 14. Four pitchers (Catfish Hunter, Don Gullett, Dick Tidrow and Andy Messersmith) were all hurting and injuries had knocked regulars Willie Randolph, Mickey Rivers, Thurman Munson and Dent out of the lineup at various times.

With pennant hopes glimmering and tensions running high one incident was likely to cause a firestorm of turbulence. When Jackson ignored Martin's change of signals and fouled out bunting after being ordered to hit away in the tenth inning of a 7–7 game at Kansas City that the Yankees lost, the fuse was there.

Martin had Jackson suspended for five games. When he rejoined the club in Chicago Jackson told reporters, "I don't know why he suspended me." Then Martin learned from White Sox owner Bill Veeck that Yankee owner George Steinbrenner, who'd given Martin a public vote of confidence less than a month earlier, had wanted to swap Martin for Lemon.

When the club reached O'Hare Airport, Martin's head was filled with Jackson, Steinbrenner and what he believed to be their deceptions. "The two of them deserve each other," Martin told two New York sportswriters. "One's a born liar, the other's convicted," alluding to Steinbrenner's contributions to the 1972 presidential election. It was a tender subject with Steinbrenner and Martin knew it. "I didn't mean it about George," he would say. "How he came into it I don't know. I meant it about the other guy. I was mad at the other guy."

When his players read those comments the next morning they realized the consequences. "He's gone," predicted pitcher Ken Clay. Steinbrenner, informed of Martin's quotes by telephone, had hinted at dismissal. "I've got to believe that no boss in his right mind would take that," he'd said.

Instead, Martin made the move. He called a press conference the next day in the lobby of the club's Kansas City hotel. He started by saying he would answer no questions. "That means now and forever, because I am a Yankee and Yankees do not talk or throw rocks.

"I don't want to hurt this team's chances for the pennant with this undue publicity," he began reading. "The team has a shot at the pennant and

I hope they win it. I owe it to my health and my mental well-being to resign. At this time I'm also sorry about those things that were written about George Steinbrenner. He does not deserve them nor did I say them. I've had my differences with George but we've been able to resolve them. I would like to thank the Yankee management ... the press, the news media, my coaches, my players and most of all ... the fans."

The final sentence had been disrupted by his own sobs. Martin left abruptly with Phil Rizzuto's arm around him, spent the afternoon in a small country-and-western bar nearby, then flew to Florida to see Mickey Mantle.

That night Steinbrenner called Martin's agent, Doug Newton. He didn't feel right, Steinbrenner said, about not having Martin as manager. So two days later Martin was sitting down with Steinbrenner in his suite at New York's Carlyle Hotel, sipping iced tea and talking about coming back for the 1979 season.

They both liked each other, they admitted. Maybe they hadn't talked enough. After both men promised to reform their idiosyncrasies and stay in better touch, they agreed that Martin would reclaim his job for the 1980 season. Lemon, whom Steinbrenner had hired after all, would be given the chance to manage for a full year more, then would become general manager.

The announcement would be made three days later at the Stadium just prior to Old Timers' Day. Management smuggled Martin, wearing dark glasses and a hat, into the Stadium through a side entrance.

"It was high drama, like a CIA maneuver," he said. "They took me to a little closet underneath the Stadium where I put on my uniform. I could hear the loudspeaker announcing the names of the old timers as I dressed. Then they sneaked me into a boiler room near the dugout."

When Martin sprinted from the dugout in pinstripes, waving his cap, the crowd cheered him for ten minutes; meanwhile, Lemon, an affable man with the unruffled nature of an Ohio town mayor, would direct a Yankee club that had already begun to come back together.

While the Red Sox, missing shortstop Rick Burleson and captain Carl Yastrzemski, lost 11 of 14 games in the second half of July, New York won 12 of 16 and whittled Boston's lead to 6½ games. When they met at Fenway Park on September 7 for a four-game series, the result turned an entire season around. The opener, before a capacity crowd that began pouring out into Yawkey Way, disgusted, after four innings, set the tone.

"It didn't matter who Boston put in there," Lyle said, "whether it was Torrez, Hassler, Drago or Campbell. Whoever was in there got pounded. To be down for so long and to have to hear about the unbeatable Red Sox all year and how they're better than the 1927 Yankees and all that crap, well, we beat them 15–3 and it was just terrific."

The next night New York led 8–0 after two innings, won 13–2 and cut the deficit to two games. The rest, played in broad weekend daylight, was easy. Ron Guidry, on his way to the best season (25–3) of any Yankee pitcher since Whitey Ford in 1961, shut out Boston, 7–0, on Saturday. No lefthander had done that to Boston in four years. "I can't believe what I've been seeing," said New York pitching coach Clyde King. "I could understand if an expansion team fell apart like that but Boston's got the best record in baseball. It can't go on."

Yet it did. New York rubbed out the Red Sox, 7–4, on Sunday and pulled into a tie for first place. It was the first time since 1968 that the Red Sox had lost a four-game series at home, and manager Don Zimmer was humiliated. "I don't know what happened," he muttered. "For four days I looked at the scoreboard in the third or fourth inning and we're trailing by five or six runs and they have twelve or fifteen hits."

A week later, New York took two of three from Boston at the Stadium, consolidated their lead at 2½ games and began printing playoff tickets. The Red Sox, who'd been 51–19 at one point, were floundering and confused. "Every day you sit in front of your locker and ask God what the hell is going on," said shortstop Rick Burleson.

Yet the Red Sox, stung by comparison to the classic "choke" teams in baseball history—the 1951 and 1962 Dodgers and the 1964 Phillies—regrouped to win 12 of their final 14 games and their last eight straight. When the Yankees stubbed their toes, 9–2, on the Indians in the season finale, the Red Sox had pulled even. "This is the way it should be," Lyle realized. A playoff at Fenway Park, Guidry versus Torrez.

For six innings the Red Sox owned it. Yastrzemski had belted a homer in the second and Jim Rice had knocked in Burleson from third in the sixth. And Torrez, who'd come to Boston from the Yankees as a free agent over the winter, had clamped down tight. In the first, fourth and fifth innings he put the leadoff man on base and then retired the side.

Then Chambliss and White nicked him for singles in the seventh and Dent hit his pop fly toward Yastrzemski. "I didn't know it cleared the wall," Dent admitted, "until I was past first base."

So it was New York 3, Boston 2 and the Yankees quickly added another run on a walk, a stolen base and a double by Munson off reliever Bob Stanley. When Jackson dumped a fastball into the center-field bleachers in the eighth it appeared mere frosting. Instead, it proved the winning run as the Red Sox pushed until the final out.

A double by second baseman Jerry Remy

in the eighth had been followed by three singles that produced two runs. Now, with the late afternoon sun covering right field with a blinding glare, Yankee outfielder Lou Piniella became a central figure.

He'd snared a drive down the line by Fred Lynn with two out in the sixth that might have scored two runs. Now with Burleson on first and one out in the ninth, Remy lashed a ball that Piniella couldn't find in the sun—but pretended to. "If you start pounding your glove like you have it," he reasoned, "then the runner can't go." So Piniella played the ball on the bounce, conceded Remy a single and held Burleson on second. Then Rice rapped a long fly which Piniella again couldn't find. "Oh no," Piniella thought. "I'm not going to catch it and they're going to win the pennant."

Somehow he located the ball. Had Burleson been on third, it was a tied game. Instead, Burleson now advanced there with two out, not one. Now Yastrzemski needed a base hit.

Goose Gossage, who'd relieved Guidry in the seventh, was determined to make Yastrzemski hit his best pitch—a fastball tailing inside—to do it. What resulted was a high pop fly barely foul behind third base that Nettles (Georgie Jessel could not have made the play) settled under as everybody inside Fenway froze. Moments later Yastrzemski was weeping, the Yankees were pounding each other in celebration and Jackson was marveling at the hair's breadth by which a season had been decided. "The 163rd game, 5–4 with a man on third and two out in the ninth," he said.

After that the pennant playoff was an anti-climax. The Yankees split the first two games in Kansas City, which was their goal, then polished the Royals off in the Bronx in four.

Was the dynasty back in full flower? "A dynasty doesn't fall fourteen games behind," Lemon figured. Or lose the first two games in the Series as New York did at Dodger Stadium by counts of 11–5 and 4–3. As dramatic punctuation Los Angeles rookie Bob Welch had struck out Jackson with two out and two on and a full count in the ninth inning of game two. "Aviation fuel all the way," Jackson admitted. "High octane. The kid came right at me."

Back in New York with a pulsating crowd behind them, the Yankees tore the Series away. "We've got 'em overconfident and tired," Nettles joked. "Tired of running around those bases." Three games and three New York victories later (5–1, 4–3 and 12–2), the Dodgers boarded a westbound jet, shattered. "I don't like this town, I don't like this park, I don't understand these people, I don't understand their existence," said center fielder Rick Monday.

The end came quickly in game six—New York 7, Los Angeles 2—and the resurrection was complete.

"What we've done," proclaimed Dent, who would become a folk hero over the winter, "will give a lot of teams years from now incentive. They'll say, 'Hey, look at the '78 Yankees. They didn't quit.' "

1979

He had decided that the commuting probably wasn't a wise idea, that a job in the Bronx and a family in Canton, Ohio linked by a private jet was impractical, probably unfair to teammates that had to travel with the club, and possibly dangerous.

"Why are you flying this thing?" Yankee manager Billy Martin had asked catcher Thurman Munson. "Does George know you're flying?"

Yes, Munson replied, the owner knew. The Cessna Citation, Munson's $1.3-million half-shuttle, half-toy, had even been written into his contract; if Munson died while piloting it, the Yankees had to pay the rest of his salary.

Still, Martin was worried. He'd flown from Albuquerque to Kansas City with Munson in an ice storm and had noticed a flash coming from an engine.

"Maybe that was when I switched on the de-icer," Munson mused.

"No way," Martin had told him. "I've never seen flames come out of an engine like that. You better check it out."

So mechanics had inspected the engine in Kansas City, found that the rotors were mashed and bent, and replaced it. Now George Steinbrenner, who'd originally given Munson permission to fly, wanted him to change his mind. He did, Martin would report; Munson and his wife would take an apartment in New Jersey. Two weeks later he was dead in a flaming wreckage after a training run had gone awry. Team publicist Mickey Morabito called Martin.

"I was standing there, holding the phone, and I started crying," Martin would say. "For five minutes all I did was cry. I couldn't say a thing."

There was nothing left to say, and with two months left in the 1979 season, no reason left to play. Munson's death was the final punctuation mark to a season that had been doomstruck from the beginning and laced through with sour incidents.

Gossage was sidelined with a torn ligament suffered in a clubhouse scuffle with reserve catcher Cliff Johnson. Rookie Ron Davis stepped in and had a 14–2 record, plus 9 saves in 44 relief jobs.

Tommy John was signed as a free agent and led Yankee pitchers with a 21–9 record, 2.96 ERA.

Bobby Murcer returned after a late-June deal, becoming one of 47 players to wear pinstripes in the season, a Yankee record, as Mickey Rivers, Chris Chambliss and Roy White played their final Yankee seasons.

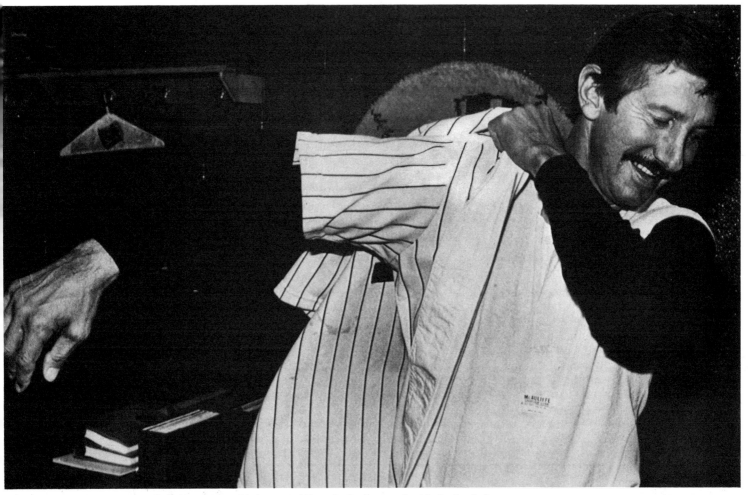

Billy Martin replaced Bob Lemon in mid-June, and Reggie Jackson asked to be traded.

THURMAN MUNSON
NEW YORK YANKEES
JUNE 7, 1947 - AUGUST 2, 1979
YANKEE CAPTAIN
"OUR CAPTAIN AND LEADER HAS NOT LEFT US-
TODAY, TOMORROW, THIS YEAR, NEXT...
OUR ENDEAVORS WILL REFLECT OUR
LOVE AND ADMIRATION FOR HIM."

The nation was stunned when Thurman Munson was killed on August 2 when the jet he was piloting crashed in his Ohio hometown. The Yankees announced neither Munson's number nor his locker would ever be used again, and a Yankee Stadium plaque was dedicated by his widow Diana the following September.

The Yankees had entered the season brimming with confidence after a 1978 campaign that had produced the most dramatic comeback in American League history (from 14 games out on July 19 to the pennant) and a world championship over the Dodgers after the loss of the first two games.

For the first time in five years there was harmony between the front office and the manager's chair, where placid Bob Lemon sat. The lineup was stable, the pitching staff even stronger since Steinbrenner had spent more than $2 million in the free-agent bazaar on Dodger lefthander Tommy John (who'd win 21) and Red Sox right-hander Luis Tiant (who'd win 13).

But this time New York fell 14 games behind the division leader (Baltimore this season) and stayed there. This time Lemon, who'd replaced Martin in mid-season the year before, was replaced by Martin in mid-season. This time reliever Goose Gossage, who'd saved 27 games including the playoff victory over Boston, tore thumb ligaments during a clubhouse scuffle with backup catcher Cliff Johnson and missed three months. Stability seemed a dozen years ago.

The Yankees would share first place for one day—April 20—then come apart during their first West Coast swing, losing seven of nine. By June 18 New York had slipped to fourth place, 8½ games behind the Orioles, and Steinbrenner was calling Martin.

"Billy, Lemon is doing a terrible job, just terrible," Martin heard Steinbrenner say. "He has no control over the players, he's not doing anything, the poor guy can't do it."

The fact that Lemon's son had recently been killed in an automobile accident no doubt played a part in Lemon's ineffectiveness. Still, Steinbrenner wanted a change and he was willing to overlook the fact that Martin wasn't due back until the 1980 season (having resigned and been rehired during July of 1978 with that understanding), that Martin had scuffled with a reporter in Reno during the off-season and that Steinbrenner had wanted him to clear himself of charges there before Martin got the job.

Nothing mattered. Martin was back in pinstripes less than a year after he'd resigned. Turmoil accompanied him. That night Jackson, who'd squabbled with Martin for much of the previous year, went to Steinbrenner and asked, unsuccessfully, to be traded. Then president Al Rosen, who'd been a teammate and close friend of Lemon, quit in July.

Meanwhile, the club plummeted further behind Baltimore each week. On August 2 the Yankees were 14 games out of first place and had been written off. As they arrived home after a midwestern road trip Munson was in Canton, practic-

ing takeoffs and landings. He failed to clear an embankment at the end of the runway, sheared off the wings on a clump of treetops and missed the runway by 1,000 feet.

The flight instructor and a friend of Munson pulled themselves clear but reserve fuel ignited and consumed Munson. A witness called the Stadium and asked for Steinbrenner. "It's a matter of life and death," he said.

"Oh my God," Steinbrenner gasped, hearing the news. "Oh, no."

Munson was only thirty-two, yet he'd been the linchpin of the franchise, its captain, its symbol, since 1970. He'd played for five managers, toasted three pennants and seen the pitching staff transformed, then transformed again.

They held a service for him at the Stadium the next night, leaving the spot behind the plate symbolically empty as a crowd of 51,150 saluted Munson's memory with an eight-minute standing ovation, and the club announced that neither his number nor his locker would ever be used again. And three days later the entire team flew to Canton for its captain's burial.

"I still can't believe it," right fielder Lou Piniella murmured. "I still can't believe I'm not going to walk into the locker room and see him standing there and it's all going to be a nightmare."

Any chance for a Yankee comeback duplicating that of 1978 died with Munson. The club lost five of its next eight games and went on to finish fourth, 13½ games behind the Orioles.

"The whole bottom fell out of the team," Martin would say. "It was difficult from then on. Wins didn't matter quite so much and the losses became tougher. Thurman's death took everything out of the club."

1980

Over in a corner of the Kansas City clubhouse, Royals owner Ewing Kauffman was mimicking his Yankee counterpart, George Steinbrenner, leaping to his feet and cursing as his third baseman grounded into a game-ending double play. And at his locker, starter and victor Dennis Leonard was explaining why his teammates were in the process of burying the Second Revival of the New York dynasty.

"The Yankees are good," he conceded, "but they're not the same team we played in '78. They don't have Chambliss swinging the bat, they don't have Rivers slapping the ball and they don't have Munson getting the clutch hit. They're just not the same."

Which was an undeniable fact. Only four New York players remained from the club that two years earlier had beaten the Red Sox in the divisional playoff, the Royals for the pennant and the Dodgers in the Series for their first world championship in sixteen years. Munson had been killed in a plane crash in August of 1979. Then Chris Chambliss, whose ninth-inning home run had won the 1976 pennant, had been traded to Toronto. Rivers had been shipped to Texas. Roy White, the last link to the dark days of the mid-sixties, had gone off reluctantly—at thirty-six—to Japan.

Meanwhile, Kansas City had retained eight men who remembered the bitter playoff losses to the Yankees in 1976, 1977 and 1978 (two of them in the final inning of the fifth game)—but did not feel haunted by them.

"Past history doesn't mean a thing," Royals third baseman George Brett repeated for newspapermen. "Doesn't mean a thing, doesn't mean a thing."

And it didn't. After wiping out New York in the first two games of the 1980 playoff series at Kansas City, the Royals interred their tormentors at the Stadium in game three and completed a sweep that left the Yankees speechless. It was that swift, that total, and all the more unexpected because New York had just completed a rousing regular season during which they'd dethroned defending American League champion Baltimore by winning 28 of their final 37 games.

By recent Yankee standards it had been a mellow summer. Billy Martin, who'd resigned, been rehired and fired all within fifteen months, had been replaced by coach Dick Howser, whose dealings with Steinbrenner were far less spiky.

Diplomatic relations between Steinbrenner and Martin had been severed irrevocably several weeks after the 1979 World Series over, of all things, a fight between Martin and a marshmallow salesman in a hotel bar near the Minneapolis airport.

Martin claimed the salesman goaded him into a fight; in any case the Marshmallow King, as he called himself, ended up with a split lip. "I stood there looking down at him and it was an old story," Martin would say. "I was saying to myself, 'How in the hell did I get into this?' "

Five days later he was out of a job. "How much can we take and still command any respect?" Steinbrenner wondered. "How can the Yankees, as an organization, keep putting their head in the sand?"

So Howser, who'd replaced Martin for a day

The Yankees had a new manager in Dick Howser (l) and a new general manager in Gene Michael.

Rich Gossage came out of the bullpen 64 times and racked up 6 victories, 33 saves and 2.27 ERA.

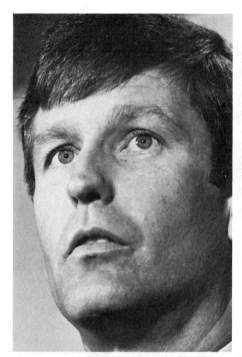

Tommy John again led Yankee pitchers with a 22–9 record, including 6 shutouts.

Rick Cerone was acquired from Toronto in the Chambliss trade to replace Munson. He hit .277 with 85 RBIs.

Joe Lefebvre homered in his first 2 major league games—the only Yankee batter ever to do so.

Lou Pinella hit one of the team's 3 homers in the League championship series.

when he'd resigned in 1978 and had turned down opportunities to replace him permanently the year before, was given the reins.

The only undue excitement during the 1980 season occurred in mid-August when the Yankees were about to blow a 9½-game lead over the Orioles and lose the grip on first place in the American League East they'd held alone since May 14.

Mired in fourth place, 11 games behind New York on July 14, Baltimore had won 25 of 34, including six of eight from the Yankees on consecutive weekends, and eventually reduced the gap to half a game.

"This is fun," Howser decided. "It's demanding and draining and nerve-wracking but it's what baseball is all about."

Yet the schedulemaker, who would not put the two clubs head-to-head at all during the final 45 games, robbed the stretch run of most of its suspense. The Yankees cleaned up in September—rebuilding their lead back to six games by the 17th—and won the divisional title by three games.

When catcher Rick Cerone and right fielder Lou Piniella crunched back-to-back homers off ex-Yankee Larry Gura in the second inning of the playoff opener, nothing seemed to have changed in five years. "Here we go again," Brett thought.

But New York shortstop Bucky Dent, the hero of the 1978 playoff game with Boston, lost a two-out blooper by Frank White with two men on base and let the Royals tie it in the bottom half of the inning. Then Willie Aikens knocked in two more with a two-out, bases-loaded single off Ron Guidry in the fourth, Brett added a 400-foot homer in the seventh and the rout was on. The final was 7–2, and Kansas City would pile it on early the next day, too. Two singles, a triple by Willie Wilson and a double by U. L. Washington got them three runs in the third inning off New York starter Rudy May.

Then, after Graig Nettles had legged out one run on an inside-the-park homer and Willie Randolph had doubled home another to cut Kansas City's lead to 3–2, came the play that would force the Yankees to the brink. With two out in the eighth inning and Randolph on first, Bob Watson bashed a ball off the left-field wall. When Wilson's throw soared over the head of shortstop and cutoff man Washington, New York third base coach Mike Ferraro waved Randolph, who'd stumbled between first and second, on to home.

But Brett, backing up Wilson as a trailer, caught the ball and nailed Randolph at the plate. "You've got to take a chance with two outs," Ferraro reasoned, "especially since we haven't been scoring. Brett had his back turned and he has to turn around and make a perfect throw."

Howser agreed. "The throw was so high I thought Brett was going to call for a fair catch," he said. "I coached third base for ten years and I would have done the same thing."

But Steinbrenner was furious. He criticized Ferraro's judgment to the national press in the clubhouse afterward, then stalked around the room trying to revive his troops. For six innings of game three, New York stayed alive and nursed a 2–1 lead. But with two out in the seventh and nobody on base, Wilson doubled and Washington singled, chasing 22-game winner Tommy John, and Brett greeted reliever Goose Gossage with a 450-foot home run that blew it apart.

"I still think we're the better team," Howser said, but his employer didn't agree. "When Cincinnati swept us in the Series in '76, I vowed to myself that that would never happen again," Steinbrenner said. "Now this. I was never so disappointed. It's embarrassing as hell to me. It was even more embarrassing than Cincinnati."

Before the fall was done Ferraro would be made coach at first base, where there would be few opportunities to send men home. And Howser would be sent packing. Gene Michael, a former Yankee shortstop now general manager at age forty-two, would be Steinbrenner's seventh manager in eight years.

1981

Moments after Bob Watson hit into the final out a typewritten statement was distributed in the Yankee Stadium press box.

"I want to sincerely apologize to the people of New York and to fans of the New York Yankees everywhere for the performance of the Yankee team in the World Series," owner George Steinbrenner had dictated. "I also want to assure you that we will be at work immediately to prepare for 1982."

This was Plan B, one of several options Steinbrenner had toyed with as New York worked its way through the American League mini-series, pennant playoff and its 33rd World Series. Had the Yankees beaten the Dodgers for their 23d world championship their owner presumably would have invoked Plan A and kept the team intact.

But now that New York had squandered a 2–0 Series lead and lost in six games to a Los Angeles club that hadn't won a championship in

Dave Winfield was signed to a record $20-million, long-term contract. The outfielder would hit .294, lead the team in hits, doubles, total bases, RBIs and game-winning RBIs, but would slump to 1-for-22, .045 in the World Series.

Bob Lemon returned as manager in early September.

Southpaw Dave Righetti was Rookie of the Year with an 8–4 record and 2.06 ERA.

Guidry led the Yankee staff with an 11–5 record, a .688 winning percentage.

The pitching staff's 2.90 ERA easily led the League, and Tommy John ranked fourth with a 2.64 mark, winning 9 and losing 8.

Rich Gossage and Ron Davis (r) were a lethal 1–2 punch out of the bullpen. Gossage had 3 victories, 20 saves and an 0.77 ERA in 32 appearances, while Davis had 4 wins, 6 saves and a 2.71 ERA in 43 games.

When injuries sidelined Willie Randolph and Bucky Dent, Larry Milbourne stepped into the lineup, hit .313, and put up a stout defense at second and shortstop.

16 years, Steinbrenner was embarrassed and speculation ran rampant that a bunch of veterans would be gone by spring training.

It was an unsettling climax to the most unsettled season in baseball history, a season broken apart by a 59-day players' strike and crowned with an unprecedented playoff system that matched first- and second-half winners in a mini-series to determine each divisional champion.

Since the overall season's record meant nothing, Cincinnati, whose 66–42 mark was the best in the majors, didn't qualify for a thing. The Yankees, who otherwise would have finished third in the AL East, earned a mini-series date with Milwaukee by winning 34 of 56 first-half games.

What followed was an uninspired second-half effort that led to the dismissal of manager Gene Michael and the rehiring of Bob Lemon, who'd managed the 1978 Yankees to a world championship after taking over from Billy Martin in July.

What Michael inherited was a wealthy but aging (eight regulars over 30) team with a $20-million leftfielder in Dave Winfield, a .284 lifetime hitter whom Steinbrenner had lured from San Diego as a free agent.

What Steinbrenner expected from Winfield and his mates were performances worthy of their paychecks. When the club was pounded at home by Cleveland before a near-capacity Jacket Day crowd in late May, Steinbrenner exploded.

Injuries to Watson, catcher Rick Cerone, centerfielder Jerry Mumphrey and pitchers Tommy John, Goose Gossage and Ron Guidry might have crippled the Yankees physically but errors and mental mistakes the owner could not excuse.

"I'm embarrassed and disgusted," he fumed. "When 55,000 people come out here and pay their hard-earned dough to see this fiasco, I'm embarrassed. But I can tell you this, these guys are the highest-paid players in baseball and if they embarrass New York in Baltimore there's gonna be hell to pay."

But once the Yankees lost three straight to the Orioles and dropped into fifth place, Steinbrenner's focus shifted to Michael.

"Right now Gene's been snakebit," Steinbrenner mused. "The decisions he has made have not been the right ones. I'm not saying the decisions are right or wrong, but they have turned out wrong."

While Michael's fate was being pondered by the owner and "his people" and debated in the tabloids, the Yankees came alive and won 11 of their next 12 games. When the strike came on June 12th, New York found itself two games ahead of Baltimore in first place.

"No other manager has sewed it up this early for George before, have they?" Michael

joked when his club was awarded its mini-series berth when the season resumed in August. But the guarantee was also a liability—New York had no incentive to win the second half.

When the club lost nine of its next 15 and fell into the division cellar, Steinbrenner leveled his gaze once again upon Michael.

"I'll always do what he wants," Michael had said of his boss in May. "He knows that." But now Michael was chafing at what he considered front-office interference, including an off-day practice ordered by Steinbrenner.

"If you're ordering me to do it, I'll do it," Michael told him. "But I'm going to tell the players it's your practice."

"Tell them anything you want," Steinbrenner replied. "I think it has to be done and I'm signing the paychecks."

Privately, Steinbrenner stewed about what he perceived as Michael's failure to be "a good soldier." Michael had hung up on the owner's intermediaries when they called. He'd told newspapermen that Steinbrenner had called him at the start of a Midwestern trip and threatened to dismiss him. "George, if you're going to fire me, do it," Michael had told him. "Tonight before the game. Do it and stop threatening me about it."

Steinbrenner, who felt such conversations should be private, didn't appreciate reading about them. "You can't say those things about your boss and expect to get away with them," Steinbrenner decided. So on September 6 Michael was dismissed. "If George ever manages a team," he would say bitterly, "I hope I own it."

The new manager would be an old manager in Lemon, who'd made up a 14-game deficit on Boston the last time he'd replaced anybody.

"How are you going to turn this thing around?" reporters wondered.

"If I turn things around," Lemon replied, "we'll be losing. I want to keep things going the way they were and they will if I don't get in the way. This is the first time I've ever been in the playoffs before managing one game."

Which turned out to be his club's main problem down the stretch. The sole reward for winning both halves of the season was an extra home game in the best-of-five mini-series. Whenever the Yankees played Milwaukee or Boston, the inequality of emotion was obvious.

"They're playing pressure baseball," outfielder Lou Piniella sighed after the Red Sox had scored seven runs in the eighth to win, 8–5, at Fenway Park in mid-September. "They're counting down. Fourteen games, thirteen. If we win or lose it doesn't make any difference. Here we are just waiting to play somebody."

That somebody was Milwaukee, which had edged Detroit and Boston by 1½ games in the second half. The Yankees had finished fifth with a 25–26 record (11–14 under Lemon), but their record was quickly forgotten as the club headed west for the mini-series opener.

If nothing else the guaranteed spot had given the Yankees a chance to get healthy and put their pitching rotation in order. With Cerone, Mumphrey, Watson and Gossage all back in form the Yankees were ready to play their kind of baseball—which meant blinding pitching, taut defense and timely hitting.

But the key was the relief work of Gossage and Ron Davis, who routinely mopped up the final four innings of most games. In the opener, after New York had climbed out of a 2–0 hole with four runs in the fourth, Davis and Gossage took over for Guidry and shut out the Brewers the rest of the way with untouchable fastballs.

The next afternoon, after rookie Dave Righetti had struck out ten Brewers and allowed only four hits in six scoreless innings, Lemon again summoned Davis and Gossage to nail down a 3–0 victory and push Milwaukee to the edge.

"There aren't five guys in the rest of the league who throw as hard as those four guys on the Yankees," moaned Brewer rightfielder Paul Molitor. "And those four guys have been out there firing at us for 18 innings in 18 hours."

With ace Pete Vuchovich down with the flu and the series shifting to the Bronx, Milwaukee appeared doomed. But another flu-ridden mate, Randy Lerch, forgot his 7–9 record, allowed only three hits in six innings and watched Rollie Fingers mop up a 5–3 triumph that kept the Brewers breathing.

On came Vuchovich for Game 4 to hold the Yankees scoreless for five innings and throw up in the dugout in between. "I'd made up my mind there'd be no way that I wouldn't pitch this," he said, after four relievers finished up a 2–1 triumph.

Meanwhile in the other clubhouse Steinbrenner was holding kangaroo court with Cerone, who'd angered the owner by going to salary arbitration during the previous winter, his primary target. Cerone's baserunning blunder in the seventh had killed a Yankee rally that might have won both game and series.

When Steinbrenner was done Cerone, humiliated and in tears, had told the owner to "go —— yourself." The catcher, Steinbrenner had warned, was "on trial." So were his teammates, who were now one loss from an embarrassing elimination. Plan B, too, was a loss away.

"Today," Steinbrenner said, "we find out which guys deserve to be Yankees and which ones don't." Cerone's fate hung in the balance. So did that of Reggie Jackson, who'd squabbled all year with Steinbrenner and was headed for free agency.

"I'm interested in finding how much of this Reggie Jackson crap is true," Jackson said before Game 5. "Everybody's always saying I come through in the big games. Well, if I'm ever gonna do anything, it'll be tonight."

After the Brewers had touched Guidry for two runs, Jackson tied the game in the fourth inning with a towering home run to rightfield off Moose Haas. "I just wanted to do something dramatic," Reggie said.

When Gamble followed with another homer, it made for a four-run inning. And after the Brewers had cut the lead back to a run, Cerome belted one of his own in the seventh off Jim Slaton (one of six Milwaukee relievers).

Once Winfield tracked down a Don Money blast to the leftfield wall with two men on in the eighth ('How scared was I?" quipped Lemon. "Only my laundryman knows for sure."), the Brewers were dead.

Later, in a jubilant (and relieved) Yankee clubhouse, Steinbrenner shook hands all around including that of Cerone, to whom he'd sent an explanatory "Dear Rick" letter before the game.

Thus aroused—and reprieved—the Yankees found the pennant playoff with Oakland something of an afterthought. "George's Gall vs. Billyball," announced the New York News.

Martin had worked for Steinbrenner twice, resigning in 1978 and being fired in 1979. Now, back in the Bay Area where he'd grown up, he'd drilled his Billyball (speed, aggressiveness, defense and complete games) into the once-pathetic A's. They'd responded by winning a record 17 of their first 18 and sweeping Kansas City in their mini-series.

"We'll beat his [Steinbrenner's] tail like a drum," Martin boasted, but Oakland vanished in three straight without ever leading once. Yankee third baseman Graig Nettles ripped a full-count, two-out, bases-loaded double in the first inning of the opener at Yankee Stadium and John, Davis and Gossage did the rest, 3–1.

The next day it was 13–3 as Piniella and Nettles each crashed three-run homers and New York fans sang "Goodbye Billy" in the ninth inning.

So the clubs boarded jets and flew 3000 miles for one game, which Yankee second baseman Willie Randolph (who'd hit only two home runs all season) won with a two-run blast to leftfield with two out in the sixth.

Once Davis and Gossage came out to relieve Righetti, three more New York runs in the ninth were unnecessary. "Maybe there'll be something called Bobbyball," Lemon cracked.

The only excitement came afterward in a nearby Oakland restaurant when Nettles knocked down Jackson after a dispute over several of

The Yanks faced Billy Martin and his "Billy Ball" A's in the League championship series and wiped them out in 3 straight.

Center fielder Jerry Mumphrey was obtained from San Diego and led Yankee batters in average with .307 and outfielders with 5 assists.

Graig Nettles stemmed a Dodger rally, diving to spear Steve Garvey's liner. He jammed a thumb in the second game, which forced him to the sidelines for games 3, 4, and 5.

George Steinbrenner, his broken hand bandaged, apologized to fans for his team's World Series performance, and looked toward the future.

Jackson's uninvited guests asking Nettles' wife to move. "That's Yankee baseball," shrugged Oriole pitcher Jim Palmer.

While the Yankees waited for the Dodgers to beat Montreal in the final inning of the final game of the National League playoffs, Nettles and Jackson patched up their differences. "It's all in the past," Nettles said. "It's forgotten." When the Series opened in New York, the Yankees were still in form.

This time Watson, in his first Series at-bat, gave the Yankees a 3–0 lead with a first-inning homer, Guidry and Gossage kept the Dodgers at bay and Nettles, who'd frustrated Los Angeles with his glove in the 1978 Series, robbed Davey Lopes and Steve Garvey this time. "You would think by now they would have learned," Lemon said, "you don't hit the ball down there."

"DON'T THE DODGERS EVER LEARN?" wondered a fan's hand-lettered sign the next night as John set them down in order for four innings. The Dodgers had let him get away as a free agent after the 1978 Series. When he left after seven innings, New York had a 1–0 lead and Los Angeles had managed only one hit.

Now came the glaring, mustachioed Gossage to strike out three of their last six batters, the final two looking at his 90-plus mile-per-hour fastball.

"Everyone in the ballpark," Gossage shrugged, "knows what I'm gonna throw." Groaned Dodgers manager Tommy Lasorda: "Don't show me Fu Manchu no more."

And his players had had a bellyful of the Bronx, where they'd now lost six straight over three Series. "We're going home with Fernando Valenzuela pitching in Dodger Stadium," reasoned Garvey. "That's the symbol of better times. You'll see a different team Friday night."

Indeed, Game 3 was worlds away from the first two. To begin with, Nettles had jammed a thumb and was sidelined. And what had been billed as a classic duel between two brilliant rookies came apart in the first inning, when Los Angeles third baseman Ron Cey dumped a Righetti fastball over the left-centerfield fence.

Then the Yankees rocked Valenzuela with home runs in the second and third to take a 4–3 lead. George Frazier had relieved Righetti in the first but Lasorda stuck with Valenzuela, his Cy Young Award winner. Valenzuela threw 146 pitches and let 17 Yankees reach base, but at the end, after the Dodgers had scrapped for two more runs, he stood on the mound with left fist high.

Thus the Series turned. The Yankees would knock out Los Angeles starter Bob Welch in the first inning of Game 4 and run up leads of 4–0 and 6–3. But bad baserunning, shabby defensive work in the outfield and questionable strategy (Lemon benched Mumphrey, used John in relief instead of Gossage and pinch hit catcher Barry Foote for third baseman Aurelio Rodriguez) brought New York to ruin, 8–7.

The next afternoon Dodgers Pedro Guerrero and Steve Yeager clouted back-to-back home runs off Guidry in the seventh, pitcher Jerry Reuss held New York to a run and the Yankees, who'd never lost a Series in six games after winning the first two, were facing an empty winter.

"We'll win it in New York," growled Steinbrenner, who said he'd been assaulted by two Los Angeles fans in a hotel elevator and had broken a hand in retaliation. That was a prelude to a more humiliating mugging at home, where the Dodgers rapped out eight runs in the middle three innings and bore off the championship, 9–2.

It was a collapse worthy of a formal apology and it began when Lemon decided to yank John for pinch hitter Bobby Murcer with the score 1–1 in the fourth inning.

"We had to get runs," Lemon explained. "All I wanted was a run. I figured our bullpen could get us to the seventh and Gossage. I guess I'm not so smart."

John, for his part, was incredulous. "I hope you have someone who can hold them," he told Lemon in disgust. Lemon's choice was Frazier, who'd begun the year in the Cardinals' farm system and had lost both Games 3 and 4 in relief.

Los Angeles hopped on him for three runs in the fifth and racked Davis and Rick Reuschel for four more in the sixth. "I couldn't get the voodoo lady off my back," moaned Frazier, who set a Series record for most losses. "She kept sticking the needle in me."

And Frazier wasn't the only one. Winfield, the $20-million man, went 1-for-23 for the Series and uncorked a throw in the finale than bounced on the infield dirt and reached the plate on three bounces. Davis, the superb middle reliever, had watched his ERA balloon to 23.14.

Nettles had been hurt and Jackson (who'd injured a calf muscle in the Oakland series) had missed the first three games.

Meanwhile the Dodgers, who'd only beaten New York twice in 10 previous Series, returned to the Coast as heroes to the vast relief of Lasorda, who knew what would have happened had his people lost another.

"The people would have cut off my head," he'd guessed, "and kicked it down Wilshire Boulevard."

What Steinbrenner would do with his Yankees was an open question as autumn turned into winter.

Tommy John.

THE RECORD

Monte Beville 1903–04
Harry Billiard 1908
Doug Bird 1980–81
Ewell Blackwell 1952–53
Rick Bladt 1975
Paul Blair 1977–80
Walter Blair 1907–11
Johnny Blanchard 1955, 1959–65
Gil Blanco 1965
Wade Blasingame 1972
Steve Blateric 1972
Gary Blaylock 1959
Curt Blefary 1970–71
Elmer Bliss 1903–04
Ron Blomberg 1969, 1971–77
Eddie Bockman 1946
Ping Bodie 1918–21
Len Boehmer 1969, 1971
Don Bollweg 1953
Bobby Bonds 1975
Ernie Bonham 1940–46
Luke Boone 1913–16
Frenchy Bordagaray 1941
Hank Borowy 1942–45
Babe Borton 1913
Jim Bouton 1962–68
Clete Boyer 1959–66
Neal Brady 1915
Ralph Branca 1954
Norm Branch 1941–42
Marshall Brant 1980
Garland Braxton 1925–26
Don Brennan 1933
Jim Brenneman 1965
Ken Brett 1976
Marv Breuer 1939–43
Fritz Brickell 1958–59
Jim Brideweser 1951–53
Marshall Bridges 1962–63
Harry Bright 1963–64
Ed Brinkman 1975
Johnny Broaca 1934–37
Lew Brockett 1907, 1909
Jim Bronstad 1959
Boardwalk Brown 1914–15
Bobby Brown 1946–52, 1954
Bobby Brown 1979–81
Hal Brown 1962
Jumbo Brown 1932–33, 1935–36
Billy Bryan 1966–67
Jess Buckles 1916
Bill Burbach 1969–71
Lew Burdette 1950
George Burns 1928–29
Alex Burr 1914
Ray Burris 1979
Joe Bush 1922–24
Tom Buskey 1973–74
Ralph Buxton 1949
Joe Buzas 1945
Harry Byrd 1954
Sammy Byrd 1929–34
Tommy Byrne 1943, 1946–51, 1954–57

Charlie Caldwell 1925
Ray Caldwell 1910–18
Johnny Callison 1972–73
Howie Camp 1917
Archie Campbell 1928
Mike Cantwell 1916
Andy Carey 1952–60

Roy Carlyle 1926
Duke Carmel 1965
Dick Carroll 1909
Ownie Carroll 1930
Tommy Carroll 1955–56
Hugh Casey 1949
Roy Castleton 1907
Bill Castro 1981
Danny Cater 1970–71
Rick Cerone 1980–81
Bob Cerv 1951–56, 1960–62
Chris Chambliss 1974–79
Frank Chance 1913–14
Spud Chandler 1937–47
Les Channell 1910
Ben Chapman 1930–36
Mike Chartak 1940
Hal Chase 1905–13
Jack Chesbro 1903–09
Al Cicotte 1957
Allie Clark 1947
George Clark 1913
Horace Clarke 1965–74
Walter Clarkson 1904–07
Ken Clay 1977–79
Tex Clevenger 1961–62
Lu Clinton 1966–67
Al Closter 1971–72
Andy Coakley 1911
Jim Coates 1956, 1959–62
Jim Cockman 1905
Rich Coggins 1975–76
Rocky Colavito 1968
King Cole 1914–15
Curt Coleman 1912
Jerry Coleman 1949–57
Rip Coleman 1955–56
Bob Collins 1944
Joe Collins 1948–57
Orth Collins 1904
Pat Collins 1926–28
Rip Collins 1920–21
Frank Colman 1946–47
Loyd Colson 1970
Earle Combs 1924–35
Tom Connelly 1920–21
Joe Connor 1905
Wid Conroy 1903–08
Doc Cook 1913–16
Dusty Cooke 1930–32
Johnny Cooney 1944
Phil Cooney 1905
Guy Cooper 1914
Dan Costello 1913
Ensign Cottrell 1915
Clint Courtney 1951
Ernie Courtney 1903
Stan Coveleski 1928
Billy Cowan 1969
Bobby Cox 1968–69
Casey Cox 1972–73
Birdie Cree 1908–15
Lou Criger 1910
Herb Crompton 1945
Frank Crosetti 1932–48
Jack Cullen 1962, 1965–66
Roy Cullenbine 1942
Nick Cullop 1916–17
Nick Cullop 1926
John Cumberland 1968–70
Jim Curry 1911
Fred Curtis 1905

Babe Dahlgren 1937–40
Bud Daley 1961–64
Tom Daley 1914–15
Bert Daniels 1910–13
George Davis 1912
Kiddo Davis 1926
Lefty Davis 1903
Ron Davis 1978–81
John Deering 1903
John Deidel 1974
Frank Delahanty 1905–06, 1908
Bobby Del Greco 1957–58
Jim Delsing 1949–50
Joe DeMaestri 1960–61
Ray Demmitt 1909
Rick Dempsey 1973–76
Bucky Dent 1977–81
Claud Derrick 1913
Russ Derry 1944–45
Jimmie DeShong 1934–35
Charlie Devens 1932–34
Al DeVormer 1921–22
Bill Dickey 1928–43, 1946
Murry Dickson 1958
Joe DiMaggio 1936–42, 1946–51
Kerry Dineen 1975–76
Art Ditmar 1957–61
Sonny Dixon 1956
Pat Dobson 1973–75
Cozy Dolan 1911–12
Atley Donald 1938–45
Mike Donovan 1908
Wild Bill Donovan 1915–16
Patsy Dougherty 1904–06
Al Downing 1961–69
Brian Doyle 1978–80
Jack Doyle 1905
Slow Joe Doyle 1906–10
Bill Drescher 1944–46
Karl Drews 1946–48
Monk Dubiel 1944–45
Joe Dugan 1922–28
Ryne Duren 1958–61
Leo Durocher 1925, 1928–29
Cedric Durst 1927–30

Rawly Eastwick 1978
Doc Edwards 1965
Foster Edwards 1930
Kid Elberfeld 1903–09
Gene Elliott 1911
Dock Ellis 1976–77
John Ellis 1969–72
Red Embree 1948
Clyde Engle 1909–10
John Enright 1917
Nick Etten 1943–46

Doc Farrell 1932–33
Alex Ferguson 1918, 1921
Frank Fernandez 1967–69
Mike Ferraro 1966, 1968
Wes Ferrell 1938–39
Tom Ferrick 1950–51
Chick Fewster 1917–22
Ed Figueroa 1976–80
Happy Finneran 1918
Gus Fisher 1912
Ray Fisher 1910–17
Mike Fitzgerald 1911
Barry Foote 1981
Russ Ford 1909–13

Whitey Ford 1950, 1953–67
Eddie Foster 1910
Jack Fournier 1918
Ray Francis 1925
George Frazier 1981
Mark Freeman 1959
Ray French 1920
Lonny Frey 1947–48
Bob Friend 1966
John Frill 1910
Dave Fultz 1903–05
Liz Funk 1929

John Gabler 1959–60
Joe Gallagher 1939
Oscar Gamble 1976, 1979–81
John Ganzel 1903–04
Mike Garbark 1944–45
Damaso Garcia 1978–79
Billy Gardner 1961–62
Earl Gardner 1908–12
Rob Gardner 1970–72
Ned Garvin 1904
Milt Gaston 1924
Mike Gazella 1923, 1926–28
Joe Gedeon 1916–17
Lou Gehrig 1923–39
Al Gettel 1945–46
Joe Giard 1927
Jake Gibbs 1962–71
Sam Gibson 1930
Frank Gilhooley 1913–18
Fred Glade 1908
Frank Gleich 1919–20
Joe Glenn 1932–33, 1935–38
Lefty Gomez 1930–42
Jesse Gonder 1960–61
Fernando Gonzalez 1974
Pedro Gonzalez 1963–65
Wilbur Good 1905
Art Goodwin 1905
Joe Gordon 1938–43, 1946
Tom Gorman 1952–54
Rich Gossage 1978–81
Dick Gossett 1913–14
Larry Gowell 1972
Johnny Grabowski 1927–29
Wayne Granger 1973
Ted Gray 1955
Eli Grba 1959–60
Willie Greene 1903
Mike Griffin 1979–81
Clark Griffith 1903–07
Bob Grim 1954–58
Burleigh Grimes 1934
Oscar Grimes 1943–46
Lee Grissom 1940
Ron Guidry 1975–81
Brad Gulden 1979–80
Don Gullett 1977–80
Randy Gumpert 1946–48
Larry Gura 1974–76

Bump Hadley 1936–40
Kent Hadley 1960
Ed Hahn 1905–06
Noodles Hahn 1906
Hinkey Haines 1923
George Halas 1919
Bob Hale 1961
Jimmie Hall 1969
Roger Hambright 1971

Steve Hamilton 1963–70
Mike Handiboe 1911
Jim Hanley 1913
Truck Hannah 1918–20
Ron Hansen 1970–71
Joe Hanson 1913
Jim Hardin 1971
Bubbles Hargrave 1930
Harry Harper 1921
Joe Harris 1914
Jim Hart 1973–74
Roy Hartzell 1911–16
Buddy Hassett 1942
Chicken Hawks 1921
Fran Healy 1976–78
Mike Heath 1978
Don Heffner 1934–37
Mike Hegan 1964, 1966–67,
    1973–74
Fred Heimach 1928–29
Woodie Held 1954
Charlie Hemphill 1908–11
Rollie Hemsley 1942–44
Bill Henderson 1930
Harvey Hendrick 1923–24
Elrod Hendricks 1976–77
Tim Hendryx 1915–17
Tommy Henrich 1937–42,
    1946–50
Billy Henry 1966
Ed Herrmann 1975
Hugh High 1915–18
Oral Hildebrand 1939–40
Jesse Hill 1935
Frank Hiller 1946, 1948–49
Mack Hillis 1924
Rich Hinton 1972
Myril Hoag 1931–32, 1934–38
Red Hoff 1911–13
Danny Hoffman 1906–07
Solly Hofman 1916
Fred Hofmann 1919–25
Bill Hogg 1905–08
Bobby Hogue 1951–52
Ken Holcombe 1945
Bill Holden 1913–14
Ken Holloway 1930
Fred Holmes 1903
Roger Holt 1980
Ken Holtzman 1976–78
Don Hood 1979
Wally Hood 1949
Johnny Hopp 1950–52
Shags Horan 1924
Ralph Houk 1947–54
Elston Howard 1955–67
Harry Howell 1903
Dick Howser 1967–68
Waite Hoyt 1921–30
Long Tom Hughes 1904
Tom Hughes 1906–07, 1909–10
John Hummel 1918
Ken Hunt 1959–60
Billy Hunter 1955–56
Catfish Hunter 1975–79
Ham Hyatt 1918

Fred Jacklitsch 1905
Grant Jackson 1976
Reggie Jackson 1977–81
Johnny James 1958, 1960–61
Jackie Jensen 1950–52

Elvio Jimenez 1964
Tommy John 1979–81
Alex Johnson 1974–75
Billy Johnson 1943, 1946–51
Cliff Johnson 1977–79
Darrell Johnson 1957–58
Deron Johnson 1960–61
Don Johnson 1947
Ernie Johnson 1923–25
Hank Johnson 1925–26, 1928–32
Johnny Johnson 1944
Ken Johnson 1969
Otis Johnson 1911
Roy Johnson 1936–37
Jay Johnstone 1978–79
Gary Jones 1970–71
Darryl Jones 1979
Ruppert Jones 1980
Sad Sam Jones 1922–26
Tim Jordan 1903
Art Jorgens 1929–39
Mike Jurewicz 1965

Jim Kaat 1979–80
Bob Kammeyer 1978–79
Frank Kane 1919
Bill Karlon 1930
Herb Karpel 1946
Benny Kauff 1912
Eddie Kearse 1942
Ray Keating 1912–16, 1918
Bob Keefe 1907
Willie Keeler 1903–09
Mike Kekich 1969–73
Charlie Keller 1939–43, 1945–49,
    1952
John Kennedy 1967
Jerry Kenney 1967, 1969–72
Dave Kingman 1977
Harry Kingman 1914
Fred Kipp 1960
Frank Kitson 1907
Ted Kleinhans 1936
Red Kleinow 1904–10
Ed Klepfer 1911
Ron Klimkowski 1969–70, 1972
Steve Kline 1970–74
Mickey Klutts 1976–78
Bill Knickerbocker 1938–40
John Knight 1909–11, 1913
Mark Koenig 1925–30
Jim Konstanty 1954–56
Andy Kosco 1968
Steve Kraly 1953
Jack Kramer 1951
Ernie Krueger 1915
Dick Kryhoski 1949
Tony Kubek 1957–65
Johnny Kucks 1955–59
Bill Kunkel 1963
Bob Kuzava 1951–54

Joe Lake 1908–09
Bill Lamar 1917–19
Hal Lanier 1972–73
Frank LaPorte 1905–10
Dave LaRoche 1981
Don Larsen 1955–59
Lyn Lary 1929–34
Gene Layden 1915
Tony Lazzeri 1926–37
Joe Lefebvre 1980

Frank Leja 1954–55
Jack Lelivelt 1912–13
Eddie Leon 1975
Louis LeRoy 1905–06
Ed Levy 1942
Duffy Lewis 1919–20
Terry Ley 1971
Paul Lindblad 1978
Johnny Lindell 1941–50
Phil Linz 1962–65
Jack Little 1912
Clem Llewellyn 1922
Gene Locklear 1976–77
Sherm Lollar 1947–48
Tim Lollar 1980
Dale Long 1960, 1962–63
Herman Long 1903
Ed Lopat 1948–55
Art Lopez 1965
Hector Lopez 1959–66
Baldy Louden 1907
Slim Love 1916–18
Johnny Lucadello 1947
Joe Lucey 1920
Ray Luebbe 1925
Jerry Lumpe 1956–59
Sparky Lyle 1972–78
Al Lyons 1944, 1946–47
Jim Lyttle 1969–71

Duke Maas 1958–61
Danny MacFayden 1932–34
Ray Mack 1947
Bunny Madden 1910
Elliot Maddox 1974–76
Dave Madison 1950
Lee Magee 1916–17
Sal Maglie 1957–58
Stubby Magner 1911
Jim Magnuson 1973
Fritz Maisel 1913–17
Hank Majeski 1946
Frank Makosky 1937
Pat Malone 1935–37
Pat Maloney 1912
Al Mamaux 1924
Rube Manning 1907–10
Mickey Mantle 1951–68
Clif Mapes 1948–51
Roger Maris 1960–66
Cliff Markle 1915–16, 1924
Jim Marquis 1925
Armando Marsans 1917–18
Cuddles Marshall 1946, 1948–49
Billy Martin 1950–53, 1955–57
Hersh Martin 1944–45
Jack Martin 1912
Tippy Martinez 1974–76
Jim Mason 1974–76
Carlos May 1976–77
Rudy May 1974–76, 1980–81
Carl Mays 1919–23
Larry McCall 1977–78
Joe McCarthy 1905
Pat McCauley 1903
Larry McClure 1910
George McConnell 1909, 1912–13
Mike McCormick 1970
Lindy McDaniel 1968–73
Mickey McDermott 1956
Danny McDevitt 1961
Dave McDonald 1969

Jim McDonald 1952–54
Gil McDougald 1951–60
Sam McDowell 1973–74
Lou McEvoy 1930–31
Herm McFarland 1903
Andy McGaffigan 1981
Bob McGraw 1917–20
Deacon McGuire 1904–07
Marty McHale 1913–15
Irish McIlveen 1908–09
Bill McKechnie 1913
Rich McKinney 1972
Frank McManus 1904
Norm McMillan 1922
Tommy McMillan 1912
Mike McNally 1921–24
Herb McQuaid 1926
George McQuinn 1947–48
Charlie Meara 1914
Doc Medich 1972–75
Fred Merkle 1925–26
Andy Messersmith 1978
Tom Metcalf 1963
Bud Metheny 1943–46
Bob Meusel 1920–29
Bob Meyer 1964
Gene Michael 1968–74
Ezra Midkiff 1912–13
Pete Mikkelsen 1964–65
Larry Milbourne 1981
Bill Miller 1952–54
Elmer Miller 1915–18, 1921–22
John Miller 1966
Buster Mills 1940
Mike Milosevich 1944–45
Paul Mirabella 1979
Willie Miranda 1953–54
Bobby Mitchell 1970
Fred Mitchell 1910
Johnny Mitchell 1921–22
Johnny Mize 1949–53
George Mogridge 1915–20
Fenton Mole 1949
Bill Monbouquette 1967–68
Ed Monroe 1917–18
Zack Monroe 1958–59
Archie Moore 1964–65
Earl Moore 1907
Wilcy Moore 1927–29, 1932–33
Ray Morehart 1927
Tom Morgan 1951–52, 1954–56
George Moriarty 1906–08
Ross Moschitto 1965, 1967
Jerry Moses 1973
Charlie Mullen 1914–16
Jerry Mumphrey 1981
Bob Muncrief 1951
Thurman Munson 1969–79
Bobby Murcer 1965–66, 1969–74,
    1979–81
Johnny Murphy 1932, 1934–43,
    1946
George Murray 1922
Larry Murray 1974–76

Jerry Narron 1979
Bots Nekola 1929
Gene Nelson 1981
Luke Nelson 1919
Graig Nettles 1973–81
Tacks Neuer 1907
Ernie Nevel 1950–51

Floyd Newkirk 1934
Bobo Newsom 1947
Doc Newton 1905–09
Gus Niarhos 1946, 1948–50
Harry Niles 1908
Irv Noren 1952–56
Don Nottebart 1969
Les Nunamaker 1914–17

Johnny Oates 1980–81
Andy O'Connor 1908
Jack O'Connor 1903
Paddy O'Connor 1918
Heinie Odom 1925
Lefty O'Doul 1919–20, 1922
John O'Dowd 1912
Rube Oldring 1905, 1916
Bob Oliver 1975
Nate Oliver 1969
Steve O'Neill 1925
Queenie O'Rourke 1909
Al Orth 1904–09
Champ Osteen 1904
Joe Ostrowski 1950–52
Bill Otis 1912
Stubby Overmire 1951

Del Paddock 1912
Dave Pagan 1973–76
Joe Page 1944–50
Ben Paschal 1924–29
Gil Patterson 1977
Mike Patterson 1981
Monte Pearson 1936–40
Roger Peckinpaugh 1913–21
Steve Peek 1941
Herb Pennock 1923–33
Joe Pepitone 1962–69
Marty Perez 1977
Cecil Perkins 1967
Cy Perkins 1931
Gaylord Perry 1980
Fritz Peterson 1966–74
Eddie Phillips 1932
Jack Phillips 1947–49
Cy Pieh 1913–15
Bill Piercy 1917
Duane Pillette 1949–50
Lou Piniella 1974–81
George Pipgras 1923–24,
   1927–33
Wally Pipp 1915–25
Jim Pisoni 1959–60
Bob Porterfield 1948–51
Jack Powell 1904–05
Jake Powell 1936–40
Mike Powers 1905
Del Pratt 1918–20
Jerry Priddy 1941–42
Johnnie Priest 1911–12
Ambrose Puttman 1903–05

Mel Queen 1942, 1944, 1946–47
Ed Quick 1903
Jack Quinn 1909–12, 1919–21

Dave Rajsich 1978
Domingo Ramos 1978
Pedro Ramos 1964–66
Lenny Randle 1979
Willie Randolph 1976–81

Vic Raschi 1946–53
Jack Reed 1961–63
Jimmy Reese 1930–31
Hal Reniff 1961–67
Bill Renna 1953
Tony Rensa 1933
Roger Repoz 1964–66
Rick Reuschel 1981
Dave Revering 1981
Allie Reynolds 1947–54
Bill Reynolds 1913–14
Gordon Rhodes 1929–32
Harry Rice 1930
Bobby Richardson 1955–66
Nolan Richardson 1935
Branch Rickey 1907
Dave Righetti 1979, 1981
Mickey Rivers 1976–79
Phil Rizzuto 1941–42, 1946–56
Roxy Roach 1910–11
Dale Roberts 1967
Andre Robertson 1981
Gene Robertson 1928–29
Aaron Robinson 1943, 1945–47
Bill Robinson 1967–69
Bruce Robinson 1979–80
Eddie Robinson 1954–56
Hank Robinson 1918
Aurelio Rodriguez 1980–81
Ellie Rodriguez 1968
Oscar Roettger 1923–24
Jay Rogers 1914
Tom Rogers 1921
Jim Roland 1972
Red Rolfe 1931, 1934–42
Buddy Rosar 1939–42
Larry Rosenthal 1944
Steve Roser 1944–46
Braggo Roth 1921
Muddy Ruel 1917–20
Dutch Ruether 1926–27
Red Ruffing 1930–42, 1945–46
Allan Russell 1915–19
Marius Russo 1939–43, 1946
Babe Ruth 1920–34
Blondy Ryan 1935
Rosy Ryan 1928

Johnny Sain 1951–55
Jack Saltzgaver 1932, 1934–37
Celerino Sanchez 1972–73
Roy Sanders 1918
Charlie Sands 1967
Fred Sanford 1949–51
Don Savage 1944–45
Rick Sawyer 1974–75
Ray Scarborough 1952–53
Germany Schaefer 1916
Harry Schaeffer 1952
Roy Schalk 1932
Art Schallock 1951–55
Wally Schang 1921–25
Bob Schmidt 1965
Butch Schmidt 1909
Johnny Schmitz 1952–53
Pete Schneider 1919
Dick Schofield 1966
Paul Schreiber 1945
Art Schult 1953
Al Schulz 1912–14
Bill Schwartz 1914

Pius Schwert 1914–15
Everett Scott 1922–25
George Scott 1979
Ken Sears 1943
Bob Seeds 1936
Kal Segrist 1952
George Selkirk 1934–42
Ted Sepkowski 1947
Hank Severeid 1926
Joe Sewell 1931–33
Howard Shanks 1925
Billy Shantz 1960
Bobby Shantz 1957–60
Bob Shawkey 1915–27
Spec Shea 1947–49, 1951
Al Shealy 1928
George Shears 1912
Tom Sheehan 1921
Rollie Sheldon 1961–62, 1964–65
Skeeter Shelton 1915
Roy Sherid 1929–31
Dennis Sherrill 1978, 1980
Ben Shields 1929–31
Dennis Sherrill 1978, 1980
Ben Shields 1924–25
Urban Shocker 1916–17, 1925–28
Tom Shopay 1967, 1969
Ernie Shore 1919–20
Bill Short 1960
Norm Siebern 1956, 1958–59
Charlie Silvera 1948–56
Ken Silvestri 1941, 1946–47
Hack Simmons 1912
Dick Simpson 1969
Harry Simpson 1957–58
Duke Sims 1973–74
Bill Skiff 1926
Camp Skinner 1922
Lou Skizas 1956
Bill Skowron 1954–62
Roger Slagle 1979
Enos Slaughter 1954–59
Walt Smallwood 1917
Charley Smith 1967–68
Elmer Smith 1922–23
Joe Smith 1913
Klondike Smith 1912
Harry Smythe 1934
Eric Soderholm 1980
Tony Solaita 1968
Steve Souchock 1945
Jim Spencer 1978–81
Charlie Spikes 1972
Bill Stafford 1960–65
Jake Stahl 1908
Roy Staiger 1979
Tuck Stainback 1942–45
Gerry Staley 1955–56
Charley Stanceu 1941
Fred Stanley 1973–80
Dick Starr 1947–48
Dutch Sterrett 1912–13
Bud Stewart 1948
Lee Stine 1938
Snuffy Stirnweiss 1943–50
Mel Stottlemyre 1964–74
Hal Stowe 1960
Gabby Street 1912
Marlin Stuart 1954
Bill Stumpf 1912–13
Tom Sturdivant 1955–59

Johnny Sturm 1941
Bill Sudakis 1974
Steve Sundra 1936, 1938–40
Ed Sweeney 1908–15
Ron Swoboda 1971–73

Fred Talbot 1966–69
Vito Tamulis 1934–35
Jesse Tannehill 1903
Zack Taylor 1934
Frank Tepedino 1967, 1969–72
Ralph Terry 1956–57, 1959–64
Dick Tettelbach 1955
Ira Thomas 1906–07
Lee Thomas 1961
Myles Thomas 1926–29
Stan Thomas 1977
Gary Thomasson 1978
Homer Thompson 1912
Tommy Thompson 1912
Jack Thoney 1904
Hank Thormahlen 1917–20
Marv Throneberry 1955, 1958–59
Luis Tiant 1979–80
Dick Tidrow 1974–79
Bobby Tiefenauer 1965
Eddie Tiemeyer 1909
Ray Tift 1907
Bob Tillman 1967
Thad Tillotson 1967–68
Dan Tipple 1915
Earl Torgeson 1961
Rusty Torres 1971–72
Mike Torrez 1977
Cesar Tovar 1976
Tom Tresh 1961–69
Gus Triandos 1953–54
Virgil Trucks 1958
Frank Truesdale 1914
Bob Turley 1955–62
Jim Turner 1942–45

George Uhle 1933–34
Tom Underwood 1908–81
Bob Unglaub 1904
Cecil Upshaw 1974

Elmer Valo 1960
Russ Van Atta 1933–35
Dazzy Vance 1915–1918
Joe Vance 1937–38
Bobby Vaughn 1909
Hippo Vaughn 1908, 1910–12
Bobby Veach 1925
Otto Velez 1973–76
Joe Verbanic 1967–68, 1970
Frank Verdi 1953
Sammy Vick 1917–20

Jake Wade 1946
Dick Wakefield 1950
Curt Walker 1919
Dixie Walker 1931, 1933–36
Mike Wallace 1974–75
Jimmy Walsh 1914
Joe Walsh 1910–11
Roxy Walters 1915–18
Danny Walton 1971
Paul Waner 1944–45
Jack Wanner 1909
Pee Wee Wanninger 1925

Aaron Ward 1917–26
Joe Ward 1909
Pete Ward 1970
Jack Warhop 1908–15
George Wasburn 1941
Gary Waslewski 1970–71
Bob Watson 1980–81
Roy Weatherly 1943
Jim Weaver 1931
Dave Wehrmeister 1981
Lefty Weinert 1931
Ed Wells 1929–32
Butch Wensloff 1943, 1947
Julie Wera 1927
Bill Werber 1930
Dennis Werth 1979–81
Steve Whitaker 1966–68
Roy White 1965–79
George Whiteman 1913
Terry Whitfield 1974–76
Kemp Wicker 1936–38
Al Wickland 1919
Bob Wiesler 1951, 1954–55
Bill Wight 1946–47
Ted Wilborn 1980
Ed Wilkinson 1911
Bob Williams 1911–14
Harry Williams 1913
Jimmy Williams 1903–07
Stan Williams 1963–64
Walt Williams 1974–75
Archie Wilson 1951–52

George Wilson 1956
Pete Wilson 1908–09
Ted Wilson 1956
Snake Wiltse 1903
Gordie Windhorn 1959
Dave Winfield 1981
Mickey Witek 1949
Whitey Witt 1922–25
Bill Wolfe 1903–04
Harry Wolter 1910–13
Harry Wolverton 1912
Dooley Womack 1966–68
Gene Wooding 1949–54
Ron Woods 1969–71
Dick Woodson 1974
Hank Workman 1950
Ken Wright 1974
Yats Wuestling 1930
John Wyatt 1968
Jimmy Wynn 1977

Joe Yeager 1905–06
Jim York 1976
Ralph Young 1913

Tom Zachary 1928–30
Jack Zalusky 1903
George Zeber 1977–78
Rollie Zeider 1913
Guy Zinn 1911–12
Bill Zuber 1943–46

Bobby Richardson scores in the 1962 World Series.

Casey Stengel in a familiar position.

POSITION LEADERS YEAR BY YEAR *(Determined by number of games played at that position)*

Year	Pitcher (starts)	Pitcher (games)	Catcher	First Baseman	Second Baseman
1903	Jack Chesbro, 36	Jack Chesbro, 40	Monte Beville, 75	John Ganzel, 129	Jimmy Williams, 132
1904	Jack Chesbro, 51	Jack Chesbro, 55	Deacon McGuire, 97	John Ganzel, 118	Jimmy Williams, 146
1905	Jack Chesbro, 38	Jack Chesbro, 41	Red Kleinow, 83	Hal Chase, 122	Jimmy Williams, 129
1906	Jack Chesbro, 42	Jack Chesbro, 49	Red Kleinow, 95	Hal Chase, 150	Jimmy Williams, 139
1907	Al Orth, 33	Al Orth, 36	Red Kleinow, 86	Hal Chase, 121	Jimmy Williams, 139
1908	Jack Chesbro, 31	Jack Chesbro, 45	Red Kleinow, 89	Hal Chase, 98	Harry Niles, 85
1909	Joe Lake, 26	Jack Warhop, 36	Red Kleinow, 77	Hal Chase, 118	Frank LaPorte, 83
1910	Russ Ford, 33	Jack Warhop, 37	Ed Sweeney, 78	Hal Chase, 130	Frank LaPorte, 79
1911	Russ Ford, 33	Ray Caldwell, 41	Walter Blair, 84	Hal Chase, 124	Earl Gardner, 101
1912	Russ Ford, 35	Jack Warhop, 39	Ed Sweeney, 108	Hal Chase, 121	Hack Simmons, 88
1913	Ray Fisher, 31	Ray Fisher, 43	Ed Sweeney, 112	John Knight, 50	Roy Hartzell, 81
1914	Ray Fisher, 26	Jack Warhop, 37	Ed Sweeney, 78	Charlie Mullen, 93	Luke Boone, 90
1915	Ray Caldwell, 35	Ray Caldwell, 36	Les Nunamaker, 77	Wally Pipp, 134	Luke Boone, 115
1916	Bob Shawkey, 27	Bob Shawkey, 53	Les Nunamaker, 79	Wally Pipp, 148	Joe Gedeon, 122
1917	Ray Caldwell, 29	Slim Love, 33*	Les Nunamaker, 91*	Wally Pipp, 155	Fritz Maisel, 100
1918	Slim Love, 29	George Mogridge, 45*	Truck Hannah, 88*	Wally Pipp, 91	Del Pratt, 126
1919	Jack Quinn, 31	Bob Shawkey, 41	Muddy Ruel, 81	Wally Pipp, 138	Del Pratt, 140
1920	Carl Mays, 37	Carl Mays, 45	Muddy Ruel, 80	Wally Pipp, 153	Del Pratt, 154
1921	Carl Mays, 38	Carl Mays, 49	Wally Schang, 132	Wally Pipp, 153	Aaron Ward, 123
1922	Bob Shawkey, 33	Sad Sam Jones, 45	Wally Schang, 119	Wally Pipp, 152	Aaron Ward, 152
1923	Bob Shawkey, 31	Sad Sam Jones, 39	Wally Schang, 81	Wally Pipp, 144	Aaron Ward, 152
1924	Herb Pennock, 34	Waite Hoyt, 46	Wally Schang, 106	Wally Pipp, 153	Aaron Ward, 120
1925	Herb Pennock, 31 Sad Sam Jones, 31	Herb Pennock, 47	Benny Bengough, 94	Lou Gehrig, 114	Aaron Ward, 113
1926	Urban Shocker, 33 Herb Pennock, 33	Urban Shocker, 41	Pat Collins, 100	Lou Gehrig, 155	Tony Lazzeri, 149
1927	Waite Hoyt, 32	Wilcy Moore, 50*	Pat Collins, 89	Lou Gehrig, 155	Tony Lazzeri, 113
1928	George Pipgras, 38	George Pipgras, 46	Johnny Grabowski, 75	Lou Gehrig, 154	Tony Lazzeri, 110
1929	George Pipgras, 33	Wilcy Moore, 41*	Bill Dickey, 127*	Lou Gehrig, 154	Tony Lazzeri, 147
1930	George Pipgras, 30	George Pipgras, 44 Hank Johnson, 44*	Bill Dickey, 101	Lou Gehrig, 153	Tony Lazzeri, 77
1931	Red Ruffing, 30	Lefty Gomez, 40 Hank Johnson, 40	Bill Dickey, 125	Lou Gehrig, 154	Tony Lazzeri, 90
1932	Lefty Gomez, 31	Lefty Gomez, 37	Bill Dickey, 108	Lou Gehrig, 155	Tony Lazzeri, 133
1933	Lefty Gomez, 30	Lefty Gomez, 35 Red Ruffing, 35 Wilcy Moore, 35*	Bill Dickey, 127	Lou Gehrig, 152	Tony Lazzeri, 138
1934	Lefty Gomez, 33	Johnny Murphy, 40†	Bill Dickey, 104	Lou Gehrig, 153	Tony Lazzeri, 92
1935	Lefty Gomez, 30	Johnny Murphy, 40**	Bill Dickey, 118	Lou Gehrig, 149	Tony Lazzeri, 118
1936	Red Ruffing, 33	Johnny Broaca, 37	Bill Dickey, 107	Lou Gehrig, 155	Tony Lazzeri, 148
1937	Lefty Gomez, 34	Johnny Murphy, 39*	Bill Dickey, 137	Lou Gehrig, 157	Tony Lazzeri, 125
1938	Lefty Gomez, 32	Lefty Gomez, 32 Johnny Murphy, 32*	Bill Dickey, 126	Lou Gehrig, 157	Joe Gordon, 126
1939	Red Ruffing, 28	Johnny Murphy, 38*	Bill Dickey, 126	Babe Dahlgren, 144	Joe Gordon, 151
1940	Red Ruffing, 30	Johnny Murphy, 35*	Bill Dickey, 102	Babe Dahlgren, 155	Joe Gordon, 155
1941	Marius Russo, 27	Johnny Murphy, 35*	Bill Dickey, 104	Johnny Sturm, 124	Joe Gordon, 131
1942	Ernie Bonham, 27	Johnny Murphy, 31*	Bill Dickey, 80	Buddy Hassett, 132	Joe Gordon, 147
1943	Spud Chandler, 30	Johnny Murphy, 37*	Bill Dickey, 71	Nick Etten, 154	Joe Gordon, 152

*Majority or all in relief.
†Half in starts, half in relief.

Shortstop	Third Baseman	Outfielder	Outfielder	Outfielder	Designated Hitter
Kid Elberfeld, 90	Wid Conroy, 123	Willie Keeler, 128	Herm McFarland, 103	Lefty Davis, 102	
Kid Elberfeld, 122	Wid Conroy, 110	Willie Keeler, 142	John Anderson, 112	Patsy Dougherty, 106	
Kid Elberfeld, 108	Joe Yeager, 90	Willie Keeler, 139	Dave Fultz, 122	Patsy Dougherty, 108	
Kid Elberfeld, 98	Frank LaPorte, 114	Willie Keeler, 152	Danny Hoffman, 98	Frank Delahanty, 92	
Kid Elberfeld, 118	George Moriarty, 91	Danny Hoffman, 135	Willie Keeler, 107	Wid Conroy, 100	
Neal Ball, 130	Wid Conroy, 119	Charlie Hemphill, 142	Willie Keeler, 88	Jake Stahl, 67	
John Knight, 78	Jimmy Austin, 111	Clyde Engle, 134	Ray Demmitt, 109	Willie Keeler, 95	
John Knight, 79	Jimmy Austin, 133	Birdie Cree, 134	Harry Wolter, 130	Charlie Hemphill, 94	
John Knight, 82	Roy Hartzell, 124	Birdie Cree, 137	Bert Daniels, 120	Harry Wolter, 113	
Jack Martin, 64	Roy Hartzell, 56	Bert Daniels, 131	Guy Zinn, 106	Roy Hartzell, 55	
Roger Peckinpaugh, 93	Ezra Midkiff, 76	Birdie Cree, 144	Harry Wolter, 121	Bert Daniels, 87	
Roger Peckinpaugh 157	Fritz Maisel, 148	Roy Hartzell, 128	Doc Cook, 126	Birdie Cree, 76	
Roger Peckinpaugh, 142	Fritz Maisel, 134	Doc Cook, 131	Hugh High, 117	Roy Hartzell, 107	
Roger Peckinpaugh, 146	Frank Baker, 96	Lee Magee, 128	Hugh High, 109	Frank Gilhooley, 57	
Roger Peckinpaugh, 148	Frank Baker, 146	Elmer Miller, 112	Tim Hendryx, 107	Hugh High, 100	
Roger Peckinpaugh, 122	Frank Baker, 126	Frank Gilhooley, 111	Ping Bodie, 90	Elmer Miller, 62	
Roger Peckinpaugh, 121	Frank Baker, 141	Duffy Lewis, 141	Ping Bodie, 134	Sammy Vick, 100	
Roger Peckinpaugh, 137	Aaron Ward, 114	Babe Ruth, 139	Ping Bodie, 129	Duffy Lewis, 99	
Roger Peckinpaugh, 149	Frank Baker, 83	Babe Ruth, 152	Bob Meusel, 147	Elmer Miller, 56	
Everett Scott, 154	Frank Baker, 60	Whitey Witt, 138	Bob Meusel, 121	Babe Ruth, 110	
	Joe Dugan, 60				
Everett Scott, 152	Joe Dugan, 146	Babe Ruth, 148	Whitey Witt, 144	Bob Meusel, 121	
Everett Scott, 153	Joe Dugan, 148	Babe Ruth, 152	Whitey Witt, 143	Bob Meusel, 143	
Pee Wee Wanninger, 111	Joe Dugan, 96	Earle Combs, 150	Bob Meusel, 131	Babe Ruth, 98	
Mark Koenig, 141	Joe Dugan, 122	Babe Ruth, 149	Earle Combs, 145	Bob Meusel, 107	
Mark Koenig, 122	Joe Dugan, 111	Earle Combs, 152	Babe Ruth, 151	Bob Meusel, 131	
Mark Koenig, 125	Joe Dugan, 91	Babe Ruth, 154	Earle Combs, 149	Bob Meusel, 131	
Leo Durocher, 93	Gene Robertson, 77	Earle Combs, 141	Babe Ruth, 133	Bob Meusel, 96	
Lyn Lary, 113	Ben Chapman, 91	Babe Ruth, 144	Earle Combs, 135	Harry Rice, 87	
Lyn Lary, 155	Joe Sewell, 121	Babe Ruth, 142	Ben Chapman, 137	Earle Combs, 129	
Frank Crosetti, 83	Joe Sewell, 122	Ben Chapman, 149	Earle Combs, 138	Babe Ruth, 127	
Frank Crosetti, 133	Joe Sewell, 131	Ben Chapman, 147	Babe Ruth, 132	Earle Combs, 104	
Frank Crosetti, 119	Jack Saltzgaver, 84	Ben Chapman, 149	Babe Ruth, 111	Myril Hoag, 86	
Frank Crosetti, 87	Red Rolfe, 136	Ben Chapman, 138	George Selkirk, 127	Jesse Hill, 94	
Frank Crosetti, 151	Red Rolfe, 133	Joe DiMaggio, 138	George Selkirk, 135	Jake Powell, 84	
Frank Crosetti, 147	Red Rolfe, 154	Joe DiMaggio, 150	Myril Hoag, 99	Jake Powell, 94	
Frank Crosetti, 157	Red Rolfe, 151	Joe DiMaggio, 145	Tommy Henrich, 130	George Selkirk, 95	
Frank Crosetti, 152	Red Rolfe, 152	George Selkirk, 124	Joe DiMaggio, 117	Charlie Keller, 105	
Frank Crosetti, 145	Red Rolfe, 138	Charlie Keller, 136	Joe DiMaggio, 130	George Selkirk, 111	
Phil Rizzuto, 128	Red Rolfe, 134	Tommy Henrich, 139	Joe DiMaggio, 139	Charlie Keller, 137	
Phil Rizzuto, 144	Frank Crosetti, 62	Joe DiMaggio, 154	Charlie Keller, 152	Tommy Henrich, 119	
Frank Crosetti, 90	Billy Johnson, 155	Charlie Keller, 141	Johnny Lindell, 122	Bud Metheny, 91	

POSITION LEADERS YEAR BY YEAR *(Determined by number of games played at that position)*

Year	Pitcher (starts)	Pitcher (games)	Catcher	First Baseman	Second Baseman
1944	Hank Borowy, 30	Hank Borowy, 35 / Jim Turner, 35*	Mike Garbark, 85	Nick Etten, 154	Snuffy Stirnweiss, 154
1945	Bill Bevens, 25	Jim Turner, 30*	Mike Garbark, 59	Nick Etten, 152	Snuffy Stirnweiss, 152
1946	Spud Chandler, 32	Spud Chandler, 34	Aaron Robinson, 95	Nick Etten, 84	Joe Gordon, 108
1947	Allie Reynolds, 30	Joe Page, 56*	Aaron Robinson, 74	George McQuinn, 142	Snuffy Stirnweiss, 148
1948	Ed Lopat, 31 / Vic Raschi, 31 / Allie Reynolds, 31	Joe Page, 55*	Gus Niarhos, 82	George McQuinn, 90	Snuffy Stirnweiss, 141
1949	Vic Raschi, 37	Joe Page, 60*	Yogi Berra, 109	Tommy Henrich, 52	Jerry Coleman, 122
1950	Ed Lopat, 32 / Vic Raschi, 32	Joe Page, 37*	Yogi Berra, 148	Johnny Mize, 72	Jerry Coleman, 152
1951	Vic Raschi, 34	Allie Reynolds, 40	Yogi Berra, 141	Johnny Mize, 93	Jerry Coleman, 102
1952	Vic Raschi, 31	Allie Reynolds, 35 / Johnny Sain, 35*	Yogi Berra, 140	Joe Collins, 119	Billy Martin, 107
1953	Whitey Ford, 30	Allie Reynolds, 41*	Yogi Berra, 133	Joe Collins, 113	Billy Martin, 146
1954	Whitey Ford, 28	Johnny Sain, 45*	Yogi Berra, 149	Joe Collins, 117	Gil McDougald, 92
1955	Bob Turley, 34	Jim Konstanty, 45*	Yogi Berra, 145	Bill Skowron, 74	Gil McDougald, 126
1956	Johnny Kucks, 31	Tom Morgan, 41*	Yogi Berra, 135	Bill Skowron, 120	Billy Martin, 105
1957	Tom Sturdivant, 28	Art Ditmar, 46* / Bob Grim, 46*	Yogi Berra, 121	Bill Skowron, 115	Bobby Richardson, 93
1958	Bob Turley, 31	Ryne Duren, 44*	Yogi Berra, 88	Bill Skowron, 118	Gil McDougald, 115
1959	Whitey Ford, 29	Ryne Duren, 41*	Yogi Berra, 116	Bill Skowron, 72	Bobby Richardson, 109
1960	Whitey Ford, 29	Bobby Shantz, 42* / Ryne Duren, 42*	Elston Howard, 91	Bill Skowron, 142	Bobby Richardson, 141
1961	Whitey Ford, 39	Luis Arroyo, 65*	Elston Howard, 111	Bill Skowron, 149	Bobby Richardson, 161
1962	Ralph Terry, 39	Marshall Bridges, 52*	Elston Howard, 129	Bill Skowron, 135	Bobby Richardson, 161
1963	Whitey Ford, 37 / Ralph Terry, 37	Hal Reniff, 48*	Elston Howard, 132	Joe Pepitone, 143	Bobby Richardson, 150
1964	Jim Bouton, 37	Pete Mikkelsen, 50*	Elston Howard, 146	Joe Pepitone, 155	Bobby Richardson, 157
1965	Mel Stottlemyre, 37	Pedro Ramos, 65*	Elston Howard, 95	Joe Pepitone, 115	Bobby Richardson, 158
1966	Mel Stottlemyre, 35	Hal Reniff, 56*	Elston Howard, 100	Joe Pepitone, 119	Bobby Richardson, 147
1967	Mel Stottlemyre, 36	Dooley Womack, 65*	Jake Gibbs, 99	Mickey Mantle, 131	Horace Clarke, 140
1968	Mel Stottlemyre, 36	Dooley Womack, 45*	Jake Gibbs, 121	Mickey Mantle, 131	Horace Clarke, 139
1969	Mel Stottlemyre, 39	Lindy McDaniel, 51*	Jake Gibbs, 66	Joe Pepitone, 132	Horace Clarke, 156
1970	Mel Stottlemyre, 37 / Fritz Peterson, 37	Lindy McDaniel, 62*	Thurman Munson, 125	Danny Cater, 131	Horace Clarke, 157
1971	Mel Stottlemyre, 35 / Fritz Peterson, 35	Lindy McDaniel, 44*	Thurman Munson, 117	Danny Cater, 78	Horace Clarke, 156
1972	Mel Stottlemyre, 36	Sparky Lyle, 59*	Thurman Munson, 132	Ron Blomberg, 95 / Felipe Alou, 95	Horace Clarke, 143
1973	Mel Stottlemyre, 38	Sparky Lyle, 51*	Thurman Munson, 142	Felipe Alou, 67	Horace Clarke, 147
1974	Pat Dobson, 39	Sparky Lyle, 66*	Thurman Munson, 137	Chris Chambliss, 106	Sandy Alomar, 76
1975	Catfish Hunter, 39	Sparky Lyle, 49*	Thurman Munson, 130	Chris Chambliss, 147	Sandy Alomar, 150
1976	Catfish Hunter, 36	Sparky Lyle, 64*	Thurman Munson, 121	Chris Chambliss, 155	Willie Randolph, 124
1977	Ed Figueroa, 32	Sparky Lyle, 72*	Thurman Munson, 136	Chris Chambliss, 157	Willie Randolph, 147
1978	Ed Figueroa, 35 / Ron Guidry, 35	Rich Gossage, 63*	Thurman Munsun, 125	Chris Chambliss, 155	Willie Randolph, 134
1979	Tommy John, 36	Ron Davis, 44*	Thurman Munson, 88	Chris Chambliss, 134	Willie Randolph, 153
1980	Tommy John, 36	Rich Gossage, 64*	Rick Cerone, 147	Bob Watson, 104	Willie Randolph, 138
1981	Rudy May, 22	Ron Davis, 43	Rick Cerone, 69	Bob Watson, 50	Willie Randolph, 93

Shortstop	Third Baseman	Outfielder	Outfielder	Outfielder	Designated Hitter
Mike Milosevich, 91	Oscar Grimes, 97	Johnny Lindell, 149	Bud Metheny, 132	Hersh Martin, 80	
Frank Crosetti, 126	Oscar Grimes, 141	Bud Metheny, 128	Hersh Martin, 102	Tuck Stainback, 83	
Phil Rizzuto, 125	Snuffy Stirnweiss, 79	Charlie Keller, 149	Joe DiMaggio, 131	Tommy Henrich, 111	
Phil Rizzuto, 151	Billy Johnson, 132	Joe DiMaggio, 139	Tommy Henrich, 132	Johnny Lindell, 118	
Phil Rizzuto, 128	Billy Johnson, 118	Joe DiMaggio, 152	Tommy Henrich, 102	Johnny Lindell, 79	
Phil Rizzuto, 152	Bobby Brown, 86	Cliff Mapes, 108	Gene Woodling, 98	Hank Bauer, 95	
Phil Rizzuto, 155	Billy Johnson, 100	Joe DiMaggio, 137	Gene Woodling, 118	Hank Bauer, 110	
Phil Rizzuto, 144	Bobby Brown, 90	Gene Woodling, 116	Joe DiMaggio, 113	Hank Bauer, 107	
Phil Rizzuto, 152	Gil McDougald, 117	Mickey Mantle, 141	Hank Bauer, 139	Gene Woodling, 118	
Phil Rizzuto, 133	Gil McDougald, 136	Hank Bauer, 126	Mickey Mantle, 121	Gene Woodling, 119	
Phil Rizzuto, 126	Andy Carey, 120	Mickey Mantle, 144	Irv Noren, 116	Hank Bauer, 108	
Billy Hunter, 98	Andy Carey, 135	Mickey Mantle, 145	Hank Bauer, 133	Irv Noren, 126	
Gil McDougald, 92	Andy Carey, 131	Hank Bauer, 146	Mickey Mantle, 144	Elston Howard, 65	
Gil McDougald, 121	Andy Carey, 81	Mickey Mantle, 139	Hank Bauer, 135	Elston Howard, 71	
Tony Kubek, 134	Andy Carey, 99	Mickey Mantle, 150	Norm Siebern, 133	Hank Bauer, 123	
Tony Kubek, 67	Hector Lopez, 76	Mickey Mantle, 143	Hank Bauer, 111	Norm Siebern, 93	
Tony Kubek, 136	Clete Boyer, 99	Mickey Mantle, 150	Roger Maris, 131	Hector Lopez, 106	
Tony Kubek, 145	Clete Boyer, 141	Roger Maris, 160	Mickey Mantle, 150	Yogi Berra, 87	
Tom Tresh, 111	Clete Boyer, 157	Roger Maris, 154	Mickey Mantle, 117	Hector Lopez, 84	
Tony Kubek, 132	Clete Boyer, 141	Tom Tresh, 144	Hector Lopez, 124	Roger Maris, 86	
Tony Kubek, 99	Clete Boyer, 123	Tom Tresh, 146	Roger Maris, 137	Mickey Mantle, 132	
Tony Kubek, 93	Clete Boyer, 147	Tom Tresh, 154	Mickey Mantle, 108	Hector Lopez, 75	
Horace Clarke, 63	Clete Boyer, 85	Mickey Mantle, 97	Roger Maris, 95	Tom Tresh, 84	
Ruben Amaro, 123	Charley Smith, 115	Joe Pepitone, 123	Tom Tresh, 118	Steve Whitaker, 114	
Tom Tresh, 119	Bobby Cox, 132	Roy White, 154	Bill Robinson, 98	Joe Pepitone, 92	
Gene Michael, 118	Jerry Kenney, 83	Roy White, 126	Bobby Murcer, 118	Bill Robinson, 62	
Gene Michael, 123	Jerry Kenney, 135	Roy White, 161	Bobby Murcer, 155	Curt Blefary, 79	
Gene Michael, 136	Jerry Kenney, 109	Roy White, 145	Bobby Murcer, 143	Felipe Alou, 80	
Gene Michael, 121	Celerino Sanchez, 68	Roy White, 155	Bobby Murcer, 151	Johnny Callison, 74	
Gene Michael, 128	Graig Nettles, 157	Roy White, 162	Bobby Murcer, 160	Matty Alou, 94	Jim Hart, 106
Jim Mason, 152	Graig Nettles, 154	Bobby Murcer, 156	Elliott Maddox, 135	Lou Piniella, 130	Ron Blomberg, 58
Jim Mason, 93	Graig Nettles, 157	Roy White, 135	Bobby Bonds, 129	Elliott Maddox, 55	Ed Herrmann, 35
Fred Stanley, 110	Graig Nettles, 158	Roy White, 156	Mickey Rivers, 136	Oscar Gamble, 104	Carlos May, 81
Bucky Dent, 157	Graig Nettles, 156	Mickey Rivers, 136	Roy White, 135	Reggie Jackson, 127	Carlos May, 51
Bucky Dent, 123	Graig Nettles, 159	Mickey Rivers, 138	Reggie Jackson, 104	Lou Piniella, 103	Cliff Johnson, 39
Bucky Dent, 141	Graig Nettles, 144	Reggie Jackson, 125	Lou Piniella, 112	Bobby Murcer, 70	Jim Spencer, 71
Bucky Dent, 141	Graig Nettles, 88	Bobby Brown, 131	Lou Piniella, 104	Reggie Jackson, 94	Eric Soderholm, 51
Bucky Dent, 73	Graig Nettles, 97	Dave Winfield, 102	Jerry Mumphrey, 79	Reggie Jackson, 61	Oscar Gamble, 33
					Reggie Jackson, 33
					Bobby Murcer, 33

YEAR BY YEAR

Year	Position	W–L	Pct.	World Series Opponent	World Series Record	Manager	Attendance
1903	4th (−17)	72–62	.537			Clark Griffith	211,808
1904	2nd (−1½)	92–59	.609			Clark Griffith	438,919
1905	6th (−21½)	71–78	.477			Clark Griffith	309,100
1906	2nd (−3)	90–61	.596			Clark Griffith	434,700
1907	5th (−21)	70–78	.473			Clark Griffith	350,020
1908	8th (−39½)	51–103	.331			C. Griffith–K. Elberfeld	305,500
1909	5th (−23½)	74–77	.490			George Stallings	501,000
1910	2nd (−14½)	88–63	.583			G. Stallings–H. Chase	355,857
1911	6th (−25½)	76–76	.500			Hal Chase	302,444
1912	8th (−55)	50–102	.329			Harry Wolverton	242,194
1913	7th (−38)	57–94	.377			Frank Chance	357,551
‡1914	†6th (−30)	70–84	.455			F. Chance–R. Peckinpaugh	359,477
1915	5th (−32½)	69–83	.454			Wild Bill Donovan	256,035
1916	4th (−11)	80–74	.519			Wild Bill Donovan	469,211
1917	6th (−28½)	71–82	.464			Wild Bill Donovan	330,294
1918	4th (−13½)	60–63	.488			Miller Huggins	282,047
1919	3rd (−7½)	80–59	.576			Miller Huggins	619,154
1920	3rd (−3)	95–59	.617			Miller Huggins	1,289,422
1921	1st (+4½)	98–55	.641	Giants	3–5	Miller Huggins	1,230,696
1922	1st (+1)	94–60	.610	Giants	0–4	Miller Huggins	1,026,134
1923	*1st (+16)	98–54	.645	Giants	4–2	Miller Huggins	1,007,066
1924	2nd (−2)	89–63	.586			Miller Huggins	1,053,533
1925	7th (−28½)	69–85	.448			Miller Huggins	697,267
1926	1st (+3)	91–63	.591	Cardinals	3–4	Miller Huggins	1,027,095
1927	*1st (+19)	110–44	.714	Pirates	4–0	Miller Huggins	1,164,015
1928	*1st (+2½)	101–53	.656	Cardinals	4–0	Miller Huggins	1,072,132
1929	2nd (−18)	88–66	.571			M. Huggins–A. Fletcher	960,148
1930	3rd (−16)	86–68	.558			Bob Shawkey	1,169,230
1931	2nd (−13½)	94–59	.614			Joe McCarthy	912,437
1932	*1st (+13)	107–47	.695	Cubs	4–0	Joe McCarthy	962,320
1933	2nd (−7)	91–59	.607			Joe McCarthy	728,014
1934	2nd (−7)	94–60	.610			Joe McCarthy	854,682
1935	2nd (−3)	89–60	.597			Joe McCarthy	657,508
1936	*1st (+19½)	102–51	.667	Giants	4–2	Joe McCarthy	976,913
1937	*1st (+13)	102–52	.662	Giants	4–1	Joe McCarthy	998,148
1938	*1st (+9½)	99–53	.651	Cubs	4–0	Joe McCarthy	970,916
1939	*1st (+17)	106–45	.702	Reds	4–0	Joe McCarthy	859,785
1940	3rd (−2)	88–66	.571			Joe McCarthy	988,975
1941	*1st (+17)	101–53	.656	Dodgers	4–1	Joe McCarthy	964,722
1942	1st (+9)	103–51	.669	Cardinals	1–4	Joe McCarthy	988,251
1943	*1st (+13½)	98–56	.636	Cardinals	4–1	Joe McCarthy	645,006
1944	3rd (−6)	83–71	.539			Joe McCarthy	822,864
1945	4th (−6½)	81–71	.533			Joe McCarthy	811,846
1946	3rd (−17)	87–67	.565			J. McCarthy–B. Dickey–J. Neun	2,265,512
1947	*1st (+12)	97–57	.630	Dodgers	4–3	Bucky Harris	2,178,937
1948	3rd (−2½)	94–60	.610			Bucky Harris	2,373,901
1949	*1st (+1)	97–57	.630	Dodgers	4–1	Casey Stengel	2,281,676

YEAR BY YEAR

Year	Position	W–L	Pct.	World Series Opponent	World Series Record	Manager	Attendance
1950	*1st (+3)	98–56	.636	Phillies	4–0	Casey Stengel	2,081,380
1951	*1st (+5)	98–56	.636	Giants	4–2	Casey Stengel	1,950,107
1952	*1st (+2)	95–59	.617	Dodgers	4–3	Casey Stengel	1,629,665
1953	*1st (+8½)	99–52	.656	Dodgers	4–2	Casey Stengel	1,537,811
1954	2nd (–8)	103–51	.669			Casey Stengel	1,475,171
1955	1st (+3)	96–58	.623	Dodgers	3–4	Casey Stengel	1,490,138
1956	*1st (+9)	97–57	.680	Dodgers	4–3	Casey Stengel	1,491,784
1957	1st (+8)	98–56	.636	Braves	3–4	Casey Stengel	1,497,134
1958	*1st (+10)	92–62	.597	Braves	4–3	Casey Stengel	1,428,438
1959	3rd (–15)	79–75	.513			Casey Stengel	1,552,030
1960	1st (+8)	97–57	.630	Pirates	3–4	Casey Stengel	1,627,349
1961	*1st (+8)	109–53	.673	Reds	4–1	Ralph Houk	1,747,736
1962	*1st (+5)	96–66	.593	Giants	4–3	Ralph Houk	1,493,574
1963	1st (+10½)	104–57	.646	Dodgers	0–4	Ralph Houk	1,308,920
1964	1st (+1)	99–63	.611	Cardinals	3–4	Yogi Berra	1,305,638
1965	6th (–25)	77–85	.475			Johnny Keane	1,213,552
1966	10th (–26½)	70–89	.440			J. Keane–R. Houk	1,124,648
1967	9th (–20)	72–90	.444			Ralph Houk	1,141,714
1968	5th (–20)	83–79	.512			Ralph Houk	1,125,124
1969	5th (–28½)	80–81	.497			Ralph Houk	1,067,996
1970	2nd (–15)	93–69	.574			Ralph Houk	1,136,879
1971	4th (–21)	82–80	.506			Ralph Houk	1,070,711
1972	4th (–6½)	79–76	.510			Ralph Houk	966,328
1973	4th (–17)	80–82	.494			Ralph Houk	1,262,077
1974	2nd (–2)	89–73	.549			Bill Virdon	1,273,075
1975	3rd (–12)	83–77	.519			B. Virdon–B. Martin	1,288,048
1976	1st (+10½)	97–62	.610	Reds	0–4	Billy Martin	2,012,434
1977	*1st (2½)	100–62	.617	Dodgers	4–2	Billy Martin	2,103,092
1978	*1st† (+1)	100–63	.613	Dodgers	4–2	B. Martin–B. Lemon	2,335,871
1979	4th (–13½)	89–71	.556			B. Lemon–B. Martin	2,537,765
1980	1st (+3)	103–59	.636			Dick Howser	2,627,417
1981 §	1st (+2)	34–22	.607	Dodgers	2–4	Gene Michael–B. Lemon	1,614,353**
	6th (–5)	25–26	.490				

*Won world championship
**Only 50 home dates because of players strike.
† Won 1-game playoff at Boston for 1978 A.L. East title.
‡ Tied with Chicago for sixth in 1914.
§ Won 1st half, then defeated 2nd half winner Milwaukee in a playoff series to win pennant.
World champions—22.
American League champions—32.
American League East champions—5.
Finished first—33; second—12; third—9; fourth—8; fifth—5; sixth—5; seventh—2; eighth—2; ninth—1; tenth—1.
Highest percentage—.714 in 1927; lowest—.329 in 1912.

YANKEE FIRST-PLACE TEAMS

1921 American League Champions

Manager: Miller Huggins
World Series Roster: Pitchers: Rip Collins, Alex Ferguson, Harry Harper, Waite Hoyt, Carl Mays, Bill Piercy, Jack Quinn, Tom Rogers, Bob Shawkey. *Catchers:* Al DeVormer, Wally Schang. *Infielders:* Frank Baker, Mike McNally, Johnny Mitchell, Roger Peckinpaugh, Wally Pipp, Aaron Ward. *Outfielders:* Chick Fewster, Chicken Hawks, Bob Meusel, Elmer Miller, Braggo Roth, Babe Ruth.

World Series

	W	L	Pct.
Giants	5	3	.625
Yankees	3	5	.375

Game 1 (Oct. 5 at Polo Grounds)

| Yankees | 100 | 011 | 000 | — | 3 | 7 | 0 |
| Giants | 000 | 000 | 000 | — | 0 | 5 | 0 |

Yankees: CARL MAYS and Wally Schang.
Giants: PHIL DOUGLAS, Jesse Barnes (9th) and Frank Snyder.
Home Runs: None.
Attendance: 30,202.

Game 2 (Oct. 6 at Polo Grounds)

| Giants | 000 | 000 | 000 | — | 0 | 2 | 3 |
| Yankees | 000 | 100 | 02X | — | 3 | 3 | 0 |

Giants: ART NEHF and Earl Smith.
Yankees: WAITE HOYT and Wally Schang.
Home Runs: None
Attendance: 34,939.

Game 3 (Oct. 7 at Polo Grounds)

| Yankees | 004 | 000 | 010 | — | 5 | 8 | 0 |
| Giants | 004 | 000 | 81X | — | 13 | 20 | 0 |

Yankees: Bob Shawkey, JACK QUINN (3d), Rip Collins (7th), Tom Rogers (7th) and Wally Schang, Al DeVormer (8th).
Giants: Fred Toney, JESSE BARNES (3d) and Frank Snyder.
Home Runs: None.
Attendance: 36,509.

Game 4 (Oct. 9 at Polo Grounds)

| Giants | 000 | 000 | 031 | — | 4 | 9 | 1 |
| Yankees | 000 | 010 | 001 | — | 2 | 7 | 1 |

Giants: PHIL DOUGLAS and Frank Snyder.
Yankees: CARL MAYS and Wally Schang.
Home Run: Babe Ruth (Yankees).
Attendance: 36,372.

Game 5 (Oct. 10 at Polo Grounds)

| Yankees | 001 | 200 | 000 | — | 3 | 6 | 1 |
| Giants | 100 | 000 | 000 | — | 1 | 10 | 1 |

Yankees: WAITE HOYT and Wally Schang.
Giants: ART NEHF and Earl Smith.
Home Runs: None.
Attendance: 35,758.

Game 6 (Oct. 11 at Polo Grounds)

| Giants | 030 | 401 | 000 | — | 8 | 13 | 0 |
| Yankees | 320 | 000 | 000 | — | 5 | 7 | 2 |

Giants: Fred Toney, JESSE BARNES (1st) and Frank Snyder.
Yankees: Harry Harper, BOB SHAWKEY (2d), Bill Piercy (9th) and Wally Schang.
Home Runs: Irish Meusel (Giants), Frank Snyder (Giants) and Chick Fewster (Yankees).
Attendance: 34,283.

NOTE: Capital letters indicate pitcher of decision.

Game 7 (Oct. 12 at Polo Grounds)

| Yankees | 010 | 000 | 000 | — | 1 | 8 | 1 |
| Giants | 000 | 100 | 10X | — | 2 | 6 | 0 |

Yankees: CARL MAYS and Wally Schang.
Giants: PHIL DOUGLAS and Frank Snyder.
Home Runs: None.
Attendance: 36,503.

Game 8 (Oct. 13 at Polo Grounds)

| Giants | 100 | 000 | 000 | — | 1 | 6 | 0 |
| Yankees | 000 | 000 | 000 | — | 0 | 4 | 1 |

Giants: ART NEHF and Frank Snyder.
Yankees: WAITE HOYT and Wally Schang.
Home Runs: None.
Attendance: 25,410

NOTE: Although owned by the Giants, the Polo Grounds was also the Yankees' home field. So the rivals alternated being the "home" team during both the 1921 and 1922 World Series—until Yankee Stadium was opened in 1923.

1922 American League Champions

Manager: Miller Huggins
World Series Roster: Pitchers: Joe Bush, Waite Hoyt, Sad Sam Jones, Carl Mays, George Murray, Lefty O'Doul, Bob Shawkey. *Catchers:* Al DeVormer, Fred Hofmann, Wally Schang. *Infielders:* Frank Baker, Joe Dugan, Mike McNally, Wally Pipp, Everett Scott, Aaron Ward. *Outfielders:* Norm McMillan, Bob Meusel, Babe Ruth, Camp Skinner, Elmer Smith, Whitey Witt.

World Series

	W	L	T	Pct.
Giants	4	0	1	1.000
Yankees	0	4	1	.000

Game 1 (Oct. 4 at Polo Grounds)

| Yankees | 000 | 001 | 100 | — | 2 | 7 | 0 |
| Giants | 000 | 000 | 03X | — | 3 | 11 | 3 |

Yankees: JOE BUSH, Waite Hoyt (8th) and Wally Schang.
Giants: Art Nehf, ROSY RYAN (8th) and Frank Snyder.
Home Runs: None.
Attendance: 36,514.

Game 2 (Oct. 5 at Polo Grounds)

| Giants | 300 | 000 | 000 | 0 | — | 3 | 8 | 1 |
| Yankees | 100 | 100 | 010 | 0 | — | 3 | 8 | 0 |

Giants: JESSE BARNES and Frank Snyder.
Yankees: BOB SHAWKEY and Wally Schang.
Home Runs: Irish Meusel (Giants) and Aaron Ward (Yankees).
Attendance: 37,020.

Game 3 (Oct. 6 at Polo Grounds)

| Yankees | 000 | 000 | 000 | — | 0 | 4 | 1 |
| Giants | 002 | 000 | 10X | — | 3 | 12 | 1 |

Yankees: WAITE HOYT, Sad Sam Jones (8th) and Wally Schang.
Giants: JACK SCOTT and Earl Smith.
Home Runs: None.
Attendance: 37,620.

Game 4 (Oct. 7 at Polo Grounds)

| Giants | 000 | 040 | 000 | — | 4 | 9 | 1 |
| Yankees | 200 | 000 | 100 | — | 3 | 8 | 0 |

Giants: HUGH McQUILLAN and Frank Snyder.
Yankees: CARL MAYS, Sad Sam Jones (9th) and Wally Schang.
Home Run: Aaron Ward (Yankees).
Attendance: 36,242.

Game 5 (Oct. 8 at Polo Grounds)

Yankees	100	010	100	—	3	5	0
Giants	020	000	03X	—	5	10	0

Yankees: JOE BUSH and Wally Schang.
Giants: ART NEHF and Frank Snyder.
Home Runs: None.
Attendance: 38,551.

1923 World Champions

Manager: Miller Huggins
World Series Roster: Pitchers: Joe Bush, Waite Hoyt, Sad Sam Jones, Carl Mays, Herb Pennock, George Pipgras, Oscar Roettger, Bob Shawkey. *Catchers:* Benny Bengough, Fred Hofmann, Wally Schang. *Infielders:* Joe Dugan, Mike Gazella, Ernie Johnson, Mike McNally, Wally Pipp, Everett Scott, Aaron Ward. *Outfielders:* Hinkey Haines, Harvey Hendrick, Bob Meusel, Babe Ruth, Elmer Smith, Whitey Witt.

World Series

	W	L	Pct.
Yankees	4	2	.667
Giants	2	4	.333

Game 1 (Oct. 10 at Yankee Stadium)

Giants	004	000	001	—	5	8	0
Yankees	120	000	100	—	4	12	1

Giants: Mule Watson, ROSY RYAN (3d) and Frank Snyder.
Yankees: Waite Hoyt, JOE BUSH (3d) and Wally Schang.
Home Run: Casey Stengel (Giants).
Attendance: 55,307.

Game 2 (Oct. 11 at Polo Grounds)

Yankees	010	210	000	—	4	10	0
Giants	010	001	000	—	2	9	2

Yankees: HERB PENNOCK and Wally Schang.
Giants: HUGH McQUILLAN, Jack Bentley (4th) and Frank Snyder.
Home Runs: Babe Ruth (Yankees) 2, Aaron Ward (Yankees) and Irish Meusel (Giants).
Attendance: 40,402.

Game 3 (Oct. 12 at Yankee Stadium)

Giants	000	000	100	—	1	4	0
Yankees	000	000	000	—	0	6	1

Giants: ART NEHF and Frank Snyder.
Yankees: SAD SAM JONES, Joe Bush (9th) and Wally Schang.
Home Run: Casey Stengel (Giants).
Attendance: 62,430.

Game 4 (Oct. 13 at Polo Grounds)

Yankees	061	100	000	—	8	13	1
Giants	000	000	031	—	4	13	1

Yankees: BOB SHAWKEY, Herb Pennock (8th) and Wally Schang.
Giants: JACK SCOTT, Rosy Ryan (2d), Hugh McQuillan (2d), Claude Jonnard (8th), Virgil Barnes (9th) and Frank Snyder.
Home Run: Ross Youngs (Giants).
Attendance: 46,302.

Game 5 (Oct. 14 at Yankee Stadium)

Giants	010	000	000	—	1	3	2
Yankees	340	100	00X	—	8	14	0

Giants: JACK BENTLEY, Jack Scott (2d), Virgil Barnes (4th), Claude Jonnard (8th) and Hank Gowdy.
Yankees: JOE BUSH and Wally Schang.
Home Run: Joe Dugan (Yankees).
Attendance: 62,817.

Game 6 (Oct. 15 at Polo Grounds)

Yankees	100	000	050	—	6	5	1
Giants	100	111	000	—	4	10	1

Yankees: HERB PENNOCK, Sad Sam Jones (8th) and Wally Schang.
Giants: ART NEHF, Rosy Ryan (8th) and Frank Snyder.
Home Runs: Babe Ruth (Yankees) and Frank Snyder (Giants).
Attendance: 34,172

1926 American League Champions

Manager: Miller Huggins
World Series Roster: Pitchers: Walter Beall, Garland Braxton, Waite Hoyt, Sad Sam Jones, Herb McQuaid, Herb Pennock, Dutch Ruether, Bob Shawkey, Urban Shocker, Myles Thomas. *Catchers:* Benny Bengough, Pat Collins, Hank Severeid. *Infielders:* Spencer Adams, Joe Dugan, Mike Gazella, Lou Gehrig, Mark Koenig, Tony Lazzeri, Aaron Ward. *Outfielders:* Roy Carlyle, Earle Combs, Bob Meusel, Ben Paschal, Babe Ruth.

World Series

	W	L	Pct.
Cardinals	4	3	.571
Yankees	3	4	.429

Game 1 (Oct. 2 at Yankee Stadium)

Cardinals	100	000	000	—	1	3	1
Yankees	100	001	00X	—	2	6	0

Cardinals: BILL SHERDEL, Jesse Haines (8th) and Bob O'Farrell.
Yankees: HERB PENNOCK and Hank Severeid.
Home Runs: None.
Attendance: 61,658.

Game 2 (Oct. 3 at Yankee Stadium)

Cardinals	002	000	301	—	6	12	1
Yankees	020	000	000	—	2	4	0

Cardinals: GROVER CLEVELAND ALEXANDER and Bob O'Farrell.
Yankees: URBAN SHOCKER, Bob Shawkey (8th), Sad Sam Jones (9th) and Hank Severeid, Pat Collins (9th).
Home Runs: Billy Southworth (Cardinals) and Tommy Thevenow (Cardinals).
Attendance: 63,600.

Game 3 (Oct. 5 at St. Louis)

Yankees	000	000	000	—	0	5	1
Cardinals	000	310	00X	—	4	8	0

Yankees: DUTCH RUETHER, Bob Shawkey (5th), Myles Thomas (8th) and Hank Severeid.
Cardinals: JESSE HAINES and Bob O'Farrell.
Home Run: Jesse Haines (Cardinals).
Attendance: 37,708.

Game 4 (Oct. 6 at St. Louis)

Yankees	101	142	100	—	10	14	1
Cardinals	100	300	001	—	5	14	0

Yankees: WAITE HOYT and Hank Severeid.
Cardinals: Flint Rhem, ART REINHART (5th), Hi Bell (5th), Wild Bill Hallahan (7th), Vic Keen (9th) and Bob O'Farrell.
Home Runs: Babe Ruth (Yankees), 3.
Attendance: 38,825.

Game 5 (Oct. 7 at St. Louis)

Yankees	000	001	001	1	—	3	9	1
Cardinals	000	100	100	0	—	2	7	1

Yankees: HERB PENNOCK and Hank Severeid.
Cardinals: BILL SHERDEL and Bob O'Farrell.
Home Runs: None.
Attendance: 39,552.

Game 6 (Oct. 9 at Yankee Stadium)

Cardinals	300	010	501	—	10	13	2
Yankees	000	100	100	—	2	8	1

Cardinals: GROVER CLEVELAND ALEXANDER and Bob O'Farrell.
Yankees: BOB SHAWKEY, Urban Shocker (7th), Myles Thomas (8th) and Hank Severeid, Pat Collins (8th).
Home Run: Les Bell (Cardinals).
Attendance: 48,615.

Game 7 (Oct. 10 at Yankee Stadium)

Cardinals	000	300	000	—	3	8	0
Yankees	001	001	000	—	2	8	3

Cardinals: JESSE HAINES, Grover Cleveland Alexander (7th) and Bob O'Farrell.
Yankees: WAITE HOYT, Herb Pennock (7th) and Hank Severeid, Pat Collins (7th).
Home Run: Babe Ruth (Yankees).
Attendance: 38,093.

1927 World Champions

Manager: Miller Huggins
World Series Roster: Pitchers: Joe Giard, Waite Hoyt, Wilcy Moore, Herb Pennock, George Pipgras, Dutch Ruether, Bob Shawkey, Urban Shocker, Myles Thomas. *Catchers:* Benny Bengough, Pat Collins, Johnny Grabowski. *Infielders:* Joe Dugan, Mike Gazella, Lou Gehrig, Mark Koenig, Tony Lazzeri, Ray Morehart, Julie Wera. *Outfielders:* Earle Combs, Cedric Durst, Bob Meusel, Ben Paschal, Babe Ruth.

World Series

	W	L	Pct.
Yankees	4	0	1.000
Pirates	0	4	.000

Game 1 (Oct. 5 at Pittsburgh)

Yankees	103	010	000	—	5	6	1
Pirates	101	010	010	—	4	9	2

Yankees: WAITE HOYT, Wilcy Moore (8th) and Pat Collins.
Pirates: RAY KREMER, Johnny Miljus (6th) and Earl Smith.
Home Runs: None.
Attendance: 41,467.

Game 2 (Oct. 6 at Pittsburgh)

Yankees	003	000	030	—	6	11	0
Pirates	100	000	010	—	2	7	2

Yankees: GEORGE PIPGRAS and Benny Bengough.
Pirates: VIC ALDRIDGE, Mike Cvengros (8th), Joe Dawson (9th) and Johnny Gooch.
Home Runs: None.
Attendance: 41,634.

Game 3 (Oct. 7 at Yankee Stadium)

Pirates	000	000	010	—	1	3	1
Yankees	200	000	60X	—	8	9	0

Pirates: LEE MEADOWS, Mike Cvengros (7th) and Johnny Gooch.
Yankees: HERB PENNOCK and Johnny Grabowski, Benny Bengough (8th).
Home Run: Babe Ruth (Yankees).
Attendance: 60,695.

Game 4 (Oct. 8 at Yankee Stadium)

Pirates	100	000	200	—	3	10	1
Yankees	100	020	001	—	4	12	2

Pirates: Carmen Hill, JOHNNY MILJUS (7th) and Earl Smith Johnny Gooch (7th).
Yankees: WILCY MOORE and Pat Collins.
Home Run: Babe Ruth (Yankees).
Attendance: 57,909.

1928 World Champions

Manager: Miller Huggins
World Series Roster: Pitchers: Fred Heimach, Waite Hoyt, Herb Pennock, George Pipgras, Rosy Ryan, Myles Thomas, Tom Zachary. *Catchers:* Benny Bengough, Pat Collins, Bill Dickey, Johnny Grabowski. *Infielders:* Joe Dugan, Leo Durocher. Mike Gazella, Lou Gehrig, Mark Koenig, Tony Lazzeri, Gene Robertson. *Outfielders:* Earle Combs, Cedric Durst, Bob Meusel, Ben Paschal, Babe Ruth.

World Series

	W	L	Pct.
Yankees	4	0	1.000
Cardinals	0	4	.000

Game 1 (Oct. 4 at Yankee Stadium)

Cardinals	000	000	100	—	1	3	1
Yankees	100	200	01X	—	4	7	0

Cardinals: BILL SHERDEL, Syl Johnson (8th) and Jimmie Wilson.
Yankees: WAITE HOYT and Benny Bengough.
Home Runs: Bob Meusel (Yankees) and Jim Bottomley (Cardinals).
Attendance: 61,425.

Game 2 (Oct. 5 at Yankee Stadium)

Cardinals	030	000	000	—	3	4	1
Yankees	314	000	10X	—	9	8	2

Cardinals: GROVER CLEVELAND ALEXANDER, Clarence Mitchell (3d) and Jimmie Wilson.
Yankees: GEORGE PIPGRAS and Benny Bengough.
Home Run: Lou Gehrig (Yankees).
Attendance: 60,714.

Game 3 (Oct. 7 at St. Louis)

Yankees	010	203	100	—	7	7	2
Cardinals	200	010	000	—	3	9	3

Yankees: TOM ZACHARY and Benny Bengough.
Cardinals: JESSE HAINES, Syl Johnson (7th), Flint Rhem (8th) and Jimmie Wilson.
Home Runs: Lou Gehrig (Yankees), 2.
Attendance: 39,602.

Game 4 (Oct. 9 at St. Louis)

Yankees	000	100	420	—	7	15	2
Cardinals	001	100	001	—	3	11	0

Yankees: WAITE HOYT and Benny Bengough, Pat Collins (7th).
Cardinals: BILL SHERDEL, Grover Cleveland Alexander (7th) and Earl Smith.
Home Runs: Babe Ruth (Yankees) 3, Cedric Durst (Yankees) and Lou Gehrig (Yankees).
Attendance: 37,331.

1932 World Champions

Manager: Joe McCarthy
World Series Roster: Pitchers: Johnny Allen, Jumbo Brown, Charlie Devens, Lefty Gomez, Danny MacFayden, Wilcy Moore, Herb Pennock, George Pipgras, Red Ruffing, Ed Wells. *Catchers:* Bill Dickey, Art Jorgens. *Infielders:* Frank Crosetti, Doc Farrell, Lou Gehrig, Lyn Lary, Tony Lazzeri, Joe Sewell. *Outfielders:* Sammy Byrd, Ben Chapman, Earle Combs, Myril Hoag, Babe Ruth.

World Series

	W	L	Pct.
Yankees	4	0	1.000
Cubs	0	4	.000

Game 1 (Sept. 28 at Yankee Stadium)

Cubs	200	000	220	—	6	10	1
Yankees	000	305	31X	—	12	8	2

Cubs: GUY BUSH, Burleigh Grimes (6th), Bob Smith (8th) and Gabby Hartnett.
Yankees: RED RUFFING and Bill Dickey.
Home Run: Lou Gehrig (Yankees).
Attendance: 41,459.

Game 2 (Sept. 29 at Yankee Stadium)

Cubs	101	000	000	—	2	9	0
Yankees	202	010	00X	—	5	10	1

Cubs: LON WARNEKE and Gabby Hartnett.
Yankees: LEFTY GOMEZ and Bill Dickey.
Home Runs: None.
Attendance: 50,709.

Game 3 (Oct. 1 at Chicago)

Yankees	301	020	001	—	7	8	1
Cubs	102	100	001	—	5	9	4

Yankees: GEORGE PIPGRAS, Herb Pennock (9th) and Bill Dickey.
Cubs: CHARLIE ROOT, Pat Malone (5th), Jakie May (8th), Bud Tinning (9th) and Gabby Hartnett.
Home Runs: Babe Ruth (Yankees) 2, Lou Gehrig (Yankees) 2, Kiki Cuyler (Cubs) and Gabby Hartnet (Cubs).
Attendance: 49,986.

Game 4 (Oct. 2 at Chicago)

Yankees	102	002	404	—	13	19	4
Cubs	400	001	001	—	6	9	1

Yankees: Johnny Allen, WILCY MOORE (1st), Herb Pennock (7th) and Bill Dickey.
Cubs: Guy Bush, Lon Warneke (1st), JAKIE MAY (4th), Bud Tinning (7th), Burleigh Grimes (9th) and Gabby Hartnett, Rollie Hemsley (9th).
Home Runs: Tony Lazzeri (Yankees) 2, Frank Demaree (Cubs) and Earle Combs (Yankees).
Attendance: 49,844.

1936 World Champions

Manager: Joe McCarthy
World Series Roster: Pitchers: Johnny Broaca, Jumbo Brown, Lefty Gomez, Bump Hadley, Pat Malone, Johnny Murphy, Monte Pearson, Red Ruffing, Kemp Wicker. *Catchers:* Bill Dickey, Joe Glenn, Art Jorgens. *Infielders:* Frank Crosetti, Lou Gehrig, Don Heffner, Tony Lazzeri, Red Rolfe, Jack Saltzgaver. *Outfielders:* Joe DiMaggio, Roy Johnson, Jake Powell, Bob Seeds, George Selkirk.

World Series

	W	L	Pct.
Yankees	4	2	.667
Giants	2	4	.333

Game 1 (Sept. 30 at Polo Grounds)

Yankees	001	000	000	—	1	7	2
Giants	000	011	04X	—	6	9	1

Yankees: RED RUFFING and Bill Dickey.
Giants: CARL HUBBELL and Gus Mancuso.
Home Runs: Dick Bartell (Giants) and George Selkirk (Yankees).
Attendance: 39,419.

Game 2 (Oct. 2 at Polo Grounds)

Yankees	207	001	206	—	18	17	0
Giants	010	300	000	—	4	6	1

Yankees: LEFTY GOMEZ and Bill Dickey.
Giants: HAL SCHUMACHER, Al Smith (3d), Dick Coffman (3d), Frank Gabler (5th), Harry Gumbert (9th) and Gus Mancuso.
Home Runs: Bill Dickey (Yankees) and Tony Lazzeri (Yankees).
Attendance: 43,543.

Game 3 (Oct. 3 at Yankee Stadium)

Giants	000	010	000	—	1	11	0
Yankees	010	000	01X	—	2	4	0

Giants: FREDDIE FITZSIMMONS and Gus Mancuso.
Yankees: BUMP HADLEY, Pat Malone (9th) and Bill Dickey.
Home Runs: Lou Gehrig (Yankees) and Jimmy Ripple (Giants).
Attendance: 64,842.

Game 4 (Oct. 4 at Yankee Stadium)

Giants	000	100	010	—	2	7	1
Yankees	013	000	01X	—	5	10	1

Giants: CARL HUBBELL, Frank Gabler (8th) and Gus Mancuso.
Yankees: MONTE PEARSON and Bill Dickey.
Home Run: Lou Gehrig (Yankees).
Attendance: 66,669.

Game 5 (Oct. 5 at Yankee Stadium)

Giants	300	001	000	1	—	5	8	3
Yankees	011	002	000	0	—	4	10	1

Giants: HAL SCHUMACHER and Gus Mancuso.
Yankees: Red Ruffing, PAT MALONE (7th) and Bill Dickey.
Home Run: George Selkirk (Yankees).
Attendance: 50,024.

Game 6 (Oct. 6 at Polo Grounds)

Yankees	021	200	017	—	13	17	2
Giants	200	010	100	—	5	9	1

Yankees: LEFTY GOMEZ, Johnny Murphy (7th) and Bill Dickey.
Giants: FREDDIE FITZSIMMONS, Slick Castleman (4th), Dick Coffman (9th), Harry Gumbert (9th) and Gus Mancuso, Harry Danning (8th).
Home Runs: Jo-Jo Moore (Giants), Mel Ott (Giants) and Jake Powell (Yankees).
Attendance: 38,427.

1937 World Champions

Manager: Joe McCarthy
World Series Roster: Pitchers: Ivy Andrews, Spud Chandler, Lefty Gomez, Bump Hadley, Frank Makosky, Pat Malone, Johnny Murphy, Monte Pearson, Red Ruffing, Kemp Wicker. *Catchers:* Bill Dickey, Joe Glenn, Art Jorgens. *Infielders:* Frank Crosetti, Lou Gehrig, Don Heffner, Tony Lazzeri, Red Rolfe, Jack Saltzgaver. *Outfielders:* Joe DiMaggio, Tommy Henrich, Myril Hoag, Jake Powell, George Selkirk.

World Series

	W	L	Pct.
Yankees	4	1	.800
Giants	1	4	.200

Game 1 (Oct. 6 at Yankee Stadium)

Giants	000	010	000	—	1	6	2
Yankees	000	007	01X	—	8	7	0

Giants: CARL HUBBELL, Harry Gumbert (6th), Dick Coffman (6th), Al Smith (8th) and Gus Mancuso.
Yankees: LEFTY GOMEZ and Bill Dickey.
Home Run: Tony Lazzeri (Yankees).
Attendance: 60,573.

Game 2 (Oct. 7 at Yankee Stadium)

Giants	100	000	000	—	1	7	0
Yankees	000	024	20X	—	8	12	0

Giants: CLIFF MELTON, Harry Gumbert (5th), Dick Coffman (6th) and Gus Mancuso.
Yankees: RED RUFFING and Bill Dickey.
Home Runs: None.
Attendance: 57,675.

Game 3 (Oct. 8 at Polo Grounds)

Yankees	012	110	000	—	5	9	0
Giants	000	000	100	—	1	5	4

Yankees: MONTE PEARSON, Johnny Murphy (9th) and Bill Dickey.
Giants: HAL SCHUMACHER, Cliff Melton (7th), Don Brennan (9th) and Harry Danning.
Home Runs: None.
Attendance: 37,385.

Game 4 (Oct. 9 at Polo Grounds)

Yankees	101	000	001	—	3	6	0
Giants	060	000	10X	—	7	12	3

Yankees: BUMP HADLEY, Ivy Andrews (2d), Kemp Wicker (8th) and Bill Dickey.
Giants: CARL HUBBELL and Harry Danning.
Home Run: Lou Gehrig (Yankees).
Attendance: 44,293.

Game 5 (Oct. 10 at Polo Grounds)

Yankees	011	020	000	—	4	8	0
Giants	002	000	000	—	2	10	0

Yankees: LEFTY GOMEZ and Bill Dickey.
Giants: CLIFF MELTON, Al Smith (6th), Don Brennan (8th) and Harry Danning.
Home Runs: Joe DiMaggio (Yankees), Myril Hoag (Yankees) and Mel Ott (Giants).
Attendance: 38,216.

1938 World Champions

Manager: Joe McCarthy
World Series Roster: Pitchers: Ivy Andrews, Spud Chandler, Wes Ferrell, Lefty Gomez, Bump Hadley, Johnny Murphy, Monte Pearson, Red Ruffing, Steve Sundra. *Catchers:* Bill Dickey, Joe Glenn, Art Jorgens. *Infielders:* Frank Crosetti, Babe Dahlgren, Lou Gehrig, Joe Gordon, Bill Knickerbocker, Red Rolfe. *Outfielders:* Joe DiMaggio, Tommy Henrich, Myril Hoag, Jake Powell. George Selkirk.

World Series

	W	L	Pct.
Yankees	4	0	1.000
Cubs	0	4	.000

Game 1 (Oct. 5 at Chicago)

Yankees	020	000	100	—	3	12	1
Cubs	001	000	000	—	1	9	1

Yankees: RED RUFFING and Bill Dickey.
Cubs: BILL LEE, Jack Russell (9th) and Gabby Hartnett.
Home Runs: None.
Attendance: 43,642.

Game 2 (Oct. 6 at Chicago)

Yankees	020	000	022	—	6	7	2
Cubs	102	000	000	—	3	11	0

Yankees: LEFTY GOMEZ, Johnny Murphy (8th) and Bill Dickey.
Cubs: DIZZY DEAN, Larry French (9th) and Gabby Hartnett.
Home Runs: Frank Crosetti (Yankees) and Joe DiMaggio (Yankees).
Attendance: 42,108.

Game 3 (Oct. 8 at Yankee Stadium)

Cubs	000	010	010	—	2	5	1
Yankees	000	022	01X	—	5	7	2

Cubs: CLAY BRYANT, Jack Russell (6th), Larry French (7th) and Gabby Hartnett.
Yankees: MONTE PEARSON and Bill Dickey.
Home Runs: Bill Dickey (Yankees), Joe Gordon (Yankees) and Joe Marty (Cubs).
Attendance: 55,236.

Game 4 (Oct. 9 at Yankee Stadium)

Cubs	000	100	020	—	3	8	1
Yankees	030	001	04X	—	8	11	1

Cubs: BILL LEE, Charlie Root (4th), Vance Page (7th), Larry French (8th), Tex Carleton (8th), Dizzy Dean (8th) and Ken O'Dea.
Yankees: RED RUFFING and Bill Dickey.
Home Runs: Tommy Henrich (Yankees) and Ken O'Dea (Cubs).
Attendance: 59,847.

1939 World Champions

Manager: Joe McCarthy
World Series Roster: Pitchers: Spud Chandler, Atley Donald, Lefty Gomez, Bump Hadley, Oral Hildebrand, Johnny Murphy, Monte Pearson, Red Ruffing, Marius Russo, Steve Sundra. *Catchers:* Bill Dickey, Art Jorgens, Buddy Rosar. *Infielders:* Frank Crosetti, Babe Dahlgren, Lou Gehrig, Joe Gordon. Bill Knickerbocker, Red Rolfe. *Outfielders:* Joe DiMaggio, Tommy Henrich, Charlie Keller, Jake Powell, George Selkirk.

World Series

	W	L	Pct.
Yankees	4	0	1.000
Reds	0	4	.000

Game 1 (Oct. 4 at Yankee Stadium)

Reds	000	100	000	—	1	4	0
Yankees	000	010	001	—	2	6	0

Reds: PAUL DERRINGER and Ernie Lombardi.
Yankees: RED RUFFING and Bill Dickey.
Home Runs: None.
Attendance: 58,541.

Game 2 (Oct. 5 at Yankee Stadium)

Reds	000	000	000	—	0	2	0
Yankees	003	100	00X	—	4	9	0

Reds: BUCKY WALTERS and Ernie Lombardi, Willard Hershberger (8th).
Yankees: MONTE PEARSON and Bill Dickey.
Home Run: Babe Dahlgren (Yankees).
Attendance: 59,791.

Game 3 (Oct. 7 at Cincinnati)

Yankees	202	030	000	—	7	5	1
Reds	120	000	000	—	3	10	0

Yankees: Lefty Gomez, BUMP HADLEY (2d) and Bill Dickey.
Reds: JUNIOR THOMPSON, Lee Grissom (5th), Whitey Moore (7th) and Ernie Lombardi, Willard Hershberger (8th).
Home Runs: Charlie Keller (Yankees) 2, Joe DiMaggio (Yankees) and Bill Dickey (Yankees).
Attendance: 32,723.

Game 4 (Oct. 8 at Cincinnati)

Yankees	000	000	202	3	—	7	7	1
Reds	000	000.	310	0	—	4	11	4

Yankees: Oral Hildebrand, Steve Sundra (5th), JOHNNY MURPHY (7th) and Bill Dickey.
Reds: Paul Derringer, BUCKY WALTERS (8th) and Ernie Lombardi.
Home Runs: Charlie Keller (Yankees) and Bill Dickey (Yankees).
Attendance: 32,794.

1941 World Champions

Manager: Joe McCarthy
World Series Roster: Pitchers: Ernie Bonham, Norm Branch, Marv Breuer, Spud Chandler, Atley Donald, Lefty Gomez, Johnny Murphy, Steve Peek, Red Ruffing, Marius Russo, Charley Stanceu. *Catchers:* Bill Dickey, Buddy Rosar, Ken Silvestri. *Infielders:* Frank Crosetti, Joe Gordon, Jerry Priddy, Phil Rizzuto, Red Rolfe, Johnny Sturm. *Outfielders:* Frenchy Bordagaray, Joe DiMaggio, Tommy Henrich, Charlie Keller, George Selkirk.

World Series

	W	L	Pct.
Yankees	4	1	.800
Dodgers	1	4	.200

Game 1 (Oct. 1 at Yankee Stadium)

Dodgers	000	010	100	—	2	6	0
Yankees	010	101	00X	—	3	6	1

Dodgers: CURT DAVIS, Hugh Casey (6th), Johnny Allen (7th) and Mickey Owen, Herman Franks (7th).
Yankees: RED RUFFING and Bill Dickey.
Home Run: Joe Gordon (Yankees).
Attendance: 68,540.

Game 2 (Oct. 2 at Yankee Stadium)

Dodgers	000	021	000	—	3	6	2
Yankees	011	000	000	—	2	9	1

Dodgers: WHITLOW WYATT and Mickey Owen.
Yankees: SPUD CHANDLER, Johnny Murphy (6th) and Bill Dickey, Buddy Rosar (9th).
Home Runs: None.
Attendance: 66,248.

Game 3 (Oct. 4 at Brooklyn)

Yankees	000	000	020	—	2	8	0
Dodgers	000	000	010	—	1	4	0

Yankees: MARIUS RUSSO and Bill Dickey.
Dodgers: Freddie Fitzsimmons, HUGH CASEY (8th), Larry French (8th), Johnny Allen (9th) and Mickey Owen.
Home Runs: None.
Attendance: 33,100.

Game 4 (Oct. 5 at Brooklyn)

Yankees	100	200	004	—	7	12	0
Dodgers	000	220	000	—	4	9	1

Yankees: Atley Donald, Marv Breuer (5th), JOHNNY MURPHY (8th) and Bill Dickey.
Dodgers: Kirby Higbe, Larry French (4th), Johnny Allen (5th), HUGH CASEY (5th) and Mickey Owen.
Home Run: Pete Reiser (Dodgers).
Attendance: 33,813.

Game 5 (Oct. 6 at Brooklyn)

Yankees	020	010	000	—	3	6	0
Dodgers	001	000	000	—	1	4	1

Yankees: ERNIE BONHAM and Bill Dickey.
Dodgers: WHITLOW WYATT and Mickey Owen.
Home Run: Tommy Henrich (Yankees).
Attendance: 34,072.

1942 American League Champions

Manager: Joe McCarthy
World Series Roster: Pitchers: Ernie Bonham, Hank Borowy, Marv Breuer, Spud Chandler, Atley Donald, Lefty Gomez, Johnny Lindell, Johnny Murphy, Red Ruffing, Marius Russo, Jim Turner. *Catchers:* Bill Dickey, Rollie Hemsley, Buddy Rosar. *Infielders:* Frank Crosetti, Joe Gordon, Buddy Hassett, Jerry Priddy, Phil Rizzuto, Red Rolfe. *Outfielders:* Roy Cullenbine, Joe DiMaggio, Charlie Keller, George Selkirk, Tuck Stainback.

World Series

	W	L	Pct.
Cardinals	4	1	.800
Yankees	1	4	.200

Game 1 (Sept. 30 at St. Louis)

Yankees	000	110	032	—	7	11	0
Cardinals	000	000	004	—	4	7	4

Yankees: RED RUFFING, Spud Chandler (9th) and Bill Dickey.
Cardinals: MORT COOPER, Harry Gumbert (8th), Max Lanier (9th) and Walker Cooper.
Home Runs: None.
Attendance: 34,769.

Game 2 (Oct. 1 at St. Louis)

Yankees	000	000	030	—	3	10	2
Cardinals	200	000	11X	—	4	6	0

Yankees: ERNIE BONHAM and Bill Dickey.
Cardinals: JOHNNY BEAZLEY and Walker Cooper.
Home Run: Charlie Keller (Yankees).
Attendance: 34,255.

Game 3 (Oct. 3 at Yankee Stadium)

Cardinals	001	000	001	—	2	5	1
Yankees	000	000	000	—	0	6	1

Cardinals: ERNIE WHITE and Walker Cooper.
Yankees: SPUD CHANDLER, Marv Breuer (9th), Jim Turner (9th) and Bill Dickey.
Home Runs: None.
Attendance: 69,123.

Game 4 (Oct. 4 at Yankee Stadium)

Cardinals	000	600	201	—	9	12	1
Yankees	100	005	000	—	6	10	1

Cardinals: Mort Cooper, Harry Gumbert (6th), Howie Pollet (6th), MAX LANIER (7th) and Walker Cooper.
Yankees: Hank Borowy, ATLEY DONALD (4th), Ernie Bonham (7th) and Bill Dickey.
Home Run: Charlie Keller (Yankees).
Attendance: 69,902.

Game 5 (Oct. 5 at Yankee Stadium)

Cardinals	000	101	002	—	4	9	4
Yankees	100	100	000	—	2	7	1

Cardinals: JOHNNY BEAZLEY and Walker Cooper.
Yankees: RED RUFFING and Bill Dickey.
Home Runs: Phil Rizzuto (Yankees), Enos Slaughter (Cardinals) and Whitey Kurowski (Cardinals).
Attendance: 69,052.

1943 World Champions

Manager: Joe McCarthy
World Series Roster: Pitchers: Ernie Bonham, Hank Borowy, Marv Breuer, Tommy Byrne, Spud Chandler, Atley Donald, Johnny Murphy, Marius Russo, Jim Turner, Butch Wensloff, Bill Zuber. *Catchers:* Bill Dickey, Rollie Hemsley, Ken Sears. *Infielders:* Frank Crosetti, Nick Etten, Joe Gordon, Oscar Grimes, Billy Johnson, Snuffy Stirnweiss. *Outfielders:* Charlie Keller, Johnny Lindell, Bud Metheny, Tuck Stainback, Roy Weatherly.

World Series

	W	L	Pct.
Yankees	4	1	.800
Cardinals	1	4	.200

Game 1 (Oct. 5 at Yankee Stadium)

Cardinals	010	010	000	—	2	7	2
Yankees	000	202	00X	—	4	8	2

Cardinals: MAX LANIER, Harry Brecheen (8th) and Walker Cooper.
Yankees: SPUD CHANDLER and Bill Dickey.
Home Run: Joe Gordon (Yankees).
Attendance: 68,676.

Game 2 (Oct. 6 at Yankee Stadium)

Cardinals	001	300	000	—	4	7	2
Yankees	000	100	002	—	3	6	0

Cardinals: MORT COOPER and Walker Cooper.
Yankees ERNIE BONHAM, Johnny Murphy (9th) and Bill Dickey.
Home Runs: Marty Marion (Cardinals) and Ray Sanders (Cardinals).
Attendance: 68,578.

Game 3 (Oct. 7 at Yankee Stadium)

Cardinals	000	200	000	—	2	6	4
Yankees	000	001	05X	—	6	8	0

Cardinals: AL BRAZLE, Howie Krist (8th), Harry Brecheen (8th) and Walker Cooper.
Yankees: HANK BOROWY, Johnny Murphy (9th) and Bill Dickey.
Home Runs: None.
Attendance: 69,990.

Game 4 (Oct. 10 at St. Louis)

Yankees	000	100	010	—	2	6	2
Cardinals	000	000	100	—	1	7	1

Yankees: MARIUS RUSSO and Bill Dickey.
Cardinals: Max Lanier, HARRY BRECHEEN (8th) and Walker Cooper.
Home Runs: None.
Attendance: 36,196.

Game 5 (Oct. 11 at St. Louis)

Yankees	000	002	000	—	2	7	1
Cardinals	000	000	000	—	0	10	1

Yankees: SPUD CHANDLER and Bill Dickey.
Cardinals: MORT COOPER, Max Lanier (8th), Murry Dickson and Walker Cooper, Ken O'Dea.
Home Run: Bill Dickey (Yankees).
Attendance: 33,872.

NOTE: Because of wartime travel restrictions, the World Series' first three games were scheduled for New York, as many of the last four as necessary for St. Louis.

1947 World Champions

Manager: Bucky Harris
World Series Roster: Pitchers: Bill Bevens, Spud Chandler, Karl Drews, Randy Gumpert, Don Johnson, Bobo Newsom, Joe Page, Vic Raschi, Allie Reynolds, Spec Shea, Butch Wensloff. *Catchers:* Yogi Berra, Ralph Houk, Sherm Lollar, Aaron Robinson. *Infielders:* Bobby Brown, Lonny Frey, Billy Johnson, George McQuinn, Jack Phillips, Phil Rizzuto, George Stirnweiss. *Outfielders:* Allie Clark, Joe DiMaggio, Tommy Henrich, Charlie Keller, Johnny Lindell.

World Series

	W	L	Pct.
Yankees	4	3	.571
Dodgers	3	4	.429

Game 1 (Sept. 30 at Yankee Stadium)

Dodgers	100	001	100	—	3	6	0
Yankees	000	050	00X	—	5	4	0

Dodgers: RALPH BRANCA, Hank Behrman (5th), Hugh Casey (7th) and Bruce Edwards.
Yankees: SPEC SHEA, Joe Page (6th) and Yogi Berra.
Home Runs: None.
Attendance: 73,365.

Game 2 (Oct. 1 at Yankee Stadium)

Dodgers	001	100	001	—	3	9	2
Yankees	101	121	40X	—	10	15	1

Dodgers: VIC LOMBARDI, Hal Gregg (5th), Hank Behrman (7th), Rex Barney (7th) and Bruce Edwards.
Yankees: ALLIE REYNOLDS and Yogi Berra.
Home Runs: Dixie Walker (Dodgers) and Tommy Henrich (Yankees).
Attendance: 69,865.

Game 3 (Oct. 2 at Brooklyn)

Yankees	002	221	100	—	8	13	0
Dodgers	061	200	00X	—	9	13	1

Yankees: BOBO NEWSOM, Vic Raschi (2d), Karl Drews (3d), Spud Chandler (4th), Joe Page (6th) and Sherm Lollar, Yogi Berra (7th).
Dodgers: Joe Hatten, Ralph Branca (5th), HUGH CASEY (7th) and Bruce Edwards.
Home Runs: Joe DiMaggio (Yankees) and Yogi Berra (Yankees).
Attendance: 33,098.

Game 4 (Oct. 3 at Brooklyn)

Yankees	100	100	000	—	2	8	1
Dodgers	000	010	002	—	3	1	3

Yankees: BILL BEVENS and Yogi Berra.
Dodgers: Harry Taylor, Hal Gregg (1st), Hank Behrman (8th), HUGH CASEY (9th) and Bruce Edwards.
Home Runs: None.
Attendance: 33,443.

Game 5 (Oct. 4 at Brooklyn)

Yankees	000	110	000	—	2	5	0
Dodgers	000	001	000	—	1	4	1

Yankees: SPEC SHEA and Aaron Robinson.
Dodgers: REX BARNEY, Joe Hatten (5th), Hank Behrman (7th), Hugh Casey (8th) and Bruce Edwards.
Home Run: Joe DiMaggio (Yankees).
Attendance: 34,379.

Game 6 (Oct. 5 at Yankee Stadium)

Dodgers	202	004	000	—	8	12	1
Yankees	004	100	001	—	6	15	2

Dodgers: Vic Lombardi, RALPH BRANCA (3d), Joe Hatten (6th), Hugh Casey (9th) and Bruce Edwards.
Yankees: Allie Reynolds, Karl Drews (3d), JOE PAGE (5th), Bobo Newsom (6th), Vic Raschi (7th), Butch Wensloff (8th) and Sherm Lollar, Aaron Robinson (4th).
Home Runs: None.
Attendance: 74,065.

Game 7 (Oct. 6 at Yankee Stadium)

Dodgers	020	000	000	—	2	7	0
Yankees	010	201	10X	—	5	7	0

Dodgers: HAL GREGG, Hank Behrman (4th), Joe Hatten (6th), Rex Barney (6th), Hugh Casey (7th) and Bruce Edwards.
Yankees: Spec Shea, Bill Bevens (2d), JOE PAGE (5th) and Aaron Robinson.
Home Runs: None.
Attendance: 71,548.

1949 World Champions

Manager: Casey Stengel
World Series Roster: Pitchers: Ralph Buxton, Tommy Byrne, Ed Lopat, Cuddles Marshall, Joe Page, Duane Pillette, Vic Raschi, Allie Reynolds, Fred Sanford. *Catchers:* Yogi Berra, Gus Niarhos, Charlie Silvera. *Infielders:* Bobby Brown, Jerry Coleman, Tommy Henrich, Billy Johnson, Johnny Mize, Phil Rizzuto, Snuffy Stirnweiss. *Outfielders:* Hank Bauer, Joe DiMaggio, Charlie Keller, Johnny Lindell, Cliff Mapes, Gene Woodling.

World Series

	W	L	Pct.
Yankees	4	1	.800
Dodgers	1	4	.200

Game 1 (Oct. 5 at Yankee Stadium)

Dodgers	000	000	000	—	0	2	0
Yankees	000	000	001	—	1	5	1

Dodgers: DON NEWCOMBE and Roy Campanella.
Yankees: ALLIE REYNOLDS and Yogi Berra.
Home Run: Tommy Henrich (Yankees).
Attendance: 66,230.

Game 2 (Oct. 6 at Yankee Stadium)

Dodgers	010	000	000	—	1	7	2
Yankees	000	000	000	—	0	6	1

Dodgers: PREACHER ROE and Roy Campanella.
Yankees: VIC RASCHI, Joe Page (9th) and Charlie Silvera, Gus Niarhos (9th).
Home Runs: None.
Attendance: 70,053.

Game 3 (Oct. 7 at Brooklyn)

Yankees	001	000	003	—	4	5	0
Dodgers	000	100	002	—	3	5	0

Yankees: Tommy Byrne, JOE PAGE (4th) and Yogi Berra.
Dodgers: RALPH BRANCA, Jack Banta (9th) and Roy Campanella.
Home Runs: Pee Wee Reese (Dodgers), Luis Olmo (Dodgers) and Roy Campanella (Dodgers).
Attendance: 32,788.

Game 4 (Oct. 8 at Brooklyn)

Yankees	000	330	000	—	6	10	0
Dodgers	000	004	000	—	4	9	1

Yankees: ED LOPAT, Allie Reynolds (6th) and Yogi Berra.
Dodgers: DON NEWCOMBE, Joe Hatten (4th), Carl Erskine (6th), Jack Banta (7th) and Roy Campanella.
Home Runs: None.
Attendance: 33,934.

Game 5 (Oct. 9 at Brooklyn)

Yankees	203	113	000	—	10	11	1
Dodgers	001	001	400	—	6	11	2

Yankees: VIC RASCHI, Joe Page (7th) and Yogi Berra.
Dodgers: REX BARNEY, Jack Banta (3d), Carl Erskine (6th), Joe Hatten (6th), Efv Palica (7th), Paul Minner (9th), and Roy Campanella.
Home Runs: Joe DiMaggio (Yankees) and Gil Hodges (Dodgers).
Attendance: 33,711.

1950 World Champions

Manager: Casey Stengel
World Series Roster: Pitchers: Tommy Byrne, Tom Ferrick, Whitey Ford, Ed Lopat, Joe Ostrowski, Joe Page, Vic Raschi, Allie Reynolds, Fred Sanford. *Catchers:* Yogi Berra, Ralph Houk, Charlie Silvera. *Infielders:* Bobby Brown, Jerry Coleman, Joe Collins, Johnny Hopp, Bllly Johnson, Billy Martin, Johnny Mize, Phil Rizzuto. *Outfielders:* Hank Bauer, Joe DiMaggio, Jackie Jensen, Cliff Mapes, Gene Woodling.

World Series

	W	L	Pct.
Yankees	4	0	1.000
Phillies	0	4	.000

Game 1 (Oct. 4 at Philadelphia)

Yankees	000	100	000	—	1	5	0
Phillies	000	000	000	—	0	2	1

Yankees: VIC RASCHI and Yogi Berra.
Phillies: JIM KONSTANTY, Russ Meyer (9th) and Andy Seminick.
Home Runs: None.
Attendance: 30,746.

Game 2 (Oct. 5 at Philadelphia)

Yankees	010	000	000	1	—	2	10	0
Phillies	000	010	000	0	—	1	7	0

Yankees: ALLIE REYNOLDS and Yogi Berra.
Phillies: ROBIN ROBERTS and Andy Seminick, Ken Silvestri (8th) and Stan Lopata (10th).
Home Run: Joe DiMaggio (Yankees).
Attendance: 32,660.

Game 3 (Oct. 6 at Yankee Stadium)

Phillies	000	001	100	—	2	10	2
Yankees	001	000	011	—	3	7	0

Phillies: Ken Heintzelman, Jim Konstanty (8th), RUSS MEYER (9th) and Andy Seminick.
Yankees: Ed Lopat, TOM FERRICK (9th) and Yogi Berra.
Home Runs: None.
Attendance: 64,505.

Game 4 (Oct. 7 at Yankee Stadium)

Phillies	000	000	002	—	2	7	1
Yankees	200	003	00X	—	5	8	2

Phillies: BOB MILLER, Jim Konstanty (1st), Robin Roberts (8th) and Andy Seminick.
Yankees: WHITEY FORD, Allie Reynolds (9th) and Yogi Berra.
Home Run: Yogi Berra (Yankees).
Attendance: 68,098.

1951 World Champions

Manager: Casey Stengel
World Series Roster: Pitchers: Bobby Hogue, Bob Kuzava, Ed Lopat, Tom Morgan, Joe Ostrowski, Stubby Overmire, Vic Raschi, Allie Reynolds, Johnny Sain, Art Schallock, Spec Shea. *Catchers:* Yogi Berra, Ralph Houk, Charlie Silvera. *Infielders:* Bobby Brown, Jerry Coleman, Joe Collins, Johnny Hopp, Billy Martin, Gil McDougald, Johnny Mize, Phil Rizzuto. *Outfielders:* Hank Bauer, Joe DiMaggio, Mickey Mantle, Gene Woodling.

World Series

	W	L	Pct.
Yankees	4	2	.667
Giants	2	4	.333

Game 1 (Oct. 4 at Yankee Stadium)

Giants	200	003	000	—	5	10	1
Yankees	010	000	000	—	1	7	1

Giants: DAVE KOSLO and Wes Westrum.
Yankees: ALLIE REYNOLDS, Bobby Hogue (7th), Tom Morgan (8th) and Yogi Berra.
Home Run: Al Dark (Giants).
Attendance: 65,673.

Game 2 (Oct. 5 at Yankee Stadium)

Giants	000	000	100	—	1	5	1
Yankees	110	000	01X	—	3	6	0

Giants: LARRY JANSEN, George Spencer (7th) and Wes Westrum, Ray Noble (7th).
Yankees: ED LOPAT and Yogi Berra.
Home Run: Joe Collins (Yankees).
Attendance: 66,018.

Game 3 (Oct. 6 at Polo Grounds)

Yankees	000	000	011	—	2	5	2
Giants	010	050	00X	—	6	7	2

Yankees: VIC RASCHI, Bobby Hogue (5th), Joe Ostrowski (7th) and Yogi Berra.
Giants: JIM HEARN, Sheldon Jones (8th) and Wes Westrum.
Home Runs: Whitey Lockman (Giants) and Gene Woodling (Yankees).
Attendance: 52,035.

Game 4 (Oct. 8 at Polo Grounds)

Yankees	010	120	200	—	6	12	0
Giants	100	000	001	—	2	8	2

Yankees: ALLIE REYNOLDS and Yogi Berra.
Giants: SAL MAGLIE, Sheldon Jones (6th), Monte Kennedy (9th) and Wes Westrum.
Home Run: Joe DiMaggio (Yankees).
Attendance: 49,010.

Game 5 (Oct. 9 at Polo Grounds)

Yankees	005	202	400	—	13	12	1
Giants	100	000	000	—	1	5	3

Yankees: ED LOPAT and Yogi Berra.
Giants: LARRY JANSEN, Monte Kennedy (4th), George Spencer (6th), Al Corwin (7th), Alex Konikowski (9th) and Wes Westrum.
Home Runs: Gil McDougald (Yankees) and Phil Rizzuto (Yankees).
Attendance: 47,530.

Game 6 (Oct. 10 at Yankee Stadium)

Giants	000	010	002	—	3	11	1
Yankees	100	003	00X	—	4	7	0

Giants: DAVE KOSLO, Jim Hearn (7th), Larry Jansen (8th) and Wes Westrum, Ray Noble (8th).
Yankees: VIC RASCHI, Johnny Sain (7th), Bob Kuzava (9th) and Yogi Berra.
Home Runs: None.
Attendance: 61,711.

1952 World Champions

Manager: Casey Stengel
World Series Roster: Pitchers: Ewell Blackwell, Tom Gorman, Bob Kuzava, Ed Lopat, Jim McDonald, Bill Miller, Joe Ostrowski, Vic Raschi, Allie Reynolds, Johnny Sain, Ray Scarborough. *Catchers:* Yogi Berra, Ralph Houk, Charlie Silvera. *Infielders:* Loren Babe, Jim Brideweser, Joe Collins, Billy Martin, Gil McDougald, Johnny Mize, Phil Rizzuto. *Outfielders:* Hank Bauer, Mickey Mantle, Irv Noren, Gene Woodling.

World Series

	W	L	Pct.
Yankees	4	3	.571
Dodgers	3	4	.429

Game 1 (Oct. 1 at Brooklyn)

Yankees	001	000	010	—	2	6	2
Dodgers	010	002	01X	—	4	6	0

Yankees: ALLIE REYNOLDS, Ray Scarborough (8th) and Yogi Berra.
Dodgers: JOE BLACK and Roy Campanella.
Home Runs: Jackie Robinson (Dodgers), Gil McDougald (Yankees), Duke Snider (Dodgers) and Pee Wee Reese (Dodgers).
Attendance: 34,861.

Game 2 (Oct. 2 at Brooklyn)

Yankees	000	115	000	—	7	10	0
Dodgers	001	000	000	—	1	3	1

Yankees: VIC RASCHI and Yogi Berra.
Dodgers: CARL ERSKINE, Billy Loes (6th), Ken Lehman (8th) and Roy Campanella.
Home Run: Billy Martin (Yankees).
Attendance: 33,792.

Game 3 (Oct. 3 at Yankee Stadium)

Dodgers	001	010	012	—	5	11	0
Yankees	010	000	011	—	3	6	2

Dodgers: PREACHER ROE and Roy Campanella.
Yankees: ED LOPAT, Tom Gorman (9th) and Yogi Berra.
Home Runs: Yogi Berra (Yankees) and Johnny Mize (Yankees).
Attendance: 66,698.

Game 4 (Oct. 4 at Yankee Stadium)

Dodgers	000	000	000	—	0	4	1
Yankees	000	100	01X	—	2	4	1

Dodgers: JOE BLACK, Johnny Rutherford (8th) and Roy Campanella.
Yankees: ALLIE REYNOLDS and Yogi Berra.
Home Run: Johnny Mize (Yankees).
Attendance: 71,787.

Game 5 (Oct. 5 at Yankee Stadium)

Dodgers	010	030	100	01	—	6	10	0
Yankees	000	050	000	00	—	5	5	1

Dodgers: CARL ERSKINE and Roy Campanella.
Yankees: Ewell Blackwell, JOHNNY SAIN (6th) and Yogi Berra.
Home Runs: Duke Snider (Dodgers) and Johnny Mize (Yankees).
Attendance: 70,536.

Game 6 (Oct. 6 at Brooklyn)

Yankees	000	000	210	—	3	9	10
Dodgers	000	001	010	—	2	8	1

Yankees: VIC RASCHI, Allie Reynolds (8th) and Yogi Berra.
Dodgers: BILLY LOES, Preacher Roe (9th) and Roy Campanella.
Home Runs: Duke Snider (Dodgers) 2, Yogi Berra (Yankees) and Mickey Mantle (Yankees).
Attendance: 30,037.

Game 7 (Oct. 7 at Brooklyn)

Yankees	000	111	100	—	4	10	4
Dodgers	000	110	000	—	2	8	1

Yankees: Ed Lopat, ALLIE REYNOLDS (4th), Vic Raschi (7th), Bob Kuzava (7th) and Yogi Berra.
Dodgers: JOE BLACK, Preacher Roe (6th), Carl Erskine (8th) and Roy Campanella.
Home Runs: Gene Woodling (Yankees) and Mickey Mantle (Yankees).
Attendance: 33,195.

1953 World Champions

Manager: Casey Stengel
World Series Roster: Pitchers: Whitey Ford, Tom Gorman, Steve Kraly, Bob Kuzava, Ed Lopat, Jim McDonald, Bill Miller, Vic Raschi, Allie Reynolds, Johnny Sain, Art Schallock. *Catchers:* Yogi Berra, Charlie Silvera, Gus Triandos. *Infielders:* Don Bollweg, Andy Carey, Jerry Coleman, Joe Collins, Billy Martin, Gil McDougald, Willie Miranda, Johnny Mize, Phil Rizzuto. *Outfielders:* Hank Bauer, Mickey Mantle, Irv Noren, Bill Renna, Gene Woodling.

World Series

	W	L	Pct.
Yankees	4	2	.667
Dodgers	2	4	.333

Game 1 (Sept. 30 at Yankee Stadium)

Dodgers	000	013	100	—	5	12	2
Yankees	400	010	13X	—	9	12	2

Dodgers: Carl Erskine, Jim Hughes (2d), CLEM LABINE (6th), Ben Wade (7th) and Roy Campanella.
Yankees: Allie Reynolds, JOHNNY SAIN (6th) and Yogi Berra.
Home Runs: Jim Gilliam (Dodgers), Yogi Berra (Yankees), Gil Hodges (Dodgers), George Shuba (Dodgers) and Joe Collins (Yankees).
Attendance: 69,374.

Game 2 (Oct. 1 at Yankee Stadium).

| Dodgers | 000 | 200 | 000 | — | 2 | 9 | 1 |
| Yankees | 100 | 000 | 12X | — | 4 | 5 | 0 |

Dodgers: PREACHER ROE and Roy Campanella.
Yankees: ED LOPAT and Yogi Berra.
Home Runs: Billy Martin (Yankees) and Mickey Mantle (Yankees).
Attendance: 66,786.

Game 3 (Oct. 2 at Brooklyn)

| Yankees | 000 | 010 | 010 | — | 2 | 6 | 0 |
| Dodgers | 000 | 011 | 01X | — | 3 | 9 | 0 |

Yankees: VIC RASCHI and Yogi Berra.
Dodgers: CARL ERSKINE and Roy Campanella.
Home Run: Roy Campanella (Dodgers).
Attendance: 35,270.

Game 4 (Oct. 3 at Brooklyn)

| Yankees | 000 | 020 | 001 | — | 3 | 9 | 0 |
| Dodgers | 300 | 102 | 10X | — | 7 | 12 | 0 |

Yankees: WHITEY FORD, Tom Gorman (2d), Johnny Sain (5th), Art Schallock (7th) and Yogi Berra.
Dodgers: BILLY LOES, Clem Labine (9th) and Roy Campanella.
Home Runs: Gil McDougald (Yankees) and Duke Snider (Dodgers).
Attendance: 36,775.

Game 5 (Oct. 4 at Brooklyn)

| Yankees | 105 | 000 | 311 | — | 11 | 11 | 1 |
| Dodgers | 010 | 010 | 041 | — | 7 | 14 | 1 |

Yankees: JIM McDONALD, Bob Kuzava (8th), Allie Reynolds (9th) and Yogi Berra.
Dodgers: JOHNNY PODRES, Russ Meyer (3d), Ben Wade (8th), Joe Black (9th) and Roy Campanella.
Home Runs: Gene Woodling (Yankees), Mickey Mantle (Yankees), Billy Martin (Yankees), Billy Cox (Dodgers), Gil McDougald (Yankees) and Jim Gilliam (Dodgers).
Attendance: 36,775.

Game 6 (Oct. 5 at Yankee Stadium)

| Dodgers | 000 | 001 | 002 | — | 3 | 8 | 3 |
| Yankees | 210 | 000 | 001 | — | 4 | 13 | 0 |

Dodgers: Carl Erskine, Bob Milliken (5th), CLEM LABINE (7th) and Roy Campanella.
Yankees: Whitey Ford, ALLIE REYNOLDS (8th) and Yogi Berra.
Home Run: Carl Furillo (Dodgers).
Attendance: 62,370.

1955 American League Champions

Manager: Casey Stengel
World Series Roster: Pitchers: Tommy Byrne, Rip Coleman, Whitey Ford, Bob Grim, Johnny Kucks, Don Larsen, Tom Morgan, Tom Sturdivant, Bob Turley, Bob Wiesler. *Catchers:* Yogi Berra, Charlie Silvera. *Infielders:* Andy Carey, Tommy Carroll, Jerry Coleman, Joe Collins, Frank Leja, Billy Martin, Gil McDougald, Phil Rizzuto, Eddie Robinson, Bill Skowron. *Outfielders:* Hank Bauer, Bob Cerv, Elston Howard, Mickey Mantle, Irv Noren.

World Series

	W	L	Pct.
Dodgers	4	3	.571
Yankees	3	4	.429

Game 1 (Sept. 28 at Yankee Stadium)

| Dodgers | 021 | 000 | 020 | — | 5 | 10 | 0 |
| Yankees | 021 | 102 | 00X | — | 6 | 9 | 1 |

Dodgers: DON NEWCOMBE, Don Bessent (6th), Clem Labine (8th) and Roy Campanella.
Yankees: WHITEY FORD, Bob Grim (9th) and Yogi Berra.
Home Runs: Joe Collins (Yankees) 2, Carl Furillo (Dodgers), Elston Howard (Yankees) and Duke Snider (Dodgers).
Attendance: 63,869.

Game 2 (Sept. 29 at Yankee Stadium)

| Dodgers | 000 | 110 | 000 | — | 2 | 5 | 2 |
| Yankees | 000 | 4000 | 00X | — | 4 | 8 | 0 |

Dodgers: BILLY LOES, Don Bessent (4th), Karl Spooner (5th), Clem Labine (8th) and Roy Campanella.
Yankees: TOMMY BYRNE and Yogi Berra.
Home Runs: None.
Attendance: 64,707.

Game 3 (Sept. 30 at Brooklyn)

| Yankees | 020 | 000 | 100 | — | 3 | 7 | 0 |
| Dodgers | 220 | 200 | 20X | — | 8 | 11 | 1 |

Yankees: BOB TURLEY, Tom Morgan (2d), Johnny Kucks (5th), Tom Sturdivant (7th) and Yogi Berra.
Dodgers: JOHNNY PODRES and Roy Campanella.
Home Runs: Roy Campanella (Dodgers) and Mickey Mantle (Yankees).
Attendance: 34,209.

Game 4 (Oct. 1 at Brooklyn)

| Yankees | 110 | 102 | 000 | — | 5 | 9 | 0 |
| Dodgers | 001 | 330 | 10X | — | 8 | 14 | 0 |

Yankees: DON LARSEN, Johnny Kucks (5th), Rip Coleman (6th), Tom Morgan (7th), Tom Sturdivant (8th) and Yogi Berra.
Dodgers: Carl Erskine, Don Bessent (4th), CLEM LABINE (5th) and Roy Campanella.
Home Runs: Gil McDougald (Yankees), Roy Campanella (Dodgers), Gil Hodges (Dodgers) and Duke Snider (Dodgers).
Attendance: 36,242.

Game 5 (Oct. 2 at Brooklyn)

| Yankees | 000 | 100 | 110 | — | 3 | 6 | 0 |
| Dodgers | 021 | 010 | 01X | — | 5 | 9 | 2 |

Yankees: BOB GRIM, Bob Turley (7th) and Yogi Berra.
Dodgers: ROGER CRAIG, Clem Labine (7th) and Roy Campanella.
Home Runs: Duke Snider (Dodgers) 2, Sandy Amoros (Dodgers), Bob Cerv (Yankees) and Yogi Berra (Yankees).
Attendance: 36,796.

Game 6 (Oct. 3 at Yankee Stadium)

| Dodgers | 000 | 100 | 000 | — | 1 | 4 | 1 |
| Yankees | 500 | 000 | 00X | — | 5 | 8 | 0 |

Dodgers: KARL SPOONER, Russ Meyer (1st), Ed Roebuck (7th) and Roy Campanella.
Yankees: WHITEY FORD and Yogi Berra.
Home Run: Bill Skowron (Yankees).
Attendance: 64,022.

Game 7 (Oct. 4 at Yankee Stadium)

| Dodgers | 000 | 101 | 000 | — | 2 | 5 | 0 |
| Yankees | 000 | 000 | 000 | — | 0 | 8 | 1 |

Dodgers: JOHNNY PODRES and Roy Campanella.
Yankees: TOMMY BYRNE, Bob Grim (6th), Bob Turley (8th) and Yogi Berra.
Home Runs: None.
Attendance: 62,465.

1956 World Champions

Manager: Casey Stengel

World Series Roster: Pitchers: Tommy Byrne, Rip Coleman, Whitey Ford, Bob Grim, Johnny Kucks, Don Larsen, Mickey McDermott, Tom Morgan, Tom Sturdivant, Bob Turley. *Catchers:* Yogi Berra, Charlie Silvera. *Infielders:* Andy Carey, Tommy Carroll, Jerry Coleman, Joe Collins, Billy Hunter, Billy Martin, Gil McDougald, Bill Skowron. *Outfielders:* Hank Bauer, Bob Cerv, Elston Howard, Mickey Mantle, Norm Siebern, Enos Slaughter, Ted Wilson.

World Series

	W	L	Pct.
Yankees	4	3	.571
Dodgers	3	4	.429

Game 1 (Oct. 3 at Brooklyn)

| Yankees | 200 | 100 | 000 | — | 3 | 9 | 1 |
| Dodgers | 023 | 100 | 00X | — | 6 | 9 | 0 |

Yankees: WHITEY FORD, Johnny Kucks (4th), Tom Morgan (6th), Bob Turley (8th) and Yogi Berra.
Dodgers: SAL MAGLIE and Roy Campanella.
Home Runs: Mickey Mantle (Yankees), Jackie Robinson (Dodgers), Gil Hodges (Dodgers) and Billy Martin (Yankees).
Attendance: 34,479.

Game 2 (Oct. 5 at Brooklyn)

| Yankees | 150 | 100 | 001 | — | 8 | 12 | 2 |
| Dodgers | 061 | 220 | 02X | — | 13 | 12 | 0 |

Yankees: Don Larsen, Johnny Kucks (2d), Tommy Byrne (2d), Tom Sturdivant (3d), TOM MORGAN (3d), Bob Turley (5th), Mickey McDermott (6th) and Yogi Berra.
Dodgers: Don Newcombe, Ed Roebuck (2d), DON BESSENT (3d) and Roy Campanella.
Home Runs: Yogi Berra (Yankees) and Duke Snider (Dodgers).
Attendance: 36,217.

Game 3 (Oct. 6 at Yankee Stadium)

| Dodgers | 010 | 001 | 100 | — | 3 | 8 | 1 |
| Yankees | 010 | 003 | 01X | — | 5 | 8 | 1 |

Dodgers: ROGER CRAIG, Clem Labine (7th) and Roy Campanella.
Yankees: WHITEY FORD and Yogi Berra.
Home Runs: Billy Martin (Yankees) and Enos Slaughter (Yankees).
Attendance: 73,977.

Game 4 (Oct. 7 at Yankee Stadium)

| Dodgers | 000 | 100 | 001 | — | 2 | 6 | 0 |
| Yankees | 100 | 201 | 20X | — | 6 | 7 | 2 |

Dodgers: CARL ERSKINE, Ed Roebuck (5th), Don Drysdale (7th) and Roy Campanella.
Yankees: TOM STURDIVANT and Yogi Berra.
Home Runs: Mickey Mantle (Yankees) and Hank Bauer (Yankees).
Attendance: 69,705.

Game 5 (Oct. 8 at Yankee Stadium)

| Dodgers | 000 | 000 | 000 | — | 0 | 0 | 0 |
| Yankees | 000 | 101 | 00X | — | 2 | 5 | 0 |

Dodgers: SAL MAGLIE and Roy Campanella.
Yankees: DON LARSEN and Yogi Berra.
Home Run: Mickey Mantle (Yankees).
Attendance: 64,519.

Game 6 (Oct. 9 at Brooklyn)

| Yankees | 000 | 000 | 000 | 0 | — | 0 | 7 | 0 |
| Dodgers | 000 | 000 | 000 | 1 | — | 1 | 4 | 0 |

Yankees: BOB TURLEY and Yogi Berra.
Dodgers: CLEM LABINE and Roy Campanella.
Home Runs: None.
Attendance: 33,224.

Game 7 (Oct. 10 at Brooklyn)

| Yankees | 202 | 100 | 400 | — | 9 | 10 | 0 |
| Dodgers | 000 | 000 | 000 | — | 0 | 3 | 1 |

Yankees: JOHNNY KUCKS and Yogi Berra.
Dodgers: DON NEWCOMBE, Don Bessent (4th), Roger Craig (7th), Ed Roebuck (7th), Carl Erskine (9th) and Roy Campanella.
Home Runs: Yogi Berra (Yankees) 2, Elston Howard (Yankees) and Bill Skowron (Yankees).
Attendance: 33,782.

1957 American League Champions

Manager: Casey Stengel

World Series Roster: Pitchers: Tommy Byrne, Al Cicotte, Art Ditmar, Whitey Ford, Bob Grim, Johnny Kucks, Don Larsen, Bobby Shantz, Tom Sturdivant, Bob Turley. *Catchers:* Yogi Berra, Darrell Johnson. *Infielders:* Andy Carey, Jerry Coleman, Joe Collins, Tony Kubek, Jerry Lumpe, Gil McDougald, Bobby Richardson, Bill Skowron. *Outfielders:* Hank Bauer, Elston Howard, Mickey Mantle, Harry Simpson, Enos Slaughter.

World Series

	W	L	Pct.
Braves	4	3	.571
Yankees	3	4	.429

Game 1 (Oct. 2 at Yankee Stadium)

| Braves | 000 | 000 | 100 | — | 1 | 5 | 0 |
| Yankees | 000 | 012 | 00X | — | 3 | 9 | 1 |

Braves: WARREN SPAHN, Ernie Johnson (6th), Don McMahon (7th) and Del Crandall.
Yankees: WHITEY FORD and Yogi Berra.
Home Runs: None.
Attendance: 69,476.

Game 2 (Oct. 3 at Yankee Stadium)

| Braves | 011 | 200 | 000 | — | 4 | 8 | 0 |
| Yankees | 011 | 000 | 000 | — | 2 | 7 | 2 |

Braves: LEW BURDETTE and Del Crandall.
Yankees: BOBBY SHANTZ, Art Ditmar (4th), Bob Grim (8th) and Yogi Berra.
Home Runs: Johnny Logan (Braves) and Hank Bauer (Yankees).
Attendance: 65,202.

Game 3 (Oct. 5 at Milwaukee)

| Yankees | 302 | 200 | 500 | — | 12 | 9 | 0 |
| Braves | 010 | 020 | 000 | — | 3 | 8 | 1 |

Yankees: Bob Turley, DON LARSEN (2d) and Yogi Berra.
Braves: BOB BUHL, Juan Pizarro (1st), Gene Conley (3d), Ernie Johnson (5th), Bob Trowbridge (7th), Don McMahon (8th) and Del Rice, Del Crandall (9th).
Home Runs: Tony Kubek (Yankees) 2, Mickey Mantle (Yankees) and Hank Aaron (Braves).
Attendance: 45,804.

Game 4 (Oct. 6 at Milwaukee)

| Yankees | 100 | 000 | 003 | 1 | — | 5 | 11 | 0 |
| Braves | 000 | 400 | 000 | 3 | — | 7 | 7 | 0 |

Yankees: Tom Sturdivant, Bobby Shantz (5th), Johnny Kucks (8th), Tommy Byrne (8th), BOB GRIM (10th) and Yogi Berra.
Braves: WARREN SPAHN and Del Crandall.
Home Runs: Hank Aaron (Braves), Frank Torre (Braves), Elston Howard (Yankees) and Eddie Mathews (Braves).
Attendance: 45,804.

Game 5 (Oct. 7 at Milwaukee)

Yankees	000	000	000	—	0	7	0
Braves	000	001	00X	—	1	6	1

Yankees: WHITEY FORD, Bob Turley (8th) and Yogi Berra
Braves: LEW BURDETTE and Del Crandall.
Home Runs: None.
Attendance: 45,811.

Game 6 (Oct. 9 at Yankee Stadium)

Braves	000	010	100	—	2	4	0
Yankees	002	000	10X	—	3	7	0

Braves: Bob Buhl, ERNIE JOHNSON (3d), Don McMahon (8th) and Del Rice.
Yankees: BOB TURLEY and Yogi Berra.
Home Runs: Yogi Berra (Yankees), Frank Torre (Braves), Hank Aaron (Braves) and Hank Bauer (Yankees).
Attendance: 61,408.

Game 7 (Oct. 10 at Yankee Stadium)

Braves	004	000	010	—	5	9	1
Yankees	000	000	000	—	0	7	3

Braves: LEW BURDETTE and Del Crandall.
Yankees: DON LARSEN, Bobby Shantz (3d), Art Ditmar (4th), Tom Sturdivant (6th), Tommy Byrne (8th) and Yogi Berra.
Home Run: Del Crandall (Braves).
Attendance: 61,207.

1958 World Champions

Manager: Casey Stengel
World Series Roster: Pitchers: Murry Dickson, Art Ditmar, Ryne Duren, Whitey Ford, Johnny Kucks, Don Larsen, Duke Maas, Zack Monroe, Bobby Shantz, Tom Sturdivant, Virgil Trucks, Bob Turley. *Catchers:* Yogi Berra, Elston Howard, Darrell Johnson. *Infielders:* Andy Carey, Tony Kubek, Jerry Lumpe, Gil McDougald, Bobby Richardson, Bill Skowron, Marv Throneberry. *Outfielders:* Hank Bauer, Mickey Mantle, Norm Siebern, Enos Slaughter.

World Series

	W	L	Pct.
Yankees	4	3	.571
Braves	3	4	.429

Game 1 (Oct. 1 at Milwaukee)

Yankees	000	120	000	0	—	3	8	1
Braves	000	200	010	1	—	4	10	0

Yankees: Whitey Ford, RYNE DUREN (8th) and Yogi Berra.
Braves: WARREN SPAHN and Del Crandall.
Home Runs: Bill Skowron (Yankees) and Hank Bauer (Yankees).
Attendance: 46,367.

Game 2 (Oct. 2 at Milwaukee)

Yankees	100	100	003	—	5	7	0
Braves	710	000	23X	—	13	15	1

Yankees: BOB TURLEY, Duke Maas (1st), Johnny Kucks (1st), Murry Dickson (5th), Zack Monroe (8th) and Yogi Berra.
Braves: LEW BURDETTE and Del Crandall.
Home Runs: Mickey Mantle (Yankees) 2, Bill Bruton (Braves), Lew Burdette (Braves) and Hank Bauer (Yankees).
Attendance: 46,367.

Game 3 (Oct. 4 at Yankee Stadium)

Braves	000	000	000	—	0	6	0
Yankees	000	020	20X	—	4	4	0

Braves: BOB RUSH, Don McMahon (7th) and Del Crandall.
Yankees: DON LARSEN, Ryne Duren (8th) and Yogi Berra.
Home Run: Hank Bauer (Yankees).
Attendance: 71,599.

Game 4 (Oct. 5 at Yankee Stadium)

Braves	000	001	110	—	3	9	0
Yankees	000	000	000	—	0	2	1

Braves: WARREN SPAHN and Del Crandall.
Yankees: WHITEY FORD, Johnny Kucks (8th), Murry Dickson (9th) and Yogi Berra.
Home Runs: None.
Attendance: 71,563.

Game 5 (Oct. 6 at Yankee Stadium)

Braves	000	000	000	—	0	5	0
Yankees	001	006	00X	—	7	10	0

Braves: LEW BURDETTE, Juan Pizarro (6th), Carlton Willey (8th) and Del Crandall.
Yankees: BOB TURLEY and Yogi Berra.
Home Run: Gil McDougald (Yankees).
Attendance: 65,279.

Game 6 (Oct. 8 at Milwaukee)

Yankees	100	001	000	2	—	4	10	1
Braves	110	000	000	1	—	3	10	4

Yankees: Whitey Ford, Art Ditmar (2d), RYNE DUREN (6th), Bob Turley (10th) and Yogi Berra.
Braves: WARREN SPAHN, Don McMahon (10th) and Del Crandall.
Home Runs: Hank Bauer (Yankees) and Gil McDougald (Yankees).
Attendance: 46,367.

Game 7 (Oct. 9 at Milwaukee)

Yankees	020	000	040	—	6	8	0
Braves	100	001	000	—	2	5	2

Yankees: Don Larsen, BOB TURLEY (3d) and Yogi Berra.
Braves: LEW BURDETTE, Don McMahon (9th) and Del Crandall.
Home Runs: Del Crandall (Braves) and Bill Skowron (Yankees).
Attendance: 46,367.

1960 American League Champions

Manager: Casey Stengel
World Series Roster: Pitchers: Luis Arroyo, Jim Coates, Art Ditmar, Ryne Duren, Whitey Ford, Eli Grba, Duke Maas, Bobby Shantz, Bill Stafford, Ralph Terry, Bob Turley. *Catchers:* Yogi Berra, Johnny Blanchard, Elston Howard. *Infielders:* Clete Boyer, Joe DeMaestri, Tony Kubek, Dale Long, Gil McDougald, Bobby Richardson, Bill Skowron. *Outfielders:* Bob Cerv, Hector Lopez, Mickey Mantle, Roger Maris.

World Series

	W	L	Pct.
Pirates	4	3	.571
Yankees	3	4	.429

Game 1 (Oct. 5 at Pittsburgh)

Yankees	100	100	002	—	4	13	2
Pirates	300	201	00X	—	6	8	0

Yankees: ART DITMAR, Jim Coates (1st), Duke Maas (5th), Ryne Duren (7th) and Yogi Berra.
Pirates: VERNON LAW, Elroy Face (8th) and Smoky Burgess.
Home Runs: Roger Maris (Yankees), Bill Mazeroski (Pirates) and Elston Howard (Yankees).
Attendance: 36,676.

Game 2 (Oct. 6 at Pittsburgh)

Yankees	002	127	301	—	16	19	1
Pirates	000	100	002	—	3	13	1

Yankees: BOB TURLEY, Bobby Shantz (9th) and Elston Howard.
Pirates: BOB FRIEND, Freddie Green (5th), Clem Labine (6th), George Witt (6th), Joe Gibbon (7th), Tom Cheney (9th) and Smoky Burgess.
Home Runs: Mickey Mantle (Yankees) 2.
Attendance: 37,308.

Game 3 (Oct. 8 at Yankee Stadium)

Pirates	000	000	000	—	0	4	0
Yankees	600	400	00X	—	10	16	1

Pirates: VINEGAR BEND MIZELL, Clem Labine (1st), Freddie Green (1st), George Witt (4th), Tom Cheney (6th), Joe Gibbon (8th) and Hal Smith.
Yankees: WHITEY FORD and Elston Howard.
Home Runs: Bobby Richardson (Yankees) and Mickey Mantle (Yankees).
Attendance: 70,001.

Game 4 (Oct. 9 at Yankee Stadium)

Pirates	000	030	000	—	3	7	0
Yankees	000	100	100	—	2	8	0

Pirates: VERNON LAW, Elroy Face (7th) and Smoky Burgess, Bob Oldis (9th).
Yankees: RALPH TERRY, Bobby Shantz (7th), Jim Coates (8th) and Yogi Berra.
Home Run: Bill Skowron (Yankees).
Attendance: 67,812.

Game 5 (Oct. 10 at Yankee Stadium)

Pirates	031	000	001	—	5	10	2
Yankees	011	000	000	—	2	5	2

Pirates: HARVEY HADDIX, Elroy Face (7th) and Smoky Burgess, Bob Oldis (9th).
Yankees: ART DITMAR, Luis Arroyo (2d), Bill Stafford (3d), Ryne Duren (8th) and Elston Howard, Yogi Berra (8th).
Home Run: Roger Maris (Yankees).
Attendance: 62,753.

Game 6 (Oct. 12 at Pittsburgh)

Yankees	015	002	220	—	12	17	1
Pirates	000	000	000	—	0	7	1

Yankees: WHITEY FORD and Elston Howard, Johnny Blanchard (2d).
Pirates: BOB FRIEND, Tom Cheney (3d), Vinegar Bend Mizell (4th), Freddie Green (6th), Clem Labine (6th), George Witt (9th) and Hal Smith.
Home Runs: None.
Attendance: 38,580.

Game 7 (Oct. 13 at Pittsburgh)

Yankees	000	014	022	—	9	13	1
Pirates	220	000	051	—	10	11	0

Yankees: Bob Turley, Bill Stafford (2d), Bobby Shantz (3d), Jim Coates (8th), RALPH TERRY (9th) and Johnny Blanchard.
Pirates: Vernon Law, Elroy Face (6th), Bob Friend (9th), HARVEY HADDIX (9th) and Smoky Burgess, Hal Smith (8th).
Home Runs: Rocky Nelson (Pirates), Bill Skowron (Yankees), Yogi Berra (Yankees), Hal Smith (Pirates) and Bill Mazeroski (Pirates).
Attendance: 36,683.

1961 World Champions

Manager: Ralph Houk
World Series Roster: Pitchers: Luis Arroyo, Tex Clevenger, Jim Coates, Bud Daley, Al Downing, Whitey Ford, Hal Reniff, Rollie Sheldon, Bill Stafford, Ralph Terry, Bob Turley. *Catchers:* Johnny Blanchard, Elston Howard. *Infielders:* Clete Boyer, Joe DeMaestri, Billy Gardner, Bob Hale, Tony Kubek, Bobby Richardson, Bill Skowron. *Outfielders:* Yogi Berra, Hector Lopez, Mickey Mantle, Roger Maris, Jack Reed.

World Series

	W	L	Pct.
Yankees	4	1	.800
Reds	1	4	.200

Game 1 (Oct. 4 at Yankee Stadium)

Reds	000	000	000	—	0	2	0
Yankees	000	101	00X	—	2	6	0

Reds: JIM O'TOOLE, Jim Brosnan (8th) and Darrell Johnson, Jerry Zimmerman (8th).
Yankees: WHITEY FORD and Elston Howard.
Home Runs: Elston Howard (Yankees) and Bill Skowron (Yankees).
Attendance: 62,397.

Game 2 (Oct. 5 at Yankee Stadium)

Reds	000	211	020	—	6	9	0
Yankees	000	200	000	—	2	4	3

Reds: JOEY JAY and Johnny Edwards.
Yankees: RALPH TERRY, Luis Arroyo (8th) and Elston Howard.
Home Runs: Gordy Coleman (Reds) and Yogi Berra (Yankees).
Attendance: 63,083.

Game 3 (Oct. 7 at Cincinnati)

Yankees	000	000	111	—	3	6	1
Reds	001	000	100	—	2	8	0

Yankees: Bill Stafford, Bud Daley (7th), LUIS ARROYO (8th) and Elston Howard.
Reds: BOB PURKEY and Johnny Edwards.
Home Runs: Johnny Blanchard (Yankees) and Roger Maris (Yankees).
Attendance: 32,589.

Game 4 (Oct. 8 at Cincinnati)

Yankees	000	112	300	—	7	11	0
Reds	000	000	000	—	0	5	1

Yankees: WHITEY FORD, Jim Coates (6th) and Elston Howard.
Reds: JIM O'TOOLE, Jim Brosnan (6th), Bill Henry (9th) and Darrell Johnson, Jerry Zimmerman (8th).
Home Runs: None.
Attendance: 32,589.

Game 5 (Oct. 9 at Cincinnati)

Yankees	510	502	000	—	13	15	1
Reds	003	020	000	—	5	11	3

Yankees: Ralph Terry, BUD DALEY (3d) and Elston Howard.
Reds: JOEY JAY, Jim Maloney (1st), Ken Johnson (2d), Bill Henry (3d), Sherman Jones (4th), Bob Purkey (5th), Jim Brosnan (7th), Ken Hunt (9th) and Johnny Edwards.
Home Runs: Johnny Blanchard (Yankees), Frank Robinson (Reds), Hector Lopez (Yankees) and Wally Post (Reds).
Attendance: 32,589.

1962 World Champions

Manager: Ralph Houk
World Series Roster: Pitchers: Luis Arroyo, Jim Bouton, Marshall Bridges, Tex Clevenger, Jim Coates, Bud Daley, Whitey Ford, Rollie Sheldon, Bill Stafford, Ralph Terry, Bob Turley. *Catchers:* Johnny Blanchard, Elston Howard. *Infielders:* Clete Boyer, Tony Kubek, Phil Linz, Dale Long, Bobby Richardson, Bill Skowron. *Outfielders:* Yogi Berra, Hector Lopez, Mickey Mantle, Roger Maris, Jack Reed, Tom Tresh.

World Series

	W	L	Pct.
Yankees	4	3	.571
Giants	3	4	.429

Game 1 (Oct. 4 at San Francisco)

Yankees	200	000	121	—	6	11	0
Giants	011	000	000	—	2	10	0

Yankees: WHITEY FORD and Elston Howard.
Giants: BILLY O'DELL, Don Larsen (8th), Stu Miller (9th) and Ed Bailey,
John Orsino (9th).
Home Run: Clete Boyer (Yankees).
Attendance: 43,852.

Game 2 (Oct. 5 at San Francisco)

Yankees	000	000	000	—	0	3	1
Giants	100	000	10X	—	2	6	0

Yankees: RALPH TERRY, Bud Daley (8th) and Yogi Berra.
Giants: JACK SANFORD and Tom Haller.
Home Run: Willie McCovey (Giants).
Attendance: 43,910.

Game 3 (Oct. 7 at Yankee Stadium)

Giants	000	000	002	—	2	4	3
Yankees	000	000	30X	—	3	5	1

Giants: BILLY PIERCE, Don Larsen (7th), Bob Bolin (8th) and Ed Bailey.
Yankees: BILL STAFFORD and Elston Howard.
Home Run: Ed Bailey (Giants).
Attendance: 71,434.

Game 4 (Oct. 8 at Yankee Stadium)

Giants	020	000	401	—	7	9	1
Yankees	000	002	001	—	3	9	1

Giants: Juan Marichal, Bob Bolin (5th), DON LARSEN (6th), Billy O'Dell
(7th) and Tom Haller.
Yankees: Whitey Ford, JIM COATES (7th), Marshall Bridges (7th) and
Elston Howard.
Home Runs: Tom Haller (Giants) and Chuck Hiller (Giants).
Attendance: 66,607.

Game 5 (Oct. 10 at Yankee Stadium)

Giants	001	010	001	—	3	8	2
Yankees	000	101	03X	—	5	6	0

Giants: JACK SANFORD, Stu Miller (8th) and Tom Haller.
Yankees: RALPH TERRY and Elston Howard.
Home Runs: Jose Pagan (Giants) and Tom Tresh (Yankees).
Attendance: 63,165.

Game 6 (Oct. 15 at San Francisco)

Yankees	000	010	010	—	2	3	2
Giants	000	320	00X	—	5	10	1

Yankees: WHITEY FORD, Jim Coates (5th), Marshall Bridges (8th) and
Elston Howard.
Giants: BILLY PIERCE and Ed Bailey.
Home Run: Roger Maris (Yankees).
Attendance: 43,948.

Game 7 (Oct. 16 at San Francisco)

Yankees	000	010	000	—	1	7	0
Giants	000	000	000	—	0	4	1

Yankees: RALPH TERRY and Elston Howard.
Giants: JACK SANFORD, Billy O'Dell (8th) and Tom Haller.
Home Runs: None.
Attendance: 43,948.

1963 American League Champions

Manager: Ralph Houk
World Series Roster: Pitchers: Jim Bouton, Marshall Bridges, Al Downing,
Whitey Ford, Steve Hamilton, Bill Kunkel, Tom Metcalf, Hal Reniff, Bill
Stafford, Ralph Terry, Stan Williams. *Catchers:* Yogi Berra, Elston
Howard. *Infielders:* Clete Boyer, Harry Bright, Tony Kubek, Phil Linz, Joe
Pepitone, Bobby Richardson. *Outfielders:* Johnny Blanchard, Hector
Lopez, Mickey Mantle, Roger Maris, Jack Reed, Tom Tresh.

World Series

	W	L	Pct.
Dodgers	4	0	1.000
Yankees	0	4	.000

Game 1 (Oct. 2 at Yankee Stadium)

Dodgers	041	000	000	—	5	9	0
Yankees	000	000	020	—	2	6	0

Dodgers: SANDY KOUFAX and John Roseboro.
Yankees: WHITEY FORD, Stan Williams (6th), Steve Hamilton (9th) and
Elston Howard.
Home Runs: John Roseboro (Dodgers) and Tom Tresh (Yankees).
Attendance: 69,000.

Game 2 (Oct. 3 at Yankee Stadium)

Dodgers	200	100	010	—	4	10	1
Yankees	000	000	001	—	1	7	0

Dodgers: JOHNNY PODRES, Ron Perranoski (9th) and John Roseboro.
Yankees: AL DOWNING, Ralph Terry (6th), Hal Reniff (9th) and Elston
Howard.
Home Run: Bill Skowron (Dodgers).
Attendance: 66,455.

Game 3 (Oct. 5 at Los Angeles)

Yankees	000	000	000	—	0	3	0
Dodgers	100	000	00X	—	1	4	1

Yankees: JIM BOUTON, Hal Reniff (8th) and Elston Howard.
Dodgers: DON DRYSDALE and John Roseboro.
Home Runs: None.
Attendance: 55,912.

Game 4 (Oct. 6 at Los Angeles)

Yankees	000	000	100	—	1	6	1
Dodgers	000	010	10X	—	2	2	1

Yankees: WHITEY FORD, Hal Reniff (8th) and Elston Howard.
Dodgers: SANDY KOUFAX and John Roseboro.
Home Runs: Frank Howard (Dodgers) and Mickey Mantle (Yankees).
Attendance: 55,912.

1964 American League Champions

Manager: Yogi Berra
World Series Roster: Pitchers: Jim Bouton, Al Downing, Whitey Ford,
Steve Hamilton, Pete Mikkelsen, Hal Reniff, Rollie Sheldon, Bill Staf-
ford, Mel Stottlemyre, Ralph Terry, Stan Williams. *Catchers:* Johnny
Blanchard, Elston Howard. *Infielders:* Clete Boyer, Pedro Gonzalez, Mike
Hegan, Tony Kubek, Phil Linz, Joe Pepitone, Bobby Richardson. *Out-
fielders:* Hector Lopez, Mickey Mantle, Roger Maris, Archie Moore, Tom
Tresh.

World Series

	W	L	Pct.
Cardinals	4	3	.571
Yankees	3	4	.429

Game 1 (Oct. 7 at St. Louis)

Yankees	030	010	010	—	5	12	2
Cardinals	110	004	03X	—	9	12	0

Yankees: WHITEY FORD, Al Downing (6th), Rollie Sheldon (8th), Pete
Mikkelsen (8th) and Elston Howard.
Cardinals: RAY SADECKI, Barney Schultz (7th) and Tim McCarver.
Home Runs: Tom Tresh (Yankees) and Mike Shannon (Cardinals).
Attendance: 30,805.

Game 2 (Oct. 8 at St. Louis)

Yankees	000	101	204	—	8	12	0
Cardinals	001	000	011	—	3	7	0

Yankees: MEL STOTTLEMYRE and Elston Howard.
Cardinals: BOB GIBSON, Barney Schultz (9th), Gordie Richardson (9th), Roger Craig (9th) and Tim McCarver.
Home Run: Phil Linz (Yankees).
Attendance: 30,805.

Game 3 (Oct. 10 at Yankee Stadium)

Cardinals	000	010	000	—	1	6	0
Yankees	010	000	001	—	2	5	2

Cardinals: Curt Simmons, BARNEY SCHULTZ (9th) and Tim McCarver.
Yankees: JIM BOUTON and Elston Howard.
Home Run: Mickey Mantle (Yankees).
Attendance: 67,101.

Game 4 (Oct. 11 at Yankee Stadium)

Cardinals	000	004	000	—	4	6	1
Yankees	300	000	000	—	3	6	1

Cardinals: Ray Sadecki, ROGER CRAIG (1st), Ron Taylor (6th) and Tim McCarver.
Yankees: AL DOWNING, Pete Mikkelsen (7th), Ralph Terry (8th) and Elston Howard.
Home Run: Ken Boyer (Cardinals).
Attendance: 66,312.

Game 5 (Oct. 12 at Yankee Stadium)

Cardinals	000	020	000	3	—	5	10	1
Yankees	000	000	002	0	—	2	6	2

Cardinals: BOB GIBSON and Tim McCarver.
Yankees: Mel Stottlemyre, Hal Reniff (8th), PETE MIKKELSEN (8th) and Elston Howard.
Home Runs: Tom Tresh (Yankees) and Tim McCarver (Cardinals).
Attendance: 65,633.

Game 6 (Oct. 14 at St. Louis)

Yankees	000	012	050	—	8	10	0
Cardinals	100	000	011	—	3	10	1

Yankees: JIM BOUTON, Steve Hamilton (9th) and Elston Howard.
Cardinals: CURT SIMMONS, Ron Taylor (7th), Barney Schultz (8th), Gordie Richardson (8th), Bob Humphreys (9th) and Tim McCarver.
Home Runs: Mickey Mantle (Yankees), Roger Maris (Yankees) and Joe Pepitone (Yankees).
Attendance: 30,805.

Game 7 (Oct. 15 at St. Louis)

Yankees	000	003	002	—	5	9	2
Cardinals	000	330	10X	—	7	10	1

Yankees: MEL STOTTLEMYRE, Al Downing (5th), Rollie Sheldon (5th), Steve Hamilton (7th), Pete Mikkelsen (8th) and Elston Howard.
Cardinals: BOB GIBSON and Tim McCarver.
Home Runs: Lou Brock (Cardinals), Mickey Mantle (Yankees), Ken Boyer (Cardinals), Clete Boyer (Yankees) and Phil Linz (Yankees).
Attendance: 30,346.

1976 American League Champions

Manager: Billy Martin
World Series Roster: Pitchers: Doyle Alexander, Dock Ellis, Ed Figueroa, Ron Guidry, Ken Holtzman, Catfish Hunter, Grant Jackson, Sparky Lyle, Dick Tidrow. *Catchers:* Fran Healy, Elrod Hendricks, Thurman Munson. *Infielders:* Sandy Alomar, Chris Chambliss, Jim Mason, Graig Nettles, Willie Randolph, Fred Stanley. *Outfielders:* Oscar Gamble, Elliott Maddox, Carlos May, Lou Piniella, Mickey Rivers, Otto Velez, Roy White.

A.L. Championship Series

	W	L	Pct.
Yankees	3	2	.600
Royals	2	3	.400

Game 1 (Oct. 9 at Kansas City)

Yankees	200	000	002	—	4	12	0
Royals	000	000	010	—	1	5	2

Yankees: CATFISH HUNTER and Thurman Munson.
Royals: LARRY GURA, Mark Littell (9th) and Buck Martinez, John Wathan (9th).
Home Runs: None.
Attendance: 41,077.

Game 2 (Oct. 10 at Kansas City)

Yankees	012	000	000	—	3	12	5
Royals	200	002	03X	—	7	9	0

Yankees: ED FIGUEROA, Dick Tidrow (6th) and Thurman Munson.
Royals: Dennis Leonard, PAUL SPLITTORFF (3d), Steve Mingori (9th) and Buck Martinez.
Home Runs: None.
Attendance: 41,091.

Game 3 (Oct. 12 at Yankee Stadium)

Royals	300	000	000	—	3	6	0
Yankees	000	203	00X	—	5	9	0

Royals: ANDY HASSLER, Marty Pattin (6th), Tom Hall (6th), Steve Mingori (6th), Mark Littell (6th) and Buck Martinez, Bob Stinson (8th).
Yankees: DOCK ELLIS, Sparky Lyle (9th) and Thurman Munson.
Home Run: Chris Chambliss (Yankees).
Attendance: 56,808.

Game 4 (Oct. 13 at Yankee Stadium)

Royals	030	201	010	—	7	9	1
Yankees	020	000	101	—	4	11	0

Royals: Larry Gura, DOUG BIRD (3d), Steve Mingori (7th) and Buck Martinez.
Yankees: CATFISH HUNTER, Dick Tidrow (4th), Grant Jackson (7th) and Thurman Munson.
Home Runs: Graig Nettles (Yankees) 2.
Attendance: 56,355.

Game 5 (Oct. 14 at Yankee Stadium)

Royals	210	000	030	—	6	11	1
Yankees	202	002	001	—	7	11	1

Royals: Dennis Leonard, Paul Splittorff (1st), Marty Pattin (4th), Andy Hassler (5th), MARK LITTELL (7th) and Buck Martinez.
Yankees: Ed Figueroa, Grant Jackson (8th), DICK TIDROW (9th) and Thurman Munson.
Home Runs: John Mayberry (Royals), George Brett (Royals) and Chris Chambliss (Yankees).
Attendance: 56,821.

World Series

	W	L	Pct.
Reds	4	0	1.000
Yankees	0	4	.000

Game 1 (Oct. 16 at Cincinnati)

Yankees	010	000	000	—	1	5	1
Reds	101	001	20X	—	5	10	1

Yankees: DOYLE ALEXANDER, Sparky Lyle (7th) and Thurman Munson.
Reds: DON GULLETT, Pedro Borbon (8th) and Johnny Bench.
Home Run: Joe Morgan (Reds).
Attendance: 54,826.

Game 2 (Oct. 17 at Cincinnati)

Yankees	000	100	200	—	3	9	1
Reds	030	000	001	—	4	10	0

Yankees: CATFISH HUNTER and Thurman Munson.
Reds: Fred Norman, JACK BILLINGHAM (7th) and Johnny Bench.
Home Runs: None.
Attendance: 54,816.

Game 3 (Oct. 19 at Yankee Stadium)

Reds	030	100	020	—	6	13	2
Yankees	000	100	100	—	2	8	0

Reds: PAT ZACHRY, Will McEnaney (7th) and Johnny Bench.
Yankees: DOCK ELLIS, Grant Jackson (4th), Dick Tidrow (8th) and Thurman Munson.
Home Runs: Dan Driessen (Reds) and Jim Mason (Yankees).
Attendance: 56,667.

Game 4 (Oct. 21 at Yankee Stadium)

Reds	000	300	004	—	7	9	2
Yankees	100	010	000	—	2	8	0

Reds: GARY NOLAN, Will McEnaney (7th) and Johnny Bench.
Yankees: ED FIGUEROA, Dick Tidrow (9th), Sparky Lyle (9th) and Thurman Munson.
Home Runs: Johnny Bench (Reds) 2.
Attendance: 56,700.

1977 World Champions

Manager: Billy Martin
World Series Roster: Pitchers: Ken Clay, Ed Figueroa, Ron Guidry, Don Gullett, Ken Holtzman, Catfish Hunter, Sparky Lyle, Dick Tidrow, Mike Torrez. *Catchers:* Fran Healy, Cliff Johnson, Thurman Munson. *Infielders:* Chris Chambliss, Bucky Dent, Mickey Klutts, Graig Nettles, Willie Randolph, Fred Stanley, George Zeber. *Outfielders:* Paul Blair, Reggie Jackson, Lou Piniella, Mickey Rivers, Roy White.

A.L. Championship Series

	W	L	Pct.
Yankees	3	2	.600
Royals	2	3	.400

Game 1 (Oct. 5 at Yankee Stadium)

Royals	222	000	010	—	7	9	0
Yankees	002	000	000	—	2	9	0

Royals: PAUL SPLITTORFF, Doug Bird (9th) and Darrell Porter.
Yankees: DON GULLETT, Dick Tidrow (3d), Sparky Lyle (9th) and Thurman Munson.
Home Runs: Hal McRae (Royals), John Mayberry (Royals), Thurman Munson (Yankees) and Al Cowens (Royals).
Attendance: 54,930.

Game 2 (Oct. 6 at Yankee Stadium)

Royals	001	001	000	—	2	3	1
Yankees	000	023	01X	—	6	10	1

Royals: ANDY HASSLER, Mark Littell (6th), Steve Mingori (8th) and Darrell Porter, John Wathan (8th).
Yankees: RON GUIDRY and Thurman Munson.
Home Run: Cliff Johnson (Yankees).
Attendance: 56,230.

Game 3 (Oct. 7 at Kansas City)

Yankees	000	010	001	—	2	4	1
Royals	011	012	10X	—	6	12	1

Yankees: MIKE TORREZ, Sparky Lyle (6th) and Thurman Munson.
Royals: DENNIS LEONARD and Darrell Porter.
Home Runs: None.
Attendance: 41,285.

Game 4 (Oct. 8 at Kansas City)

Yankees	121	100	001	—	6	13	0
Royals	002	200	000	—	4	8	2

Yankees: Ed Figueroa, Dick Tidrow (4th), SPARKY LYLE (4th), and Thurman Munson.
Royals: LARRY GURA, Marty Pattin (3d), Steve Mingori (9th), Doug Bird (9th) and Darrell Porter.
Home Runs: None.
Attendance: 41,135.

Game 5 (Oct. 9 at Kansas City)

Yankees	001	000	013	—	5	10	0
Royals	201	000	000	—	3	10	1

Yankees: Ron Guidry, Mike Torrez (3d), SPARKY LYLE (8th) and Thurman Munson.
Royals: Paul Splittorff, Doug Bird (8th), Steve Mingori (8th), DENNIS LEONARD (9th), Larry Gura (9th), Mark Littell (9th) and Darrell Porter.
Home Runs: None.
Attendance: 41,133.

World Series

	W	L	Pct.
Yankees	4	2	.667
Dodgers	2	4	.333

Game 1 (Oct. 11 at Yankee Stadium)

Dodgers	200	000	001	000	—	3	6	0
Yankees	100	001	010	001	—	4	11	0

Dodgers: Don Sutton, Lance Rautzhan (8th), Elias Sosa (8th), Mike Garman (9th), RICK RHODEN (12th) and Steve Yeager, Jerry Grote (9th).
Yankees: Don Gullett, SPARKY LYLE (9th) and Thurman Munson.
Home Run: Willie Randolph (Yankees).
Attendance: 56,668.

Game 2 (Oct. 12 at Yankee Stadium)

Dodgers	212	000	001	—	6	9	0
Yankees	000	100	000	—	1	5	0

Dodgers: BURT HOOTON and Steve Yeager.
Yankees: CATFISH HUNTER, Dick Tidrow (3d), Ken Clay (6th), Sparky Lyle (9th) and Thurman Munson.
Home Runs: Ron Cey (Dodgers), Steve Yeager (Dodgers), Reggie Smith (Dodgers) and Steve Garvey (Dodgers).
Attendance: 56,691.

Game 3 (Oct. 14 at Los Angeles)

Yankees	300	110	000	—	5	10	0
Dodgers	003	000	000	—	3	7	1

Yankees: MIKE TORREZ and Thurman Munson.
Dodgers: TOMMY JOHN, Charlie Hough (7th) and Steve Yeager.
Home Run: Dusty Baker (Dodgers).
Attendance: 55,992.

Game 4 (Oct. 15 at Los Angeles)

Yankees	030	001	000	—	4	7	0
Dodgers	002	000	000	—	2	4	0

Yankees: RON GUIDRY and Thurman Munson.
Dodgers: DOUG RAU, Rick Rhoden (2d), Mike Garman (9th) and Steve Yeager.
Home Runs: Dave Lopes (Dodgers) and Reggie Jackson (Yankees).
Attendance: 55,995.

Game 5 (Oct. 16 at Los Angeles)

Yankees	000	000	220	—	4	9	2
Dodgers	100	432	00X	—	10	13	0

Yankees: DON GULLETT, Ken Clay (5th), Dick Tidrow (6th), Catfish Hunter (7th) and Thurman Munson, Cliff Johnson (8th).
Dodgers: DON SUTTON and Steve Yeager, Johnny Oates (7th).
Home Runs: Steve Yeager (Dodgers), Reggie Smith (Dodgers), Thurman Munson (Yankees) and Reggie Jackson (Yankees).
Attendance: 55,955.

Game 6 (Oct. 18 at Yankee Stadium)

Dodgers	201	000	001	—	4	9	0
Yankees	020	320	01X	—	8	8	1

Dodgers: BURT HOOTON, Elias Sosa (4th), Doug Rau (5th), Charlie Hough (7th) and Steve Yeager.
Yankees: MIKE TORREZ and Thurman Munson.
Home Runs: Reggie Jackson (Yankees) 3, Chris Chambliss (Yankees) and Reggie Smith (Dodgers).
Attendance: 56,407.

1978 World Champions

Manager: Bob Lemon
World Series Roster: Pitchers: Jim Beattie, Ken Clay, Ed Figueroa, Rich Gossage, Ron Guidry, Catfish Hunter, Paul Lindblad, Sparky Lyle, Dick Tidrow. *Catchers:* Mike Heath, Cliff Johnson, Thurman Munson. *Infielders:* Chris Chambliss, Bucky Dent, Brian Doyle, Graig Nettles, Jim Spencer, Fred Stanley. *Outfielders:* Paul Blair, Reggie Jackson, Jay Johnstone, Lou Piniella, Mickey Rivers, Gary Thomasson, Roy White.

°*Lemon was named manager on July 25, succeeding Billy Martin, who resigned the previous day.*

American League East Playoff

(One game to break deadlock after New York and Boston finished schedule tied for first place with matching 99–63 records.)

(Oct. 2 at Boston)

Yankees	000	000	410	—	5	8	0
Red Sox	010	001	020	—	4	11	0

Yankees: RON GUIDRY, Rich Gossage (7th) and Thurman Munson.
Red Sox: MIKE TORREZ, Bob Stanley (7th), Andy Hassler (8th), Dick Drago (9th) and Carlton Fisk.
Home Runs: Carl Yastrzemski (Red Sox), Bucky Dent (Yankees) and Reggie Jackson (Yankees).
Attendance: 32,925.

A.L. Championship Series

	W	L	Pct.
Yankees	3	1	.750
Royals	1	3	.250

Game 1 (Oct. 3 at Kansas City)

Yankees	011	020	030	—	7	16	0
Royals	000	001	000	—	1	2	2

Yankees: JIM BEATTIE, Ken Clay (6th) and Thurman Munson.
Royals: DENNIS LEONARD, Steve Mingori (5th), Al Hrabosky (8th), Doug Bird (9th) and Darrell Porter.
Home Run: Reggie Jackson (Yankees).
Attendance: 41,143.

Game 2 (Oct. 4 at Kansas City)

Yankees	000	000	220	—	4	12	1
Royals	140	000	32X	—	10	16	1

Yankees: ED FIGUEROA, Dick Tidrow (2d), Sparky Lyle (7th) and Thurman Munson.
Royals: LARRY GURA, Marty Pattin (7th), Al Hrabosky (8th) and Darrell Porter.
Home Run: Freddie Patek (Royals).
Attendance: 41,158.

Game 3 (Oct. 6 at Yankee Stadium)

Royals	101	010	020	—	5	10	1
Yankees	010	201	02X	—	6	10	0

Royals: Paul Splittorff, DOUG BIRD (8th), Al Hrabosky (8th) and Darrell Porter.
Yankees: Catfish Hunter, RICH GOSSAGE (7th) and Thurman Munson.
Home Runs: George Brett (Royals) 3, Reggie Jackson (Yankees) and Thurman Munson (Yankees).
Attendance: 55,535.

Game 4 (Oct. 7 at Yankee Stadium)

Royals	100	000	000	—	1	7	0
Yankees	010	001	00X	—	2	4	0

Royals: DENNIS LEONARD and Darrell Porter.
Yankees: RON GUIDRY, Rich Gossage (9th) and Thurman Munson.
Home Runs: Graig Nettles (Yankees) and Roy White (Yankees).
Attendance: 56,356.

World Series

	W	L	Pct.
Yankees	4	2	.667
Dodgers	2	4	.333

Game 1 (Oct. 10 at Los Angeles)

Yankees	000	000	320	—	5	9	1
Dodgers	030	310	31X	—	11	15	2

Yankees: ED FIGUEROA, Ken Clay (2d), Paul Lindblad (5th), Dick Tidrow (7th) and Thurman Munson.
Dodgers: TOMMY JOHN, Terry Forster (8th) and Steve Yeager.
Home Runs: Dave Lopes (Dodgers) 2, Dusty Baker (Dodgers) and Reggie Jackson (Yankees).
Attendance: 55,997.

Game 2 (Oct. 11 at Los Angeles)

Yankees	002	000	100	—	3	11	0
Dodgers	000	103	00X	—	4	7	0

Yankees: CATFISH HUNTER, Rich Gossage (7th) and Thurman Munson.
Dodgers: BURT HOOTON, Terry Forster (7th), Bob Welch (9th) and Steve Yeager.
Home Run: Ron Cey (Dodgers).
Attendance: 55,982.

Game 3 (Oct. 13 at Yankee Stadium)

Dodgers	001	000	000	—	1	8	0
Yankees	110	000	30X	—	5	10	1

Dodgers: DON SUTTON, Lance Rautzhan (7th), Charlie Hough (8th) and Steve Yeager, Jerry Grote (6th), Joe Ferguson (8th).
Yankees: RON GUIDRY and Thurman Munson.
Home Run: Roy White (Yankees).
Attendance: 56,447.

Game 4 (Oct. 14 at Yankee Stadium)

Dodgers	000	030	000	0	—	3	6	1
Yankees	000	002	010	1	—	4	9	0

Dodgers: Tommy John, Terry Forster (8th), BOB WELCH (8th) and Steve Yeager, Jerry Grote (9th).
Yankees: Ed Figueroa, Dick Tidrow (6th), RICH GOSSAGE (9th) and Thurman Munson.
Home Run: Reggie Smith (Dodgers).
Attendance: 56,445.

Game 5 (Oct. 15 at Yankee Stadium)

Dodgers	101	000	000	—	2	9	3
Yankees	004	300	41X	—	12	18	0

Dodgers: BURT HOOTON, Lance Rautzhan (3d), Charlie Hough (4th) and Steve Yeager, Johnny Oates (7th).
Yankees: JIM BEATTIE and Thurman Munson, Mike Heath (9th).
Home Runs: None.
Attendance: 56,448.

Game 6 (Oct. 17 at Los Angeles)

Yankees	030	002	200	—	7	11	0
Dodgers	101	000	000	—	2	7	1

Yankees: CATFISH HUNTER, Rich Gossage (8th) and Thurman Munson.
Dodgers: DON SUTTON, Bob Welch (6th), Doug Rau (8th) and Joe Ferguson.
Home Runs: Dave Lopes (Dodgers) and Reggie Jackson (Yankees).
Attendance: 55,985.

1980 American League East Champions

Manager: Dick Howser
Regular-Season Roster (Minimum 10 games): Pitchers: Doug Bird, Ron Davis, Ed Figueroa, Rich Gossage, Mike Griffin, Ron Guidry, Tommy John, Tim Lollar, Rudy May, Gaylord Perry, Luis Tiant, Tom Underwood. *Catchers:* Rick Cerone, Johnny Oates, Dennis Werth. *Infielders:* Bucky Dent, Brian Doyle, Graig Nettles, Willie Randolph, Aurelio Rodriguez, Eric Soderholm, Jim Spencer, Fred Stanley, Bob Watson. *Outfielders:* Paul Blair, Bobby Brown, Oscar Gamble, Reggie Jackson, Ruppert Jones, Joe Lefebvre, Bobby Muncer, Lou Piniella.

A.L. Championship Series

	W	L	Pct.
Royals	3	0	1.000
Yankees	0	3	.000

Game 1 (Oct. 8 at Kansas City)

Yankees	020	000	000	—	2	10	1
Royals	022	000	12X	—	7	10	0

Yankees: RON GUIDRY, Ron Davis (4th), Tom Underwood (8th) and Rick Cerone.
Royals: LARRY GURA and Darrell Porter.
Home Runs: Rick Cerone (Yankees), Lou Piniella (Yankees) and George Brett (Royals).
Attendance: 42,598.

Game 2 (Oct. 9 at Kansas City)

Yankees	000	020	000	—	2	8	0
Royals	003	000	00X	—	3	6	0

Yankees: RUDY MAY and Rick Cerone.
Royals: DENNIS LEONARD, Dan Quisenberry (9th) and Darrell Porter.
Home Run: Graig Nettles (Yankees).
Attendance: 42,633.

Game 3 (Oct. 10 at Yankee Stadium)

Royals	000	010	300	—	4	12	1
Yankees	000	002	000	—	2	8	0

Royals: Paul Splittorff, DAN QUISENBERRY (6th) and Darrell Porter.
Yankees: Tommy John, RICH GOSSAGE (7th), Tom Underwood (8th) and Rick Cerone.
Home Runs: Frank White (Royals) and George Brett (Royals).
Attendance: 56,588.

1981 American League Champions

**Manager:* Bob Lemon
World Series Roster: Pitchers: Ron Davis, George Frazier, Rich Gossage, Ron Guidry, Tommy John, Dave LaRoche, Rudy May, Rick Reuschel, Dave Righetti. *Catchers:* Rick Cerone, Barry Foote. *Infielders:* Bucky Dent,** Larry Milbourne, Graig Nettles, Willie Randolph, Dave Revering, Andre Robertson, Aurelio Rodriguez, Bob Watson. *Outfielders:* Bobby Brown, Oscar Gamble, Reggie Jackson, Jerry Mumphrey, Bobby Murcer, Lou Piniella, Dave Winfield.

**Lemon was named manager on September 6, replacing Gene Michael.
**Dent on the disabled list.*

A.L. East Playoffs

(Best-of-five series between the division's first- and second-half winners. New York (34–22) won the first half, Milwaukee (31–22) the second half of the schedule interrupted nearly two months at midseason by a players' strike.)

	W	L	Pct.
Yankees	3	2	.600
Brewers	2	3	.400

Game 1 (Oct. 7 at Milwaukee)

Yankees	000	400	001	—	5	13	1
Brewers	011	010	000	—	3	8	3

Yankees: Ron Guidry, RON DAVIS (5th), Rich Gossage (8th) and Rick Cerone.
Brewers: MOOSE HAAS, Dwight Bernard (4th), Bob McClure (5th), Jim Slaton (6th), Rollie Fingers (8th) and Ted Simmons.
Home Run: Oscar Gamble (Yankees).
Attendance: 35,064.

Game 2 (Oct. 8 at Milwaukee)

Yankees	000	100	002	—	3	7	0
Brewers	000	000	000	—	0	7	0

Yankees: DAVE RIGHETTI, Ron Davis (7th), Rich Gossage (7th) and Rick Cerone.
Brewers: MIKE CALDWELL, Jim Slaton (9th) and Ted Simmons.
Home Runs: Lou Piniella (Yankees) and Reggie Jackson (Yankees).
Attendance: 26,395.

Game 3 (Oct. 9 at Yankee Stadium)

Brewers	000	000	320	—	5	9	0
Yankees	000	100	200	—	3	8	2

Brewers: Randy Lerch, ROLLIE FINGERS (7th) and Ted Simmons.
Yankees: TOMMY JOHN, Rudy May (8th) and Rick Cerone.
Home Runs: Ted Simmons (Brewers) and Paul Molitor (Brewers).
Attendance: 56,411.

Game 4 (Oct. 10 at Yankee Stadium)

Brewers	000	200	000	—	2	4	2
Yankees	000	001	000	—	1	5	0

Brewers: PETE VUCKOVICH, Jamie Easterly (6th), Jim Slaton (7th), Bob McClure (8th), Rollie Fingers (9th) and Ted Simmons.
Yankees: RICK REUSCHEL, Ron Davis (7th) and Rick Cerone.
Home Runs: None.
Attendance: 52,077.

Game 5 (Oct. 11 at Yankee Stadium)

Brewers	011	000	100	—	3	8	0
Yankees	000	400	12X	—	7	13	0

Brewers: MOOSE HAAS, Mike Caldwell (4th), Dwight Bernard (4th), Bob McClure (6th), Jim Slaton (7th), Jamie Easterly (8th), Pete Vuckovich (8th) and Ted Simmons.
Yankees: Ron Guidry, DAVE RIGHETTI (5th), Rich Gossage (8th) and Rick Cerone.
Home Runs: Gorman Thomas (Brewers), Reggie Jackson (Yankees), Oscar Gamble (Yankees) and Rick Cerone (Yankees).
Attendance: 47,105.

A.L. Championship Series

	W	L	Pct.
Yankees	3	0	1.000
A's	0	3	.000

Game 1 (Oct. 13 at Yankee Stadium)

A's	000	010	000	—	1	6	1
Yankees	300	000	00X	—	3	7	1

A's: MIKE NORRIS, Tom Underwood (8th) and Jeff Newman.
Yankees: TOMMY JOHN, Ron Davis (7th), Rich Gossage (8th) and Rick Cerone.
Home Runs: None.
Attendance: 55,740.

Game 2 (Oct. 14 at Yankee Stadium)

A's	001	200	000	—	3	11	1
Yankees	100	701	40X	—	13	19	0

A's: STEVE McCATTY, Dave Beard (4th), Jeff Jones (5th), Brian Kingman (7th), Bob Owchinko (7th) and Mike Heath.
Yankees: Rudy May, GEORGE FRAZIER (4th) and Rick Cerone.
Home Runs: Lou Piniella (Yankees) and Graig Nettles (Yankees).
Attendance: 48,497.

Game 3 (Oct. 15 at Oakland)

Yankees	000	001	003	—	4	10	0
A's	000	000	000	—	0	5	0

Yankees: DAVE RIGHETTI, Ron Davis (7th), Rich Gossage (9th) and Rick Cerone.
A's: MATT KEOUGH, Tom Underwood (9th) and Jeff Newman.
Home Run: Willie Randolph (Yankees).
Attendance: 47,302.

World Series

	W	L	Pct.
Dodgers	4	2	.667
Yankees	2	4	.333

Game 1 (Oct. 20 at Yankee Stadium)

Dodgers	000	010	020	—	3	5	0
Yankees	301	100	00X	—	5	6	0

Dodgers: JERRY REUSS, Bob Castillo (3d), Dave Goltz (4th), Tom Niedenfuer (5th), Dave Stewart (8th) and Steve Yeager.
Yankees: RON GUIDRY, Ron Davis (8th), Rich Gossage (8th) and Rick Cerone.
Home Runs: Bob Watson (Yankees) and Steve Yeager (Dodgers).
Attendance: 56,470.

Game 2 (Oct. 21 at Yankee Stadium)

Dodgers	000	000	000	—	0	4	2
Yankees	000	010	02X	—	3	6	1

Dodgers: BURT HOOTON, Terry Forster (7th), Steve Howe (8th), Dave Stewart (8th) and Steve Yeager, Mike Scioscia (8th).
Yankees: TOMMY JOHN, Rich Gossage (8th) and Rick Cerone.
Home Runs: None.
Attendance: 56,505.

Game 3 (Oct. 23 at Los Angeles)

Yankees	022	000	000	—	4	9	0
Dodgers	300	020	00X	—	5	11	1

Yankees: Dave Righetti, GEORGE FRAZIER (3d), Rudy May (5th), Ron Davis (8th) and Rick Cerone.
Dodgers: FERNANDO VALENZUELA and Steve Yeager, Mike Scioscia (3d).
Home Runs: Ron Cey (Dodgers), Bob Watson (Yankees) and Rick Cerone (Yankees).
Attendance: 56,236.

Game 4 (Oct. 24 at Los Angeles)

Yankees	211	002	010	—	7	13	1
Dodgers	002	013	20X	—	8	14	2

Yankees: Rick Reuschel, Rudy May (4th), Ron Davis (5th), GEORGE FRAZIER (6th), Tommy John (7th) and Rick Cerone.
Dodgers: Bob Welch, Dave Goltz (1st), Terry Forster (4th), Tom Niedenfuer (5th), STEVE HOWE (7th) and Mike Scioscia, Steve Yeager (7th).
Home Runs: Willie Randolph (Yankees), Jay Johnstone (Dodgers) and Reggie Jackson (Yankees).
Attendance: 56,242.

Game 5 (Oct. 25 at Los Angeles)

Yankees	010	000	000	—	1	5	0
Dodgers	000	000	20X	—	2	4	3

Yankees: RON GUIDRY, Rich Gossage (8th) and Rick Cerone.
Dodgers: JERRY REUSS and Steve Yeager.
Home Runs: Pedro Guerrero (Dodgers) and Steve Yeager (Dodgers).
Attendance: 56,115.

Game 6 (Oct. 28 at Yankee Stadium)

Dodgers	000	134	010	—	9	13	1
Yankees	001	001	000	—	2	7	2

Dodgers: BURT HOOTON, Steve Howe (6th) and Steve Yeager.
Yankees: Tommy John, GEORGE FRAZIER (5th), Ron Davis (6th), Rick Reuschel (6th), Rudy May (7th), Dave LaRoche (9th) and Rick Cerone.
Home Runs: Willie Randolph (Yankees) and Pedro Guerrero (Dodgers).
Attendance: 56,513.

Bobby Murcer scores.

YANKEES' WORLD SERIES SHARES

1921	$3,510.00 (L)	8	New York Giants
1922	$2,842.86 (L)	5*	New York Giants
1923	$6,143.49 (W)	6	New York Giants
1926	$3,417.75 (L)	7	St. Louis Cardinals
1927	$5,782.24 (W)	4	Pittsburgh Pirates
1928	$5,813.20 (W)	4	St. Louis Cardinals
1932	$5,231.77 (W)	4	Chicago Cubs
1936	$6,430.55 (W)	6	New York Giants
1937	$6,471.11 (W)	5	New York Giants
1938	$5,728.76 (W)	4	Chicago Cubs
1939	$5,541.89 (W)	4	Cincinnati Reds
1941	$5,943.31 (W)	5	Brooklyn Dodgers
1942	$3,351.77 (L)	5	St. Louis Cardinals
1943	$6,139.46 (W)	5	St. Louis Cardinals
1947	$5,830.03 (W)	7	Brooklyn Dodgers
1949	$5,626.74 (W)	5	Brooklyn Dodgers
1950	$5,737.95 (W)	4	Philadelphia Phillies
1951	$6,446.09 (W)	6	New York Giants
1952	$5,982.65 (W)	7	Brooklyn Dodgers
1953	$8,280.68 (W)	6	Brooklyn Dodgers
1955	$5,598.58 (L)	7	Brooklyn Dodgers
1956	$8,714.76 (W)	7	Brooklyn Dodgers
1957	$5,606.06 (L)	7	Milwaukee Braves
1958	$8,759.10 (W)	7	Milwaukee Braves
1960	$5,214.64 (L)	7	Pittsburgh Pirates
1961	$7,389.13 (W)	5	Cincinnati Reds
1962	$9,882.74 (W)	7	San Francisco Giants
1963	$7,874.32 (L)	4	Los Angeles Dodgers
1964	$5,309.29 (L)	7	St. Louis Cardinals
1976	†$19,935.48 (L)	4	Cincinnati Reds
1977	†$27,758.04 (W)	6	Los Angeles Dodgers
1978	†$31,236.99 (W)	6	Los Angeles Dodgers
1981	‡$39,609.20 (L)	6	Los Angeles Dodgers

*Five games in 1922 World Series included one tie.
† Total combined share for both league championship series and World Series.
‡ Total combined share for division playoffs, league championship series, and World Series.

MAJOR LEAGUE AND AMERICAN LEAGUE RECORDS AND HONORS BY YANKEES

TRIPLE CROWN WINNERS

Year	Player	Pos.	Ave.	HR	RBI
1934	Lou Gehrig	1B	.363	49	165
1956	Mickey Mantle	CF	.353	52	130
1962	Mickey Mantle	CF	.321	30	89
1963	Elston Howard	C	.287	28	85
1976	Thurman Munson	C	.302	17	105

Note: There have been only nine Triple Crown winners in major league history.

AMERICAN LEAGUE MOST VALUABLE PLAYER (Originated in 1922)

Year	Player	Pos.	Ave.	HR	RBI
1923	Babe Ruth	RF	.393	41	130
1927	Lou Gehrig	1B	.373	47	175
1936	Lou Gehrig	1B	.354	49	152
1939	Joe DiMaggio	CF	.381	30	126
1941	Joe DiMaggio	CF	.357	30	125
1942	Joe Gordon	2B	.322	18	103
1943	Spud Chandler	P	20–4	1.64 ERA	
1947	Joe DiMaggio	CF	.315	20	97
1950	Phil Rizzuto	SS	.324	7	66
1951	Yogi Berra	C	.294	27	88
1954	Yogi Berra	C	.307	22	125
1955	Yogi Berra	C	.272	27	108
1956	Mickey Mantle	CF	.353	52	130
1957	Mickey Mantle	CF	.365	34	94
1960	Roger Maris	RF	.283	39	112
1961	Roger Maris	RF	.269	61	142

AMERICAN LEAGUE CY YOUNG AWARD (Originated in 1956)

Year	Player	W-L	Saves	Pct.	ERA	LP	SO	BB
1958	*Bob Turley	21–7	1	.750	2.97	245⅓	168	128
1961	*Whitey Ford	25–4	0	.862	3.21	283	209	92
1977	Sparky Lyle	13–5	26	.722	2.17	137	68	33
1978	Ron Guidry	25–3	0	.893	1.74	274	248	72

*Combined choice for both major leagues. Only one Cy Young Award was voted through 1966. Beginning in 1967, two awards were made, one for each league.

AMERICAN LEAGUE ROOKIE OF THE YEAR (Originated in 1947)

Year	Player	Pos.	Ave.	HR	RBI
1951	Gil McDougald	3B–2B	.306	14	63
1954	Bob Grim	P	20–6	3.26 ERA	
1957	Tony Kubek	IF–OF	.297	3	39
1962	Tom Tresh	SS–OF	.286	20	93
1968	Stan Bahnsen	P	17–12	2.05 ERA	
1970	Thurman Munson	C	.302	6	53
1981	Dave Righetti	P	8–4	2.05 ERA	

BABE RUTH AWARD (World Series MVP) (Originated in 1949)

Year	Player	Pos.
1949	Joe Page	P
1950	Jerry Coleman	2B
1951	Phil Rizzuto	SS
1952	Johnny Mize	PH–1B
1953	Billy Martin	2B
1956	Don Larsen	P
1958	Elston Howard	LF–PH
1961	Whitey Ford	P
1962	Ralph Terry	P
1977	Reggie Jackson	RF
1978	Bucky Dent	SS

DAWSON AWARD (Outstanding Yankee rookie in spring training)

Year	Player	Pos.
1956	Norm Siebern	OF
1957	Tony Kubek	SS
1958	Johnny Blanchard	C
1959	Gordie Windhorn	OF
1960	Johnny James	P
1961	Rollie Sheldon	P
1962	Tom Tresh	SS
1963	Pedro Gonzalez	2B
1964	Pete Mikkelsen	P
1965	Art Lopez	OF
1966	Roy White	OF
1967	Bill Robinson	OF
1968	Mike Ferraro	3B
1969	Jerry Kenney	OF
	Bill Burbach	P
1970	John Ellis	C–1B
1971	(none selected)	
1972	Rusty Torres	OF
1973	Otto Velez	OF
1974	Tom Buskey	P
1975	Tippy Martinez	P
1976	Willie Randolph	2B
1977	George Zeber	IF
1978	Jim Beattie	P
1979	Paul Mirabella	P
1980	Mike Griffin	P
1981	Gene Nelson	P

AMERICAN LEAGUE MOST VALUABLE PLAYER (1929–45)

1931	Lou Gehrig	1941	Joe DiMaggio
1934	Lou Gehrig	1942	Joe Gordon
1936	Lou Gehrig	1943	Spud Chandler
1939	Joe DiMaggio		

AMERICAN LEAGUE PLAYER OF THE YEAR (Originated in 1948)

1950	Phil Rizzuto	1961	Roger Maris
1956	Mickey Mantle	1962	Mickey Mantle
1960	Roger Maris	1976	Thurman Munson

AMERICAN LEAGUE PITCHER OF THE YEAR (Originated in 1948)

1955	Whitey Ford	1963	Whitey Ford
1958	Bob Turley	1978	Ron Guidry
1961	Whitey Ford		

AMERICAN LEAGUE FIREMAN OF THE YEAR (Originated in 1960)

1961	Luis Arroyo	1978	Rich Gossage
1972	Sparky Lyle		

AMERICAN LEAGUE ROOKIE OF THE YEAR (Originated in 1946)

1950	Whitey Ford*	1962	Tom Tresh
1954	Bob Grim	1968	Stan Bahnsen
1957	Tony Kubek	1981	Dave Righetti**
1958	Ryne Duren		

*Ford was a combined choice for both major leagues.
**Righetti was named Rookie Pitcher of the Year.
Note: Two rookies—one pitcher, one non-pitcher—have been chosen most years since 1958.

SPORTING NEWS AWARDS

MAJOR LEAGUE EXECUTIVE OF THE YEAR (Originated in 1936)

1937	Ed Barrow	1952	George Weiss
1941	Ed Barrow	1960	George Weiss
1950	George Weiss	1961	Dan Topping
1951	George Weiss	1974	Gabe Paul

MAJOR LEAGUE MANAGER OF THE YEAR (Originated in 1936)

1936	Joe McCarthy	1953	Casey Stengel
1938	Joe McCarthy	1958	Casey Stengel
1943	Joe McCarthy	1961	Ralph Houk
1947	Bucky Harris	1974	Bill Virdon
1949	Casey Stengel		

MAJOR LEAGUE PLAYER OF THE YEAR (Originated in 1936)

1939	Joe DiMaggio	1958	Bob Turley
1943	Spud Chandler	1961	Roger Maris
1950	Phil Rizzuto	1978	Ron Guidry
1956	Mickey Mantle		

ALL-STAR SELECTIONS (Originated in 1926)

Year	Player	Position	Year	Player	Position
1926	Herb Pennock	P	1938	Bill Dickey	C
	Babe Ruth	OF		Joe DiMaggio	OF
1927	Lou Gehrig	1B		Lefty Gomez	P
	Babe Ruth	OF		Red Rolfe	3B
1928	Lou Gehrig	1B		Red Ruffing	P
	Waite Hoyt	P	1939	Bill Dickey	C
	Babe Ruth	OF		Joe DiMaggio	OF
1929	Babe Ruth	OF		Joe Gordon	2B
1930	Babe Ruth	OF		Red Rolfe	3B
1931	Lou Gehrig	1B		Red Ruffing	P
	Babe Ruth	OF	1940	Joe DiMaggio	OF
1932	Bill Dickey	C		Joe Gordon	2B
	Tony Lazzeri	2B	1941	Bill Dickey	C
1933	Bill Dickey	C		Joe DiMaggio	OF
1934	Lou Gehrig	1B		Joe Gordon	2B
	Lefty Gomez	P	1942	Ernie Bonham	P
1936	Bill Dickey	C		Joe DiMaggio	OF
	Lou Gehrig	1B		Joe Gordon	2B
1937	Joe DiMaggio	OF	1943	Spud Chandler	P
	Lou Gehrig	1B		Billy Johnson	3B
	Red Rolfe	3B	1945	Snuffy Stirnweiss	2B
	Red Ruffing	P	1946	Aaron Robinson	C
			1947	Joe DiMaggio	OF
			1948	Joe DiMaggio	OF

Year	Player	Position	Year	Player	Position
1949	Tommy Henrich	OF–1B	1963	Whitey Ford	P
	Joe Page	P		Elston Howard	C
	Phil Rizzuto	SS		Joe Pepitone	1B
1950	Yogi Berra	C		Bobby Richardson	2B
	Vic Raschi	P	1964	Elston Howard	C
	Phil Rizzuto	SS		Mickey Mantle	OF
1951	Allie Reynolds	P		Bobby Richardson	2B
	Phil Rizzuto	SS	1965	Bobby Richardson	2B
1952	Yogi Berra	C		Mel Stottlemyre	P
	Mickey Mantle	OF	1966	Bobby Richardson	2B
	Allie Reynolds	P	1971	Bobby Murcer	OF
	Phil Rizzuto	SS	1972	Bobby Murcer	OF
1954	Yogi Berra	C	1973	Thurman Munson	C
1955	Whitey Ford	P		Bobby Murcer	OF
1956	Yogi Berra	C	1974	Thurman Munson	C
	Whitey Ford	P	1975	Thurman Munson	C
	Mickey Mantle	OF		Graig Nettles	3B
1957	Yogi Berra	C	1976	Chris Chambliss	1B
	Mickey Mantle	OF		Thurman Munson	C
	Gil McDougald	SS		Mickey Rivers	OF
1958	Bob Turley	P	1977	Graig Nettles	3B
1960	Roger Maris	OF		Willie Randolph	2B
	Bill Skowron	1B	1978	Ron Guidry	P
1961	Whitey Ford	P		Graig Nettles	3B
	Elston Howard	C	1980	Rick Cerone	C
	Tony Kubek	SS		Reggie Jackson	OF–DH
	Mickey Mantle	OF		Tommy John	P
	Roger Maris	OF		Willie Randolph	2B
	Bobby Richardson	2B	1981	Ron Guidry	P
1962	Mickey Mantle	OF			
	Bobby Richardson	2B			
	Ralph Terry	P			
	Tom Tresh	SS			

Note: The Sporting News' *All-Star selections are made at season's end.*

HALL OF FAMERS

Hall of Famer/Yankee Years/Capacity	Elected
Babe Ruth (1920–34 player)	1936
Lou Gehrig (1923–39 player)	1939
Willie Keeler (1903–09 player)	1939
Clark Griffith (1903–07 player–manager)	1945
Frank Chance (1913–14 player–manager)	1946
Jack Chesbro (1903–09 player)	1946
Herb Pennock (1923–33 player)	1948
Ed Barrow (1920–45 executive)	1953
Bill Dickey (*1928–43 player, 1946 player, manager)	1954
Frank Baker (1916–19, 1921–22 player)	1955
Joe DiMaggio (*1936–42, 1946–51 player)	1955
Joe McCarthy (1931–46 manager)	1957
Bill McKechnie (1913 player)	1962
Miller Huggins (1918–29 manager)	1964
Casey Stengel (1949–60 manager)	1966
Branch Rickey (1907 player)	1967
Red Ruffing (*1930–42, 1945–46 player)	1967
Waite Hoyt (1921–30 player)	1969
Earle Combs (1924–35 player)	1970
George Weiss (1932–60 executive)	1970
Yogi Berra (1946–63 player, 1964 manager)	1971
Lefty Gomez (1930–42 player)	1972
Whitey Ford (*1950, 1953–67 player)	1974
Mickey Mantle (1951–68 player)	1974
Bucky Harris (1947–48 manager)	1975
Bob Lemon (1978–79, 1981 manager)	1976
Joe Sewell (1931–33 player)	1977
Larry MacPhail (1945–47 executive)	1978
Johnny Mize (1949–53 player)	1981

*Yankee career interrupted by military service.

NOTES:

A number of Hall of Famers listed here also served as Yankee coaches. However, time served in that capacity is not included under "Yankee Years" column.

Three other Hall of Famers wore Yankee uniforms briefly, a dozen or fewer games. Dazzy Vance pitched in eight games (0–3) for the Yankees in 1915 and in two games (0–0) in 1918 before resurfacing in the majors four years later with the Brooklyn Dodgers and blossoming as a star pitcher at age thirty-one. And Stan Coveleski, Burleigh Grimes and Paul Waner concluded their careers in pinstripes. Coveleski had a 5–1 record while pitching in 12 games for the 1928 Yankees; Grimes was 1–2 in 10 games in 1934; and Waner batted .143 in nine games in 1944 and was walked as a pinch hitter in his only 1945 appearance before retiring.

Longtime Yankee broadcasters Mel Allen (1939–64) and Red Barber (1954–66) also have special niches at Cooperstown.

RETIRED NUMBERS

No.	Player	Year
3	Babe Ruth	1948
4	Lou Gehrig	1939
5	Joe DiMaggio	1952
7	Mickey Mantle	1969
8	Yogi Berra & Bill Dickey	1972
15	Thurman Munson	1979
16	Whitey Ford	1974
37	Casey Stengel	1970

DiMaggio, Mantle and Berra wore different numbers as rookies— DiMaggio 9, Mantle 6 and Berra 35.

After Babe Ruth, No. 3 was worn by George Selkirk, Allie Clark, Joe Medwick (during spring training), Bud Metheny and Cliff Mapes until the number was retired in1948, shortly before Ruth's death.

Mapes had the distinction of wearing two now-retired numbers during his less than four full seasons as a Yankee.

Labeled the "next Babe Ruth," the big outfielder was presented Ruth's No. 3 as a rookie in 1948—only to have it taken away and retired during that season. Mapes then wore No. 7 until July 31, 1951, when he was traded to the St. Louis Browns. Mantle, meanwhile, wore No. 6 for a few months that 1951 season before being sent back to the minors. When he was recalled after 40 games at Triple-A Kansas City, Mapes was gone and Mantle was issued No. 7—the last Yankee ever to wear that number.

ALL-STAR GAME SELECTIONS (All-Star Game Originated in 1933)

YANKEE ALL-STARS

1933 (6)—Ben Chapman, outfield; *Bill Dickey, catcher; Lou Gehrig, first base; Lefty Gomez, pitcher; *Tony Lazzeri, second base; Babe Ruth, outfield.

1934 (6)—Ben Chapman, outfield; Bill Dickey, catcher; Lou Gehrig, first base; Lefty Gomez, pitcher; Red Ruffing, pitcher; Babe Ruth, outfield.

1935 (3)—Ben Chapman, outfield; Lou Gehrig, first base; Lefty Gomez, pitcher.

1936 (7)—Frank Crosetti, shortstop; Bill Dickey, catcher; Joe DiMaggio, outfield; Lou Gehrig, first base; *Lefty Gomez, pitcher; *Monte Pearson, pitcher; George Selkirk, outfield.

1937 (6)—Bill Dickey, catcher; Joe DiMaggio, outfield; Lou Gehrig, first base; Lefty Gomez, pitcher; *Johnny Murphy, pitcher; Red Rolfe, third base.

1938 (6)—Bill Dickey, catcher; Joe DiMaggio, outfield; Lou Gehrig, first base; Lefty Gomez, pitcher; *Red Rolfe, third base; *Red Ruffing, pitcher.

1939 (9)—*Frank Crosetti, shortstop; *Bill Dickey, catcher; Joe DiMaggio, outfield; *Lefty Gomez, pitcher; Joe Gordon, second base; *Johnny Murphy, pitcher; Red Rolfe, third base; Red Ruffing, pitcher; George Selkirk, outfield.

1940 (7)—Bill Dickey, catcher; Joe DiMaggio, outfield; Joe Gordon, second base; Charlie Keller, outfield; *Monte Pearson, pitcher; *Red Rolfe, third base; Red Ruffing, pitcher.

1941 (6)—Bill Dickey, catcher; Joe DiMaggio, outfield; Joe Gordon, second base; Charlie Keller, outfield; *Red Ruffing, pitcher; *Marius Russo, pitcher.

1942 (9)—*Ernie Bonham, pitcher; Spud Chandler, pitcher; *Bill Dickey, catcher; Joe DiMaggio, outfield; Joe Gordon, second base; Tommy Henrich, outfield; *Phil Rizzuto, shortstop; *Buddy Rosar, catcher; *Red Ruffing, pitcher.

†1943 (6)—*Ernie Bonham, pitcher; *Spud Chandler, pitcher; *Bill Dickey, catcher; *Joe Gordon, second base; *Charlie Keller, outfield; *Johnny Lindell, outfield.

1944 (3)—Hank Borowy, pitcher; Rollie Hemsley, catcher; *Joe Page, pitcher.

1945—No game.

1946 (6)—*Spud Chandler, pitcher; Bill Dickey, catcher; *Joe DiMaggio, outfield; Joe Gordon, second base; Charlie Keller, outfield; Snuffy Stirnweiss, third base.

1947 (9)—*Spud Chandler, pitcher; Joe DiMaggio, outfield; Tommy Heinrich, outfield; Billy Johnson, third base; *Charlie Keller, outfield; George McQuinn, first base; Joe Page, pitcher; *Aaron Robinson, catcher; Spec Shea, pitcher.

1948 (6)—*Yogi Berra, catcher; Joe DiMaggio, outfield; Tommy Henrich, outfield; George McQuinn, first base; *Joe Page, pitcher; Vic Raschi, pitcher.

1949 (5)—Yogi Berra, catcher; Joe DiMaggio, outfield; *Tommy Henrich, outfield; Vic Raschi, pitcher; *Allie Reynolds, pitcher.

1950 (8)—Yogi Berra, catcher; *Tommy Byrne, pitcher; Jerry Coleman, second base; Joe DiMaggio, outfield; Tommy Henrich, first base; Vic Raschi, pitcher; Allie Reynolds, pitcher; Phil Rizzuto, shortstop.

1951 (4)—Yogi Berra, catcher; *Joe DiMaggio, outfield; Ed Lopat, pitcher; Phil Rizzuto, shortstop.

1952 (7)—Hank Bauer, outfield; Yogi Berra, catcher; *Mickey Mantle, outfield; Vic Raschi, pitcher; *Allie Reynolds, pitcher; Phil Rizzuto, shortstop; Gil McDougald, second base.

1953 (7)—Hank Bauer, outfield; Yogi Berra, catcher; Mickey Mantle, outfield; Johnny Mize, first base; Allie Reynolds, pitcher; Phil Rizzuto, shortstop; *Johnny Sain, pitcher.

1954 (6)—Hank Bauer, outfield; Yogi Berra, catcher; Whitey Ford, pitcher; Mickey Mantle, outfield; Irv Noren, outfield; *Allie Reynolds, pitcher.

1955 (4)—Yogi Berra, catcher; Whitey Ford, pitcher; Mickey Mantle, outfield; *Bob Turley, pitcher.

1956 (6)—Yogi Berra, catcher; Whitey Ford, pitcher; *Johnny Kucks, pitcher; Mickey Mantle, outfield; Billy Martin, second base; *Gil McDougald, shortstop.

1957 (8)—Yogi Berra, catcher; Bob Grim, pitcher; *Elston Howard, catcher; Mickey Mantle, outfield; Gil McDougald, shortstop; *Bobby Richardson, second base; *Bobby Shantz, pitcher; Bill Skowron, first base.

1958 (9)—Yogi Berra, catcher; *Ryne Duren, pitcher; *Whitey Ford, pitcher; *Elston Howard, catcher; *Tony Kubek, shortstop; Mickey Mantle, outfield; Gil McDougald, second base; Bill Skowron, first base; Bob Turley, pitcher.

1959 (9)—Yogi Berra, catcher; Ryne Duren, pitcher; Whitey Ford, pitcher; *Elston Howard, catcher; Tony Kubek, shortstop; Mickey Mantle, outfield; Gil McDougald, shortstop; *Bobby Richardson, second base; Bill Skowron, first base.

1960 (7)—Yogi Berra, catcher; Jim Coates, pitcher; Whitey Ford, pitcher; Elston Howard, catcher; Mickey Mantle, outfield; Roger Maris, outfield; Bill Skowron, first base.

1961 (8)—*Luis Arroyo, pitcher; Yogi Berra, catcher; Whitey Ford, pitcher; Elston Howard, catcher; Tony Kubek, shortstop; Mickey Mantle, outfield; Roger Maris, outfield; *Bill Skowron, first base.

1962 (7)—Yogi Berra, catcher; Elston Howard, catcher; *Mickey Mantle, outfield; Roger Maris, outfield; Bobby Richardson, second base; *Ralph Terry, pitcher; Tom Tresh, shortstop.

1963 (6)—Jim Bouton, pitcher; Elston Howard, catcher; *Mickey Mantle, outfield; Joe Pepitone, first base; Bobby Richardson, second base; Tom Tresh, outfield.

1964 (5)—*Whitey Ford, pitcher; Elston Howard, catcher; Mickey Mantle, outfield; Joe Pepitone, first base; Bobby Richardson, second base.

1965 (5)—*Elston Howard, catcher; *Mickey Mantle, outfield; Joe Pepitone, first base; Bobby Richardson, second base; *Mel Stottlemyre, pitcher.

1966 (2)—Bobby Richardson, second base; Mel Stottlemyre, pitcher.

1967 (2)—Al Downing, pitcher; Mickey Mantle, first base.

1968 (2)—Mickey Mantle, first base; Mel Stottlemyre, pitcher.

1969 (2)—Mel Stottlemyre, pitcher; Roy White, outfield.

1970 (3)—Fritz Peterson, pitcher; Mel Stottlemyre, pitcher; *Roy White, outfield.

1971 (2)—Bobby Murcer, outfield; Thurman Munson, catcher.

1972 (1)—Bobby Murcer, outfield.

1973 (3)—Sparky Lyle, pitcher; Bobby Murcer, outfield; Thurman Munson, catcher.

1974 (2)—Bobby Murcer, outfield; Thurman Munson, catcher.

1975 (4)—Bobby Bonds, outfield; Catfish Hunter, pitcher; Thurman Munson, catcher; Graig Nettles, third base.

1976 (6)—Chris Chambliss, first base; Catfish Hunter, pitcher; *Sparky Lyle, pitcher; Thurman Munson, catcher; *Willie Randolph, second base; Mickey Rivers, outfield.

1977 (5)—Reggie Jackson, outfield; Sparky Lyle, pitcher; Thurman Munson, catcher; Graig Nettles, third base; Willie Randolph, second base.

1978 (3)—Rich Gossage, pitcher; Ron Guidry, pitcher; Graig Nettles, third base.

1979 (4)—Ron Guidry, pitcher; Reggie Jackson, outfield; *Tommy John, pitcher; Graig Nettles, third base.

1980 (6)—Bucky Dent, shortstop; Rich Gossage, pitcher; Reggie Jackson, outfield; Tommy John, pitcher; Graig Nettles, third base; Willie Randolph, second base.

1981 (6)—Ron Davis, pitcher; Bucky Dent, shortstop; *Rich Gossage, pitcher; Reggie Jackson, outfield; Willie Randolph, second base; and Dave Winfield, outfield.

*Did not play.
†1943 was the only year in which a Yankee didn't play in the All-Star Game—despite (1) six being chosen, and (2) Joe McCarthy being the American League manager.

YANKEE ALL-STAR GAME MANAGERS

Year	Manager	Winner	Score
1936	Joe McCarthy	N.L.	4–3
1937	Joe McCarthy	A.L.	8–3
1938	Joe McCarthy	N.L.	4–1
1939	Joe McCarthy	A.L.	3–1
1943	Joe McCarthy	A.L.	5–3
1944	Joe McCarthy	N.L.	7–1
1948	Bucky Harris	A.L.	5–2
1950	Casey Stengel	N.L.	4–3
1951	Casey Stengel	N.L.	8–3
1952	Casey Stengel	N.L.	3–2
1953	Casey Stengel	N.L.	5–1
1954	Casey Stengel	A.L.	11–9
1956	Casey Stengel	N.L.	7–3
1957	Casey Stengel	A.L.	6–5
1958	Casey Stengel	A.L.	4–3
1959	Casey Stengel	N.L.	5–4 (1st)
		A.L.	5–3 (2d)
1962	Ralph Houk	N.L.	3–1 (1st)
		A.L.	9–4 (2d)
1963	Ralph Houk	N.L.	5–3
1977	Billy Martin	N.L.	7–5
1978	Billy Martin	N.L.	7–3
1979	Bob Lemon	N.L.	7–6

MANAGERS' ALL-STAR GAME RECORDS

Manager	G	W	L	Pct.
Casey Stengel	10	4	6	.400
Joe McCarthy	6	3	3	.500
Ralph Houk	3	1	2	.333
Billy Martin	2	0	2	.000
Bucky Harris	1	1	0	1.000
Bob Lemon	1	0	1	.000

ALL-STAR GAME WINNING PITCHERS

1933—Lefty Gomez (A.L. 4–2), at Comiskey Park, Chicago.
1935—Lefty Gomez (A.L. 4–1), at Municipal Stadium, Cleveland.
1937—Lefty Gomez (A.L. 8–3), at Griffith Stadium, Washington.
1942—Spud Chandler (A.L. 3–1), at the Polo Grounds, New York.
1947—Spec Shea (A.L. 2–1), at Wrigley Field, Chicago.
1948—Vic Raschi (A.L. 5–2), at Sportsman's Park, St. Louis.

ALL-STAR GAME LOSING PITCHERS

1938—Lefty Gomez (N.L. 4–1), at Crosley Field, Cincinnati.
1940—Red Ruffing (N.L. 4–0), at Sportsman's Park, St. Louis.
1951—Ed Lopat (N.L. 8–3), at Briggs Stadium, Detroit.
1953—Allie Reynolds (N.L. 5–1), at Crosley Field, Cincinnati.
1959—Whitey Ford (N.L. 5–4), at Forbes Field, Pittsburgh.*
1960—Whitey Ford (N.L. 6–0), at Yankee Stadium, New York.†
1969—Mel Stottlemyre (N.L. 9–3), at RFK Stadium, Washington.
1975—Catfish Hunter (N.L. 6–3), at County Stadium, Milwaukee.
1978—Rich Gossage (N.L. 4–3), at San Diego Stadium.
1980—Tommy John (N.L. 4–2), at Dodger Stadium, Los Angeles.

*First of two games that season.
†Second of two games that season.

ALL-STAR GAME HOME RUNS

1933—Babe Ruth (one on; A.L. 4–2), at Comiskey Park, Chicago.
1936—Lou Gehrig (none on; N.L. 4–3), at Braves Field, Boston.
1937—Lou Gehrig (one on; A.L. 8–3), at Griffith Stadium, Washington.
1939—Joe DiMaggio (none on; A.L. 3–1), at Yankee Stadium, New York.
1946—Charlie Keller (one on; A.L. 12–0), at Fenway Park, Boston.
1955—Mickey Mantle (two on; N.L. 6–5), at County Stadium, Milwaukee.
1956—Mickey Mantle (none on; N.L. 7–3), at Griffith Stadium, Washington.
1959—Yogi Berra (one on; A.L. 5–3), at the Coliseum, Los Angeles.*

*Second of two games that season.

ALL-STAR GAMES AT YANKEE STADIUM

July 11, 1939

National League	001	000	000	—	1	7	1
American League	000	210	00X	—	3	6	1

N.L.: Paul Derringer (Reds), BILL LEE (Cubs) (4th), Lou Fette (Braves) (7th) and Ernie Lombardi (Reds).
A.L.: Red Ruffing (Yankees), TOMMY BRIDGES (Tigers) (4th), Bob Feller (Indians) (6th) and Bill Dickey (Yankees).
Home Run: Joe DiMaggio (Yankees).
Managers: Joe McCarthy (Yankees), Gabby Hartnett (Cubs).
Attendance: 62,892.

July 13, 1960

(Second All-Star Game that year)

National League	021	000	102	—	6	10	0
American League	000	000	000	—	0	8	0

N.L.: VERN LAW (Pirates), Johnny Podres (Dodgers) (3d), Stan Williams (Dodgers) (5th), Larry Jackson (Cardinals) (7th), Bill Henry (Reds) (8th), Lindy McDaniel (Cardinals) (9th) and Del Crandall (Braves), Ed Bailey (Reds), Smoky Burgess (Pirates).
A.L.: WHITEY FORD (Yankees), Early Wynn (White Sox) (4th), Gerry Staley (White Sox) (6th), Frank Lary (Tigers) (8th), Gary Bell (Indians) (9th) and Yogi Berra (Yankees), Sherm Lollar (White Sox).
Home Runs: Eddie Mathews (Braves), Willie Mays (Giants), Stan Musial (Cardinals) and Ken Boyer (Cardinals).
Managers: Al Lopez (White Sox), Walter Alston (Dodgers).
Attendance: 38,362.

July 19, 1977

National League	401	000	020	—	7	9	1
American League	000	002	102	—	5	8	0

N.L.: DON SUTTON (Dodgers) Gary Lavelle (Giants) (4th), Tom Seaver (Reds) (6th), Rick Reuschel (Cubs) (8th), Rich Gossage (Pirates) (9th) and Johnny Bench (Reds), Ted Simmons (Cardinals), John Stearns (Mets).
A.L.: JIM PALMER (Orioles), Jim Kern (Indians) (3d), Dennis Eckersley (Indians) (4th), Dave LaRoche (Angels) (6th), Bill Campbell (Red Sox) (7th), Sparky Lyle (Yankees) (8th) and Carlton Fisk (Red Sox), Butch Wynegar (Twins).
Home Runs: Joe Morgan (Reds), Greg Luzinski (Phillies), Steve Garvey (Dodgers) and George Scott (Red Sox).
Managers: Billy Martin (Yankees), Sparky Anderson (Reds).
Attendance: 56,683.

Note: Capital letters indicate pitchers of decision.

YANKEE AMERICAN LEAGUE LEADERS

HITTING CHAMPIONS

Batting

Year	Player	Pos.	Ave.
1924	Babe Ruth	OF	.378
1934	Lou Gehrig	1B	.363*
1939	Joe DiMaggio	CF	.381*
1940	Joe DiMaggio	CF	.352
1945	Snuffy Stirnweiss	2B	.309
1956	Mickey Mantle	CF	.353*

*Led both major leagues.

Home Runs

Year	Player	Pos.	Homers
1916	Wally Pipp	1B	12†
1917	Wally Pipp	1B	9
1920	Babe Ruth	OF	54*
1921	Babe Ruth	OF	59*
1923	Babe Ruth	OF	41†
1924	Babe Ruth	OF	46*
1925	Bob Meusel	OF	33
1926	Babe Ruth	OF	47*
1927	Babe Ruth	OF	60*
1928	Babe Ruth	OF	54*
1929	Babe Ruth	OF	46*
1930	Babe Ruth	OF	49
1931	Lou Gehrig	1B	46†
	Babe Ruth	OF	46†
1934	Lou Gehrig	1B	49*
1936	Lou Gehrig	1B	49*
1937	Joe DiMaggio	CF	46*
1944	Nick Etten	1B	22
1948	Joe DiMaggio	CF	39
1955	Mickey Mantle	CF	37
1956	Mickey Mantle	CF	52*
1958	Mickey Mantle	CF	42
1960	Mickey Mantle	CF	40
1961	Roger Maris	RF	61*
1976	Graig Nettles	3B	32
1980	Reggie Jackson	RF–DH	41‡

Slugging

Year	Player	Pos.	Ave.
1920	Babe Ruth	OF	.847*
1921	Babe Ruth	OF	.846*
1922	Babe Ruth	OF	.672
1923	Babe Ruth	OF	.764*
1924	Babe Ruth	OF	.739*
1926	Babe Ruth	OF	.737*
1927	Babe Ruth	OF	.772*
1928	Babe Ruth	OF	.709*
1929	Babe Ruth	OF	.697*
1930	Babe Ruth	OF	.732*
1931	Babe Ruth	OF	.700*
1934	Lou Gehrig	1B	.706*
1936	Lou Gehrig	1B	.696*
1937	Joe DiMaggio	CF	.673*
1945	Snuffy Stirnweiss	2B	.476
1950	Joe DiMaggio	CF	.585
1955	Mickey Mantle	CF	.611
1956	Mickey Mantle	CF	.705*
1960	Roger Maris	RF	.581
1961	Mickey Mantle	CF	.687*
1962	Mickey Mantle	CF	.605

Runs Batted In

Year	Player	Pos.	RBI
1920	Babe Ruth	OF	137*
1921	Babe Ruth	OF	170*
1923	Babe Ruth	OF	130†
1925	Bob Meusel	OF	138
1926	Babe Ruth	OF	155*
1927	Lou Gehrig	1B	175*
1928	Lou Gehrig	1B	142†
	Babe Ruth	OF	142†
1930	Lou Gehrig	1B	174
1931	Lou Gehrig	1B	184*
1934	Lou Gehrig	1B	165*
1941	Joe DiMaggio	CF	125*
1945	Nick Etten	1B	111
1948	Joe DiMaggio	CF	155*
1956	Mickey Mantle	CF	130*
1960	Roger Maris	RF	112
1961	Roger Maris	RF	142†

Runs

Year	Player	Pos.	Runs
1904	Patsy Dougherty	OF	113
1920	Babe Ruth	OF	158*
1921	Babe Ruth	OF	177*
1923	Babe Ruth	OF	151*
1924	Babe Ruth	OF	143*
1926	Babe Ruth	OF	139*
1927	Babe Ruth	OF	158*
1928	Babe Ruth	OF	163*
1931	Lou Gehrig	1B	163*
1933	Lou Gehrig	1B	138*
1935	Lou Gehrig	1B	125
1936	Lou Gehrig	1B	167*
1937	Joe DiMaggio	CF	151*
1939	Red Rolfe	3B	139*
1944	Snuffy Stirnweiss	2B	125*
1945	Snuffy Stirnweiss	2B	107
1948	Tommy Henrich	OF–1B	138*
1954	Mickey Mantle	CF	129*
1956	Mickey Mantle	CF	132*
1957	Mickey Mantle	CF	121*
1958	Mickey Mantle	CF	127*
1960	Mickey Mantle	CF	119*
1961	Mickey Mantle	CF	132*
	Roger Maris	RF	132*
1972	Bobby Murcer	CF	102
1976	Roy White	OF	104

NOTE: Dougherty played in 106 games for New York and in 49 for the Boston Americans in 1904.

Hits

Year	Player	Pos.	Hits
1927	Earle Combs	CF	231
1931	Lou Gehrig	1B	211
1939	Red Rolfe	3B	213*
1944	Snuffy Stirnweiss	2B	205*
1945	Snuffy Stirnweiss	2B	195
1962	Bobby Richardson	2B	209

Singles

Year	Player	Pos.	Hits
1904	Willie Keeler	OF	164*
1905	Willie Keeler	OF	147
1906	Willie Keeler	OF	166*
1927	Earle Combs	CF	166
1929	Earle Combs	CF	151
1944	Snuffy Stirnweiss	2B	146*
1950	Phil Rizzuto	SS	150*
1961	Bobby Richardson	2B	148
1962	Bobby Richardson	2B	158
1964	Bobby Richardson	2B	148
1967	Horace Clarke	2B	140
1969	Horace Clarke	2B	146
1975	Thurman Munson	C	151

Doubles

Year	Player	Pos.	No.
1927	Lou Gehrig	1B	52*
1928	Lou Gehrig	1B	47‡
1939	Red Rolfe	3B	46

Triples

Year	Player	Pos.	No.
1924	Wally Pipp	1B	19
1926	Lou Gehrig	1B	20
1927	Earle Combs	CF	23*
1928	Earle Combs	CF	21*
1930	Earle Combs	CF	22
1934	Ben Chapman	CF	13
1936	Joe DiMaggio	CF	15†
	Red Rolfe	3B	15†
1943	Johnny Lindell	OF	12‡
1944	Johnny Lindell	OF	16
	Snuffy Stirnweiss	2B	16
1945	Snuffy Stirnweiss	2B	22*
1947	Tommy Henrich	OF–1B	13
1948	Tommy Henrich	OF–1B	14
1955	Andy Carey	3B	11
	Mickey Mantle	CF	11
1957	Hank Bauer	OF	9
	Gil McDougald	IF	9
	Harry Simpson	OF–1B	9

Total Bases

Year	Player	Pos.	Bases
1921	Babe Ruth	OF	457*
1923	Babe Ruth	OF	399*
1924	Babe Ruth	OF	391*
1926	Babe Ruth	OF	365*
1927	Lou Gehrig	1B	447*
1928	Babe Ruth	OF	380*
1930	Lou Gehrig	1B	419
1931	Lou Gehrig	1B	410*
1934	Lou Gehrig	1B	409*
1937	Joe DiMaggio	CF	418*
1941	Joe DiMaggio	CF	348*
1944	Johnny Lindell	OF	297
1945	Snuffy Stirnweiss	2B	301
1948	Joe DiMaggio	CF	355
1956	Mickey Mantle	CF	376*
1958	Mickey Mantle	CF	307
1960	Mickey Mantle	CF	294
1961	Roger Maris	RF	366*
1972	Bobby Murcer	CF	314

Stolen Bases

Year	Player	Pos.	No.
1914	Fritz Maisel	3B	74*
1931	Ben Chapman	OF–IF	61*
1932	Ben Chapman	OF	38*
1933	Ben Chapman	OF	27*
1938	Frank Crosetti	SS	27*
1944	Snuffy Stirnweiss	2B	55*
1945	Snuffy Stirnweiss	2B	33*

Walks

Year	Player	Pos.	No.
1920	Babe Ruth	OF	148*
1921	Babe Ruth	OF	144*
1922	Whitey Witt	OF	89*
1923	Babe Ruth	OF	170*
1924	Babe Ruth	OF	142*
1926	Babe Ruth	OF	144*
1927	Babe Ruth	OF	138*
1928	Babe Ruth	OF	135*
1930	Babe Ruth	OF	136*
1931	Babe Ruth	OF	128*
1932	Babe Ruth	OF	130*
1933	Babe Ruth	OF	114*
1935	Lou Gehrig	1B	132*
1936	Lou Gehrig	1B	130*

*Led major leagues.
† Shared major league lead.
‡ Shared league lead.

1937	Lou Gehrig	1B	127*
1940	Charlie Keller	OF	106
1943	Charlie Keller	OF	106
1944	Nick Etten	1B	97
1955	Mickey Mantle	CF	113*
1957	Mickey Mantle	CF	146*
1958	Mickey Mantle	CF	129*
1961	Mickey Mantle	CF	126*
1962	Mickey Mantle	CF	122*
1972	Roy White	OF	99†
1980	Willie Randolph	2B	119*

Struck Out
(Strikeouts not included in American League batting records until 1913.)

Year	Player	Pos.	No.
1916	Wally Pipp	1B	82
1920	Aaron Ward	3B	84
1921	Bob Meusel	OF	88*
1923	Babe Ruth	OF	93*
1924	Babe Ruth	OF	81*
1926	Tony Lazzeri	2B	96*
1927	Babe Ruth	OF	89*
1928	Babe Ruth	OF	87
1937	Frank Crosetti	SS	105
1938	Frank Crosetti	SS	97
1942	Joe Gordon	2B	95*
1946	Charlie Keller	OF	101‡
1952	Mickey Mantle	CF	111‡
1954	Mickey Mantle	CF	107*
1958	Mickey Mantle	CF	120†
1959	Mickey Mantle	CF	126*
1960	Mickey Mantle	CF	125

Led major leagues.
† Shared major league lead.
‡ Shared league lead.

PITCHING LEADERS
Games

Year	Player		No.
1904	Jack Chesbro		55*
1906	Jack Chesbro		49*
1918	George Mogridge		45†
1921	Carl Mays		49*
1935	Russ Van Atta		58*
1948	Joe Page		55
1949	Joe Page		60*
1961	Luis Arroyo		65†
1977	Sparky Lyle		72

Note: Van Atta's 58 games in 1935 were divided between the Yankees (5) and St. Louis Browns (53).

Innings

Year	Player	Innings
1904	Jack Chesbro	455*
1906	Al Orth	339
1921	Carl Mays	337*
1925	Herb Pennock	277
1928	George Pipgras	301
1934	Lefty Gomez	282
1961	Whitey Ford	283*
1962	Ralph Terry	299
1963	Whitey Ford	269
1965	Mel Stottlemyre	291
1975	Catfish Hunter	328*

Victories

Year	Player	Record
1904	Jack Chesbro	41–13*
1906	Al Orth	25–17
1921	Carl Mays	27–9†
1927	Waite Hoyt	22–7‡
1928	George Pipgras	24–13‡
1934	Lefty Gomez	26–5
1937	Lefty Gomez	21–11
1938	Red Ruffing	21–7
1943	Spud Chandler	20–4‡
1955	Whitey Ford	18–7‡
1958	Bob Turley	21–7
1961	Whitey Ford	25–4*
1962	Ralph Terry	23–12
1963	Whitey Ford	24–7
1975	Catfish Hunter	23–14†
1978	Ron Guidry	25–3*

Year	Player	Percentage	
1904	Jack Chesbro	.759	(41–13)
1921	Carl Mays	.750*	(27–9)
1922	Joe Bush	.788*	(26–7)
1923	Herb Pennock	.760	(19–6)
1927	Waite Hoyt	.759*	(22–7)
1932	Johnny Allen	.810*	(17–4)
1934	Lefty Gomez	.839*	(26–5)
1936	Monte Pearson	.731	(19–7)
1938	Red Ruffing	.750*	(21–7)
1941	Lefty Gomez	.750	(15–5)
1942	Ernie Bonham	.808*	(21–15)
1943	Spud Chandler	.833*	(20–4)
1947	Allie Reynolds	.704	(19–8)
1950	Vic Raschi	.724	(21–8)
1953	Ed Lopat	.800*	(16–4)
1955	Tommy Byrne	.762	(16–5)

1956	Whitey Ford	.760	(19–6)
1957	Tom Sturdivant	.727†	(16–6)
1958	Bob Turley	.750*	(21–7)
1961	Whitey Ford	.862*	(25–4)
1963	Whitey Ford	.774	(24–7)
1978	Ron Guidry	.893*	(25–3)

Strikeouts

Year	Player	Strikeouts
1932	Red Ruffing	190
1933	Lefty Gomez	163
1934	Lefty Gomez	158
1937	Lefty Gomez	194*
1951	Vic Raschi	164†
1952	Allie Reynolds	160
1964	Al Downing	217

Earned Run Average

Year	Player	ERA
1920	Bob Shawkey	2.45
1927	Waite Hoyt	2.63
1934	Lefty Gomez	2.33
1937	Lefty Gomez	2.33*
1943	Spud Chandler	1.64*
1947	Spud Chandler	2.46
1952	Allie Reynolds	2.06*
1953	Ed Lopat	2.42
1956	Whitey Ford	2.47*
1957	Bobby Shantz	2.45*
1958	Whitey Ford	2.01*
1978	Ron Guidry	1.74*
1979	Ron Guidry	2.78
1980	Rudy May	2.47

Saves

Year	Player	No.
1916	Bob Shawkey	9*
1919	Allan Russell	5*
1921	Carl Mays	7†
1922	Sad Sam Jones	8*
1927	Wilcy Moore	13†
1928	Waite Hoyt	8*
1936	Pat Malone	9
1938	Johnny Murphy	11
1939	Johnny Murphy	19*
1941	Johnny Murphy	15*
1942	Johnny Murphy	11
1945	Jim Turner	10
1947	Joe Page	17‡
1949	Joe Page	27*
1954	Johnny Sain	22
1957	Bob Grim	19*
1958	Ryne Duren	20†
1961	Luis Arroyo	29*
1972	Sparky Lyle	35
1976	Sparky Lyle	23
1978	Rich Gossage	27
1980	Rich Gossage	33†

Note: Russell pitched in 23 games for the Yankees and in 21 for the Red Sox in 1919.

Shutouts

Year	Player	No.
1920	Carl Mays	6
1928	Herb Pennock	5*
1930	George Pipgras	3‡
1934	Lefty Gomez	6†
1937	Lefty Gomez	6*
1938	Lefty Gomez	4
1939	Red Ruffing	5
1942	Ernie Bonham	6
1943	Spud Chandler	5‡
1951	Allie Reynolds	7†
1952	Allie Reynolds	6
1958	Whitey Ford	7*
1960	Whitey Ford	4‡
1978	Ron Guidry	9*
1980	Tommy John	6†

Complete Games

Year	Player	No.
1904	Jack Chesbro	48*
1906	Al Orth	36
1934	Lefty Gomez	25*
1942	Ernie Bonham	22‡
1943	Spud Chandler	20‡
1955	Whitey Ford	18
1958	Bob Turley	19‡
1963	Ralph Terry	18‡
1965	Mel Stottlemyre	18
1969	Mel Stottlemyre	24
1975	Catfish Hunter	30*

*Led major leagues.
† Shared major league lead.
‡ Shared league lead.

YANKEE CLUB RECORDS

BATTING

Most years with Yankees	Yogi Berra	18
	Mickey Mantle	18
Most games, season	Bobby Richardson	162 (1961)
	Roy White	162 (1970)
	Chris Chambliss	162 (1978)
Most at bats, season	Bobby Richardson	692 (1952)†
Most runs, season	Babe Ruth	177 (1921)*
Most hits, season	Earle Combs	231 (1927)
Most singles, season	Willie Keeler	166 (1906)
	Earle Combs	166 (1927)
Most doubles, season	Lou Gehrig	52 (1927)
Most triples, season	Earle Combs	23 (1927)
Most home runs, right hander, season	Joe DiMaggio	46 (1937)
Most home runs, left hander, season	Babe Ruth	60 (1927)*
	Roger Maris	61 (1961)*
Most home runs, rookie, season	Joe DiMaggio	29 (1936)
Most grand slam home runs, season	Lou Gehrig	4 (1934)
	Tommy Henrich	4 (1948)
Most grand slam home runs, career	Lou Gehrig	23*
Most home runs, season, at home	Babe Ruth	32 (1921) (PG)
	Lou Gehrig	30 (1934) (YS)
	Roger Maris	30 (1961) (YS)
Most home runs, season, on the road	Babe Ruth	32 (1927)*
Most home runs, one month, right hander	Joe DiMaggio	15 (7/37)
Most home runs, one month, left hander	Babe Ruth	17 (9/27)*
Most total bases, season	Babe Ruth	457 (1921)*
Most sacrifice hits, season	Willie Keeler	42 (1905)
Most sacrifice flies, season	Roy White	17 (1971)†
Most stolen bases, season	Fritz Maisel	74 (1914)
Most caught stealing, season	Ben Chapman	23 (1931)
Most walks, season	Babe Ruth	170 (1923)*
Most strikeouts, season	Bobby Bonds	137 (1975)
Fewest strikeouts, season	Joe Sewell	3 (1932)
Most hit by pitch, season	Frank Crosetti	15 (1938)
Most runs batted in, season	Lou Gehrig	184 (1931)†
Most consecutive games with an RBI	Babe Ruth	11 (1931)
Highest batting average, season	Babe Ruth	.393 (1923)
Highest slugging average, season	Babe Ruth	.847 (1920)*
Longest hitting streak	Joe DiMaggio	56 (1941)*
Most grounded into double plays, season	Billy Johnson	27 (1943)
Fewest grounded into double plays, season	Mickey Mantle	2 (1961)
	Mickey Rivers	2 (1977)

*Major league record.
†American League record.
(PG) Polo Grounds; (YS) Yankee Stadium.

PITCHING

Most years with Yankees	Whitey Ford	16
Most games, righthander, season	Pedro Ramos	65 (1965)
	Dooley Womack	65 (1967)
Most games, lefthander, season	Sparky Lyle	72 (1977)
Most games started, season	Jack Chesbro	51 (1904)
Most complete games, season	Jack Chesbro	48 (1904)
Most games finished, RHP, season	Rich Gossage	58 (1980)
Most games finished, LHP, season	Sparky Lyle	60 (1977)
Most innings pitched, season	Jack Chesbo	454 (1904)
Most victories, season	Jack Chesbro	41 (1904)*
Most 20-victory seasons	Bob Shawkey	4
	Lefty Gomez	4
	Red Ruffing	4
Most losses, season	Al Orth	21 (1907)
	Sad Sam Jones	21 (1925)
	Joe Lake	21 (1908)
	Russ Ford	21 (1912)
Highest winning percentage, season	Ron Guidry (25–3)	.893 (1978)
Most consecutive victories, season	Jack Chesbro	14 (1904)
	Whitey Ford	14 (1961)
Most consecutive losses, season	Fritz Peterson	8 (1967)
	Fred Talbot	8 (1968)
Most saves, lefthander, season	Sparky Lyle	35 (1972)
Most saves, righthander, season	Rich Gossage	33 (1980)
Most walks, lefthander, season	Tommy Byrne	179 (1949)
Most walks, righthander, season	Bob Turley	177 (1955)
Most strikeouts, season	Ron Guidry	248 (1978)
Most strikeouts, 9-inning game	Ron Guidry	18 (6/17/78)
Most strikeouts, extra-inning game	Whitey Ford	15 (4/22/59)
Most shutouts, season	Ron Guidry	9 (1978)
Most 1–0 shutouts won, career	Bob Shawkey	7
Most shutouts, lost, season	Bill Zuber	7 (1945)
Most runs allowed, season	Russ Ford	165 (1912)
Most earned runs allowed, season	Sad Sam Jones	127 (1925)
Most hits allowed, season	Jack Chesbro	337 (1904)
Most hit batsmen, season	John Warhop	26 (1909)
Most wild pitches, season	Al Downing	14 (1964)
Most home runs allowed, season	Ralph Terry	40 (1962)
Lowest ERA, season, RHP	Spud Chandler	1.64 (1943)
Lowest ERA, season, LHP	Ron Guidry	1.74 (1978)

*Major league record.

ALL-TIME TEAM RECORDS

Most players: 47 in 1979
Fewest players: 25 in 1923,1927
Most games: 164 in 1964, 1968
Most at-bats: 5705 in 1964
Most runs: 1067 in 1931
Fewest runs: 459 in 1908
Most opponents runs: 898 in 1930
Most hits: 1683 in 1930
Fewest hits: 1137 in 1968
Most singles: 1157 in 1931
Most doubles: 315 in 1936
Most triples: 110 in 1930
Most homers: 240 in 1961
Most home runs by pinch-hitters: 10 in 1961
Most home runs with bases filled: 7 in 1948
Most total bases: 2703 in 1936
Most sacrifices (sacrifice hits and flies): 218 in 1922, 1926
Most sacrifice hits: 178 in 1906
Most sacrifice flies: 72 in 1974
Most stolen bases: 289 in 1910
Most caught stealing: 82 in 1920
Most bases on balls: 766 in 1932
Most strikeouts: 1043 in 1967
Fewest strikeouts: 420 in 1924
Most hit by pitch: 46 in 1955
Fewest hit by pitch: 14 in 1969
Most runs batted in: 995 in 1936
Highest batting average: .309 in 1930
Lowest batting average: .214 in 1968
Highest slugging average: .489 in 1927
Lowest slugging average: .287 in 1914
Most grounded into double play: 147 in 1979
Fewest grounded into double play: 91 in 1963
Most left on bases: 1239 in 1934
Fewest left on bases: 1010 in 1920
Most .300 hitters: 9 in 1930
Most putouts: 4520 in 1964
Fewest putouts: 3993 in 1935
Most assists: 2086 in 1904
Fewest assists: 1493 in 1948
Most chances accepted: 6382 in 1980
Fewest chances accepted: 5551 in 1935
Most errors: 386 in 1912
Fewest errors: 109 in 1947, 1964
Most errorless games: 91 in 1964
Most consecutive errorless games: 10 in 1977
Most double plays: 214 in 1956
Fewest double plays: 81 in 1912
Most consecutive games, one or more double plays: 18 (23 double plays)
    in 1941
Most passed balls: 32 in 1913
Fewest passed balls: 0 in 1931
Highest fielding average: .983 in 1964
Lowest fielding average: .939 in 1912
Most games won: 110 in 1927
Most games lost: 103 in 1908
Highest percentage games won: .714 in 1927
Lowest percentage games won: .329 in 1912
Most shutouts won, season: 24 in 1951
Most shutouts lost, season: 27 in 1914
Most 1–0 games won: 6 in 1908, 1968
Most 1–0 games lost: 9 in 1914
Most consecutive games won, season: 19 in 1947
Most consecutive games lost, season: 13 in 1913
Most times league champions: 32
Most runs, game: New York, 25, Philadelphia 2, May 24, 1936
Most runs, game, by opponent, on road: Cleveland 24, New York 6,
    July 29, 1928
Most runs, game, by opponent, at home: Detroit 19, New York 1, June
    17, 1925; Toronto 19, New York 3, Sept. 10, 1977

Most runs, shutout game: New York 21, Philadelphia 0, Aug. 13, 1939,
    2nd game, 8 innings
Most runs, shutout game, by opponent: Chicago 15, N.Y. 0, July 15, 1907;
    Chicago 15, N.Y. 0, May 4, 1950
Most runs, inning: 14, N.Y. vs. Washington, July 6, 1920, fifth inning.
Most hits, game: 30, New York vs. Boston, Sept. 28, 1923
Most home runs, game: 8, New York vs. Philadelphia, June 28, 1939,
    first game
Most consecutive games, one or more home runs: 25 (40 homers),
    1941
Most home runs in consecutive games in which home runs were made:
    40 (25 games), 1941
Most total bases, game: 53, New York vs. Philadelphia, June 28, 1939,
    first game

YANKEES' LONGEST WINNING STREAKS

19—1947	15—1906, 1960
18—1953	14—1941
16—1926	13—1954

YANKEES' LONGEST LOSING STREAKS

13—1913	8—1973
9—1912 (twice), 1945, 1953	

Bat day at Yankee Stadium.

PITCHING LEADERS YEAR BY YEAR

Year	Pitcher (W–L #1)	Pitcher (W–L #2)	Pitcher (W–L #3)	Saves
1903	Jack Chesbro, 21–15	Jesse Tannehill, 15–15	Clark Griffith, 14–10	Doc Adkins, 1
				Snake Wiltse, 1
1904	Jack Chesbro, 41–12*	Jack Powell, 23–19	Al Orth, 11–3	Clark Griffith, 1
1905	Jack Chesbro, 20–15	Al Orth, 18–18	Bill Hogg, 9–12	Clark Griffith, 3
1906	Al Orth, 27–17	Jack Chesbro, 24–16	Bill Hogg, 14–13	Clark Griffith, 2
1907	Al Orth, 14–21	Bill Hogg, 11–8	Slow Joe Doyle, 11–11	Bob Keefe, 2
1908	Jack Chesbro, 14–20	Rube Manning, 13–16	Joe Lake, 9–22	Jack Chesbro, 3
1909	Joe Lake, 14–11	Jack Warhop, 13–15	Lew Brockett, 10–8	Jack Warhop, 4
1910	Russ Ford, 26–6	Jack Quinn, 18–12	Jack Warhop, 14–14	Ray Caldwell, 2
				Hippo Vaughn, 2
				Jack Warhop, 2
1911	Russ Ford, 22–11	Ray Caldwell, 14–14	Jack Warhop, 12–13	Ray Caldwell, 3
				Jack Quinn, 3
1912	Russ Ford, 13–21	Jack Warhop, 10–19	George McConnell, 8–12	Jack Warhop, 3
1913	Ray Fisher, 11–17	Russ Ford, 11–18	Ray Caldwell, 9–8	Russ Ford, 3
1914	Ray Caldwell, 17–9	King Cole, 11–9	Ray Fisher, 10–12	Ray Caldwell, 2
				Marty McHale, 2
1915	Ray Caldwell, 19–16	Ray Fisher, 18–11	Jack Warhop, 7–9	King Cole, 1
				Cy Pieh, 1
1916	Bob Shawkey, 24–14	Nick Cullop, 13–6	Ray Fisher, 10–8	Bob Shawkey, 9*
1917	Bob Shawkey, 13–15	Ray Caldwell, 13–16	George Mogridge, 9–11	Allan Russell, 2
1918	George Mogridge, 16–13	Slim Love, 13–12	Ray Caldwell, 9–8	George Mogridge, 5
1919	Bob Shawkey, 20–11	Jack Quinn, 15–15	Hank Thormahlen, 13–9	Bob Shawkey, 4
1920	Carl Mays, 26–11	Bob Shawkey, 20–13	Jack Quinn, 18–10	Jack Quinn, 3
1921	Carl Mays, 27–9†	Waite Hoyt, 19–13	Bob Shawkey, 18–12	Carl Mays, 7†
1922	Joe Bush, 26–7	Bob Shawkey, 20–12	Waite Hoyt, 19–12	Sad Sam Jones, 8*
1923	Sad Sam Jones, 21–8	Herb Pennock, 19–6	Joe Bush, 19–15	Sad Sam Jones, 4
1924	Herb Pennock, 21–9	Waite Hoyt, 18–13	Joe Bush, 17–16	Waite Hoyt, 4
1925	Herb Pennock, 16–17	Sad Sam Jones, 15–21	Urban Shocker, 12–12	Waite Hoyt, 6
1926	Herb Pennock, 23–11	Urban Shocker, 19–11	Waite Hoyt, 16–12	Sad Sam Jones, 5
1927	Waite Hoyt, 22–7†	Wilcy Moore, 19–7	Herb Pennock, 19–8	Wilcy Moore, 13†
1928	George Pipgras, 24–13†	Waite Hoyt, 23–7	Herb Pennock, 17–6	Waite Hoyt, 8*
1929	George Pipgras, 18–12	Ed Wells, 13–9	Tom Zachary, 12–0	Wilcy Moore, 8
1930	Red Ruffing, 15–5	George Pipgras, 15–15	Hank Johnson, 14–11	George Pipgras, 4
				Roy Sherid, 4
1931	Lefty Gomez, 21–9	Red Ruffing, 16–14	Hank Johnson, 13–8	Hank Johnson, 4
1932	Lefty Gomez, 24–7	Red Ruffing, 18–7	Johnny Allen, 17–4	Johnny Allen, 4
				Wilcy Moore, 4
1933	Lefty Gomez, 16–10	Johnny Allen, 15–7	Russ Van Atta, 12–4	Wilcy Moore, 8
1934	Lefty Gomez, 26–5*	Red Ruffing, 19–11	Johnny Murphy, 14–10	Johnny Murphy, 4
1935	Red Ruffing, 16–11	Johnny Broaca, 15–7	Johnny Allen, 13–6	Johnny Murphy, 5
1936	Red Ruffing, 20–12	Monte Pearson, 19–7	Bump Hadley, 14–4	Pat Malone, 9*
1937	Lefty Gomez, 21–11*	Red Ruffing, 20–7	Johnny Murphy, 13–4	Johnny Murphy, 10
1938	Red Ruffing, 21–7*	Lefty Gomez, 18–12	Monte Pearson, 16–7	Johnny Murphy, 11*
1939	Red Ruffing, 21–7*	Atley Donald, 13–3	Monte Pearson, 12–5	Johnny Murphy, 19*

PITCHING LEADERS YEAR BY YEAR

Earned Run Average	Innings	Strikeouts
Clark Griffith, 2.70	Jack Chesbro, 325	Jack Chesbro, 147
Jack Chesbro, 1.82	Jack Chesbro, 455*	Jack Chesbro, 239
Jack Chesbro, 2.20	Al Orth, 305	Jack Chesbro, 156
Walter Clarkson, 2.32	Al Orth, 339*	Jack Chesbro, 152
Jack Chesbro, 2.53	Al Orth, 249	Slow Joe Doyle, 94
Jack Chesbro, 2.93	Jack Chesbro, 289	Jack Chesbro, 124
Joe Lake, 1.88	Jack Warhop, 243	Joe Lake, 117
Russ Ford, 1.65	Russ Ford, 300	Russ Ford, 209
Russ Ford, 2.28	Russ Ford, 281	Russ Ford, 158
George McConnell, 2.75	Russ Ford, 292	Russ Ford, 112
Ray Caldwell, 2.43	Ray Fisher, 246	Ray Fisher, 92
Ray Caldwell, 1.94	Jack Warhop, 217	Ray Keating, 109
Ray Fisher, 2.11	Ray Caldwell, 305	Ray Caldwell, 130
Nick Cullop, 2.05	Bob Shawkey, 277	Bob Shawkey, 122
Ray Fisher, 2.19	Bob Shawkey, 236	Ray Caldwell, 102
George Mogridge, 2.27	George Mogridge, 230	Slim Love, 95
George Mogridge, 2.50	Jack Quinn, 264	Bob Shawkey, 122
Bob Shawkey, 2.45*	Carl Mays, 312	Bob Shawkey, 126
Carl Mays, 3.04	Carl Mays, 337*	Bob Shawkey, 126
Bob Shawkey, 2.91	Bob Shawkey, 300	Bob Shawkey, 130
Waite Hoyt, 3.01	Joe Bush, 276	Joe Bush, 125
		Bob Shawkey, 125
Herb Pennock, 2.83	Herb Pennock, 286	Bob Shawkey, 114
Herb Pennock, 2.96	Herb Pennock, 277*	Sad Sam Jones, 92
Urban Shocker, 3.38	Herb Pennock, 266	Waite Hoyt, 79
Wilcy Moore, 2.28*	Waite Hoyt, 256	Waite Hoyt, 86
Herb Pennock, 2.56	George Pipgras, 301	George Pipgras, 139
Tom Zachary, 2.47	George Pipgras, 225	George Pipgras, 125
George Pipgras, 4.11	Red Ruffing, 222	Red Ruffing, 117
Lefty Gomez, 2.63	Lefty Gomez, 243	Lefty Gomez, 150
Red Ruffing, 3.09	Lefty Gomez, 265	Red Ruffing, 190*
Lefty Gomez, 3.18	Lefty Gomez, 235	Lefty Gomez, 163*
	Red Ruffing, 235	
Lefty Gomez, 2.33*	Lefty Gomez, 282*	Lefty Gomez, 158*
Red Ruffing, 3.12	Lefty Gomez, 246	Lefty Gomez, 138
Monte Pearson, 3.71	Red Ruffing, 271	Monte Pearson, 118
Lefty Gomez, 2.33*	Lefty Gomez, 278	Lefty Gomez, 194*
Red Ruffing, 3.32	Red Ruffing, 247	Lefty Gomez, 129
Red Ruffing, 2.94	Red Ruffing, 233	Lefty Gomez, 102

Yogi Berra scrambles in the outfield during the 1962 World Series.

PITCHING LEADERS YEAR BY YEAR

Year	Pitcher (W–L #1)	Pitcher (W–L #2)	Pitcher (W–L #3)	Saves
1940	Red Ruffing, 15–12	Marius Russo, 14–8	Ernie Bonham, 9–3	Johnny Murphy, 9
1941	Lefty Gomez, 15–5	Red Ruffing, 15–6	Marius Russo, 14–10	Johnny Murphy, 15*
1942	Ernie Bonham, 21–5	Spud Chandler, 16–5	Hank Borowy, 15–4	Johnny Murphy, 11*
1943	Spud Chandler, 20–4 †	Ernie Bonham, 15–8	Hank Borowy, 14–9	Johnny Murphy, 8
1944	Hank Borowy, 17–12	Atley Donald, 13–10	Monk Dubiel, 13–13	Jim Turner, 7
1945	Bill Bevens, 13–9	Hank Borowy, 10–5	Monk Dubiel, 10–9	Jim Turner, 10*
1946	Spud Chandler, 20–8	Bill Bevens, 16–13	Randy Gumpert, 11–3	Johnny Murphy, 7
1947	Allie Reynolds, 19–8	Spec Shea, 14–5	Joe Page, 14–8	Joe Page, 17 †
1948	Vic Raschi, 19–8	Ed Lopat, 17–11	Allie Reynolds, 16–7	Joe Page, 16
1949	Vic Raschi, 21–10	Allie Reynolds, 17–6	Tommy Byrne, 15–7	Joe Page, 27*
1950	Vic Raschi, 21–8	Ed Lopat, 18–8	Allie Reynolds, 16–12	Joe Page, 13
1951	Ed Lopat, 21–9	Vic Raschi, 21–10	Allie Reynolds, 17–8	Allie Reynolds, 7
1952	Allie Reynolds, 20–8	Vic Raschi, 16–6	Johnny Sain, 11–6	Johnny Sain, 7
1953	Whitey Ford, 18–6	Ed Lopat, 16–4	Johnny Sain, 14–7	Allie Reynolds, 13
1954	Bob Grim, 20–6	Whitey Ford, 16–8	Allie Reynolds, 13–4	Johnny Sain, 22*
1955	Whitey Ford, 18–7	Bob Turley, 17–13	Tommy Byrne, 16–5	Jim Konstanty, 11
1956	Whitey Ford, 19–6	Johnny Kucks, 18–9	Tom Sturdivant, 16–8	Tom Morgan, 11
1957	Tom Sturdivant, 16–6	Bob Turley, 13–6	Bob Grim, 12–8	Bob Grim, 19*
1958	Bob Turley, 21–7*	Whitey Ford, 14–7	Don Larsen, 9–6	Ryne Duren, 20*
1959	Whitey Ford, 16–10	Duke Maas, 14–8	Art Ditmar, 13–9	Ryne Duren, 14
1960	Art Ditmar, 15–9	Jim Coates, 13–3	Whitey Ford, 12–9	Bobby Shantz, 11
1961	Whitey Ford, 25–4*	Ralph Terry, 16–3	Luis Arroyo, 15–5	Luis Arroyo, 29*
1962	Ralph Terry, 23–12*	Whitey Ford, 17–8	Bill Stafford, 14–9	Marshall Bridges, 18
1963	Whitey Ford, 24–7	Jim Bouton, 21–7	Ralph Terry, 17–15	Hal Reniff, 18
1964	Jim Bouton, 18–13	Whitey Ford, 17–6	Al Downing, 13–8	Pete Mikkelsen, 12
1965	Mel Stottlemyre, 20–9	Whitey Ford, 16–13	Al Downing, 12–14	Pedro Ramos, 19
1966	Fritz Peterson, 12–11	Mel Stottlemyre, 12–20	Al Downing, 10–11	Pedro Ramos, 13
1967	Mel Stottlemyre, 15–15	Al Downing, 14–10	Fritz Peterson, 8–14	Dooley Womack, 18
1968	Mel Stottlemyre, 21–12	Stan Bahnsen, 17–12	Fritz Peterson, 12–11	Steve Hamilton, 11
1969	Mel Stottlemyre, 20–14	Fritz Peterson, 17–16	Stan Bahnsen, 9–16	Jack Aker, 11
1970	Fritz Peterson, 20–11	Mel Stottlemyre, 15–13	Stan Bahnsen, 14–11	Lindy McDaniel, 29
1971	Mel Stottlemyre, 16–12	Fritz Peterson, 15–13	Stan Bahnsen, 14–12	Jack Aker, 4
				Lindy McDaniel, 4
1972	Fritz Peterson, 17–15	Steve Kline, 16–9	Mel Stottlemyre, 14–18	Sparky Lyle, 35*
1973	Mel Stottlemyre, 16–16	Doc Medich, 14–9	Lindy McDaniel, 12–6	Sparky Lyle, 27
1974	Pat Dobson, 19–15	Doc Medich, 19–15	Dick Tidrow, 11–9	Sparky Lyle, 15
1975	Catfish Hunter, 23–14	Doc Medich, 16–16	Rudy May, 14–12	Tippy Martinez, 8
1976	Ed Figueroa, 19–10	Dock Ellis, 17–8	Catfish Hunter, 17–15	Sparky Lyle, 23
1977	Ron Guidry, 16–7	Ed Figueroa, 16–11	Don Gullett, 14–4	Sparky Lyle, 26
1978	Ron Guidry, 25–3*	Ed Figueroa, 20–9	Catfish Hunter, 12–6	Rich Gossage, 27*
1979	Tommy John, 21–9	Ron Guidry, 18–8	Ron Davis, 14–2	Rich Gossage, 18
1980	Tommy John, 22–9	Ron Guidry, 17–10	Rudy May, 15–5	Rich Gossage, 33*
1981	Ron Guidry, 11–5	Tommy John, 9–8	Dave Righetti, 8–4	Rich Gossage, 20

PITCHING LEADERS YEAR BY YEAR

Earned Run Average	Innings	Strikeouts
Marius Russo, 3.29	Red Ruffing, 226	Red Ruffing, 97
Marius Russo, 3.09	Marius Russo, 210	Marius Russo, 105
Ernie Bonham, 2.27	Spud Chandler, 201	Hank Borowy, 85
Spud Chandler, 1.64*	Spud Chandler, 253	Spud Chandler, 134
Hank Borowy, 2.63	Hank Borowy, 253	Hank Borowy, 107
Ernie Bonham, 3.28	Bill Bevens, 184	Bill Bevens, 76
Spud Chandler, 2.10	Spud Chandler, 257	Spud Chandler, 138
Spud Chandler, 2.46*	Allie Reynolds, 242	Allie Reynolds, 129
Spec Shea, 3.40	Allie Reynolds, 236	Vic Raschi, 124
Ed Lopat, 3.27	Vic Raschi, 275	Tommy Byrne, 129
Ed Lopat, 3.47	Vic Raschi, 257	Allie Reynolds, 160
Ed Lopat, 2.91	Vic Raschi, 258	Vic Raschi, 164*
Allie Reynolds, 2.07*	Allie Reynolds, 244	Allie Reynolds, 160*
Ed Lopat, 2.43	Whitey Ford, 207	Whitey Ford, 110
Whitey Ford, 2.82	Whitey Ford, 211	Whitey Ford, 125
Whitey Ford, 2.62	Whitey Ford, 254	Bob Turley, 210
Whitey Ford, 2.47*	Whitey Ford, 226	Whitey Ford, 141
Bobby Shantz, 2.45	Tom Sturdivant, 202	Bob Turley, 152
Whitey Ford, 2.01*	Bob Turley, 245	Bob Turley, 168
Art Ditmar, 2.90	Whitey Ford, 204	Whitey Ford, 114
Art Ditmar, 3.06	Art Ditmar, 200	Ralph Terry, 92
Bill Stafford, 2.68	Whitey Ford, 283*	Whitey Ford, 209
Whitey Ford, 2.90	Ralph Terry, 299*	Ralph Terry, 176
Jim Bouton, 2.53	Whitey Ford, 269	Whitey Ford, 189
Whitey Ford, 2.13	Jim Bouton, 271	Al Downing, 217*
Mel Stottlemyre, 2.63	Mel Stottlemyre, 291	Al Downing, 179
Fritz Peterson, 3.31	Mel Stottlemyre, 251	Al Downing, 152
Al Downing, 2.63	Mel Stottlemyre, 255	Al Downing, 171
Stan Bahnsen, 2.06	Mel Stottlemyre, 279	Stan Bahnsen, 162
Fritz Peterson, 2.55	Mel Stottlemyre, 303	Fritz Peterson, 150
Fritz Peterson, 2.91	Mel Stottlemyre, 271	Fritz Peterson, 127
Mel Stottlemyre, 2.87	Fritz Peterson, 274	Fritz Peterson, 139
Steve Kline, 2.40	Mel Stottlemyre, 200	Mel Stottlemyre, 110
Doc Medich, 2.95	Mel Stottlemyre, 273	Doc Medich, 145
Pat Dobson, 3.07	Pat Dobson, 281	Pat Dobson, 157
Catfish Hunter, 2.58	Catfish Hunter, 328	Catfish Hunter, 177
Ed Figueroa, 3.02	Catfish Hunter, 299	Catfish Hunter, 173
Ron Guidry, 2.82	Ed Figueroa, 239	Ron Guidry, 176
Ron Guidry, 1.74*	Ron Guidry, 274	Ron Guidry, 248
Ron Guidry, 1.78*	Tommy John, 276	Ron Guidry, 201
Rudy May, 2.47*	Tommy John, 265	Ron Guidry, 166
Dave Righetti, 2.05	Rudy May, 148	Ron Guidry, 104

*Led league.
†Tied for league lead.

Phil Rizzuto turns a double play.

ALL-TIME PITCHING LEADERS

Games

1.	W. Ford	498
2.	Ruffing	426
3.	Lyle	420
4.	Shawkey	415
5.	Murphy	383
6.	Gomez	367
7.	Hoyt	365
8.	Stottlemyre	360
9.	Pennock	346
10.	Hamilton	311
11.	Reynolds	295
12.	Peterson	288
13.	Page	278
14.	Chesbro	269
15.	Caldwell	248
16.	Pipgras	247
17.	Reniff	247
18.	Turley	234
19.	Quinn	228
20.	Byrne	221
	Warhop	221

Innings

W. Ford	3171
Ruffing	3169
Stottlemyre	2662
Gomez	2498
Shawkey	2489
Hoyt	2273
Pennock	2190
Chesbro	1953
Peterson	1856
Caldwell	1718
Reynolds	1700
Raschi	1537
Lopat	1497
Chandler	1485
Warhop	1423
Fisher	1380
Pipgras	1352
Quinn	1279
Turley	1269
Downing	1236

Victories

1.	W. Ford	236
2.	Ruffing	231
3.	Gomez	189
4.	Shawkey	168
5.	Stottlemyre	164
6.	Pennock	162
7.	Hoyt	157
8.	Chesbro	131
9.	Reynolds	126
10.	Raschi	120
11.	Lopat	113
12.	Peterson	109
13.	Chandler	109
14.	Caldwell	96
15.	Murphy	93
16.	Pipgras	93
17.	Guidry	87
18.	Turley	82
19.	Mays	79
20.	Bonham	79

Percentage
(100 decisions)

Guidry	.719
Chandler	.717
Raschi	.706
W. Ford	.690
Reynolds	.686
Mays	.670
Lopat	.657
Gomez	.652
Ruffing	.651
Pennock	.643
Byrne	.643
Murphy	.637
Hoyt	.616
Bonham	.612
Turley	.612
Pipgras	.595
Chesbro	.577
Terry	.569
Pipgras	.595
Downing	.559

Strikeouts

1.	W. Ford	1956
2.	Ruffing	1526
3.	Gomez	1468
4.	Stottlemyre	1257
5.	Shawkey	1163
6.	Downing	1028
7.	Reynolds	967
8.	Chesbro	913
9.	Turley	909
10.	Peterson	893
11.	Raschi	832
12.	Guidry	818
13.	Caldwell	803
14.	Hoyt	713
15.	Pennock	656
16.	Pipgras	652
17.	Terry	615
18.	Chandler	614
19.	Byrne	592
20.	Bouton	561

Shutouts

W. Ford	45
Stottlemyre	40
Ruffing	40
Gomez	28
Reynolds	27
Chandler	26
Shawkey	24
Raschi	24
Turley	21
Lopat	20
Guidry	19
Pennock	19
Peterson	18
Bonham	17
Chesbro	16
Terry	16
Hoyt	15
Pipgras	13
Caldwell	13
Downing	12

Complete Games

1.	Ruffing	261
2.	Gomez	173
3.	Chesbro	169
4.	Pennock	165
5.	Shawkey	161
6.	W. Ford	156
7.	Hoyt	156
8.	Stottlemyre	152
9.	Caldwell	151
10.	Chandler	109
11.	Warhop	105
12.	R. Ford	103
13.	Orth	102
14.	Raschi	99
15.	Reynolds	96
16.	Bonham	91
17.	Lopat	91
18.	Pipgras	84
19.	Quinn	82
20.	Peterson	81

ERA *(800 innings)*

R. Ford	2.54
Chesbro	2.58
Orth	2.72
Guidry	2.73
Bonham	2.73
W. Ford	2.74
Chandler	2.84
Fisher	2.91
Stottlemyre	2.99
Caldwell	2.99
Warshop	3.09
Peterson	3.10
Shawkey	3.10
Bahnsen	3.10
Quinn	3.12
Lopat	3.25
Downing	3.25
Mays	3.25
Reynolds	3.30
Gomez	3.34

LEADING RELIEF PITCHERS (since 1943)

		W	S	Pts.
1943	Murphy	12	8	20
1944	Turner	4	7	11
1945	Turner	3	10	13
1946	Murphy	4	7	11
1947	Page	14	17*	31
1948	Page	7	16	23
1949	Page	13	27*	40*
1950	Ferrick	8	9	17
1951	Kuzava	5	5	10
1952	Sain	3	7	10
1953	Reynolds	7	13	20
1954	Sain	6	22*	28
1955	Konstanty	7	11	18
1956	Morgan	6	11	17
1957	Grim	12	19*	31*
1958	Duren	6	20*	26
1959	Duren	3	14	17
1960	Shantz	5	11	16
1961	Arroyo	15	29*	44*
1962	Bridges	8	18	26
1963	Reniff	4	13	17
1964	Mikkelson	7	9	16
1964	Ramos	5	14	19
1966	Ramos	3	12	15
1967	Womack	5	17	22
1968	McDaniel	4	10	14
1969	Aker	8	11	19
1970	McDaniel	9	29	38
1971	McDaniel	5	4	9
1972	Lyle	9	35*	44*
1973	Lyle	5	27	32
1974	Lyle	9	15	24
1975	Tidrow	6	5	11
	Lyle	5	6	11
1976	Lyle	7	23	30
1977	Lyle	13	26	39
1978	Gossage	10	27*	37*
1979	Davis	14	9	23
	Gossage	5	18	23
1980	Gossage	6	33*	39
1981	Gossage	3	20	23

**Led league.*

20-GAME WINNERS *(Final standing of team in parentheses under pitcher's name.)*

Year	Pitcher	W	L	Year	Pitcher	W	L
1903	Jack Chesbro (4)	21	15	1938	Red Ruffing (1)	21	7
1904	Jack Chesbro (2)	41	12	1939	Red Ruffing (1)	21	7
	Jack Powell (2)	23	19	1942	Ernie Bonham (1)	21	5
1906	Al Orth (2)	27	17	1943	Spud Chandler (1)	20	4
	Jack Chesbro (2)	24	16	1946	Spud Chandler (3)	20	8
1910	Russ Ford (2)	26	6	1949	Vic Raschi (1)	21	10
1911	Russ Ford (6)	22	11	1950	Vic Raschi (1)	21	8
1916	Bob Shawkey (4)	23	14	1951	Eddie Lopat (1)	21	9
1919	Bob Shawkey (3)	20	13		Vic Raschi (1)	21	10
1920	Carl Mays (3)	26	11	1952	Allie Reynolds (1)	20	8
	Bob Shawkey (3)	20	13	1954	Bob Grim (2)	20	6
1921	Carl Mays (1)	27	9	1958	Bob Turley (1)	21	7
1922	Joe Bush (1)	26	7	1961	Whitey Ford (1)	25	4
	Bob Shawkey (1)	20	12	1962	Ralph Terry (1)	23	12
1923	Sad Sam Jones (1)	21	8	1963	Whitey Ford (1)	24	7
1924	Herb Pennock (2)	21	9		Jim Bouton (1)	21	7
1926	Herb Pennock (1)	23	11	1965	Mel Stottlemyre (6)	20	9
1927	Waite Hoyt (1)	22	7	1968	Mel Stottlemyre (5)	21	12
1928	George Pipgras (1)	24	13	1969	Mel Stottlemyre (5)	20	14
	Waite Hoyt (1)	23	7	1970	Fritz Peterson (2)	20	11
1931	Lefty Gomez (2)	21	9	1975	Catfish Hunter (3)	23	14
1932	Lefty Gomez (1)	24	7	1978	Ron Guidry (1)	25	3
1934	Lefty Gomez (2)	26	5		Ed Figueroa (1)	20	9
1936	Red Ruffing (1)	20	12	1979	Tommy John (4)	21	9
1937	Lefty Gomez (1)	21	11	1980	Tommy John (1)	22	9
	Red Ruffing (1)	20	7				

NO-HIT GAMES BY YANKEES

		Site	N.Y.	Opponent
1910	Tom Hughes vs. Cleveland, Aug. 30 (9 innings, lost in 11th)	H	0	5
1917	George Mogridge* vs. Boston, April 24	A	2	1
1923	Sad Sam Jones vs. Philadelphia, Sept. 4	A	2	0
1938	Monte Pearson vs. Cleveland, Aug. 27 (2d game)	H	13	0
1951	Allie Reynolds vs. Cleveland, July 12 (night)	A	1	0
	Allie Reynolds vs. Boston, Sept. 28 (1st game)	H	8	0
1956	Don Larsen vs. Brooklyn, Oct. 8 † (Game 5 of W.S.)	H	2	0

*Only Yankee left-hander to pitch a no-hitter.
† Only perfect game in World Series history.

NO-HIT GAMES AGAINST YANKEES

		Site	N.Y.	Opponent
1908	Cy Young of Boston, June 30	H	0	8
1916	George Foster of Boston, June 21	A	0	2
1919	Ray Caldwell of Cleveland, Sept. 10 (1st game)	H	0	3
1946	Bob Feller of Cleveland, April 30	H	0	1
1952	Virgil Trucks of Detroit, Aug. 25	H	0	1
1958	Hoyt Wilhelm of Baltimore, Sept. 20	A	0	1

ONE-HITTERS

Yankee pitchers have tossed 48 one-hitters, the most recent by Luis Tiant on July 8, 1979, at Oakland.

Whitey Ford and Bob Turley each pitched three one-hitters for the Yankees, and both pitchers participated in a fourth. Tiant also threw three. Bob Shawkey, Rip Collins, Lefty Gomez, Bill Bevens and Vic Raschi each pitched two; one of Bevens' came at Brooklyn in game four

of the 1947 World Series; his no-hitter was spoiled by Cookie Lavagetto's game-winning double with two out in the last of the ninth.

The Yankees have been one-hit 41 times, the last two by Nolan Ryan—both in California. Ryan one-hit them there on July 13, 1979, with Reggie Jackson hitting a ninth-inning single; and on August 20, 1973, with Thurman Munson getting a first-inning single. The Yankees have been one-hit thirteen times since they were last a no-hit victim in 1958.

Ryan, Boston's Smoky Joe Wood and Earl Hamilton of the St. Louis Browns are the only opponents with two one-hitters against the Yankees. Both of Hamilton's came in 1913, both of Wood's also in the early 1900's. Baltimore's Hoyt Wilhelm one-hit the Yankees in 1959, the year after the Oriole knuckleballer no-hit them.

Horace Clarke is believed to be the only Yankee to twice spoil no-hitters, breaking up bids by Baltimore's Jim Palmer and Detroit's Joe Niekro. Further, in 1970, Clarke shattered three no-hitters in the ninth inning in one month, two winding up being more than one-hitters.

PITCHERS WITH 30 VICTORIES AGAINST YANKEES

Pitcher	Wins	Pitcher	Wins
*Walter Johnson	60	Stan Coveleski	32
Eddie Cicotte	35	Chief Bender	30
Lefty Grove	35	Hooks Dauss	30
Hal Newhouser	33	Bob Feller	30
Early Wynn	33	George Mullin	30
Red Faber	32		

*Johnson and Mel Parnell share the distinction of shutting out the Yankees most times in a season—four. Johnson did it for Washington in 1908, Parnell for Boston in 1953.

OPPOSING PITCHERS WITH TOP WINNING PCT. AGAINST YANKEES

Pitcher	W	L	Pct.	Pitcher	W	L	Pct.
Dickie Kerr	14	4	.778	John Hiller	12	7	.632
Babe Ruth	17	5	.773	Schoolboy Rowe	20	12	.625
Bill Lee	12	5	.706	Denny McLain	15	9	.625
Bernie Boland	16	7	.696	Mike Cuellar	18	11	.621
Frank Lary	28	13	.683	Ellis Kinder	14	9	.609
Firpo Marberry	22	11	.667	Steve Barber	17	11	.607
Vida Blue	14	7	.667	Dean Chance	15	10	.600
Dave Boswell	10	5	.667	*Luis Tiant	22	15	.595
Jim Palmer	25	14	.641	Sam McDowell	14	10	.583
Dick Hall	12	7	.632				

*Tiant is the only pitcher to defeat the Yankees five times in a season since expansion in 1961. He was 5–1 for the Red Sox against his future teammates in 1974.

BATTING LEADERS

YEAR BY YEAR

Year	Batting Average	Hits	Doubles	Triples	Home Runs
1903	Keeler, .313	Keeler, 164	Williams, 30	Williams, Conroy, 12	McFarland, 5
1904	Keeler, .343	Keeler, 185	Williams, 31	Anderson, Conroy, 12	Ganzel, 6
1905	Keeler, .302	Keeler, 169	Williams, 20	Williams, 8	Williams, Keeler, 4
1906	Chase, .323	Chase, 193	Williams, 25	Chase, Conroy, 10	Conroy, 4
1907	Chase, .287	Chase, 143	Chase, 23	Conroy, LaPorte, Williams, 11	Hoffman, 4
1908	Hemphill, .297	Hemphill, 150	Conroy, 22	Hemphill, 9	Niles, 4
1909	LaPorte, .298	Engle, 137	Engle, 20	Demmitt, 12	Chase, Demmitt, 4
1910	Knight, .312	Cree, 134	Knight, 25	Cree, 16	Wolter, Cree, 4
1911	Cree, .348	Cree, 181	Chase, 32	Cree, 22	Wolter, Cree, 2
1912	Paddock, .288	Chase, 143	Daniels, 25	Hartzell, Daniels, 11	Zinn, 6
1913	Cree, .272	Cree, 145	Cree, 25	Peckinpaugh, 7	Wolter, Sweeney, 2
1914	Cree, .309	Cook, 133	Maisel, 23	Maisel, Hartzell, 9	Peckinpaugh, 3
1915	Maisel, .281	Maisel, 149	Peckinpaugh, 18	High, Peckinpaugh, 7	Peckinpaugh, 5
1916	Pipp, .262	Pipp, 143	Baker, 23	Pipp, 14	Pipp*, 12
1917	Baker, .282	Baker, 156	Pipp, 29	Pipp, 12	Pipp*, 9
1918	Baker, .306	Baker, 154	Baker, 24	Pipp, 2	Baker, 8
1919	Peckinpaugh, .305	Baker, 166	Pratt, Bodie, 27	Pipp, 10	Baker, 10
1920	Ruth, .376	Pratt, 180	Ward, 40	Peckinpaugh, 14	Ruth*, 54
1921	Ruth, .378	Ruth, 204	Ruth, 44	Ruth, 16	Ruth*, 59
1922	Pipp, .329	Pipp, 190	Pipp, 32	Meusel, 11	Ruth, 35
1923	Ruth, .393	Ruth, 205	Ruth, 45	Ruth, 13	Ruth*, 41
1924	Ruth*, .378	Ruth, 200	Meusel, 40	Pipp*, 19	Ruth, 46
1925	Combs, .343	Combs, 203	Combs, 36	Combs, 13	Meusel*, 33
1926	Ruth, .372	Gehrig, 210	Gehrig, 47	Gehrig*, 20	Ruth*, 47
1927	Gehrig, .373		Gehrig*, 52	Combs*, 23	Ruth*, 60
1928	Gehrig, .374		Gehrig*, 47	Combs, 21	Ruth*, 54
		Combs*, 231	Lazzeri, 37	Combs, 15	Ruth*, 46
		Gehrig, 210	Gehrig, 42	Gehrig, 17	Ruth*, 49
1929	Lazzeri, .354	Combs, 202	Lary, 35	Combs*, 22	Ruth*, Gehrig*, 46
1930	Gehrig, .379	Gehrig, 220	Gehrig, 42	Chapman, 15	Ruth, 41
1931	Ruth, .373	Gehrig*, 211	Gehrig, 41	Combs, 15	Ruth, 34
1932	Gehrig, .349	Gehrig, 208	Gehrig, 40	Chapman*, 13	Gehrig*, 49
1933	Gehrig, .334	Gehrig, 198	Chapman, 38	Selkirk, 12	Gehrig, 30
1934	Gehrig*, .363	Gehrig, 210	DiMaggio, 44	DiMaggio*, 15	Gehrig*, 49
1935	Gehrig, .329	Rolfe, 192	Gehrig, 37	DiMaggio, 15	DiMaggio*, 46
1936	Dickey, .362	DiMaggio, 206	Rolfe*, 36	DiMaggio, 13	DiMaggio, 32
1937	Gehrig, .351	DiMaggio, 215	Rolfe*, 46	Rolfe, 10	DiMaggio, 30
1938	DiMaggio, .324	DiMaggio, 194	Gordon, 32	Keller, 15	DiMaggio, 31
1939	DiMaggio*, .381	Rolfe*, 213			
1940	DiMaggio*, .352	DiMaggio, 179			
1941	DiMaggio, .357	DiMaggio, 193	DiMaggio, 43	DiMaggio, 11	Keller, 33
1942	Gordon, .322	DiMaggio, 186	Henrich, 30	DiMaggio, 13	Keller, 26
1943	Johnson, .280	Johnson*, 166	Etten, 35	Linde*, 12	Keller, 31
1944	Stirnweiss, .319	Stirnweiss*, 205	Stirnweiss, 35	Stirnweiss*, 22	Etten*, 22
1945	Stirnweiss*, .309	Stirnweiss*, 195	Stirnweiss, 32	Stirnweiss*, Lindell*, 16	Etten, 18

BATTING LEADERS

YEAR BY YEAR

RBIs	Runs	Stolen Bases
Williams, 82	Keeler, 98	Conroy, 33
Anderson, 82	Dougherty*, 80	Conroy, 30
Williams, 60	Keeler, 81	Fultz, 44
Williams, 77	Keeler, 96	Hoffman, 33
Chase, 68	Hoffman, 81	Conroy, 41
Hemphill, 44	Hemphill, 62	Hemphill, 42
Engle, 71	Demmitt, 68	Austin, 30
Chase, 73	Daniels, 72	Daniels, 41
Hartzell, 91	Cree, 90	Cree, 48
Chase, 58	Daniels, 68	Daniels, 37
Cree, 63	Hartzell, 60	Daniels, 27
Peckinpaugh, 51	Maisel, 78	Maisel, 74
Pipp, 58	Maisel, 77	Maisel, 51
Pipp*, 99	Pipp, 70	Magee, 29
Pipp, 72	Pipp, 82	Maisel, 29
Baker, 68	Baker, Pratt, 65	Bodie, 16
Baker, 78	Peckinpaugh, 89	Pratt, 22
Ruth*, 137	Ruth*, 158	Ruth, 14
Ruth*, 170	Ruth*, 177	Meusel, Pipp, Ruth, 17
Ruth, 96	Witt, 98	Meusel, 13
Ruth*, 130	Ruth*, 151	Ruth, 17
Ruth*, 121	Ruth*, 143	Meusel, 26
Meusel*, 138	Combs, 117	Paschal, 14
Ruth*, 155	Ruth*, 139	Meusel, 16
Gehrig*, 175	Ruth*, 158	Meusel, 24
Gehrig*, Ruth*, 142	Ruth*, 163	Lazzeri, 15
Ruth, 154	Gehrig, 127	Combs, Lazzeri, 11
Gehrig*, 174	Ruth, 150	Combs, 16
Gehrig*, 184	Gehrig*, 163	Chapman*, 61
Gehrig, 151	Combs, 143	Chapman*, 38
Gehrig, 139	Gehrig*, 138	Chapman*, 27
Gehrig*, 165	Gehrig, 128	Chapman, 26
Gehrig, 119	Gehrig, 125	Chapman, 17
Gehrig, 152	Gehrig*, 167	Crosetti, 18
DiMaggio, 167	DiMaggio*, 151	Crosetti, 13
DiMaggio, 140	Rolfe, 132	Crosetti*, 27
DiMaggio, 126	Rolfe*, 139	Selkirk, 12
DiMaggio, 133	Gordon, 112	Gordon, 18
DiMaggio*, 125	DiMaggio, 122	Rizzuto, 14
DiMaggio, 114	DiMaggio, 123	Rizzuto, 22
Etten, 107	Keller, 97	Rizzuto, 14
Lindell, 103	Stirnweiss*, 125	Stirnweiss*, 55
Etten*, 111	Stirnweiss*, 107	Stirnweiss*, 33

*Led league.

Dave Winfield.

Elston Howard.

BATTING LEADERS

YEAR BY YEAR

Year	Batting Average	Hits	Doubles	Triples	Home Runs
1946	DiMaggio, .290	Keller, 148	Keller, 29	Keller, 10	Keller, 30
1947	DiMaggio, .315	DiMaggio, 168	Henrich, 35	Henrich*, 13	DiMaggio, 20
1948	DiMaggio, .320	DiMaggio, 190	Henrich, 42	Henrich*, 14	DiMaggio*, 39
1949	Henrich, .287	Rizzuto, 169	Rizzuto, 22	Rizzuto, Woodling, 7	Henrich, 24
1950	Rizzuto, .324	Rizzuto, 200	Rizzuto, 36	Woodling, DiMaggio, 10	DiMaggio, 32
1951	McDougald, .306	Berra, 161	McDougald, 23	Woodling, 8	Berra, 27
1952	Mantle, .311	Mantle, 171	Mantle, 37	Rizzuto, 10	Berra, 30
1953	Bauer, .304	McDougald, 154	McDougald, 27	McDougald, 7	Berra, 27
1954	Noren, .319	Berra, 179	Berra, 28	Mantle, 12	Mantle, 27
1955	Mantle, .306	Mantle, 158	Mantle, 25	Mantle*, 11	Mantle*, 37
1956	Mantle*, .353	Mantle, 188	Berra, 29	Bauer, 7	Mantle*, 52
1957	Mantle, .365	Mantle, 173	Mantle, 28	Bauer*, Simpson*, McDougald*, 9	Mantle, 34
1958	Mantle, .304	Mantle, 158	Bauer, Skowron, 22	Bauer, 6	Mantle*, 42
1959	Richardson, .301	Mantle, 154	Lopez, 27	McDougald, 8	Mantle, 31
1960	Skowron, .309	Skowron, 166	Skowron, 34	Maris, 7	Mantle*, 40
1961	Howard, .348	Richardson, 173	Kubek, 38	Mantle, Kubek, 6	Maris*, 61
1962	Mantle, .321	Richardson*, 209	Richardson, 38,	Skowron, 6	Maris, 33
1963	Howard, .287	Richardson, 167	Tresh, 28	Howard, Richardson, 6	Howard, 28
1964	Howard, .318	Richardson, 181	Howard, 27	Tresh, Boyer, 5	Mantle, 35
1965	Tresh, .279	Tresh, 168	Tresh, 29	Tresh, Boyer, 6	Tresh, 26
1966	Mantle, .288	Richardson, 153	Boyer, 22	Boyer, Clarke, Tresh, Pepitone, 4	Pepitone, 31
1967	Clarke, .272	Clarke, 160	Tresh, 23	Pepitone, Smith, Tresh, Whitaker, 3	Mantle, 22
1968	White, .267	White, 154	White, 20	White, Robinson, 7	Mantle, 18
1969	White, .290	Clarke, 183	White, 30	Clarke, 7	Pepitone, 27
1970	Munson, .302	White, 180	White, 31	Kenney, 7	Murcer, 23
1971	Murcer, .331	Murcer, 175	Murcer, 25	Clarke, White, 7	Murcer, 25
1972	Murcer, .292	Murcer, 171	Murcer, 30	Murcer, 7	Murcer, 33
1973	Murcer, .304	Murcer, 187	Murcer, Munson, 29	Munson, 4	Murcer, Nettles, 22
1974	Piniella, .305	Murcer, 166	Maddox, Piniella, 26	White, 8	Nettles, 22
1975	Munson, .318	Munson, 190	Chambliss, 38	White, 5	Bonds, 32
1976	Rivers, .312	Chambliss, 188	Chambliss, 32	Rivers, 8	Nettles*, 32
1977	Rivers, .326	Rivers, 184	Jackson, 39	Randolph, 11	Nettles, 37
1978	Piniella, .314	Munson, 183	Piniella, 34	Rivers, 8	Jackson, Nettles, 27
1979	Piniella, Jackson, .297	Randolph, Chambliss, 155	Chambliss, 27	Randolph, 13	Jackson, 29
1980	Watson, .307	Jackson, 154	Cerone, 30	Randolph, 7	Jackson*, 41
1981	Mumphrey, .307	Winfield, 114	Winfield, 25	Mumphrey, 5	Jackson, Nettles, 15

BATTING LEADERS

YEAR BY YEAR

RBIs	Runs	Stolen Bases
Keller, 101	Keller, 98	Stirnweiss, 18
Henrich, 98	Henrich, 109	Rizzuto, 11
DiMaggio*, 155	Henrich*, 138	Rizzuto, 6
Berra, 91	Rizzuto, 110	Rizzuto, 18
Berra, 124	Rizzuto, 125	Rizzuto, 12
Berra, 88	Berra, 92	Rizzuto, 18
Berra, 98	Berra, 97	Rizzuto, 17
Berra, 108	Mantle, 105	Mantle, 8
Berra, 125	Mantle*, 129	Mantle, Carey, 5
Berra, 108	Mantle, 121	Hunter, 9
Mantle*, 130	Mantle*, 132	Mantle, 10
Mantle, 94	Mantle*, 121	Mantle, 16
Mantle, 97	Mantle*, 127	Mantle, 18
Lopez, 93	Mantle, 104	Mantle, 21
Maris*, 112	Mantle*, 119	Mantle, 14
Maris*, 142	Mantle*, Maris*, 132	Mantle, 12
Maris, 100	Richardson, 99	Richardson, 11
Pepitone, 89	Tresh, 91	Richardson, 15
Mantle, 111	Mantle, 92	Tresh, 13
Tresh, 74	Tresh, 94	Richardson, 7
Pepitone, 83	Pepitone, 85	White, 14
Pepitone, 64	Clarke, 74	Clarke, 21
White, 62	White, 89	Clarke, White, 20
Murcer, 82	Clarke, Murcer, 82	Clarke, 33
White, 94	White, 109	White, 24
Murcer, 94	Murcer, 94	Clarke, 17
Murcer, 96	Murcer*, 102	White, 23
Murcer, 95	White, 88	White, 16
Murcer, 88	Maddox, 75	White, 15
Munson, 102	Bonds, 93	Bonds, 30
Munson, 105	White*, 104	Rivers, 43
Jackson, 110	Nettles, 99	Rivers, 22
Jackson, 97	Randolph, 87	Randolph, 36
Jackson, 89	Randolph, 98	Randolph, 32
Jackson, 111	Randolph, 99	Randolph, 30
Winfield, 68	Randolph, 59	Randolph, 14

*Led league.

Roy White.

ALL-TIME BATTING LEADERS

	Games			At Bats			Runs			RBIs	
1.	Mantle	2401		Mantle	8102		Ruth	1959		Gehrig	1991
2.	Gehrig	2164		Gehrig	8001		Gehrig	1888		Ruth	1970
3.	Berra	2116		Berra	7546		Mantle	1677		DiMaggio	1537
4.	Ruth	2084		Ruth	7217		DiMaggio	1390		Mantle	1509
5.	White	1881		DiMaggio	6821		Combs	1186		Berra	1430
6.	Dickey	1789		White	6650		Berra	1174		Dickey	1209
7.	DiMaggio	1736		Dickey	6300		Crosetti	1006		Lazzeri	1154
8.	Crosetti	1682		Crosetti	6277		White	964		Meusel	1005
9.	Rizzuto	1661		Lazzeri	6094		Lazzeri	952		Pipp	825
10.	Lazzeri	1659		Rizzuto	5816		Rolfe	942		Henrich	795
11.	Howard	1492		Combs	5748		Dickey	930		White	758
12.	Pipp	1488		Pipp	5594		Henrich	901		Howard	732
13.	Combs	1455		Richardson	5386		Rizzuto	877		Keller	723
14.	Munson	1423		Munson	5344		Pipp	820		Nettles	704
15.	Richardson	1412		Howard	5044		Bauer	792		Munson	701
16.	Bauer	1406		Meusel	5032		Meusel	764		Skowron	672
17.	McDougald	1336		Rolfe	4827		Keller	714		Murcer	656
18.	Meusel	1294		Bauer	4784		McDougald	697		Bauer	654
19.	Henrich	1284		Clarke	4723		Munson	696		Crosetti	649
20.	Nettles	1284		McDougald	4676		Peckinpaugh	670		Combs	629

	Hits			Doubles			Triples			Home Runs	
1.	Gehrig	2721		Gehrig	535		Gehrig	162		Ruth	659
2.	Ruth	2518		Ruth	424		Combs	154		Mantle	536
3.	Mantle	2415		DiMaggio	389		DiMaggio	131		Gehrig	493
4.	DiMaggio	2214		Mantle	344		Pipp	121		DiMaggio	361
5.	Berra	2148		Dickey	343		Lazzeri	115		Berra	358
6.	Dickey	1969		Meusel	338		Ruth	106		Nettles	212
7.	Combs	1866		Lazzeri	327		Meusel	87		Maris	203
8.	White	1803		Berra	321		Henrich	73		Dickey	202
9.	Lazzeri	1784		Combs	309		Mantle	72		Keller	184
10.	Rizzuto	1588		White	300		Dickey	72		Henrich	183
11.	Pipp	1577		Henrich	269		Keller	69		Lazzeri	169
12.	Meusel	1565		Crosetti	260		Rolfe	67		Murcer	167
13.	Munson	1558		Pipp	259		Stirnweiss	66		Pepitone	166
14.	Crosetti	1541		Rolfe	257		Crosetti	65		Skowron	165
15.	Richardson	1432		Rizzuto	239		Chapman	64		Howard	161
16.	Howard	1405		Munson	229		Rizzuto	62		White	160
17.	Rolfe	1394		Howard	211		Cree	62		Bauer	158
18.	Bauer	1326		Bauer	211		Conroy	59		Gordon	153
19.	Henrich	1297		Chapman	209		Bauer	56		Meusel	146
20.	McDougald	1291		Richardson	196		Peckinpaugh	53		Tresh	140

BATTING AVERAGE *(500 or more games)*

1.	Ruth	.349	11.	Lazzeri	.293
2.	Gehrig	.340	12.	Munson	.292
3.	DiMaggio	.325	13.	Selkirk	.290
4.	Combs	.325	14.	Rolfe	.289
5.	Dickey	.312	15T.	Keller	.285
6.	Meusel	.311	15T.	Berra	.285
7.	Chapman	.305	17.	Chase	.284
8.	Mantle	.298	18T.	Pipp	.282
9.	Schang	.297	18T.	Henrich	.282
10.	Skowron	.294	20.	Murcer	.281

TOP TEN, SINGLE SEASON

At Bats

Richardson	692	1962
Clarke	686	1970
Richardson	679	1964
Richardson	664	1965
Richardson	662	1961
Crosetti	656	1939
Combs	648	1927
Rolfe	648	1939
Dugan	644	1923
Stirnweiss	643	1944

Batting Average

Ruth	.393	1923
DiMaggio	.381	1939
Gehrig	.379	1930
Ruth	.378	1921
Ruth	.378	1924
Ruth	.376	1920
Gehrig	.374	1928
Gehrig	.373	1927
Ruth	.373	1931
Ruth	.372	1925

Hits

Combs	231	1927
Gehrig	220	1930
Gehrig	218	1927
DiMaggio	215	1937
Rolfe	213	1939
Gehrig	211	1931
Gehrig	210	1928
Gehrig	210	1934
Richardson	209	1962
Gehrig	208	1932

Doubles

Gehrig	52	1927
Gehrig	47	1926
Gehrig	47	1928
Meusel	47	1927
Rolfe	46	1939
Ruth	45	1923
Meusel	45	1928
Ruth	44	1921
DiMaggio	44	1936
DiMaggio	43	1941

Triples

Combs	23	1927
Combs	22	1930
Stirnweiss	22	1945
Cree	22	1911
Combs	21	1928
Gehrig	20	1926
Pipp	19	1924
Gehrig	18	1927
Gehrig	17	1930
Four tied	16	

Home Runs

Maris	61	1961
Ruth	60	1927
Ruth	59	1921
Ruth	54	1928
Ruth	54	1920
Mantle	54	1961
Mantle	52	1956
Ruth	49	1930
Gehrig	49	1934
Gehrig	49	1936

Total Bases

Ruth	457	1921
Gehrig	447	1927
Gehrig	419	1931
DiMaggio	418	1937
Ruth	417	1927
Gehrig	410	1931
Gehrig	409	1934
Gehrig	403	1936
Ruth	399	1923
Ruth	391	1924

Runs

Ruth	177	1921
Gehrig	167	1936
Ruth	163	1928
Gehrig	163	1931
Ruth	158	1920
Ruth	158	1927
Ruth	151	1923
DiMaggio	151	1937
Ruth	150	1930
Gehrig	149	1927
Ruth	149	1931

Runs Batted In

Gehrig	184	1931
Gehrig	175	1927
Gehrig	174	1930
Ruth	170	1921
DiMaggio	167	1937
Gehrig	165	1934
Ruth	164	1927
Ruth	163	1931
Gehrig	159	1937
Ruth	155	1926
DiMaggio	155	1948

Strikeouts *(Batter)*

Bonds	137	1975
Jackson	133	1978
Jackson	129	1977
Mantle	126	1959
Mantle	125	1960
Jackson	122	1980
Mantle	120	1958
Mantle	111	1952
Mantle	107	1954
Jackson	107	1979

Hitting Streaks

DiMaggio	56	1941
Peckinpaugh	29	1919
Combs	29	1931
Gordon	29	1942
Chase	27	1907
Ruth	26	1921
DiMaggio	23	1940
DiMaggio	22	1937
DiMaggio	20	1937
Hassett	20	1942
Rivers	20	1976

Walks

Ruth	170	1923
Ruth	148	1920
Mantle	146	1957
Ruth	144	1921
Ruth	144	1926
Ruth	142	1924
Ruth	138	1927
Ruth	136	1930
Ruth	135	1928
Gehrig	132	1935

Stolen Bases

Maisel	74	1914
Chapman	61	1931
Stirnweiss	55	1944
Maisel	51	1915
Cree	48	1911
Fultz	44	1905
Rivers	43	1976
Hemphill	42	1908
Conroy	41	1907
Daniels	41	1910

Games Pitched

Lyle	72	1977
Lyle	66	1974
Arroyo	65	1961
Ramos	65	1965
Womack	65	1967
Gossage	64	1980
Lyle	64	1976
Gossage	63	1978
McDaniel	62	1970
Page	60	1949

Complete Games

Chesbro	48	1904
Powell	38	1904
Orth	36	1906
Chesbro	33	1903
R. Ford	32	1912
Mays	30	1921
Hunter	30	1975
R. Ford	29	1910
Orth	26	1905
Mays	26	1920

Victories

Chesbro	41	1904
Orth	27	1906
Mays	27	1921
R. Ford	26	1910
Mays	26	1920
Bush	26	1922
Gomez	26	1934
Guidry	25	1978
W. Ford	25	1961
Chesbro	24	1906
Shawkey	24	1916
Pipgras	24	1928
W. Ford	24	1963

Saves

Lyle	35	1972
Gossage	33	1980
Arroyo	29	1961
McDaniel	29	1970
Gossage	27	1978
Lyle	27	1973
Page	27	1949
Lyle	26	1977
Lyle	23	1976
Sain	22	1954

Shutouts

Guidry	9	1978
R. Ford	8	1910
W. Ford	8	1964
Reynolds	7	1951
W. Ford	7	1958
Stottlemyre	7	1971
Stottlemyre	7	1972
Hunter	7	1975
Thirteen tied	6	

Strikeouts

Guidry	248	1978
Chesbro	239	1904
Downing	217	1964
Turley	210	1955
R. Ford	209	1910
W. Ford	209	1961
Powell	202	1904
Guidry	201	1979
Ruffing	194	1937
Ruffing	190	1932

Earned Run Average

Chandler	1.64	1943
R. Ford	1.65	1910
Guidry	1.74	1978
Chesbro	1.82	1904
Vaughn	1.83	1910
Lake	1.88	1909
Caldwell	1.94	1914
W. Ford	2.01	1958
Cullop	2.05	1916
Bahnsen	2.06	1968

ALL-TIME STOLEN-BASE LEADERS

1.	Chase	248	11.	Daniels	145
2.	White	233	12.	Peckinpaugh	143
3.	Chapman	184	13.	Cree	132
4.	Conroy	184	14.	Meusel	131
5.	Maisel	183	15.	Stirnweiss	130
6.	Mantle	153	16.	Keeler	118
7.	Clarke	151	17.	Pipp	114
8.	Rizzuto	149	18.	Crosetti	113
9.	Randolph	148	19.	Ruth	110
10.	Lazzeri	147	20.	Gehrig	102

HOME RUNS

60 Home Runs in a Season

61	Roger Maris, 1961*
60	Babe Ruth, 1927*

50 Home Runs in a Season

59	Babe Ruth, 1921*
54	Babe Ruth, 1920*
	Babe Ruth, 1928*
	Mickey Mantle, 1961
52	Mickey Mantle, 1956*

40 Home Runs in a Season

49	Babe Ruth, 1930†
	Lou Gehrig, 1934*
	Lou Gehrig, 1936*
47	Babe Ruth, 1926*
	Lou Gehrig, 1927
46	Babe Ruth, 1924*
	Babe Ruth, 1929*
	Babe Ruth, 1931**
	Lou Gehrig, 1931**
	Joe DiMaggio, 1937*
42	Mickey Mantle, 1958†
41	Babe Ruth, 1923*
	Lou Gehrig, 1930
	Babe Ruth, 1932
	Reggie Jackson, 1980‡
40	Mickey Mantle, 1960†

30 Home Runs in a Season

39	Joe DiMaggio, 1948†
	Roger Maris, 1960
37	Lou Gehrig, 1937
	Mickey Mantle, 1955†
	Graig Nettles, 1977
35	Babe Ruth, 1922
	Lou Gehrig, 1929
	Mickey Mantle, 1964
34	Lou Gehrig, 1932
	Babe Ruth, 1933
	Mickey Mantle, 1957
33	Bob Meusel, 1925†
	Charlie Keller, 1941
	Roger Maris, 1962
	Bobby Murcer, 1972
32	Lou Gehrig, 1933
	Joe DiMaggio, 1938
	Joe DiMaggio, 1950
	Graig Nettles, 1976†
	Reggie Jackson, 1977
31	Joe DiMaggio, 1940
	Tommy Henrich, 1941
	Charlie Keller, 1943
	Mickey Mantle, 1959
	Joe Pepitone, 1966
30	Lou Gehrig, 1935
	Joe DiMaggio, 1939
	Joe Gordon, 1940
	Joe DiMaggio, 1941
	Charlie Keller, 1946
	Mickey Mantle, 1962

20 Home Runs in a Season

29	Bill Dickey, 1937
	Lou Gehrig, 1938
	Reggie Jackson, 1979
28	Joe Gordon, 1939
	Yogi Berra, 1950
	Bill Skowron, 1961
	Elston Howard, 1963
	Joe Pepitone, 1964
27	Lou Gehrig, 1928
	Bill Dickey, 1938
	Yogi Berra, 1951
	Yogi Berra, 1953
	Mickey Mantle, 1954
	Yogi Berra, 1955
	Reggie Jackson, 1978
	Graig Nettles, 1978
26	Charlie Keller, 1942
	Hank Bauer, 1956
	Bill Skowron, 1960
	Roger Maris, 1964
	Tom Tresh, 1965
	Bobby Murcer, 1969
25	Babe Ruth, 1925
	Joe Gordon, 1938
	Joe DiMaggio, 1946
	Tommy Henrich, 1948
	Johnny Mize, 1950
	Tom Tresh, 1963
	Bobby Murcer, 1971
24	Bob Meusel, 1921
	Bill Dickey, 1939
	Joe Gordon, 1941
	Tommy Henrich, 1949
	Yogi Berra, 1957
23	Mickey Mantle, 1952
	Bill Skowron, 1956
	Bill Skowron, 1962
	Roger Maris, 1963
	Mickey Mantle, 1966
	Bobby Murcer, 1970
	Jim Spencer, 1979
22	Babe Ruth, 1934
	Tommy Henrich, 1938
	Nick Etten, 1944†
	Yogi Berra, 1954
	Yogi Berra, 1958
	Yogi Berra, 1961
	Mickey Mantle, 1967
	Roy White, 1970
	Graig Nettles, 1973
	Bobby Murcer, 1973
	Graig Nettles, 1974
21	George Selkirk, 1939
	Charlie Keller, 1940
	Joe DiMaggio, 1942
	Mickey Mantle, 1953
	Elston Howard, 1961
	Johnny Blanchard, 1961
20	Graig Nettles, 1975
	Lou Gehrig, 1925
	Joe DiMaggio, 1947
	Yogi Berra, 1949
	Hank Bauer, 1955
	Tom Tresh, 1962
	Thurman Munson, 1973
	Graig Nettles, 1979

*Led major leagues.
**Shared majors' lead.
†Led American League.
‡Shared league lead.

4 Home Runs in a Game

Lou Gehrig, 1932*

*Consecutive.
(Gehrig was the first player in modern major league history to hit four homers in a game.)

4 Consecutive Home Runs

Lou Gehrig, 1932
Johnny Blanchard, 1961
Mickey Mantle, 1963
Bobby Murcer, 1970
Reggie Jackson, 1977 (WS)

(WS) World Series.

3 Home Runs in a Game

Babe Ruth 1926 (WS)	Charlie Keller, 1940
Tony Lazzeri, 1927	Joe DiMaggio, 1948*
Lou Gehrig, 1927	Joe DiMaggio, 1950
Babe Ruth, 1928 (WS)*	Johnny Mize, 1950*
Lou Gehrig, 1929	Mickey Mantle, 1955
Babe Ruth, 1930	Tom Tresh, 1965*
Lou Gehrig, 1930	Bobby Murcer, 1970*†
Ben Chapman, 1932	Bobby Murcer, 1973
Tony Lazzeri, 1936	Cliff Johnson, 1977
Joe DiMaggio, 1937	Reggie Jackson, 1977 (WS)*‡
Bill Dickey, 1939	

*Consecutive.
†Murcer's three home runs in the second game of a Yankee Stadium doubleheader against the Indians followed a homer in his last at-bat in the opener, tieing him for the major league record of hitting home runs in four consecutive official times at bat.
‡Jackson's three home runs against the Dodgers, interrupted only by a walk, at Yankee Stadium in Game 6 of the World Series, followed a homer in his final at-bat in Game 5 at Los Angeles. So Jackson hit a Series record four home runs in four successive official trips.
(WS) World Series.

2 Home Runs in a Game

Babe Ruth, 72 times*
Mickey Mantle, 46 times
Lou Gehrig, 43 times
Joe DiMaggio, 35 times

All-time major league leader, nine more than runner-up Willie Mays.

Switch-Hitting Home Runs in a Game

Mickey Mantle	10 times
Roy White	5 times
Tom Tresh	3 times

2 Home Runs in One Inning

Joe DiMaggio	1936
Joe Pepitone	1962
Cliff Johnson	1977

2 Consecutive Pinch-Hit Home Runs

Ray Caldwell	1915
Charlie Keller	1948
Johnny Blanchard	1961
Ray Barker	1965

Most Home Runs in a Month

Babe Ruth, 17 (September 1927)
Mickey Mantle, 16 (May 1956)

(Ruth hit 15 homers in a month three other times, Joe DiMaggio once and Roger Maris once.)

Most Career Grand-Slam Home Runs

Lou Gehrig*	23
Babe Ruth	16
Joe DiMaggio	13
Yogi Berra	9
Mickey Mantle	9
Bill Dickey	8
Tony Lazzeri	8
Charlie Keller	7
Joe Pepitone	7

All-time major league leader, five more than runner-up Willie McCovey.
Notes: Babe Ruth twice hit grand slams on consecutive days.
Four Yankee pitchers have hit grand slams: Red Ruffing (1933), Spud Chandler (1940), Don Larsen (1956) and Mel Stottlemyre (1965).

Home Run in First Major League At-Bat

John Miller, 1966

Home Runs in First Two Major League Games

Joe Lefebvre, 1980

Landmark Home Runs in New Yankee Stadium
Into center-field bleachers:

Ken Singleton, Orioles,	1977	
Reggie Jackson, Yankees	1977*	
Reggie Jackson, Yankees	1981	

World Series

Into bullpen:

Dan Ford, Twins	1976
Thurman Munson, Yankees	1976
Doug DeCinces, Orioles	1978
Thurman Munson, Yankees	1978*
Jim Rice, Red Sox	1979
Greg Luzkinsi, White Sox	1981

American League Championship Series.

MISCELLANEOUS CLUB RECORDS

200 Hits in Rookie Season

Earle Combs, 203	1925
Joe DiMaggio, 206	1936

Most Hits in a Game

Myril Hoag, 6	1934

Most Singles in a Game

Myril Hoag, 6	1934

Most Doubles in a Game

Johnny Lindell, 4	1944
Jim Mason, 4	1974

Most Triples in a Game

Hal Chase, 3	1906
Earle Combs, 3	1927
Joe DiMaggio, 3	1938

Most Total Bases in a Game

Lou Gehrig, 16	1932

Most RBIs in a Game

Tony Lazzeri, 11	1936

Hitting for the Cycle

Bob Meusel (twice)
Lou Gehrig (twice)
Joe DiMaggio (twice)
Bert Daniels
Tony Lazzeri
Joe Gordon
Buddy Rosar
Mickey Mantle
Bobby Murcer

Elston Howard in the 1964 World Series.

BABE RUTH'S RECORD 60 HOME RUNS IN 1927 *(Yankees played a 154-game schedule plus a tie game on April 14)*

Home Run	Yankee Game	Ruth's Game	Date	Inning	Opponent	Pitcher
1	4	4	April 15	1	Philadelphia	Ehmke
2	11	11	April 23	1	at Philadelphia	Walberg (L)
3	12	12	April 24	6	at Washington	Thurston
4	14	14	April 29	5	at Boston	Harriss
5	16	16	May 1	1	Philadelphia	Quinn
6	16	16	May 1	8	Philadelphia	Walberg (L)
7	24	24	May 10	1	at St. Louis	Gaston
8	25	25	May 11	1	at St. Louis	Nevers
9	29	29	May 17	8	at Detroit	Collins
10	33	33	May 22	6	at Cleveland	Karr
11	34	34	May 23	1	at Washington	Thurston
12	37	37	May 28	7	Washington	Thurston
13	39	39	May 29	8	Boston	MacFayden
14	41	41	May 30	11	at Philadelphia	Walberg (L)
15	42	42	May 31	1	at Philadelphia	Quinn
16	43	43	May 31	5	at Philadelphia	Ehmke
17	47	47	June 5	6	Detroit	Whitehill (L)
18	48	48	June 7	4	Chicago	Thomas
19	52	52	June 11	3	Cleveland	Buckeye (L)
20	52	52	June 11	5	Cleveland	Buckeye (L)
21	53	53	June 12	7	Cleveland	Uhle
22	55	55	June 16	1	St. Louis	Zachary (L)
23	60	60	June 22	5	at Boston	Wiltse (L)
24	60	60	June 22	7	at Boston	Wiltse (L)
25	70	66	June 30	4	Boston	Harriss
26	73	69	July 3	1	at Washington	Lisenbee
27	78	74	July 8	2	at Detroit	Hankins
28	79	75	July 9	1	at Detroit	Holloway
29	79	75	July 9	4	at Detroit	Holloway
30	83	79	July 12	9	at Cleveland	Shaute (L)
31	94	90	July 24	3	at Chicago	Thomas
32	95	91	July 26	1	St. Louis	Gaston
33	95	91	July 26	6	St. Louis	Gaston
34	98	94	July 28	8	St. Louis	Stewart (L)
35	106	102	August 5	8	Detroit	Smith
36	110	106	August 10	3	at Washington	Zachary (L)
37	114	110	August 16	5	at Chicago	Thomas
38	115	111	August 17	11	at Chicago	Connally
39	118	114	August 20	1	at Cleveland	Miller (L)
40	120	116	August 22	6	at Cleveland	Shaute (L)
41	124	120	August 27	8	at St. Louis	Nevers
42	125	121	August 28	1	at St. Louis	Wingard (L)
43	127	123	August 31	8	Boston	Welzer
44	128	124	September 2	1	at Philadelphia	Walberg (L)
45	132	128	September 6	6	at Boston	Welzer
46	132	128	September 6	7	at Boston	Welzer
47	133	129	September 6	9	at Boston	Russell

Home Run	Yankee Game	Ruth's Game	Date	Inning	Opponent	Pitcher
48	134	130	September 7	1	at Boston	MacFayden
49	134	130	September 7	8	at Boston	Harriss
50	138	134	September 11	4	St. Louis	Gaston
51	139	135	September 13	7	Cleveland	Hudlin
52	140	136	September 13	4	Cleveland	Shaute (L)
53	143	139	September 16	3	Chicago	Blankenship
54	147	143	September 18	5	Chicago	Lyons
55	148	144	September 21	9	Detroit	Gibson
56	149	145	September 22	9	Detroit	Holloway
57	152	148	September 27	6	Philadelphia	Grove (L)
58	153	149	September 29	1	Washington	Lisenbee
59	153	149	September 29	5	Washington	Hopkins
60	154	150	September 30	8	Washington	Zachary (L)

(L) Indicates lefthanded pitcher.

Notes: Ruth's 60th home run came on the second-last game of the Yankees' regular-season schedule. In the final game, on Oct. 1, Ruth went hitless in three at-bats.

A lefthanded batter, Ruth hit 41 of his homers off righthanded pitchers, 19 off lefthanders.

Ruth hit 28 of his home runs at Yankee Stadium, 32 on the road: 8 in Boston, 5 in Philadelphia, 4 each in Cleveland, Detroit, St. Louis and Washington, and 3 in Chicago.

Ruth's homers by month: 4 in April, 12 in May, 9 each in June, July and August, and 17 in September.

Ruth had eight two-homer games.

All 60 of Ruth's home runs were hit in day games, there being no night baseball in the majors during his playing career.

ROGER MARIS'S RECORD 61 HOME RUNS IN 1962 *(Yankees played a 162-game schedule plus a tie game on April 22)*

Home Run	Yankee Game	Maris' Game	Date	Inning	Opponent	Pitcher
1	11	11	April 26	5	at Detroit	Foytack
2	17	17	May 3	7	at Minnesota	Ramos
3	20	20	May 6 (N)	5	at Los Angeles	Grba
4	29	29	May 17	8	Washington	Burnside (L)
5	30	30	May 19 (N)	1	at Cleveland	Perry
6	31	31	May 20	3	at Cleveland	Bell
7	32	32	May 21	1	Baltimore	Estrada
8	35	35	May 24	4	Boston	Conley
9	38	38	May 28	2	Chicago	McLish
10	40	40	May 30	6	at Boston	Conley
11	40	40	May 30	8	at Boston	Fornieles
12	41	41	May 31 (N)	3	at Boston	Muffett
13	43	43	June 2 (N)	3	at Chicago	McLish
14	44	44	June 3	8	at Chicago	Shaw
15	45	45	June 4	3	at Chicago	Kemmerer
16	48	48	June 6 (N)	6	Minnesota	Palmquist
17	49	49	June 7	3	Minnesota	Ramos
18	52	52	June 9 (N)	7	Kansas City	Herbert
19	55	55	June 11	3	Los Angeles	Grba
20	55	55	June 11	7	Los Angeles	James
21	57	57	June 13 (N)	6	at Cleveland	Perry
22	58	58	June 14 (N)	4	at Cleveland	Bell
23	61	61	June 17 (N)	4	at Detroit	Mossi (L)
24	62	62	June 18	8	at Detroit	Casale
25	63	63	June 19 (N)	9	at Kansas City	Archer (L)

Home Run	Yankee Game	Maris' Game	Date	Inning	Opponent	Pitcher
26	64	64	June 20 (N)	1	at Kansas City	Nuxhall (L)
27	66	66	June 22 (N)	2	at Kansas City	Bass
28	74	74	July 1	9	Washington	Sisler
29	75	75	July 2	3	Washington	Burnside (L)
30	75	75	July 2	7	Washington	Klippstein
31	77	77	July 4	8	Detroit	Lary
32	78	78	July 5	7	Cleveland	Funk
33	82	82	July 9	7	Boston	Monbouquette
34	84	84	July 13 (N)	1	at Chicago	Wynn
35	86	86	July 15	3	at Chicago	Herbert
36	92	92	July 21 (N)	1	at Boston	Monbouquette
37	95	95	July 25 (N)	4	Chicago	Baumann (L)
38	95	95	July 25 (N)	8	Chicago	Larsen
39	96	96	July 25 (N)	4	Chicago	Kemmerer
40	96	96	July 25 (N)	6	Chicago	Hacker
41	106	105	August 4 (N)	1	Minnesota	Pascual
42	114	113	August 11 (N)	5	at Washington	Burnside (L)
43	115	114	August 12	4	at Washington	Donovan
44	116	115	August 13	4	at Washington	Daniels
45	117	116	August 13	1	at Washington	Kutyna
46	118	117	August 15 (N)	4	Chicago	Pizarro (L)
47	119	118	August 16	1	Chicago	Pierce (L)
48	119	118	August 16	3	Chicago	Pierce (L)
49	123	122	August 20	3	at Cleveland	Perry
50	125	124	August 22 (N)	6	at Los Angeles	McBride
51	129	128	August 26	6	at Kansas City	Walker
52	135	134	September 2	6	Detroit	Lary
53	135	134	September 2	8	Detroit	Aguirre (L)
54	140	139	September 6	4	Washington	Cheney
55	141	140	September 7 (N)	3	Cleveland	Stigman (L)
56	143	142	September 9	7	Cleveland	Grant
57	151	150	September 16	3	at Detroit	Lary
58	152	151	September 17	12	at Detroit	Fox
59	155	154	September 20 (N)	3	at Baltimore	Pappas
60	159	158	September 26 (N)	3	Baltimore	Fisher
61	163	161	October 1	4	Boston	Stallard

(L) Indicates lefthanded pitcher.

Notes: Maris's 61st home run came on the final game of the Yankees' regular-season schedule.

A left-handed batter, Maris hit 49 of his homers off righthanded pitchers, 12 off lefthanders.

Maris hit 30 of his home runs at Yankee Stadium, 31 on the road: 5 each in Chicago, Cleveland and Detroit, 4 each in Boston, Kansas City and Washington, 2 in Los Angeles, and 1 each in Baltimore and Bloomington, Minnesota.

Maris' homers by month: one in April, 11 in May, 15 in June, 13 in July, 11 in August, 9 in September and one in October.

Maris had seven two-homer games.

Thirty-six of Maris's home runs were hit during day games, 25 during night games.

JOE DIMAGGIO'S RECORD BATTING STREAK *(56 Consecutive Games, May 15–July 16, 1941)*

Date	Opposing Team and Pitcher	AB	R	H	2B	3B	HR	RBI
May 15	Chicago—Smith (L)	4	0	1	0	0	0	1
May 16	Chicago—Lee (L)	4	2	2	0	1	1	1
May 17	Chicago—Rigney	3	1	1	0	0	0	0
May 18	St. Louis—Harris (2), Niggeling (1)	3	3	3	1	0	0	1
May 19	St. Louis—Galehouse	3	0	1	1	0	0	0
May 20	St. Louis—Auker	5	1	1	0	0	0	1
May 21	Detroit—Rowe (1), Benton (1)	5	0	2	0	0	0	1
May 22	Detroit—McKain (L)	4	0	1	0	0	0	1
May 23	Boston—Newsome	5	0	1	0	0	0	2
May 24	Boston—Johnson (L)	4	2	1	0	0	0	2
May 25	Boston—Grove (L)	4	0	1	0	0	0	0
May 27	at Washington—Chase (L) (1), Anderson (2), Carrasquel (1)	5	3	4	0	0	1	3
May 28	at Washington—Hudson (night)	4	1	1	0	1	0	0
May 29	at Washington—Sundra	3	1	1	0	0	0	0
May 30	at Boston—Johnson (L)	2	1	1	0	0	0	0
May 30	at Boston—Harris (L)	3	0	1	1	0	0	0
June 1	at Cleveland—Milnar (L)	4	1	1	0	0	0	0
June 1	at Cleveland—Harder	4	0	1	0	0	0	0
June 2	at Cleveland—Feller	4	2	2	1	0	0	0
June 3	at Detroit—Trout	4	1	1	0	0	1	1
June 5	at Detroit—Newhouser (L)	5	1	1	0	1	0	1
June 7	at St. Louis—Muncrief (1), Allen (1), Caster (1)	5	2	3	0	0	0	1
June 8	at St. Louis—Auker	4	3	2	0	0	2	4
June 8	at St. Louis—Caster (1), Kramer (1)	4	1	2	1	0	1	3
June 10	at Chicago—Rigney	5	1	1	0	0	0	0
June 12	at Chicago—Lee (L) (night)	4	1	2	0	0	1	1
June 14	Cleveland—Feller	2	0	1	1	0	0	1
June 15	Cleveland—Bagby	3	1	1	0	0	1	1
June 16	Cleveland—Milnar (L)	5	0	1	1	0	0	0
June 17	Chicago—Rigney	4	1	1	0	0	0	0
June 18	Chicago—Lee (L)	3	0	1	0	0	0	0
June 19	Chicago—Smith (L) (1), Ross (2)	3	2	3	0	0	1	2
June 20	Detroit—Newsom (2), McKain (L) (2)	5	3	4	1	0	0	1
June 21	Detroit—Trout	4	0	1	0	0	0	1
June 22	Detroit—Newhouser (L) (1), Newsom (1)	5	1	2	1	0	1	2
June 24	St. Louis—Muncrief	4	1	1	0	0	0	0
June 25	St. Louis—Galehouse	4	1	1	0	0	1	3
June 26	St. Louis—Auker	4	0	1	1	0	0	1
June 27	at Philadelphia—Dean (L)	3	1	2	0	0	1	2
June 28	at Philadelphia—Babich (1), Harris (1)	5	1	2	1	0	0	0
June 29	at Washington—Leonard	4	1	1	1	0	0	0
June 29	at Washington—Anderson	5	1	1	0	0	0	1
July 1	Boston—Harris (L) (1), Ryba (1)	4	0	2	0	0	0	1
July 1	Boston—Wilson	3	1	1	0	0	0	1
July 2	Boston—Newsome	5	1	1	0	0	1	3
July 5	Philadelphia—Marchildon	4	2	1	0	0	1	2
July 6	Philadelphia—Babich (1), Hadley (3)	5	2	4	1	0	0	2
July 6	Philadelphia—Knott	4	0	2	0	1	0	2

Date	Opposing Team and Pitcher	AB	R	H	2B	3B	HR	RBI
July 10	at St. Louis—Niggeling (night)	2	0	1	0	0	0	0
July 11	at St. Louis—Harris (3), Kramer (1)	5	1	4	0	0	1	2
July 12	at St. Louis—Auker (1), Muncrief (1)	5	1	2	1	0	0	1
July 13	at Chicago—Lyons (2), Hallet (1)	4	2	3	0	0	0	0
July 13	at Chicago—Lee (L)	4	0	1	0	0	0	0
July 14	at Chicago—Rigney	3	0	1	0	0	0	0
July 15	at Chicago—Smith (L)	4	1	2	1	0	0	2
July 16	at Cleveland—Milnar (L) (2), Krakauskas (L) (1)	4	3	3	1	0	0	0
	Totals (Batting Ave.: .408 Pct.) .223		56	91	16	4	15	55

(L) Indicates lefthanded pitcher.

Notes: DiMaggio's streak was halted on July 17 at Cleveland in a night game won by the Yankees, 4–3. He hit the ball hard on the ground all three official at-bats and was walked once.

DiMaggio was thrown out in the first and seventh innings on sparkling plays by third baseman Ken Keltner on balls drilled off lefthander Al Smith, who walked him in the fourth. And batting against righthander Jim Bagby Jr. in the eighth inning, DiMaggio ripped one of the hardest grounders of his career, he would reflect years later; but shortstop Lou Boudreau turned it into a double play despite a last-instant bad hop.

A righthanded batter, DiMaggio hit safely against 63 righthanded pitchers and 28 left-handers while totaling 91 hits in the 56 games.

Of the 56 games, 53 were during the day and 3 at night.

DiMaggio hit safely in 29 games in Yankee Stadium, 27 on the road.

DiMaggio did not attempt to bunt his way on base during his streak and struck out only seven times in 223 official at-bats—246 trips to the plate including being hit by pitches twice and walked 21 times.

During the streak the Yankees won 41, tied 2 and lost 13—a .759 clip that promoted them from fourth place, 5½ games behind Cleveland, to first place, 6 games ahead of the Indians.

The day after DiMaggio's streak ended, he began another that lasted 16 games before being stopped by St. Louis Browns knuckleballer Johnny Niggeling. It was the first time in 84 games since May 2 that DiMaggio had failed to reach base and only the second time in 74 games that he failed to hit safely.

DiMaggio went on to hit .357 for the season, second only to his .381 of 1939 in his 13-year Yankee career.

DON LARSEN'S PERFECT GAME 5 OF 1956 WORLD SERIES

MONDAY, OCTOBER 8, AT YANKEE STADIUM

Dodgers	AB	R	H	O	A	E	Yankees	AB	R	H	O	A	E
Gilliam, 2b	3	0	0	2	0	0	Bauer, rf	4	0	1	4	0	0
Reese, ss	3	0	0	4	2	0	Collins, 1b	4	0	1	7	0	0
Snider, cf	3	0	0	1	0	0	Mantle, cf	3	1	1	4	0	0
Robinson, 3b	3	0	0	2	4	0	Berra, c	3	0	0	7	0	0
Hodges, 1b	3	0	0	5	1	0	Slaughter, lf	2	0	0	1	0	0
Amoros, lf	3	0	0	3	0	0	Martin, 2b	3	0	1	3	4	0
Furillo, rf	3	0	0	0	0	0	McDougald, ss	2	0	0	0	2	0
Campanella, c	3	0	0	7	2	0	Carey, 3b	3	1	1	1	1	0
Maglie, p	2	0	0	0	1	0	Larsen, p	2	0	0	0	1	0
ᵃMitchell	1	0	0	0	0	0	Totals	26	2	5	27	8	0
Totals	27	0	0	24	10	0							

```
Dodgers    000   000   000   0
Yankees     000   101   00X   2
```

ᵃCalled out on strikes for Maglie in ninths. Runs batted in—Mantle, Bauer. Home run—Mantle. Sacrifice hit—Larsen. Double plays—Reese and Hodges; Hodges, Campanella, Robinson, Campanella and Robinson. Left on bases—Brooklyn 0, New York 3. Earned runs—New York 2, Brooklyn 0. Bases on balls—Off Maglie 2. Struck out—By Larsen 7, by Maglie 5. Winning pitcher—Larsen. Losing pitcher—Maglie. Umpires—Pinelli (N. L.), Soar (A. L.), Boggess (N. L.), Napp (A. L.), Gorman (N. L.), Runge (A. L.). Time—2:06. Attendance—64,519.

Note: The game stands not only as the lone perfect game in World Series history, but the only no-hitter.

BILL BEVEN'S NEAR NO-HITTER IN GAME 4 OF 1947 WORLD SERIES

FRIDAY, OCTOBER 3, AT EBBETS FIELD, BROOKLYN

Yankees	AB	R	H	O	A	E
Stirnweiss, 2b	4	1	2	2	1	0
Henrich, rf	5	0	1	2	0	0
Berra, c	4	0	0	6	1	1
DiMaggio, cf	2	0	0	2	0	0
McQuinn, 1b	4	0	1	7	0	0
Johnson, 3b	4	1	1	3	2	0
Lindell, lf	3	0	2	3	0	0
Rizzuto, ss	4	0	1	1	2	0
Bevens, p	3	0	0	0	1	0
Totals	33	2	8	26f	7	1

Dodgers	AB	R	H	O	A	E
Stanky, 2b	1	0	0	2	3	0
Lavagetto	1	0	1	0	0	0
Reese, ss	4	0	0	3	5	1
Robinson, 1b	4	0	0	11	1	0
Walker, rf	2	0	0	0	1	0
Hermanski, lf	4	0	0	2	0	0
Edwards, c	4	0	0	7	1	1
Furillo, cf	3	0	0	2	0	0
bGionfriddo	0	1	0	0	0	0
Jorgensen, 3b	2	1	0	0	1	1
Taylor, p	0	0	0	0	0	0
Gregg, p	1	0	0	0	1	0
aVaughan	0	0	0	0	0	0
Berhman, p	0	0	0	0	1	0
Casey, p	0	0	0	0	1	0
cReiser	0	0	0	0	0	0
dMiksis	0	1	0	0	0	0
Totals	26	3	1	27	15	3

```
Yankees   100  100  000   2
Dodgers   000  010  002   3
```

aWalked for Gregg in seventh. bRan for Furillo in ninth. cWalked for Casey in ninth. dRan for Reiser in ninth. eDoubled for Stanky in ninth. fTwo out when winning run was scored. Two-base hits—Lindell, Lavagetto. Three-base hit—Johnson. Sacrifice hits—Stanky, Bevens. Runs batted in—DiMaggio, Lindell, Reese, Lavagetto 2. Stolen bases—Rizzuto, Reese, Gionfriddo. Double plays—Reese, Stanky and Robinson: Gregg, Reese and Robinson; Casey, Edwards and Robinson. Bases on balls—Off Taylor 1; off Gregg 3; off Bevens 10. Struck out—By Gregg 5; by Bevens 5. Pitching record—Off Taylor 2 hits, 1 run in 0 inning (pitched to four batters); off Gregg 4 hits, 1 run in 7 innings; off Berman 2 hits, 0 runs in 1⅓ innings; off Casey 0 hits, 0 runs in ⅔ inning. Wild pitch—Bevens. Earned runs—Brooklyn 3, New York 1. Left on base—New York 9, Brooklyn 8. Winning pitcher—Casey. Umpires—Goetz (N. L.); McGowan (A. L.); Pinelli (N. L.); Rommel (A. L.); Boyer (A. L.); Magerkurth (N. L.). Time of game—2:20. Attendance—33,433.

Note: Bevens's no-hit bid was ruined by pinch-hitter Cookie Lavagetto's double with two out in the ninth inning which drove home the tying and winning runs, the two runners aboard via walks.

ALL-TIME POSITION LEADERS

MOST GAMES (At that position as a Yankee)

Pos.	Player		Games
1B	Lou Gehrig (1923–39)		2,136
2B	Tony Lazzeri (1926–37)		1,446
SS	Phil Rizzuto (1941–42, 1946–56)*		1,647 (a)
3B	Graig Nettles (1973–81)		1,284
OF	Babe Ruth (1920–34)		2,042 (b)
OF	Mickey Mantle (1951–68)		2,019
OF	Joe DiMaggio (1936–42, 1946–51)*		1,721 (c)
C	Bill Dickey (1928–43, 1946)*		1,712 (d)
DH	Lou Piniella (1974–81)		164
LHP	Whitey Ford (1950, 1953–67)*	(games)	498
RHP	Red Ruffing (1930–42, 1945–46)*	(games)	426
LHP	Whitey Ford (1950, 1953–67)*	(starts)	438
RHP	Red Ruffing (1930–42, 1945–46)*	(starts)	390

(a) Frank Crosetti played in 21 more games for the Yankees than Rizzuto, 1,682–1,661; but Rizzuto played 132 more games at shortstop, 1,647–1,515.

(b) Mickey Mantle played in 317 more games for the Yankees than Ruth, 2,401–2,084; but Ruth played 23 more games in the outfield, 2,042–2,019.

(c) Roy White played in 145 more games for the Yankees than Di-Maggio, 1,881–1,736; but DiMaggio played more games in the outfield.

(d) Yogi Berra played in 327 more games for the Yankees than Dickey, 2,116–1,789; but Dickey caught 18 more games, 1,712–1,694.

*Career interrupted by military service.

ALL-TIME YANKEE TEAM (Selected by fans in 1969)

First Team	Pos.	Second Team
Lou Gehrig	1B	Joe Pepitone
Tony Lazzeri	2B	Bobby Richardson
Phil Rizzuto	SS	Frank Crosetti
Red Rolfe	3B	Clete Boyer
Mickey Mantle	LF	Charlie Keller
Joe DiMaggio	CF	Mickey Mantle
Babe Ruth	RF	Mickey Mantle
Bill Dickey	C	Yogi Berra
Red Ruffing	RHP	Allie Reynolds
Whitey Ford	LHP	Lefty Gomez

MOST HOME RUNS (As a Yankee)

Pos.	Player	Homers
1B	Lou Gehrig (1923–39)	493
2B	Joe Gordon (1938–43, 1946)	253
SS	Frank Crosetti (1932–48)	98
3B	Graig Nettles (1973–80)	212
OF	Babe Ruth (1920–34)	659
OF	Mickey Mantle (1951–68)	536
OF	Joe DiMaggio (1936–42, 1946–51)	361
C	Yogi Berra (1946–63)	358
P	Red Ruffing (1930–42, 1945–46)	31

Note: Some home runs may have come while playing another position—such as Berra while in the lineup as an outfielder or pinch hitter, Mantle as a first baseman, etc.

SINGLE-SEASON LEADERS BY POSITION

Batting Average

1B	Lou Gehrig, .379 (1930)
2B	Tony Lazzeri, .354 (1929)
SS	Phil Rizzuto, .324 (1950)
3B	Red Rolfe, .329 (1939)
OF	*Babe Ruth, .393 (1923)
OF	Joe DiMaggio, .381 (1939)
OF	Mickey Mantle, .365 (1957)
C	Bill Dickey, .362 (1936)
P	Red Ruffing, .339 (1935)

Home Runs

1B	Lou Gehrig, 49 (1934)
2B	Joe Gordon, 30 (1940)
SS	Tom Tresh, 15 (1962)
3B	Graig Nettles, 37 (1977)
OF	Roger Maris, 61 (1961)
OF	**Babe Ruth, 60 (1927)
OF	Mickey Mantle, 54 (1961)
C	Yogi Berra, 30 (1952, 1956)
P	Red Ruffing, 5 (1936)

RBIs

1B	Lou Gehrig, 184 (1931)
2B	Tony Lazzeri, 114 (1926)
SS	Lyn Lary, 107 (1931)
3B	Graig Nettles, 107 (1977)
OF	†Babe Ruth, 170 (1921)
OF	Joe DiMaggio, 167 (1931)
OF	Roger Maris, 142 (1961)
C	Bill Dickey, 133 (1937)
p	Red Ruffing, 22 (1936, 1941)

Fielding

1B	Joe Pepitone, .997 (1965)
	Chris Chambliss, .997 (1978)
	Bob Watson, .997 (1981)
2B	Snuffy Stirnweiss, .993 (1948)
SS	Fred Stanley, .983 (1976)
3B	Graig Nettles, .975 (1978)
OF	Roy White, 1.000 (1971)
C	Elston Howard, .998 (1964)
	Thurman Munson, .998 (1971)
P‡	*Harry Howell, 1.000 (1903)

*Ruth had six of the top seven batting averages ever compiled by a Yankee outfielder. Besides his .393 in 1923, he batted .378 in both 1921 and 1924, .376 in 1920, .373 in 1931 and .372 in 1926.

** Ruth also hit 59 homers in 1921 and 54 in 1920 and 1928.

† Ruth had seven of the top eight RBI totals ever compiled by a Yankee outfielder. Besides driving in 170 runs in 1921, he had 164 in 1927, 163 in 1931, 155 in 1926, 154 in 1929, 153 in 1930 and 142 in 1928.

‡ Minimum of 110 chances.

YANKEES' LEAGUE FIELDING LEADERS

1B

John Ganzel, 1903	Bill Skowron, 1958	Joe Pepitone, 1969
Wally Pipp, 1915	Joe Pepitone, 1965	Chris Chambliss, 1978
Wally Pipp, 1924	Joe Pepitone, 1966	

2B

Aaron Ward, 1923	Jerry Coleman, 1949	Horace Clarke, 1967
Snuffy Stirnweiss, 1944	Gil McDougald, 1955	Sandy Alomar, 1975
Snuffy Stirnweiss, 1948		

SS

Everett Scott, 1922	Frank Crosetti, 1939	Phil Rizzuto, 1950
Everett Scott, 1923	Phil Rizzuto, 1949	Bucky Dent, 1980

3B

Joe Dugan, 1923	Red Rolfe, 1935	Red Rolfe, 1936

OF

Birdie Cree, 1913	Joe DiMaggio, 1947	Mickey Mantle, 1959
Whitey Witt, 1923	Gene Woodling, 1952	Tom Tresh, 1964
Sammy Byrd, 1934	Gene Woodling, 1953	Roy White, 1971
George Selkirk, 1939		

C

Ed Sweeney, 1912	Bill Dickey, 1939	Elston Howard, 1962
Bill Dickey, 1931	Bill Dickey, 1941	Elston Howard, 1964
Bill Dickey, 1935	Yogi Berra, 1957	Thurman Munson, 1971
Bill Dickey, 1937	Yogi Berra, 1959	

P

Harry Howell, 1903
Clark Griffith, 1906
Herb Pennock, 1924

Spud Chandler, 1938
Ralph Terry, 1961

Whitey Ford, 1965
Mel Stottlemyre, 1968

GOLDEN GLOVE WINNERS

1957	Bobby Shantz	P		1965	Joe Pepitone	1B
1958	Bobby Shantz	P			Bobby Richardson	2B
	Norm Siebern	OF			Tom Tresh	OF
1959	Bobby Shantz	P		1966	Joe Pepitone	1B
1960	Roger Maris	OF		1969	Joe Pepitone	1B
	Bobby Shantz	P		1972	Bobby Murcer	OF
1961	Bobby Richardson	2B		1973	Thurman Munson	C
1962	Mickey Mantle	OF		1974	Thurman Munson	C
	Bobby Richardson	2B		1975	Thurman Munson	C
1963	Elston Howard	C		1977	Graig Nettles	3B
	Bobby Richardson	2B		1978	Chris Chambliss	1B
1964	Elston Howard	C			Graig Nettles	3B
	Bobby Richardson	2B				

Note: The Yankees have had Golden Glove winners at every position except shortstop since the award was born in the mid-1950s.

YANKEE ADMINISTRATION AND LEADERSHIP

TEAM OWNERS

1903–14	Frank Farrell and William Devery
1915–22	Jacob Ruppert and Tillinghast L'Hommedieu Huston
1922–39	Jacob Ruppert
1939–45	Ruppert Estate (through Ed Barrow)
1945–47	Larry MacPhail, Dan Topping and Del Webb
1947–64	Dan Topping and Del Webb
1964–73	Columbia Broadcasting System (CBS)
1973–81	Group headed by George Steinbrenner

TEAM PRESIDENTS

1903–06	Joseph Gordon		1966–73	Mike Burke
1907–14	Frank Farrell		1973–77	Gabe Paul
1915–38	Jacob Ruppert		1978–79	Al Rosen
1939–44	Ed Barrow		1980	None
1945–47	Larry MacPahil		1981	Lou Saban
1948–66	Dan Topping			

MANAGERS' RECORDS

	G*	W	L	Pct.	Years
Yogi Berra	164	99	63	.611	1964
Frank Chance	293	118	170	.410	1913–14
Hal Chase	164	85	78	.522	1910–11
Bill Dickey	105	57	48	.543	1846
Wild Bill Donovan	465	220	239	.479	1915–17
Kid Elberfeld	98	27	71	.276	1908
Art Fletcher	11	6	5	.546	1929
Clark Griffith	807	419	370	.531	1903–08
Bucky Harris	309	191	117	.620	1947–48
Ralph Houk	1,756	944	806	.539	1961–63; 1966–73
Dick Howser	162	103	59	.636	1980
Miller Huggins	1,796	1,067	719	.597	1918–29
Johnny Keane	182	81	101	.445	1965–66
Bob Lemon	158	93	65	.589	1978–79; 1981
Billy Martin	566	334	232	.590	1975–78; 1979
Joe McCarthy	2,347	1,460	867	.627	1931–46
Gene Michael	82	48	34	.585	1981
Johnny Neun	14	8	6	.571	1946
Roger Peckinpaugh	17	9	8	.529	1914
Bob Shawkey	154	86	68	.558	1930
George Stallings	298	153	138	.526	1909–10
Casey Stengel	1,851	1,149	696	.623	1949–60
Bill Virdon	266	142	124	.534	1974–75
Harry Wolverton	153	50	102	.329	1912

Includes tie games.

SCOUTS

Director of Scouting: Bobby Hofman

*Luis Arroyo, Ponce, Puerto Rico
Hank Bauer, Overland Park, Kansas
Joe Begani, Chicago, Illinois
Howard (Hopalong) Cassady, Tampa, Florida
Harry Craft, Conroe, Texas
Al Cuccinello, Elmont, New York
Joe DiCarlo, Ringwood, New Jersey
Henry Dotterer, Syracuse, New York
Fred Ferreira, Fort Lauderdale, Florida
*Whitey Ford, Lake Success, New York
Jack Gillis, Worcester, Massachusetts
Tom Greenwade, Willard, Missouri
Jim Gruzdis, Thomasville, North Carolina
†Roy Hamey, Tucson, Arizona
Jim Hegan, Swampscott, Massachusetts
Gary Hughes, Novato, California
*John Kennedy, Peabody, Massachusetts
Don Lindeberg, Anaheim, California
Jack Llewellyn, Englewood, Florida
Jim Naples Sr., Buffalo, New York
Bob Nieman, Anaheim, California
Frank O'Rourke, Hillside, New Jersey
Meade Palmer, Wyncote, Pennsylvania
Gust Poules, Clearwater, Florida
Stan Sanders, Maumee, Ohio
Russ Sehon, Lawrence, Kansas
Bob Shaw, Westerville, Ohio
Birdie Tebbetts, Anna Maria, Florida
Mickey Vernon, Wallingford, Pennsylvania
Stan Williams, Lakewood, California

*Former Yankee player.
†Former Yankee general manager.

YANKEE CAPTAINS

Roger Peckinpaugh	1914–21	Lou Gehrig	1935–41
Babe Ruth	1922*	Thurman Munson	1976–79
Everett Scott	1922–25	Graig Nettles	1982

Ruth captained the Yankees less than a week, May 20–25, 1922. He was named captain upon rejoining the team from a suspension decreed by the commissioner for barnstorming following the 1921 season against the commissioner's orders. Five days after his return, Ruth was stripped of the captaincy and fined for climbing into the stands in pursuit of an insulting customer.

YANKEE PLAYER REPRESENTATIVES

1946	Johnny Murphy	1972–73	Bernie Allen
1947–54	Allie Reynolds	1973–74	Mike Hegan
1955–57	Jerry Coleman	1974	Bobby Murcer
1958–60	Bob Turley	1975	Doc Medich
1960–61	Bobby Richardson	1975	Ed Herrmann
1962	Whitey Ford	1976	Larry Gura
1963–66	Clete Boyer	1976	Dock Ellis
1967	Mel Stottlemyre	1977	Ken Holtzman
1967–70	Steve Hamilton	1978–81	Reggie Jackson
1970–72	Jack Aker		

YANKEE FREE AGENT SIGNINGS

Player	Pos.	Date
Catfish Hunter	P	Dec. 31, 1974
Don Gullett	P	Nov. 18, 1976
Reggie Jackson	OF	Nov. 29, 1976
Rich Gossage	P	Nov. 22, 1977
Rawly Eastwick	P	Dec. 9, 1977
Luis Tiant	P	Nov. 13, 1978
Tommy John	P	Nov. 22, 1978
Rudy May	P	Nov. 8, 1979
Bob Watson	1B	Nov. 8, 1979
Dave Winfield	OF	Dec. 15, 1980
Bill Castro	P	Feb. 17, 1981
Ron Guidry	P	Dec. 15, 1981
Dave Collins	OF–1B	Dec. 23, 1981

TOP YANKEE CHOICES IN JUNE AMATEUR DRAFT

Year	Player	Pos.	Year	Player	Pos.
1965	Bill Burbach	P	1974	Dennis Sherrill	SS
1966	Jim Lyttle	OF	1975	Jim McDonald	1B
1967	Ron Blomberg	1B-OF	1976	Pat Tabler	OF
1968	Thurman Munson	C	1977	Steve Taylor	P
1969	Charlie Spikes	3B	1978	Rex Hudler	SS
1970	Dave Cheadle	P	1979	Todd Demeter	1B
1971	Terry Whitfield	OF	1980	No first-round choice	
1972	Scott McGregor	P	1981	John Elway	OF
1973	Doug Heinold	P			

YANKEE ATTENDANCE RECORDS

Largest home season attendance: 1980	2,627,417 †
Largest road season attendance: 1980	2,461,240*
Largest combined home-road attendance: 1980	5,088,657 †
Largest day doubleheader home attendance: vs. Boston, May 30, 1938	81,841
Largest twi-night doubleheader home attendance: vs. Milwaukee, July 22, 1980	53,668
Largest regular-season single day-game home attendance: vs. Boston, Sept. 26, 1948	69,755
Largest regular-season single night-game home attendance: vs. Boston, May 16, 1947	74,747
Largest opening day home attendance: April 9, 1981	55,123
Largest Yankee Old-Timers' Day attendance: vs. Boston, Aug. 9, 1958	67,916
Largest crowd in baseball history, Yankees vs. Dodgers exhibition game at Los Angeles, May 7, 1959	93,103*
Largest home series attendance: four games vs. Boston, June 29, 30, July 1, 2, 1979	206,016

*Major League record
†American League record.

ATTENDANCE AT NEW YANKEE STADIUM *(Opened April 1976)*

Largest attendance: final game of the A.L. championship series vs. Kansas City, Thursday night, Oct. 14, 1976	56,821
Largest doubleheader attendance: vs. Detroit, Saturday, Oct. 4, 1980	55,410
Largest regular-season single day-game attendance: vs. Toronto, Saturday, May 27, 1978	55,367
Largest regular-season weekday day-game attendance: vs. California, Tuesday, July 26, 1977	43,136
Largest regular-season night-game attendance: vs. Boston, Tuesday, Sept. 13, 1977	55,269
Largest four-game series attendance: vs. Boston, June 29, 30, July 1, 2, 1979	206,016
Largest three-game regular-season attendance: vs. Boston, Sept. 15, 16, 17, 1978	165,080

TOP 20 CROWDS AT NEW YANKEE STADIUM

1. 56,821 Oct. 14, 1976: Game 5 of A.L. championship series vs. Kansas City
2. 56,808 Oct. 12, 1976: Game 3 of A.L. championship series vs. Kansas City
3. 56,700 Oct. 21, 1976: Game 4 of World Series vs. Cincinnati
4. 56,691 Oct. 12, 1977: Game 2 of World Series vs. Los Angeles
5. 56,683 July 19, 1977: All-Star Game
6. 56,668 Oct. 11, 1977: Game 1 of World Series vs. Los Angeles
7. 56,667 Oct. 19, 1976: Game 3 of World Series vs. Cincinnati
8. 56,588 Oct. 10, 1980: Game 3 of A.L. championship series vs. Kansas City
9. 56,513 Oct. 28, 1981: Game 6 of World Series vs. Los Angeles
10. 56,505 Oct. 21, 1981: Game 2 of World Series vs. Los Angeles
11. 56,470 Oct. 20, 1981: Game 1 of World Series vs. Los Angeles
12. 56,448 Oct. 15, 1978: Game 5 of World Series vs. Los Angeles
13. 56,447 Oct. 13, 1978: Game 3 of World Series vs. Los Angeles
14. 56,445 Oct. 14, 1978: Game 4 of World Series vs. Los Angeles
15. 56,407 Oct. 18, 1977: Game 6 of World Series vs. Los Angeles
16. 56,411 Oct. 9, 1981: Game 3 of Eastern Division Series vs. Milwaukee
17. 56,356 Oct. 7, 1978: Game 4 of A.L. championship series vs. Kansas City
18. 56,355 Oct. 13, 1976: Game 4 of A.L. championship series vs. Kansas City
19. 56,230 Oct. 6, 1977: Game 2 of A.L. championship series vs. Kansas City
20. 56,140 Oct. 13, 1981: Game 1 of A.L. championship series vs. Oakland

YANKEE HOME BALLPARKS AND ALL-TIME TOTAL ATTENDANCES

1903–12	Hilltop Park 168th Street & Broadway Manhattan	3,451,542
1913–22	Polo Grounds 155th Street & 8th Avenue Manhattan	6,220,031
1923–73	Yankee Stadium 161st Street & River Avenue Bronx	64,788,405
1974–75	Shea Stadium 126th Street & Roosevelt Avenue Flushing	2,561,123
1976–81	Remodeled Yankee Stadium 161st Street & River Avenue Bronx	13,231,112
	79 seasons:	90,252,213

SPRING TRAINING SITES

1903–04	Atlanta, Georgia
1905	Montgomery, Alabama
1906	Birmingham, Alabama
1907–08	Atlanta, Georgia
1909	Macon, Georgia
1910–11	Athens, Georgia
1912	Atlanta, Georgia
1913	Hamilton, Bermuda
1914	Houston, Texas
1915	Savannah, Georgia
1916–18	Macon, Georgia
1919–20	Jacksonville, Florida
1921	Shreveport, Louisiana
1922–24	New Orleans, Louisiana
1925–42	St. Petersburg, Florida
1943	Asbury Park, New Jersey
1944–45	Atlantic City, New Jersey
1946–50	St. Petersburg, Florida
1951	Phoenix, Arizona
1952–61	St. Petersburg, Florida
1962–	Fort Lauderdale, Florida

YANKEES AND METS

The Yankees and Mets have played 64 times, with the Yankees winning 39, losing 26 and tying one. The Yankees hold a 30–19 advantage in spring training games, a 9–7–1 edge in Mayor's Trophy games.

Twenty-five men have played for both the Yankees and Mets: Jack Aker, Sandy Alomar, Yogi Berra, Ray Burris, Duke Carmel, Billy Cowan, Dock Ellis, Rob Gardner, Jesse Gonder, Bob Friend, Dave Kingman, Phil Linz, Elliott Maddox, Doc Medich, Lenny Randle, Hal Reniff, Bill Short, Charlie Smith, Roy Staiger, Tom Sturdivant, Bill Sudakis, Ron Swoboda, Ralph Terry, Marv Throneberry and Gene Woodling.

Casey Stengel and Yogi Berra have managed both teams.

SELECTED YANKEE DATES

March 12, 1903	Officially approved as members of the American League in a franchise move from Baltimore to New York.
April 22, 1903	First game. Lose at Washington, 3–1.
April 30, 1903	First home game. Defeat Washington, 6–2, at Hilltop Park, 168th Street at Broadway.
April 1913	Team changes its name from Highlanders to Yankees and moves into the Polo Grounds as tenant of the National League's New York Giants.
April 22, 1915	Pinstripes first appear on Yankee uniforms.
June 17, 1917	First Sunday game at home. Lose to St. Louis Browns, 2–1.
May 11, 1919	First legalized Sunday game at home—a scoreless 12-inning tie with Washington.
September 1921	Clinch first pennant.
October 5, 1921	Play in World Series for the first time. Shut out New York Giants, 3–0, behind Carl Mays' 5-hitter, before 30,202 at the Polo Grounds.
April 18, 1923	Open Yankee Stadium. Defeat Boston Red Sox, 4–1, as Babe Ruth fittingly christens "The House That Ruth Built" with its first home run. (The Stadium's left-field stands would be enlarged in 1928, its right-field stands in 1937.)
October 15, 1923	Win first world championship, eliminating New York Giants, 4 games to 2.
June 1, 1925	Lou Gehrig replaces Wally Pipp at first base, launching Gehrig's record for consecutive games played.
September 30, 1927	Babe Ruth's record 60th home run climaxes season-long barrage by Yankees' "Murderers' Row" lineup.
April 16, 1929	Yankees appear with numbers on their uniforms, the first major league team to do so on a permanent basis.
May 2, 1939	Lou Gehrig's playing streak of 2,130 consecutive games ends, the dying "Ironman" never to play in another game.
June 26, 1939	Play in night game for the first time. Lose to the A's, 3–2, in Philadelphia.
June 2, 1941	Lou Gehrig dies at age 37.
July 17, 1941	Joe DiMaggio's 56-game hitting streak ends in Cleveland.
May 28, 1946	First night game at home. Lose to Washington, 2–1, at Yankee Stadium.
April 27, 1947	Babe Ruth Day at Yankee Stadium.
June 13, 1948	Dying Babe Ruth's uniform is retired in Yankee Stadium farewell.
April 17, 1953	Mickey Mantle wallops 565-foot home run in Washington.
October 5, 1953	Yankees eliminate Brooklyn Dodgers, 4 games to 2, to win record fifth consecutive world championship.
October 8, 1956	Don Larsen pitches the only perfect game in World Series history.
October 1, 1961	Roger Maris' 61st homer of the season (this one off Boston's Tracy Stallard) establishes a record.
June 24, 1962	Longest game in Yankee history. Jack Reed's 2-run homer, the only home run of his career, decides the 22-inning, 7-hour marathon at Detroit. Jim Bouton is the winning pitcher, Phil Regan the loser in the 9–7 Yankee victory.
June 8, 1969	No. 7 is retired during Mickey Mantle Day at Yankee Stadium.

April 6, 1974	The club begins its first of two seasons at Shea Stadium while Yankee Stadium is reconstructed.
December 31, 1974	Catfish Hunter signs a record 5-year contract.
April 15, 1976	Reconstructed Yankee Stadium opens.
November 18, 1976	Don Gullett becomes the first free agent signed by Yankees in baseball's first re-entry draft.
October 2, 1978	Defeat Red Sox, 5–4, at Boston in only the second playoff game in American League history—climaxing a Yankee comeback from 14 games out.
August 2, 1979	Thurman Munson dies at age 32 in the crash of a plane he was piloting in Ohio during an open date on the schedule.
December 15, 1980	Free agent Dave Winfield signs a record long-term contract with the Yankees.

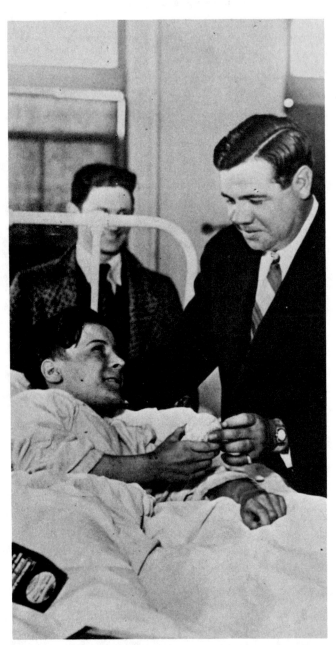

Babe Ruth visits the hospital.

READING LIST

Allen, Maury. *Where Have You Gone, Joe DiMaggio?* New York: E.P. Dutton, 1971.

Anderson, Dave and Milton Lancelot. *Upset.* Garden City, N.Y.: Doubleday, 1967.

Anderson, Dave, Murray Chass, Robert Creamer, and Harold Rosenthal. *The Yankees.* New York: Random House, 1981.

Angell, Roger. *Five Seasons.* New York: Simon & Schuster, 1977.

Angell, Roger. *The Summer Game.* New York: Viking Press, 1971.

Barber, Red. *The Broadcasters.* New York: Dial Press, 1970.

Berkow, Ira. *Beyond the Dream.* New York: Atheneum, 1975.

Bouton, Jim. *Ball Four.* New York: World Publishing Co., 1970.

Bouton, Jim. *I Managed Good, But Boy Did They Play Bad.* Chicago: Playboy Press, 1973.

Broeg, Bob. *Super Stars of Baseball.* St. Louis: The Sporting News, 1971.

Brown, Gene and Arleen Keylin. *Sports as Reported by the New York Times.* New York: Arno Press, 1976.

Buchanan, Lamont. *The World Series and Highlights of Baseball.* New York: E.P. Dutton, 1951.

Carmichael, John P. *My Greatest Day in Baseball.* New York: Grosset & Dunlap, 1963.

Devaney, John and Burt Goldblatt. *The World Series, a Complete Pictorial History.* Chicago: Rand McNally, 1972.

Dickey, Glenn. *The History of American League Baseball.* New York: Stein and Day, 1980.

DiMaggio, Joe. *Lucky to Be a Yankee.* New York: Rudolph Field, 1946.

Durant, John. *The Yankees.* New York: Hastings House, 1949.

Durso, Joseph. *Yankee Stadium.* Boston: Houghton Mifflin, 1972.

Einstein, Charles (ed.). *The Fireside Book of Baseball.* New York: Simon & Schuster, 1956.

Einstein, Charles (ed.). *The Second Fireside Book of Baseball.* New York: Simon & Schuster, 1958.

Einstein, Charles (ed.). *The Third Fireside Book of Baseball.* New York: Simon & Schuster, 1968.

Fischler, Stan and Richard Friedman. *The Comeback Yankees.* New York: Grosset and Dunlap, 1979.

Ford, Edward, Mickey Mantle, and Joseph Durso. *Whitey and Mickey.* New York: Viking Press, 1977.

Goldstein, Richard. *Spartan Seasons.* New York: MacMillan, 1980.

Golenbock, Peter. *Dynasty.* Englewood Cliffs, N.J.: Prentice-Hall, Inc., 1975.

Graham Frank, Jr. *Great Pennant Races of the Major Leagues.* New York: Random House, 1967.

Graham, Frank, Jr. *The New York Yankees.* New York: G.P. Putnam's Sons, 1943.

Greenspan, Bud. *Play It Again, Bud!* New York: Peter H. Wyden, Inc., 1973.

Heyn, Ernest V. *Twelve Sport Immortals.* New York: Batholomew House, 1949.

Holmes, A. Lawrance. *More Than a Game.* New York: MacMillan, 1967.

Honig, Donald. *Baseball Between the Lines.* New York: Coward, McCann and Geoghegan, 1976.

Honig, Donald. *Baseball When the Grass Was Real.* New York: Coward, McCann and Geoghegan, 1975.

Honig, Donald. *The Man in the Dugout.* Chicago: Follett Publishing Co., 1977.

Honig, Donald. *The October Heroes.* New York: Simon & Schuster, 1979.

Izenberg, Jerry. *At Large.* New York: Simon & Flynn, 1968.

Izenberg, Jerry. *The Rivals.* New York: Holt, Rinehart and Winston, 1968.

Jacobson, Steve. *The Best Team Money Could Buy.* New York: Atheneum, 1978.

Jennison, Christopher. *Wait 'Til Next Year.* New York: W.W. Norton, 1974.

Kahn, Roger. *The Boys of Summer.* New York: Harper & Row, 1971.

Koufax, Sandy (with Ed Linn). *Koufax.* New York: Viking Press, 1966.

Lieb, Frederick G. *The Boston Red Sox.* New York: G.P. Putnam's Sons, 1947.

Lieb, Frederick G. *The Story of the World Series.* New York: G.P. Putnam's Sons, 1965.

Lyle, Albert and Peter Golenbock. *The Bronx Zoo.* New York: Crown Publishers, 1979.

Mantle, Mickey. *The Education of a Baseball Player.* New York: Simon & Schuster, 1967.

Marsh, Irving T. and Edward Ehre. *Best Sports Stories,* 1949 edition. New York: E.P. Dutton, 1950.

Marsh, Irving T. and Edward Ehre. *Best Sports Stories,* 1957 edition. New York: E.P. Dutton, 1958.

Marsh, Irving T. and Edward Ehre. *Best Sports Stories,* 1958 edition. New York: E.P. Dutton, 1959.

Marsh, Irving T. and Edward Ehre. *Best Sports Stories,* 1962 edition. New York: E.P. Dutton, 1963.

Marsh, Irving T. and Edward Ehre. *Best Sports Stories,* 1978 edition. New York: E.P. Dutton, 1979.

Martin, Billy and Peter Golenbock. *Number 1.* New York: Delacorte Press, 1980.

Meany, Tom. *The Yankee Story.* New York: E.P. Dutton, 1962.

Metz, Robert. *CBS: Reflections in a Bloodshot Eye.* Chicago: Playboy Press, 1975.

Miers, Earl Schenk. *Baseball.* New York: Grosset and Dunlap, 1970.

Moreland, George L. *Balldom.* New York: Balldom Publishing Co., 1914.

Munson, Thurman (with Martin Appel). *Thurman Munson.* New York: Coward, McCann and Geoghegan, 1979.

Osborne, Charles (ed.). *Yesterday in Sport.* New York: Time-Life Books, 1968.

Pepe, Phil. *The Wit and Wisdom of Yogi Berra.* New York: Hawthorne Books, 1974.

Reichler, Joe (ed.). *The Game and the Glory.* Englewood Cliffs, N.J.: Prentice-Hall, 1976.

Reichler, Joe (ed.). *The World Series.* New York: Simon & Schuster, 1978.

Ritter, Lawrence S. *The Glory of Their Times.* New York: MacMillan, 1966.

Rosenbaum, Art and Bob Stevens. *The Giants of San Francisco.* New York: Coward, McCann and Geoghegan, 1963.

Rosenthal, Harold. *The Yankees.* New York: Random House, 1981.

Sahadi, Lou. *Year of the Yankees.* Chicago: Contemporary Books, 1979.

Schaap, Dick. *Sport.* New York: Arbor House, 1975.

Schoor, Gene. *Joe DiMaggio: A Biography.* Garden City, N.Y.: Doubleday, 1980.

Silverman, Al. *Joe DiMaggio: The Golden Year 1941.* Englewood Cliffs, N.J.: Prentice-Hall, 1969.

Smith, Ken. *Baseball's Hall of Fame.* New York: Grosset and Dunlap, 1974.

Smith, Robert. *The Illustrated History of Baseball.* New York: Grosset and Dunlap, 1973.

Stengel, Casey and Harry T. Payton. *Casey at the Bat.* New York: Random House, 1962.

Sullivan, George. *The Picture History of the Boston Red Sox.* New York: Bobbs-Merrill, 1979.

Tuite, James (ed.). *Sports of the Times: The Arthur Daley Years.* New York: Quadrangle, 1975.

Vecsey, George (ed.). *The Way it Was.* New York: McGraw-Hill, 1974.

Veeck, Bill (with Ed Linn). *Veeck—as in Wreck.* New York: G.P. Putnam's Sons, 1962.

Luis Tiant speaking frankly.